Dressing Up

Ulinka Rublack teaches early modern European history at Cambridge University and is a Fellow of St John's College. One of the most original scholars of her generation, she has previously published *The Crimes of Women in Early Modern Germany* and *Reformation Europe*. She is editor of *Gender in Early Modern German History* and the Oxford University Press *Concise Companion to History* (2011).

Praise for Dressing Up

'A thrilling investigation . . . hugely accomplished . . . What is really stunning... is the extraordinarily deft way in which [Rublack] has stitched together all these fragments, selvedges and even stray threads. The result is a narrative quilt that doesn't simply shimmer with surface detail but dazzles with its deep, original thought.'
Kathryn Hughes, *The Guardian*

'Insightful and original'
Maria Hayward Times Literary Supplement

'Remarkable... Rublack turns the wardrobe into a place of almost magical powers of revelation, opening up vistas into the imaginative and emotional lives of men and women in Renaissance Europe. And with more than 150 magnificent colour illustrations, this dazzling book is as much a feast for the eye as for the mind.'
John Adamson, *The Sunday Telegraph*

This stunning book transforms the way we understand clothes and the concern for appearance in Germany and Europe more generally in the sixteenth and seventeenth centuries. Garments and their wearers take us into the changing realms of personal play, religious argument, national identity, and curiosity. Richly illustrated and deeply researched, *Dressing Up* provides an exciting new mirror for early modern times.
Natalie Zemon Davis, University of Toronto

'Rublack combines deep knowledge with a remarkable subtlety of interpretation, alive always to the desires, passions and longings that made dress so profoundly important to European culture in this period. Packed with vivid vignettes and stories - from the riches to rags of a German patrician in Brazil to the riddle of Luther's Reformation choice of a red doublet - this book shows how a global economy underpinned the transformation of fashion. A major achievement, Rublack changes how we think about culture in the early modern world.'
Lyndal Roper, University of Oxford

'Rublack's wonderful new book on 'Dressing up' is both readable and compelling. While focused on Germany, she deals with fashion as a global phenomenon, exploring the many complexities that communities faced when deciding what to wear. Ranging across issues of identity, social control and cohesion, religious conflict and sumptuary laws, Rublack shows that clothing and fashion are serious and challenging topics that lead to often unexpected results.'
Evelyn Welch, Queen Mary University of London

'Viewing dress codes as cultural codes, and arguments about clothes as arguments about values, Ulinka Rublack shows us in this lively and fascinating essay how the history of costume forms part of cultural history.'
Peter Burke, University of Cambridge

Dressing Up

1.   Detail of Anonymous, *Augsburger Monatsbilder, January–March*, c.1530 (after drawings and glass roundels by Jörg Breu), oil on canvas

Dressing Up

CULTURAL IDENTITY IN RENAISSANCE EUROPE

Ulinka Rublack

OXFORD

UNIVERSITY PRESS

Great Clarendon Street, Oxford, OX2 6DP,
United Kingdom

Great Clarendon Street, Oxford OX2 6DP
Oxford University Press is a department of the University of Oxford.
It furthers the University's objective of excellence in research, scholarship,
and education by publishing worldwide in

Oxford New York

Auckland Bangkok Buenos Aires Cape Town Chennai
Dar es Salaam Delhi Hong Kong Istanbul Karachi Kolkata
Kuala Lumpur Madrid Melbourne Mexico City Mumbai Nairobi
São Paulo Shanghai Taipei Tokyo Toronto

With offices in

Argentina Austria Brazil Chile Czech Republic France Greece
Guatemala Hungary Italy Japan Poland Portugal Singapore
South Korea Switzerland Thailand Turkey Ukraine Vietnam
Oxford is a registered trade mark of Oxford University Press
in the UK and in certain other countries

Published in the United States
by Oxford University Press Inc., New York

British Library Cataloguing in Publication Data
Data available

Library of Congress Cataloging in Publication Data
Data available

Printed in China by
C & C Offset Printing Co. Ltd

ISBN 978-0-19-929874-7 (Hardback)
ISBN 978-0-19-964518-3 (Paperback)

1 3 5 7 9 10 8 6 4 2

Meiner Mutter, Dr Ursula Nelle,
in großer Liebe und Dankbarkeit gewidmet

Acknowledgements

This book was written from a fascination with life and the cultural forms it has been given. I have worked on it in several places, without any other than sabbatical leave, and over many years. Everything began in the Warburg Library in Hamburg, a few metres from where I grew up. On its largely empty shelves I found the catalogue of the *Freiherr zur Lipperheidischen Kostümbibliothek* and a reference to Sigmund Heldt's manuscript. This took me to Berlin, and I spent many weeks immersed in the splendid holdings of this library that specializes in the history of costume. I next received a visiting scholarship at the *Maison de L'Homme*, which allowed me to spend time with a copy of Matthäus Schwarz's costume book. Afterwards, I continued to live in Paris, in a district that has already been sociologically studied to analyse how bourgeois women create the 7eme street look. *Dressing Up* was finally written up in Cambridge, where in 2006 our university magazine gave space to the following request of a television company: 'ITV have approached the University in the hope that they might strike upon a couple who are good at expressing themselves verbally, but less good at expressing themselves sartorially...in other words, are you and your partner articulate, but badly dressed?'

Cambridge students are members of colleges as well as the university, and this is still marked with a process of investiture, as it is for academic college and university staff. We need to wear black gowns for many formal occasions, which define belonging and rank through different lengths of sleeves and particular accessories. Cambridge, moreover, is part of a world in which non-academic clothing is prescribed on many occasions, and I have been asked countless times to appear in a black or white tie. The world even of Oxbridge scholars hence is one in which attitudes to the material are part of a wider view of life. Students, of course, have historically been more inventive than scholars. In 1565, for instance, a report to the crown about my own college, St John's, complained about 'great disorders of apparel'. Much later, the term 'blazer' probably gained currency with reference to the bright red 'blazing' jackets worn by members of its boat club. Finally, it is said that the tie was invented by the rowing students of Corpus Christi college, when they took maroon bands from their boaters and tied them round their necks.[1] So Cambridge, in its own way, has been a perfectly inspiring place to finish this book.

It could not have been written in this way, however, without regular trips to London in order to attend sessions of the AHRC-funded network on early modern dress and textiles, expertly directed by Evelyn Welch and administered by Hilary Davidson. Here we handled objects, made ruffs, listened to Jenny Tiramani, whose knowledge about sixteenth-century clothes is legendary, went to the V&A to look at lace and embroidery sourced by its expert curators, saw shoes, and thus systematically engaged with the importance of sumptuary detail in this period. The network is a testimony to how fruitful it is to bring together university scholars from different disciplines (as well as at different stages of their careers), curators, and practitioners involved in the theatre or serious historical re-enactment. It made me appreciate the significance of accessories, and I am very grateful to Evelyn Welch for inviting me to participate and to all participants for creating such a stimulating environment.

Dressing Up has also been written with the aid of many people who lent their houses, food, drink, ears, emotional warmth, or superb critical minds. I thank them all. Students cheered me in their view that this was a 'cool' subject. David Lowe and Christian Staufenbiel at the University Library speedily ordered books and supported me in every possible way. John Dolan at the faculty computer office was wonderfully helpful in scanning slides and giving advice; so was Judith Robb. Curators, image librarians, and librarians were helpful in sending me pictures and permissions; I hope they will forgive me for not naming them individually in every case; the list is long. My college and faculty provided the calm for me to write this book during my final period of sabbatical leave, and I am deeply grateful for the unique environment they both create.

I am grateful to seminar audiences in England, Germany, Switzerland, and Spain, and all colleagues who invited me to present papers. I wish to thank Erdmute Alber, James Amelang, Diana Barrowclough, Peter Burke, Chris Clark, Hilary Davidson, Dr Adelheid Rasche of the Lipperheidische costume library, Dagmar Drinkler (for meeting with me in the Bavarian National Museum), Jack Goody, Kaspar von Greyerz, Daniela Hacke, Philip Hahn, Caspar Hirschi, Ludmilla Jordanova, John Kerrigan, Sachiko Kusukawa, Mary Laven, Beverly Lemire, Janine Maegraith, Lisa Monnas, Ruth Mohrmann, Joe McDermott, David McKitterick, Sheilagh Ogilvie, Adam Tooze, and Pamela Smith in particular for their support, engagement, or for reading parts of the manuscript. I fondly recall exchanges with my late father, Hans-Christoph Rublack, about the emerging book. Evelyn Welch read all the manuscript and offered very helpful advice. Lyndal Roper was invaluable in helping me to get a sense of the book as a whole and offered closely focused feedback when she read the draft manuscript. Marion Kant and Jonathan Steinberg gave constant encouragement from the beginning, asked pertinent questions at the end, while Jonathan, in particular, brought his extraordinary editorial experience to the manuscript in its final stages. I would like to record my tremendous gratitude for his friendship, exceptional involvement, and time. All remaining faults are entirely my own. Laura Kounine most generously proofread the manuscript and commented on it with great insight. Christopher Wheeler has been a wonderful editor to work with, and Matthew Cotton was always available for thoroughly reliable, instant help. They both are very special editors, and know what it takes to make special books. So this book in part is also a brilliant team effort, and a further person in the team has been my copy-editor, Kay Clement, who cheerfully worked with complete dedication and utter professionalism and so have been Claire Thompson and Nick Clarke.

Francisco Bethencourt has changed the way I envisage history. He also filled the years in which this book has been written with so much love and happiness. João and Sophie are our beloved children. They all are the inspiration of my life.

Contents

Acknowledgements   viii

List of Illustrations   xiii

Prologue   xix

  1. Introduction   1

  2. Looking at the Self   33

  3. The Look of Religion   81

  4. Nationhood   125

  5. Looking at Others   177

  6. Clothes and Consumers   211

  7. Bourgeois Taste and Emotional Styles   231

Epilogue: An Old Regime of Dress?   259

Notes   286

Select Bibliography   317

Index   347

List of Illustrations

1. Detail of Anonymous, *Augsburger Monatsbilder, January–March, c.*1530 (after drawings and glass roundels by Jörg Breu), oil on canvas
2. Doublet, South-Tirol (?), 1610–1625, originally red
3. Albrecht Dürer, *Self-portrait aged 26*, 1498, oil on panel
4. Albrecht Dürer, *Self-portrait in a fur-trimmed coat (Pelzrock)*, 1500, oil on panel
5. Anonymous, *Wolfgang Thenn of Augsburg and Ratisbon*, 10 October 1531, pear-wood panel, carved in relief
6. Linen shirt with embroidery and lace-work using gold-threads, south-German, mid-sixteenth century
7. Doublet of lampas silk, allegedly worn by Charles of Blois, duke of Brittany (1345–1364)
8. Jan van Eyck, *Portrait of a Man in a Turban*, (possible self-portrait), 1433, oil on wood panel
9. Netherlandish Master, *Portrait of the Anabaptist David Joris, c.*1550/1555, oil on panel
10. Petrarch, *Von der Artzney bayder Glück*, Augsburg: Heinrich Steiner 1532, frontispiece
11. Ambrogio Lorenzetti, detail of The Dancers in the *Allegory of Good Government*
12. Matthäus Schwarz, Book of Clothes, nude picture from the front, July 1526
13. Matthäus Schwarz, Book of Clothes, nude picture from the back, July 1526
14. Albrecht Dürer, *Self-portrait 1493*, oil on canvas
15. Hans Maler (active from 1500–1529), *Matthäus Schwarz 1526*, oil on canvas
16. Matthäus Schwarz, Book of Clothes, frontispiece
17. Matthäus Schwarz, Book of Clothes, aged 5 in 1502, learning the alphabet, his mother had just died
18. Matthäus Schwarz, Book of Clothes, aged 9, having run away
19. Matthäus Schwarz, Book of Clothes, aged 12, engrossed in religious worship and on his way to becoming a monk
20. Matthäus Schwarz, Book of Clothes, aged 14, trampling on his school books and finishing with school
21. *Aerial view of Augsburg*, 1521, produced by the goldsmith Jörg Seld and the Petrarch Master, woodcut from twelve printing-blocks
22. Matthäus Schwarz, Book of Clothes, aged 15, as a flirtatious boy (*Gassenbuhler*), who nonetheless remains 'clean'
23. Matthäus Schwarz, Book of Clothes, aged 17, riding to Milan

24. Matthäus Schwarz, Book of Clothes, aged 19, as Jacob Fugger's accountant in 1516
25. Anonymous, *Augsburger Monatsbilder, October–December*, oil on canvas
26. Anonymous, *Augsburger Monatsbilder, July–September*, oil on canvas
27. *Augsburger Geschlechtertanz*, 1550, with sixteen participants and seven representatives of the old patriciate
28. Matthäus Schwarz, Book of Clothes, aged 23, mourning his father in four different kinds of dress
29. Matthäus Schwarz, Book of Clothes, aged 26, wearing a doublet with 4,000 slashes (*Schnitz*)
30. Matthäus Schwarz, Book of Clothes, aged 23, in love with a lady from the Netherlands
31. Matthäus Schwarz, Book of Clothes, aged 27 in 1524, with lute and a beret from an Italian duke
32. Matthäus Schwarz, Book of Clothes, aged 33 in 1530, dressed to please Ferdinand at the Imperial Diet of Augsburg
33. Matthäus Schwarz, Book of Clothes, a sledge painted with couples dancing and a couple spinning
34. Matthäus Schwarz, Book of Clothes, aged 38, August 1535, 'when the plague started in Augsburg', standing on a fool's cap
35. Matthäus Schwarz, Book of Clothes, aged 23, with a traditional Franconian embroidered shirt, his waist measuring 60 cm
36. Matthäus Schwarz, Book of Clothes, aged 41, image on his birthday recording that as he had decided to marry this coat had been made
37. Matthäus Schwarz, Book of Clothes, Schwarz as a married man in August 1538
38. Matthäus Schwarz, Book of Clothes, aged 44, 1541
39. Christoph Amberger, *Portrait of Matthäus Schwarz*, 1542, oil on panel
40. Matthäus Schwarz, Book of Clothes, in armour to defend his city
41. Matthäus Schwarz, Book of Clothes, aged 52, at home after suffering a stroke
42. Matthäus Schwarz, Book of Clothes, aged 56, when Moritz of Saxony was shot
43. Matthäus Schwarz, Book of Clothes, final image aged 63 in 1560, at Anton Fugger's funeral
44. Matthäus Schwarz, Book of Clothes, aged 30 in 1527, at Anton Fugger's wedding
45. Georg Pencz, *Mercury and his Children*, broadsheet
46. Veit Konrad Schwarz, Book of Clothes, aged 19, 1561, for Hans Herwart's wedding
47. Panel from the Benedict-cycle, Lüneburg, 1495
48. North-German (Stralsund?) dalmatic, fourteenth century
49. Workshop of Lucas Cranach the Elder, *Satirical Coat of Arms for the Pope*, Wittenberg, 1538, text by Martin Luther, hand-coloured woodcut
50. Martin Luther/Hans Sachs, *Das Papsthum mit seinen Gliedern*, 1526: Pope
51. Martin Luther/Hans Sachs, *Das Papsthum mit seinen Gliedern*, 1526: Benedictine
52. Martin Luther/Hans Sachs, *Das Papsthum mit seinen Gliedern*, 1526: Thumbherrn
53. Martin Luther/Hans Sachs, *Das Papsthum mit seinen Gliedern*, 1526: Luther as Augustinian
54. Petrarch Master, *Von der Artzney beyder Glück*, Augsburg: Heinrich Steiner 1532, BL C39.h.25
55. Petrarch Master, *Von der Artzney beyder Glück*, Augsburg: Heinrich Steiner 1532, BL C39.h.25

56. Lucas Cranach the Elder, *Portrait of Martin Luther as Junker Jörg*, second edition woodcut 1522

57. Johann Daniel Müller, *Martinus Lutherus*, coloured broadsheet, Magdeburg: Johann Daniel Müller (1546/7)

58. *Der gestryfft Schwitzer Baur*, frontispiece

59. Martin Luther, *Wider die Mordischen und Reubischen Rotten der Bawren*, Landshut: Weissenburger 1525, frontispiece

60. Martin Luther, *Eyn Sermon von dem Wucher*, Wittenberg: Rau-Grunenberg 1519

61. Andreas Musculus, *Hosenteufel*, frontispiece, Frankfurt-on-Main: 1563

62. Epitaph of a fashionable Lutheran couple, detail, late sixteenth century, Marienkirche, Frankfurt (Oder)

63. Matthias Gerung, *Apocalypse and Satirical Allegories of the Church, Allegory on Indulgences*, 1546

64. Matthias Gerung, *Apocalypse and Satirical Allegories of the Church, The heavenly Protestant and earthly Church*, 1548

65. Lucas Cranach, *Wittenberg Altar Piece*, 1547, oil on panels, Baptism, Lord's Supper, Confession, and Luther preaching to the Congregation (Predella)

66. Lucas Cranach, *Wittenberg Altar Piece*, Predella

67. Andreas Herrneisen, *Historia der Augspurgischen Confession (1530)*, with fashionably dressed Lutherans attending the Eucharist, 1602, Kasendorf church

68. Albrecht Dürer, *Nürnberg woman and Venetian woman*, c.1495, pen and ink drawing

69. Wolfgang Lazius, *De aliquot gentium migrationibus…*, Basle: Oporiniana 1572, T.1.14, p. 443, Swabians

70. Wolfgang Lazius, *De aliquot gentium migrationibus…*, Basle: Oporiniana 1572, T.1.14, p. 785, Scottish and Irish warriors

71. Melchior Lorck/Hans Sachs, *Honour and praise of a beautifully decorated woman…* Nuremberg: 1551, broadsheet

72. Georg Herwart, mayor, in a *Schaube*, 1544, from the Herwart's family *Book of Honour*

73. Veronica Bimlin, Georg Herwart's wife in the female equivalent of a *Schaube*, from the Herwart's family *Book of Honour*

74. Hans Sachs/Eberhard Schön, *Hans Widerporst*, coloured broadsheet 1534

75. Hans Burgkmair the Elder, *Maximilian I on horseback*, in armour with peacock feathers, 1518, woodcut from two blocks

76. Lucas Cranach the Elder, *Landsquenet decorated with feathers*, c.1506, woodcut

77. Jost Amman, illustration to Leonhard Fronsperger, *Order of War*, Frankfurt: Feyerabend & Hüter 1563, soldier with a lance and a canteen woman carrying poultry

78. Albrecht Altdorfer, detail of the *Triumph of Maximilian I, Utrecht Campaign*

79. Chimney-hanging from the Leipzig town-hall, 1571, embroidery with linen, silk, metal threads, wood, paper and metal pieces

80. The naked German, at the close of Wilhelm IV of Bavaria's *Book of Court Costumes* (*Hofkleiderbuch*)

81. Silk-embroidery with costume scenes of men and Italian women as in Bertelli and Vecellio, south-German, late sixteenth century

82. Nicolas de Nicolay, *Von der Schiffart unnd Raiisz in die Türckey…*, Nuremberg 1572: designed by C. Saldoerffer, noble Turkish woman at home

83. Nicolas de Nicolay, *Von der Schiffart unnd Raiisz in die Türckey…*, Nuremberg 1572: designed by C. Saldoerffer, Janissary

84. Hans Weigel, *Trachtenbuch (Book of Costumes)*, frontispiece

85. Hans Weigel, *Trachtenbuch*, a German *Landtsfürst* (territorial ruler)

86. Hans Weigel, *Trachtenbuch*, Nuremberg woman

87. Hans Weigel, *Trachtenbuch*, Nuremberg woman attending an invitation to a meal

88. Hans Weigel, *Trachtenbuch*, Persian lord

89. Hans Weigel, *Trachtenbuch*, a Biscay couple

90. Hans Weigel, *Trachtenbuch*, Cologne maidservant

91. Hans Weigel, *Trachtenbuch*, French lady

92. Hans Weigel, *Trachtenbuch*, Lorraine woman of Metz

93. Hans Weigel, *Trachtenbuch*, Neapolitan woman

94. Hans Weigel, *Trachtenbuch*, Saxon courtier

95. Hans Weigel, *Trachtenbuch*, French peasant

96. Hans Weigel, *Trachtenbuch*, horse-carter from Flammerspach and the Allgäu-region

97. Hans Weigel, *Trachtenbuch*, Swiss man

98. Hans Weigel, *Trachtenbuch*, a Spanish priest's concubine

99. Marcus zum Lamm, *Thesaurus Picturarum*, Frisian woman

100. *A la modo monsiers* and ladies who reject traditional German values, 1628, broadsheet

101. *Alla modo Meßieurs*, with the naked German in the middle of winter and summer clothing and a parody of the German Messieurs who affected French speech, broadsheet, 1628

102. Irish soldiers as true warrior tribe, contracted for the Protestant cause by Gustav Adolf of Sweden during the Thirty Years' War, Nuremberg 1632

103. *Revanche*, broadsheet, 1641

104. Felt-hat of Pfalzgraf August (1582–1632) with several layers of dyed ostrich feathers

105. Doublet and breeches of brown velvet, Pfalzgraf Johann Friedrich (1587–1644)

106. After Hans Burgkmair the Elder, *Inhabitants of the West Coast of Africa, South-East Coast of Africa and Arabia*: Augsburg: Georg Glockendon 1511

107. Hans Burgkmair the Elder, *Inhabitants of the South-East Coast of Africa*, 1508

108. Hans Burgkmair the Elder, *Kaiser Maximilians I Triumph*, 1522

109. Albrecht Dürer, *Irish warriors and peasants*, 1521, pen and watercolour drawing

110. Albrecht Dürer, *Katherina aged 20*, drawing 1521

111. Christoph Weiditz, *Indian performance with a wooden block (second phase)*

112. Christoph Weiditz, *Manner of Dress of Indian women*

113. Christoph Weiditz, *Morisco woman sweeping*

114. Christoph Weiditz, *Morisco man*

115. Christoph Weiditz, *Galician woman going to the spinning-bee*

116. Christoph Weiditz, *Castilian peasant going to the market*

117. *Slaves in Barcelona taking in water for ships*

118. Hieronymus Koeler, *Order of the escort*

119. Sigmund Heldt, *Natives after Burgkmair*

120. Sigmund Heldt, *Nuremberg bathing master*

121. Sigmund Heldt, *Ordinary Nuremberg craftsman*
122. Sigmund Heldt, *Peasant women bringing onions and carrots to the Nuremberg market*
123. Sigmund Heldt, *Nuremberg captain of the foot-servants*
124. Sigmund Heldt, *Nuremberg house-servant*
125. Sigmund Heldt, *Berlin maidservant*
126. Sigmund Heldt, *Man making sauerkraut*
127. Sigmund Heldt, *German carter*
128. *Hausbuch der Mendelschen Zwölfbrüderstiftung*, the hat-maker Hanns Eckel
129. Album Amicorum of Paul Behaim, entry Gienger 1575, Florentine lady
130. Album Amicorum of Portner, honourable lady
131. Album Amicorum of Johannes Thomas Örtel, Italian lady with ostrich feather fan
132. Album Amicorum, The German gentleman chooses the German lady over Italian women
133. Abraham Bach, *Parable of the Prodigal Son*, Augsburg Broadsheet
134. Medal of Lucia Dorer wearing a beret, as an ornament of Germany, 1523
135. Wedding-bowl of the Augsburg Pahler–Imhof families, 1572, Augsburg
136. Jost Amman, *Ständebuch (Book of Trades)*, fool
137. Jost Amman, *Ständebuch (Book of Trades)*, furrier
138. Jost Amman, *Ständebuch (Book of Trades)*, mirror-maker. © Germanisches Nationalmuseum, Nürnberg
139. Jost Amman, *Ständebuch (Book of Trades)*, silk-embroiderer
140. Jost Amman, *Ständebuch (Book of Trades)*, bag-makers
141. Leather-bag with seams using gold-thread, south-German, mid-sixteenth century
142. Hans Weigel, *Trachtenbuch*, Nuremberg daughter of a craftsman going to a dance
143. Lorenz Strauch, *Portrait of Clara Praun* (1565–1638) with red braided hairpiece and beret without brim
144. *Hausbuch der Landauer Zwölfbrüderstiftung*, the braid maker Wolff Rummel (d. 1663)
145. *Abriß, Entwerffung vnd Erzehlung, was in dem, von Anna Köferlin zu Nürnberg, lang zusammen getragenem Kinder-Hauß…anzutreffen*, 1631, Broadside made from two blocks
146. Doll's house, Nuremberg 1611, original parrot in cage now removed
147. Detail of first Nuremberg doll's house, 1611
148. *Hausbuch der Mendelschen Zwölfbrüderstiftung*, the baker Jorg Urlaub and a maidservant, 1568
149. *Hausbuch der Mendelschen Zwölfbrüderstiftung*, the carpenter Hans Stenger, 1607
150. Albrecht Schmidt, *Die Butzenbercht*, broadsheet
151. Adriaen van de Venne, *Carousing Couple with Cat*, early seventeenth-century, watercolour and body-colour over black chalk
152. Albrecht Schmidt, *Der Rothgerber (tanner)*, broadsheet
153. Doublet, south-German (?), *c.*1625–1640, silk damask with a delicate pattern of leaves and flowers in yellow on green
154. *Hausbuch der Mendelschen Zwölfbrüderstiftung*, the braid- and glove-maker and piper Hans Zauscher (d. 1655)
155. Back of a doublet, Netherlands (?), *c.*1630–1640
156. *Markgrave Sibylla Augusta as Slave*, tempera on parchment, mounted on wood, German, *c.*1700–1710

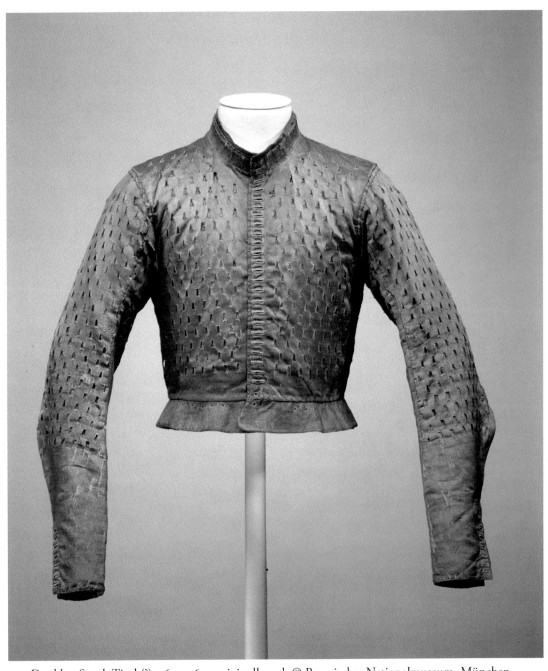

2. Doublet, South-Tirol (?), 1610–1625, originally red. © Bayerisches Nationalmuseum, München

Prologue

This book imagines the Renaissance afresh by considering people's appearances: what they wore, how this made them move, what images they created of their looks, and how all this shaped men and women's identities. It rediscovers appearances as part of a rich symbolic world capable of transmitting compact information that people responded to, misunderstood, had fun with, or fought over. I became fascinated by this subject over a decade ago when looking at images of the period I was supposed to be familiar with, and found I was not. What is happening?, I asked myself, as I looked closely at an African gondoliere with striped hose and a violet wig in one of the Venetian artist Carpaccio's paintings. What is going on?, I wondered, when I discovered a hardly known Nuremberg manuscript from the 1560s depicting three kinds of street sweepers in flamboyant dress. I began to take note of intriguing comments, like the French essayist Michel de Montaigne's noting that he felt closer to a naked savage than to overdressed peasants in the next village. Then there was the amusing fact that the notion of the 'blonde' appeared in seventeenth-century France with reference to bewigged male fops, the 'blond-ins'.[1] Sixteenth-century Spanish men meanwhile were known for their use of glasses to create a discerning look. The richer they were, the larger the glasses could be. This explains why El Greco painted Cardinal Fernando Niño de Guevara in 1600 as advancing General Inquisitor with the coldest, most distancing, and frightening look imaginable, a look achieved by his enormous black-rimmed spectacles.[2]

Vignettes of this kind from different parts of Europe relate to larger historical changes. The term Renaissance means 'rebirth' and was coined by Jules Michelet in the nineteenth century. I am using it to refer to a long period, from c.1300 to 1600. This Renaissance was about more than an Italian cultural movement that expressed itself in fine art. It marks a time when Europeans noticed huge changes in their sense of where they stood in the world and what life was about. This happened most notably through the intensified interest in a past, pagan tradition, through a renewed engagement with a broad range of visual media, and an increased interaction with overseas worlds. The Protestant and Catholic Reformations, the rise of cities and a commercial, bourgeois world, the centralization of governance, and the greater dissemination of travel experiences through print equally contributed to vibrant cultural arguments about different ways of being. Such arguments were further fuelled by a process that has been aptly termed the Renaissance discovery of 'things'. A much greater variety and quantity of goods was produced and consumed across the globe after 1300. Textiles, furnishings, and all items of apparel formed a key part of this unprecedented involvement with objects. Governing men, in fact, were so worried about the impact of this kind of consumption that they began to issue 'sumptuary' laws, after the Latin word *sumptus*, meaning expense, to restrict who should spend how much money on clothes, or be allowed to wear what. Yet fashion was a term now coined in many languages to encapsulate the experience that taste appeared to change faster than ever before.

Most of my closely researched evidence comes from sixteenth-century Germany, and uniquely connects us with everyday experiences during a transformative period. Some of my arguments will concern the place of Germany in this period. I seek to recover its considerable social and cultural aliveness and connections with other countries, in contrast to accounts that have presented post-Reformation Germany as overly rigid, inward-looking, and stagnant. I also recast our vision of Lutheranism by analysing its engagement with material culture. Yet, in looking at appearances, I have mostly wanted to know about more general questions, which are of relevance to European as well as many non-European cultures at this time. How did an interest in consumption interrelate with changing notions of the self, or even ideals of friendship and love? Did people now define themselves more strongly by what they earned, what they liked to buy, and how they looked? What was the effect of the many more images of people that were being produced for the first time?

This book, then, is an invitation to readers to enjoy thinking through appearances, and to see how this hitherto neglected subject must form an important part of the new cultural history of this period, to explore the ways in which men and women across society gave meaning to their world through visual practices, changed or challenged conventions, and thereby created culture in myriad ways. My intention is not to provide a style guide to what all Renaissance men and women, or even what all nobles, burghers, and peasants looked like at a given time. What I want to explain is how and why looks in this expanding commercial society became embedded more deeply in how people felt about themselves or others, a process which links this period to our own. New consumer and visual worlds conditioned new emotional cultures. A young man engaged in courtship, for instance, could produce an image of himself as fashionably slim and precisely note his waist measures. Parents began to use fashionable clothes as a reward even for young children; teenagers could endlessly bargain with parents for more clothes. So family exchanges became more akin to the realm of economic exchanges, while the meaning of dress could become intensely emotionalized, as when dress became a symbol of 'good' behaviour, or encapsulated romantic ideals.

The material expression of such new emotional worlds—heart-shaped bags for men, artificial braids for women, or red silk stockings for young boys—may strike us as odd. Yet their messages of self-esteem, erotic appeal, or social advancement are all familiar still, as are their effects, which ranged from delight in ingenious crafting to doubts about deception. In these parts of our lives the Renaissance becomes a mirror that leads us back in time to disturb the notion that the world in which we live was made in a modern age.

U.R.

CHAPTER ONE

Introduction

DISCOVERING THINGS

When the Nuremberg artist Albrecht Dürer depicted himself in 1498, he cut a strik-ing figure (Fig. 3). Look at his almost transparently thin leather gloves and the applied gold band at the neck of his unusually low cut linen shirt. For most contemporaries, this would have allowed for far too much nudity. Whereas he had painted his father, a goldsmith, in a modest cloak, Dürer himself put on an extravagant black and white silk or very soft leather cap. It matched with the black velvet trims on his doublet. This was refined. Yet two years later, Dürer's self-representation changed. In this millennial year, Dürer depicted himself as mature, manly master painter and in more conventional clothes. For this final self-portrait in oil, Dürer dressed up in a brown gown generously trimmed with precious marten fur and fashionable slashes on the upper arms (Fig. 4). His shirt once more was relatively low cut, and displayed fashionable slashes just below the slashes in his gown. This made him look more similar to respectable governing elites, and documented once more how financially successful he had become to be able to afford such clothes. By 1509, Dürer would indeed be spectacularly honoured with a place in the Nuremberg 'Great Council', usually a reserve of high-born men.[1] Long, carefully groomed locks and a beautiful beard nonetheless gave Dürer's appearance a twist. Some art historians argue that this presented him as a Christ look-a-like and neat-ly embodied Dürer's not so very humble sense that his artistic genius was God-given.[2] Others argue that he simply pictured the 'common spiritual goal' of imitating Christ as well as recording his fame and skill to produce a realistic likeness.[3] It has even been suggested that Dürer might have provoked being teased for his hair and beard-style, so as to more fully imitate Christ's sufferings.[4] Contemporaries were sure that he needed a

3. (*opposite*) Albrecht Dürer, *Self-Portrait aged 26*, 1498, oil on panel, 52 × 41 cm. © Museo Nacional del Prado, Madrid

servant to wave and curl the hair every day.⁵ Yet Dürer seems to have used appearances above all to assert his inventiveness in manipulating his body and clothes and images of them to create a distinctive impression. He got tailors, barbers, and shoemakers to do just what he wanted. Nobody in Nuremberg would have looked like him.⁶ Nor would his clothes have made him look identical to Christ, whom everyone believed to have worn a seamless robe. Dürer articulated his claim that highly skilled artisans should be regarded as artists in his later theoretical writings. It would turn on this God-like ability to inexhaustibly create novel inventions, rather than to reproduce all that was.⁷ His appearances embodied this ingenuity and decorousness, which contemporaries so valued, and he was the first to ever produce such a series of self-portrayals.

Dürer was part of a world in which fashion could be used as a tool to suggest different images of oneself in ever quicker succession. His work followed the long periods after 1300, when more people had become interested in possessing more and more things. 'Consumerism', it has been suggested, was 'parent and child to the Renaissance'.⁸ Richard Goldthwaite has proposed that this greater variety of goods began to objectify people's sense of self for the first time—who they were and wanted to be. 'If', he concludes with reference to the celebrated cultural history of the Renaissance written by Jacob Burckhardt in 1860, 'the Renaissance saw the development of the individual and the discovery of what he called "the full, whole nature of man," this happened largely because man attached himself in a dynamic and creative way to things'. Just like Burckhardt, Goldthwaite focuses his account on Italian Renaissance elites. He sees them as newly fascinated by large scale consumption of expensive and refined art, furniture, furnishings, and other durable wares, and regards this process as crucial for the birth of modern civilization: 'man embarked on the adventure of creating that dynamic world of goods in which he has found his characteristic identity'.⁹ The argument, in other words, is that humans create a sense of being not only in relation to other people, work, nature, space, or religion, but through creative exchange with the material world. Objects impart their qualities (say colour, or texture) to us and we relate to them emotionally and think that they represent our tastes, values, wishes, and spirituality, our connection with others and to our past. It is this dialogue which makes them meaningful, inspires to creativity, and flourishes where there is a greater range of goods. Consequently, our account of past societies must be concerned with the life of objects in people's lives. Central here must be clothes alongside images of clothes, because they played such an immediate role in constituting identities.

But if this is so, the story of the 'birth of modern civilization' can not centre yet again on urban men and women in Venice, Tuscany, Genoa, and Rome up to 1600 and any notion of Italian Renaissance or European materialist exceptionalism. For during the Renaissance and early modern period, Europe was only one of the centres of accelerated cultural development in the world, and not necessarily the most significant. Recent research has established without doubt that parts of Ming China (1368–1644),

4. (*opposite*) Albrecht Dürer, *Self-portrait in a fur-trimmed coat (Pelzrock)*, 1500, oil on panel, 67 × 49 cm, Alte Pinakothek, Munich. © Bayerische Staatsgemäldesammlungen

Momoyama and Edo/Togukawa Japan (1573–1868) were also societies in which consumption and an investment in durable goods and clothing became important not only to elites, but to larger sections of society.[10] In China, a whole genre of writings on 'superfluous things' enjoyed great popularity. It reflected moralist anxieties about the value of unnecessary luxuries. Both Chinese and Japanese regimes put their own sumptuary legislation into place.[11] In spite of such elite concerns, fashion proved to be a key agent of change in Japan. In late sixteenth-cxentury Japan a remarkable variety of designs for textile patterns were created in 'picture shops' (e-ya). Ingenious dyeing and embroidery techniques transferred them onto garments that all levels of society wore.[12] The Edo/Togukawa (1615–1886) period 'harboured a growing population of aesthetic individualists who assumed the importance of beauty in their personal attire as a necessity of life'.[13] We clearly need to look at the emergence of cultural practices commonly identified with the rise of modernity in a multi-centric way. This means looking at Italy in comparison to other countries and at Europe as a major and distinctive, but not the only, centre of change.[14]

What were the key components of a significant involvement with the consumption of 'non-necessities' in different parts of the early modern world? For a start, several societies experienced marked processes of urbanization. In 1500, 109 German, French, Italian, English, Spanish and Netherlandish cities had at least 10,000 inhabitants; by 1600 their number had risen to 137. Lisbon counted 100,000 inhabitants already by the mid-sixteenth century, while London, Paris, and Naples remained the largest urban agglomerates up into the eighteenth century, led by London with 676,000 inhabitants in 1750.[15] Edo in Japan was set to become the first city in the world with about one million inhabitants by the early eighteenth century. Urban dwellers created concentrated markets for goods, and towns obviously held markets and fairs, which were attractive for whole regions that relied on increasingly productive economic hinterlands. Towns housed diversifying groups of professions, such as wealthy traders, doctors, instrument makers, scribes, artists, illuminators, printers and other affluent artisans, scholars, religious men and women, as well as a diverse service industry of skilled cooks, child minders, seamstresses, embroiderers, or tailors. These groups provided much of the social context within which market consumption unfolded, often with great intensity (Fig. 5). In Japan, as in parts of Europe, a rooted elite of governing families could seek to restrict the political influence of such groups. In turn they used status-conferring goods to demonstrate their sense of social worth.[16]

Like Dürer, aspiring men in new professions—from artists to clock-workers, mercenary soldiers to perfumers and inventors—clearly were intrigued by possibilities of experimenting with social roles as much as with aesthetic experiences through visual practices. Think of a Landsquenet soldier in 1609 who went to a female inn-keeper in 'blue breeches, yellow stockings, a yellow doublet and nail-coloured sleeves'.[17] Or imagine the inventor Conrad Drebbel in his fifties, experimenting with a camera obscura in a dark room in London:

5.   Anonymous, *Wolfgang Thenn of Augsburg and Ratisbon*, 10 October 1531, pear-wood panel, carved in relief, 17.1 × 13.7 cm, AN409316001. © The Trustees of the British Museum

> First I change the appearance of my clothing in the eyes of all who see me. I am clad at first in black velvet, and in a second, as fast as a man can think, I am clad in green velvet, in red velvet, changing myself into all the colours of the world. And this is not all, for I can change my clothing so that I appear to be clad in satin of all colours, then in cloths of all colours, now cloth of gold and now cloth of silver, and I present myself as a king, adorned in diamonds and all sorts of precious stones, and then in a moment become a beggar, all my clothing in rags.[18]

Such groups typically had more disposable income in their hands during particular periods of their life-cycle. It is also important not to forget how often people would be paid in kind—with cloth, for instance—as well as in cash. In fact, coins were often avoided in Europe by those exposed to currencies with no gold and little silver content. These could lose their value as quickly as a squirrel hopped from tree to tree. Even textiles stored value far more effectively, and could be pawned, rented, or sold when necessary, which made care, cleanliness, and conservation from insects a key concern of domestic oversight. Pawning, second-hand markets, renting, gift giving, theft, lotteries, auctions, as well as inheritance practices all made goods accessible to broader sections of society.[19] Already in 1403, for instance, a woman called Maroie Le Grand in Douai had decided to invest most of her middling wealth in movables rather than real estate. Marriage contracts stipulated that clothes and jewellery were a woman's 'inalienable' possession. They possessed full control over them, a further incentive for spending on them. In the commercialized cities of fifteenth-century Flanders, which profitably produced luxury cloth from English wool, widows like Maroie particularly loved to use their goods to 'make social relationships concrete'.[20] Would she hint to a neighbouring artisan's daughter that in return for kind help 'this red cap will be yours when I am gone'? We do not know, but it is clear that these women almost hoarded goods to give them away and be remembered. They thus infused exchange with human value. En masse, such small bequests further confused conventions about how social rank was to be materialized if a lower ranking person inherited clothes from a higher ranking one. Meanwhile, entrepreneurs ensured that cheaper imitations of desired goods came on the market, so rare objects could turn into something familiar. Canons of taste needed to be redefined more rapidly. In an increasingly diverse society there were in any case competing attempts to define taste, and we can by no means assume that courts always dictated fashion, so that taste only diffused top-down through emulation.[21] By the early fourteenth century, fashion in a large number of Italian cities had already become 'an urban pursuit with any number of players, any of whom could make fashion statements using less than opulent materials. Labour-intensive trims like glass beads substituted rich materials and created eye-catching effects; what looked like gold was often gilt.'[22] Florentines were supremely fashion-conscious urbanites since the fourteenth century.[23] Much of the economy was structured around textile and luxury production, so much so that in 1427, 866 clothiers and 909 beret- and hatmakers as well as goat-hair manufacuters were officially counted. A weaver of brocaded velvet earned more in a year than the second chancellor. Up to forty per cent of a patrician family's income was devoted to clothing, extravagantly so on feasts like weddings, which asserted a family's status. Sumptuary laws were written in Latin, and never kept up with technological inventions. A constantly changing street vocabulary for items and colours made it easy for people to circumvent legislation. Florentine tailors in the sixteenth century made their business profitable through an entrepreneurial skill in inventing new styles of clothing and decorations.[24] Merchants were interested in encouraging new tastes, and thus the very absence of a local court trying to uphold fashion leadership and stable status displays meant that there were diverse styles among urban men and women. Fashion innovation was not restricted to aristocratic elites; it moved in 'multiple directions'.[25] As a result of such developments we can not be sure about where and when exactly one of the most intriguing luxury hallmarks of

Renaissance style was invented—small, precise, and geometrically entered slashes in upper garments (Fig. 2). These were then sewn around the edges, which made it difficult for the cloth to be reused. Perhaps this style was invented by northern Italian aristocrats in the 1480s, or quite likely by Swiss and German soldiers, who significantly developed the fashion alongside entrepreneurial tailors in the early sixteenth century; but not, it seems, by any particular court.

Of course, well resourced courts had ways of sponsoring specific trends, and European courts had increasingly invested in their displays of magnificence since the twelfth century.[26] The medieval encounter with dress was principally shaped by four processes: growing urbanization, an increase in skilled luxury craft production and marketing, alongside the development of a distinct burgher identity; the growth of clerical elites, part of whom extremely vocally equated dress with sinful vanity, while others developed an aesthetic of sacred beauty focusing on the idea of luminosity; the multiplication of courts, the emergence of ideals of courtly behaviour, as well as competitive courtly consumption. Last, but not least, the crusades led to an intensified experience of Oriental worlds and their costly goods.[27] Courts brought with them sponsorship for writers. Their romances and epics helped to define the ideals of new social groups. Hence the figure of the French-speaking, internationally successful, pious, 'courteoise' knight in glamorous clothing emerged. He was matched by the gracious, courtly lady, who displayed delicate dress, beauty, and posture with virtuosity when she entered courts to evoke a sensation close to epiphany. Writers created an emphatic evaluation of 'newness' and 'freshness' linked to dress elegance, and used such words abundantly.[28]

In this world, then, public appearance and behaviour established and maintained identity.[29] These were not just literary ideals. As exquisite garments became a vital part of ceremonial gift-giving at courts, Roger II (d. 1154) cleverly set up silk manufactures in Sicily with captured Byzantine craftsmen. They produced almost exclusively for the court, while other courts did their best to source the best silks from Islamic and Byzantine Mediterranean silks.[30] Eastern and later Mongol luxury fabrics were essential to create Western elite identities at least until the production of high-quality silks in larger quantities gradually became possible by the fourteenth and fifteenth centuries in Italy and Spain.[31] This awe of, and pleasure in, Eastern splendour visualized courtliness as 'cross-cultural phenomena' and shows how much dress was a tool of cultural exchange. 'Western' fashion, quite simply, was invented in dialogue with the East. Western merchants from the late twelfth century in turn created a demand at Muslim princely courts for Western woollens, silver, and arms.[32] It makes little sense therefore, to think of this period as witnessing the birth of fashion as a specifically Western phenomenon—rather, we need to emphasize once more how change was multi-centric and interconnected across the Western and non-Western world. Horizontal looms, too, were Oriental in origin and spread in Europe after the eleventh century. They allowed for the production of far better quality woollen cloths and could easily be extended to broad looms on which two weavers worked.[33] Meanwhile, Eastern precious fabrics continued to be used especially to establish loyalty and affirm splendour in courtly give-away events, often before a knight rode away, to mark his triumph. As courts became less itinerant and more noblemen and noblewomen regularly attended courts, such practices could turn into more systematic manipulative tools. Burgundians and Armagnacs used elaborate clothes with intricate symbolic devices to construct as well as visualize courtly clientele-systems.[34] These power strategies found their lasting visual duplication in the rich illuminations for Jean de Berry's books of hours, which abound with detailed depictions of dress and devices. Rather than being a 'mere' prayer book, as one might think, the famous *Très Riches Heures* therefore elaborated the 'new fashion system … that of the courtier, no longer to be solely understood by feats of arms, but in the representation of self, manifested by his mastery of social codes and his belonging to the courtly elite'.[35] Not surprisingly, then, not too long after the advent of printing in Europe, the Italian Count Castiglione's *Book of the Courtier* in 1528 became a bestseller. It reflected the enduring concern to explore how men and women of the upper classes should appropriately behave, dress, converse, or gesture.[36]

Yet the notion that ingenuity, manners, and taste were the benchmark of civilization certainly was not a uniquely European elite obsession either. At around the same time as Castiglione was writing the *Courtier*, the founder of the Mughal Empire, Babur (1483–1530), strikingly commented on the lack of charm of Hindustan in his autobiography:

> Its people have no good looks; of social intercourse, of paying and receiving visits there is none; of genius and capacity there is none; of manners none; in handicraft and work, there is no form or symmetry, method or quality. There are no good horses, no good dogs, no grapes, musk melons or first-rate fruit, no ice or cold water, no good bread or cooked food in the bazaars, no hammams, no colleges, no candles, torches or candlesticks.[37]

A 'controlled diversity' of styles and elegant consumption rather than uniformity was taken to symbolize and enhance Mughal power, too. Here, rulers demanded a flow of precious things from their domains through elaborate systems of ritual presentation and manifested their magnificence as 'great consumers'. Fine cloth was central to these exchanges.[38] By 1575, the Mughal Emperor Akbar was known for his love of Portuguese dress. He proudly presented the Portuguese governor of Goa with two fine brocade robes as well as a velvet cap embroidered with gold in the Portuguese style.[39]

Courts in different parts of the early modern world hence would spend increasing amounts of money on liveries, jewellery, or smaller accessories like perfumed gloves. In Europe, clothing was usually given out to everyone at court twice a year, in winter and summer, to ensure a homogenous visual display. German dukes, landgraves also were given drawings of the clothes in which Maximilian I expected them to attend solemn rituals at Imperial Diets.[40] Rulers took an active interest in determining the look of their court, and dressed up splendidly for special occasions of diplomatic relevance. In England, Henry VIII, when he was eighteen, made slashed German garments that symbolized German 'Almain' virility integral to courtly youth culture. A chronicler notes that Henry spent 200 marks on a lavish feast with twenty-four young men all dressed in the Almain fashion: 'their Vitter [outer] garmentes all of yealow Satyne [Satin], yealow hosen, yealow shoes, gyrdels, scaberdes and bonettes with yealow fethers, their garments and hosen all cutte and lined with white Satyn'.[41]

What a show! Court society in turn was commonly associated with an affected display of constant novelty to entertain with visual delight. By 1663, Molière would poetically advise his muse that at court, 'people wish to see objects that delight the eyes'.[42] In Versailles and its copies these people would feast on their reflections in halls of mirrors. Correspondingly, the claim that pompous clothes and etiquette underpinned a despondent world of affected dissimulation and wasted resources continued to be a standard theme of European anti-court literature from Philippe de Commynes, who served at the Burgundian court in the fifteenth century, on to Fray Antonio de Guevara, Franciscan court preacher in sixteenth century Spain, and finally an enlightened German bourgeois dramatist, Friedrich Schiller, who demanded that a state should be based on reasoned principles. Schiller despaired of the 'few shallow cavaliers' he met at the Weimar court, but also felt acutely ill-clad.[43] Commentators differed in whether they attributed more blame to the ruler, or his courtiers and aristocrats. Yet by the late sixteenth century the French essayist Michel de Montaigne already followed a well established blaming strategy when he, in desperation, demanded that the court should

> stop liking those vulgar codpieces, which make a parade of our hidden parts, those heavily padded doublets which make our shape look different and our armour so hard to put on; those long effeminate tresses; the custom of kissing any gift offered to our companions, allowing a nobleman to appear in respectable company with no sword at his side, untidy and unbuttoned, as though he had just come straight from the privy ... [44]

Montaigne, in other words, wanted the court to endorse a formal, manly appearance which emphasized natural shapes, convenience to the body, and the usefulness of clothing at all times. Naturalism was similarly endorsed by the English writer John Bulwer, whose extraordinary book *Anthropometamorphosis* (1654) would deftly treat everything departing from the 'God-given natural shape' as 'deformation'. Bulwer used woodcuts as a clever visual strategy to represent fashionable Europeans as similar to non-European natives. He claimed that modishness was no sign of civilization, but merely imitated forms of primitive adornment.[45]

Montaigne's plea, meanwhile, is also a rare reflection of the fact that men in his period needed to be laced or buttoned up after they had been to the toilet. Their lower garment, the hose, was usually connected to the upper garment, the doublet, with a series of 'points'. Sixteenth-century men then wore mock erect penises attached to their hose. These were made out of two pieces of stiff material, which were often additionally padded, and seamed to provide a three dimensional effect.[46] Such codpieces helped for small business, because men could quickly untie or unbutton it and put it back on. Yet

Montaigne and many others disliked the great expectations these extensions raised, and for the same reason disliked the graffiti of huge genitals that boys made on 'corridors and staircases of our royal palaces'.[47]

Courts in this period were one major influence on the ways in which clothing was imbued with meaning, but not the only one. They moreover inspired counter fashions, as in the French anti-courtier movement, to which Montaigne belonged in his calls for natural, and yet formal, displays of *majesté*. In late sixteenth-century Japan, by contrast, groups of young men from the fringes of samurai culture created a distinctive 'non-straight' (kabuki) style of dress. They were seen to be sometimes dancing and singing in the open streets, proudly showing off velvet collars imported from Europe and large belts. One of them carried a sword inscribed with the words 'Twenty-five is too long to live.' By 1619, seventy of these youngsters had been arrested in Kyoto, one lot disclosing themselves as the 'Leather Trousers Group'.[48] Youth cultures as well as alternative cultures typically create new conventions through their opposition to traditional rules and aesthetic experimentation.[49] Early modern society knew several distinctive cultures and was a young rather than an ageing society. One German ordinance in 1431, for instance, forbade all journeymen to wear coloured shoes as a sign of belonging.[50] These were group displays, and usefully remind us that collective interests alongside a greater interest in 'individual' self-display could be the driving force of changing consumption patterns.

We certainly need to qualify a Burckhardtian reverence for idealized Renaissance men who autonomously decided what was aesthetically right or wrong, as Georg Simmel did by pioneering a sociology of fashion in 1905.[51] Then as now people experienced themselves in relation to a variety of groups, from family to friends, and in relation to their age, body and sexual identity, abilities, ethnicity, religious beliefs, and status. They were more likely to use clothes to decide whom they wanted to connect with rather than whom they wanted to be separated from. Yet such experiences were often contradictory, likely to create messiness, fears about inconsistency, self-negation, or conflict, as well as sometimes resolve into comedy and experiment.[52] For, as Guido Ruggiero puts it,

> family, friends, neighbours, fellow citizens, and other social solidarities such as guilds and confraternities each constructed in dialogue with a person a socially recognized personal identity for that individual. Identities based upon 'consensus realities' could be quite different for the same person depending on the group that shared them.[53]

Hence, we see not so much a controlled process of assured self-fashioning, but people who tried to create identifications in dialogue with different groups, available self-images, and different types of objects. That is why clothes could already form an important part of what we can call people's 'psychic landscapes'. Wardrobes could become storehouses of fantasies and anxieties, as well as accommodations to expectations of what a person ought to look and be like. This made it difficult for men and women to achieve and project a unified sense of themselves through their use of consumer objects. We hence do well to see human identity as grounded in care about and vulnerability towards other people's feelings, as well as in the imagination, rather than in a human ability to gain self-assurance through detachment from others. This perspective also shows why it is too simplistic to treat fashion, as the French sociologist Lipovetsky does, as an engine of Western modernity since the Middle Ages—because it exploded tradition, encouraged self-determination, individual dignity, and opinion-making.[54] It did this in part, and importantly so, but not in uniform and uni-linear directions, let alone just in the West. What we need is a humane and nuanced depiction of how men and women lived in the past, and how their interrelation with objects added another dimension to their typically more fluid, composite self-perception, marked by a balance of the desire to fit in with different groups and yet be recognized as distinctive, so as not to be interchangeable, a mere double.

Historically, this also affirms that people across early modern society were not just absorbed in large collective cultures dictating uniformity, such as 'peasants', 'artisans', or 'Protestants'. Hats, caps, bonnets with feathers, velvet brims, that little bit of gold thread, embroideries, or bags associated people with small groups or distinguished them from peers.[55] Everyone had an eye for the make of clothes and the precise location of value, so that the English traveller Thomas Coryat, for instance, feared that two 'clownes' in rags he met might rob him 'of my gold that was quilted in my jerkin'—that is, gold metal threads which were frequently worked into showy garments. Below the jerkin, he only wore 'mean' fustian clothes.[56] Varied accessories and detail could create pleasure in change and endorse the notion of fashion as positive inventiveness in a universe of goods (Fig. 6). The Portuguese Francisco Henriques even turned biblical scenes such as the collecting of manna in the desert into a study of headwear. Twenty-three different kinds of head coverings can be counted on this medium sized panel painting dating from around 1510.[57]

Later in the sixteenth century, Montaigne, in his country gentlemen's voice, turned to the Greeks and thundered in his essay *On Sumptuary Laws*:

> In his *Laws* Plato concludes that no plague in this world can do more damage to his city than allowing liberty to the young to change from fashion to fashion in their dress, comportment, dances, sports and songs, constantly changing the basis of their ideas in this way and that, running after novelties and honouring those who invent them; by such things are morals corrupted and all ancient principles brought into disdain and contempt.[58]

Montaigne was typical of the way in which Western literary elites in this period lived in dialogue with an extensive commentary by classical Greek and Roman writers on bodily comportment, which added another important layer to their engagement with appearances. In fact, this retrieval of the classical search for civic morality loaded almost everything people did in their daily lives with extra meaning.[59] But these extra meanings, too, were far from straightforward. Classical writers in any case had not spoken with one voice on the subject of clothing. Even in republican Rome, the toga-clad male citizen had been an ideal rather than an everyday reality.[60] The Roman satirist Juvenal commented darkly: 'it's purple cloth, whatever it is, foreign and newfangled, that leads

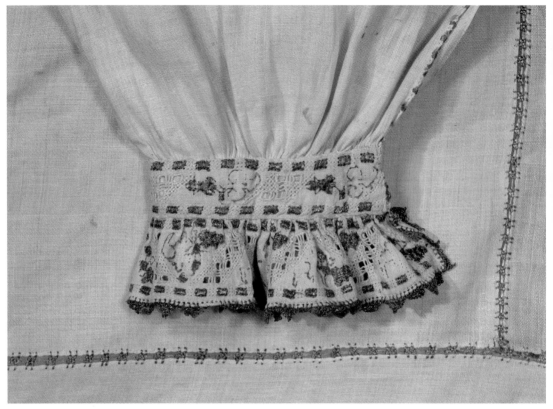

6.   Linen shirt with embroidery and lace-work using gold-threads, south-German, mid-sixteenth century. © Bayerisches Nationalmuseum, München

people into crime and wickedness'.[61] On the whole, just as in cooking, delicacy and complexity could be understood by classical writers, and in the early modern period, as a sign of civilization, but also regarded as too luxurious, tainting, and corrupting, something that took one away from an imagined origin of pure simplicity. 'Thinking through dress' during the early modern period became a way to reflect yet again on larger experiences such as urbanization in its relation to communal ideals, the greater militarization and political organization of society, as well as empire-building and cosmopolitanism. It implied the relationship of what was imagined to be 'native', pure, rural, and 'ancient' in contrast to the 'foreign' or over-civilized. For Renaissance people, ruffs, lace, silk, and pinking on perfumed doublets could be the equivalent of stew for Roman moralists: too mixed, diverse, 'spiced', excessive, inconsistent, denatured, false, or mysterious. It was entirely plausible to claim that republican liberty or foreign tyranny might hinge on what you wore.[62]

But the greater diffusion of efficient printing techniques, increased use of vernacular languages, rising literacy rates among the urban populations, and consolidation of audiences interested in secular themes all meant that woodcuts and books about divergent clothing styles in Europe certainly impacted on people's imagination. More people were better informed about clothing customs elsewhere, even if woodcuts often presented one type of dress for a region or country. 'Costume books' took off as a distinctive genre in the 1560s. They mostly consisted of images and were written simply. Readers were entertained through lively urban scenes or amusing pop-ups, such as that of a Venetian courtesan, who would reveal linen breeches underneath her petticoat if you lifted the flap. Within forty years the Venetian Cesare Vecellio had compiled an extraordinary summa of world clothing from different sources with sections on China, Japan, India, the Ottoman Empire, and America—a total of 500 woodcuts.[63] These picked up cleverly on the presence and records of a wider range of travellers than in earlier times. Travelling, missions, and printed and painted information offered more points of interconnection among different civilizations. Something that happened in one continent could resonate in another.

A particularly good example for such intercultural resonances dates from 1584, when a Jesuit called Alessandro Valignano arrived in Europe with four young Japanese men. They had converted to Christianity and were proudly presented to the pope one year later. In 1586, a coloured newssheet in Augsburg depicted these 'highly cultivated and intelligent men' together with the royal ambassador. Among the gifts they brought back to Japan were mirrors and crucifixes, which instantly sparked off a 'vogue for Western exotica'.[64] As Christianity was repressed by the rulers, crosses became a fashion symbol and counter-culture accessory for the first time in history. In 1605, for instance, one actress of the emerging kabuki theatre tradition was depicted with a colourful kimono and long dangling crucifix.[65] Objects could be appropriated in unintended ways through the ironies of cultural exchange. Images of new styles circulated. Soon during the seventeenth century, a Japanese painter, who presumably had been schooled in Western painting techniques in a Jesuit workshop, created an extraordinary world map for a shogun or high official. It depicted the globe on eight folding screens. The parts of the globe were surrounded by no fewer than forty-four insets of couples from all over the world, drawn from a variety of sources.[66] There was a great interest in manuals, encyclopaedia, and particularly in geographic information. These too popularized crude depictions of a smaller selection of people from around the world, including Europeans.[67] As early as 1585, the Portuguese Jesuit Luís Fróis wrote down a precise comparison of European and Japanese everyday practices, including all manners of dress and appearance.[68] The Spanish Jesuit Adriano de las Cortes in 1625 sent back from China an immensely detailed description of male Chinese gowns, hose, very many hats, and even girdles with countless drawings. A Japanese woodblock printed book in 1787 illustrated and described different parts of a Dutchman's dress. Communications about cross-cultural clothing customs, in short, gained in interest and could be surprisingly detailed.[69] Clothing could therefore be expected to render societies legible and condition how people would seek to understand a society when they travelled. A young French humanist, called Philippe du Fresne-Canaye, in 1573 thus spent a lot of time with his travel companions in Constantinople sitting 'by the door of our house, and there lazily we watched the foreign costumes of those who passed by; we derived so much pleasure from this'. He claimed that they had thereby successfully trained themselves to distinguish different status groups.[70] In 1614, the Italian Pietro della Valle did exactly the same. He was one of a number of foreigners who commissioned books of 'coloured figures' from local miniaturists, 'in which all the diverse clothes of every sort, both of the men and of the women of this city will be drawn from life'.[71] By the eighteenth century, Ottoman elites themselves asked artists for costume books.[72]

Already in sixteenth-century Japan, another key factor promoting fashion, apart from urbanization, social diversification, more travelling and recorded information, was the extending production of cotton.[73] Half of the region near Osaka was already taken up by cotton fields. Far more indigo was planted.[74] This dramatically increased commercial weaving and the textile trade. Cotton was more receptive to dyes than previously used hemp fabrics. Pleasing, warm, and affordable kimono with far more varied patterns could be worn by ordinary seventeenth-century Japanese. Indian block printing techniques, which the Japanese had adapted, proved similarly attractive in the Ottoman Empire as well as in Europe by the later seventeenth century.[75] By the eighteenth century, light cottons with inventive, colourful patterns became so diffused in England that even lower-class mothers could leave their babies at a London foundling hospital wrapped in cottons with playing cards or flowers on them.[76] These were not shiftless mums in rags, then, as depicted by Hogarth's famous engraving *Gin Lane*. And one uncomfortable issue to note from a study of an eighteenth-century German Pietist village engaged in textile production must be that a high fertility rate was matched here by a particularly staggering rate of child mortality up to the age of five. Meanwhile men and especially women markedly increased their expenditure on fashion and especially on new cotton textiles in the second half of the eighteenth century, a golden age in the village's proto-industrial production.[77] In the 1790s, some couples belonging to the lowest social groups even advanced into the circle of those with the most clothes by the time they married.[78] It would therefore appear that even Pietist couples in relatively rural areas could already make choices between spending on the next generation or the aesthetic quality of their own lives.

Given all of these processes, then, it is no surprise that the word 'fashion' itself gained currency in different languages at this time. Whereas 'costume' denoted more stable customs, *moda* was the word adapted from Latin in Italian. Mode in the sense of new fashion was talked about in French since the sixteenth century, having taken over from the Old French expression *cointerie* as being in-style. It was then adapted in German as 'à-la-mode' during the seventeenth century.[79] The etymologically distinctive English word 'fashion' (from the Latin word for making), as referring to a temporary mode of dress, was used by the physician Andrew Boorde in his *c.*1550 *Book of Knowledge*. Boorde used a woodcut to depict an almost naked and clearly unwise Englishman. He cheerily announces 'Now I wyl were I cannot tel what./ All new fashions be plesaunt to me [Now I will wear I cannot tell what, all fashions be pleasant to me].' Boorde thought that the English would never be a role model for other nations if they assimilated other fashions.[80] Boorde's book was also the first to enter woodcut depictions of people across Europe in different dress. In 1570, the Chinese student Chen Yao wrote how hairstyles, accessories, and cuts of clothes in his Chinese region changed 'without warning. It's what they call fashion', as in *shiyang*, which literally translates as 'look of the moment'.[81] Late Togukawa Japan even created a word for being elegantly chic—'*iki*'.[82]

These expressions matched the world a greater number of people lived in—one in which style mattered, merchants and tailors had their eyes on income, and everyone knew that people looked totally different from those one generation ago. In 1573, for instance, the Nuremberg student Paul Behaim could cleverly claim that Leipzig tailors were unwilling to use 'one stitch' to mend clothes if one never bought anything new. 'I am not writing you this because I wish to wear stately clothes with velvet and silk', he explained to his mother: 'No, not at all. I would like to follow your opinion that I should be able to wear clothes for 3, 4, 5, 6 years, like you. But I know that you would not approve if one walks around like someone who has fallen off the gallows.'[83] The English playwright Ben Jonson even created a student character for one of his plays suffering from 'disease of the flux of apparel'. He would walk observantly through London with his tailor on the lookout for new, beautiful fashion displays.[84]

Clothes were fragile in their durable value. Yet rising populations, the growing appeal of consumption, customers' commitment to look decent and to have members of their households and workshops look decent, as well as clever profit-raising strategies deployed by tailors and merchants explain why textiles played such an enormous role in trade figures. An authoritative chapter on silk trade in the Ottoman Empire thus appropriately opens: 'the motto "commerce is the wheel of the economy" should be modified to "fashion is the wheel of the economy"'.[85] The European thirst for silk continued to form a crucial basis of Iranian and Ottoman prosperity. Florentine firms, in particular, bartered Western woollen cloths for silk, and sold them in agencies in France, Britain, and the Netherlands. To avoid having to use up cash resources, agents kept on asking for the kinds of colours (red and blue) and cloth types that were most in demand in the Asian market. But cloth of different quality arrived, and this in turn must have drawn broader sections of Ottoman society, and those with whom they traded, into the possession of Western woollen cloths and market exchanges, rather than producing fabrics at home. Behind any trade figure—for example cloth valued at 4,000 ducats exchanged for raw silk and cloth from four Muslim merchants in 1478—lay in turn a whole history of environmental and social change which had already shaped much of the medieval economy. Now, even larger areas of Iran were drawn into silk production; Mexican Indians painstakingly scraped cochineal insects from fields of cacti to serve the European desire for scarlet dyes;[86] Brazilian Indians loaded Brazilwood onto Portuguese ships. Imports of indigo damaged a long-standing specialization in the east-German region of Thuringia to cultivate and prepare woad as blue dyestuff through an exceedingly complicated process involving substantial migrant labour.[87] As merchants further expanded into European villages to produce yet more and different types of cloth European societies uncomfortably wrestled with the idea that women might become independent wage-earners and masterless as full time spinners, for any further expansion of weaving depended on a greater supply of thread.[88]

Clothing consumption proved a powerful agent of change, and many societies across the world attempted to regulate its transformative elements through sumptuary laws, while lamenting the difficulties of implementing them.[89] Most European countries at some point seriously debated whether or not to introduce national dress. Sweden did so in the eighteenth century.[90] Fashion was a high political issue, and a widening production and diffusion of goods meant that its importance increased rather than decreased during this period and after. Dress, we can easily remind ourselves, played a key role in Peter the Great's attempts to 'Europeanize' Russia in 1700, in the French Revolution, the American Revolution, and the homespun Indian nationalist movements, as well as in communist policies in our own times. Its full significance only becomes explicable once we survey the complex ways in which dress had become a central idiom through which specific groups in many societies symbolized ideas about a vast range of subjects—power, property, political independence, government, gender, belief, and social belonging—in former times.[91]

THE DRAPED AND THE SEWN

In Europe, a greater awareness of and engagement with dress since the twelfth century was generated, too, by a great shift in what clothes looked like. It distinguishes much clothing predominant in the West from many other cultures up to this day. From the Carolingian period until the twelfth century there had been few changes in the shape of tunics, which were the main garment for all classes. Fabrics were produced and processed in innovative ways for clerical and secular elites in particular. Far more fitted clothing began to be frequently used in French court circles from the early twelfth century onwards to emphasize the human figure. From the early fourteenth century upper garments became much shorter, too, even though the robe similarly retained its significance.[92] An author of the quasi-official *Grandes Chroniques*, written between 1344–50, could therefore be absolutely sure that the French aristocracy had been defeated in 1346 at Crécy because God had been enraged by their new look.

> Some wore their clothing so short that it hardly covered their rumps, with the result that when they bent down to serve their lords they showed their breeches [*braies*] as well as what was inside them to those who stood behind. In addition to this, their clothes were so tight that they needed help both in dressing and undressing; it seemed as though, when one was being undressed, he was literally being skinned [*escourchoit*].[93]

One fourteenth-century German poet wittily imagined Lady Love (*Minne*) awaking from a ten-year slumber to have a new knight presented to her. She simply broke out into laughter and greeted him: 'Welcome, Mr Bare-bottom!' *Minne* told this silly knight then and there to leave her beautiful garden, only to see him stumble over a stone and be unable to get up again. His upper body was 'tightly bound like a sack'.

7. Doublet of lampas silk, allegedly worn by Charles of Blois, duke of Brittany (1345–1364) MT 30307. © Musée des Tissus de Lyon – D.R.

Love asked her ladies to help him get up again.[94]

All this was polemic, but we only need to take one look at the still existent pourpoint jacket allegedly worn by Charles de Blois from *c*.1364 to gasp at its tightness (Fig. 7). It was skilfully made from 32 pieces of white silk cloth from Iran or Iraq, brocaded in gold, closed with 32 buttons at the front, and had very narrow sleeves.[95] It was entirely cotton padded and rigidly encased, which projected the body underneath, probably requiring corseting, and instantly gave a man posture. Even though male clothing often moved away from this extreme tightness in subsequent centuries, the relative closeness of such clothes to the skin explains in part why the humanist Erasmus could think of clothing as 'the body's body'.[96] Belts and buttons became important, and bottoms in turn. Women's bodices clung to the chest, revealing the shape of breasts. There soon existed a whole vocabulary relating to a body nicely laced into a shirt.[97] Thus the body was 'invented'.[98] To understand better the implications of this major change, it is best to refer to a brilliant spark in a conversation between the French anthropologist Claude Levi-Strauss and the historian Lucien Febvre. 'I recall' wrote Levi-Strauss in 1983,

> how I talked to Lucien Febvre thirty years ago, and he said he wished historians would address problems such as the origin and spread of the button. He was absolutely clear about the fact that the presence or absence of this modest item demarcated important ways of human behaviour: it divided the draped and the sewn, two styles of clothing, one of which posing greater demands on the body, the other posing greater demands on the material—but also reflecting on bodily posture, the art of life, ways of integrating in the world, which distinguish different civilisations.[99]

In other words, tightly sewn and shorter clothing for men brought different parts of the body separately into view for the first time. This was uniquely so in the West, imposing a different awareness of what that body should look like and how it should act gracefully in doublet and hose. During the period up to the diffusion of much more generously constructed French clothing in the first decades of the seventeenth century, men in particular were confronted with an intense sense of shape and body weight. The codpiece, or the peas body, which padded the belly, created this awareness for much of the sixteenth century, stabilizing an impression of male prowess. Tightly tailored and intricately constructed clothes newly accentuated sexual difference as embodied. They reinvented masculinity and femininity, as well as a sense of what critics regarded as effeminate. Rulers like Henry VIII clearly used appearances as a power strategy. His enlarged shoulders, strong upper body and asserting pose created the image of a strong, steadfast, and supremely masculine ruler.[100] Women, by contrast, Henry valued for their small, slender bust and the erotic appeal of their partly visible breasts. This explains why sighting his bride-to-be Anne of Cleves wearing a high-cut German dress so displeased Henry. As we have seen from Montaigne's response to the codpiece, which somewhat frivolously might well be called the Renaissance man's Wonderbra, hyper-masculinity could nonetheless also raise anxiety about how dress created illusions which could not be controlled in their effects on others, as well as the question whether and which clothes were meant to cover, conceal, double, or exaggerate bodily traits. Male rulers began to look at each other's portraits to compare legs (which denoted civility) or shoulders. They worried about being outranked in appearance before meeting.[101] Praise of the 'knightly' or 'imperial' leg had in fact become a poetic trope since the high Middle Ages, and it was linked to overarching notions of a man's success and fortune in life. 'Just look at that young man', one poet imagined ladies saying at a court feast, 'what a fortunate man he is. How splendidly he succeeds in everything he does! How handsome he is! How straight his imperial legs are!'[102] Tight-fitting clothes now divided many parts of Christian and Islamic cultures far more visibly, as Islamic law forbade bodily contours being displayed. By the early sixteenth century there lay worlds between the delicate and generously curved cream caftan made from Italian satin and silks that the Ottoman ruler Süleyman the Magnificent (1494–1566) wore, which we could easily take for a woman's dress, and clothes made for the English king Henry VIII or the French ruler Francis I. Both invested unheard of sums to create magnificence with the very same exquisite Italian textiles as Süleyman, but through a different emphasis on fit and fashion.[103] For Henry it is therefore possible to precisely detail his transformation from a handsome youth into a bulky overweight man. He wore clothes made to exact measure. Fit changed the way these men were able to move and feel. Fit fuelled the production of clothes, because they had to be changed and replaced so much more often as teenagers grew or adults bulged. Caftans and kimonos were also sewn from a number of panes, and had fastenings, such as buttons. Hence the divide between civilizations based on the draped or the sewn needs to be approached with great care and does not in itself equate to a divide between Western and non-Western customs.[104] In 1377, the scholar Ibn Khaldûn already reminded Muslims to leave behind 'luxury customs, such as perfume, women, sewn garments, or boots' when they returned to 'God as He created us in the beginning' in white seamless cloth on pilgrimages to Mecca. Khaldûn distinguished between desert people, who used one piece of woven cloth simply to protect themselves from cold, and sedentary people, who cut woven cloth into pieces

> of the right size to cover the form of the body and all of its numerous limbs in their various locations. They then put the different pieces together with thread, until they turn out to be a complete garment that fits the body and can be worn by people. The craft that makes things fit is tailoring.[105]

Mughals distinguished themselves from the draped Hindu tradition through a tailored look that fitted the upper part of tunics to the chest. They introduced tightly fitted breeches up to the ankles below the wide, lower parts of a tunic, which reached down to the knees and was tied around the waist with a belt.[106] Seventeenth-century elite European male dress up to 1650 certainly became softer and less tightly structured, but then returned to the definite, structured lines of a three-piece suit, which relentlessly revealed men's waists and even emphasized them through the waistcoat. Female dress likewise became more constricting though Western neo-classical styles later of course revived draped elements. But a generally far more tightly fitted construction became uniquely common across most parts of Western culture from 1400. In the 1580s, a French traveller certainly aroused a Muslim stallholder's fury in Cairo when he turned his back towards him, thus revealing an outlined bottom.[107] This construction had more outer seams, and this made it more fragile. In addition, men's hose were now typically tailored from a number of panes and underlying fabric. Seams tore with use, or were ripped, especially in areas where tightness put more strain on material in movement. Everyone was exposed to the likelihood of bursting seams or ripped cloth, whereas the great anxiety attached to draped clothes or cloaks was that they might fall or be blown off.

Tighter clothes gave rise to a particular rhetoric of the torn, ragged, or ridiculously short, the demise of form. This could do wonders for children wishing to manipulate parents into buying them new clothes, or comedies about foolish men of a certain age. Machiavelli, in his comedy *La Mandragola* from *c.*1518, thus portrayed an old lawyer called Nicia in disguise to find out about his wife's infidelity saying to himself 'Actually, I look rather good in this disguise. Who'd recognize me? I seem taller, younger, thinner, and there's not a woman in Florence who'd charge me to take her to bed.' Meanwhile, the cunning plotter Ligurio revels in ridiculing Nicia's illusions: 'Who wouldn't laugh? He has on a short little cloak that doesn't even cover his arse. And what the hell is this thing he's wearing on his head? It looks like one of these fur hoods that church canons wear. And he has a puny little sword sticking out between his legs.'[108] His was an incongruous, insufficient, impotent appearance.

Boys—who received their first pair of hose or breeches as a rite of passage from incontinence to control of their bowels—and men were even more exposed to these issues than women, whose dresses remained long and were only tightly fitted around their upper body, emphasizing the ideal of a slim upper waist. Men in these centuries must have been aware of the quality of cuts and construction to an unprecedented extent. Monsieur Jourdain in Molière's 1670 comedy *Bourgeois Gentilhomme* certainly aroused laughter through playing on familiar sentiments when he complained to his tailor about too tight shoes and silk stockings. He was hardly able to put these expensive stockings on, and two stitches had already fallen. In addition, the small flowers on his pretend new court dress had been embroidered upside down! The scene betrays the anxiety many men must have felt to suddenly look ridiculous rather than perfect, because they had not been well informed enough about what was in fashion, or because their clothes dissolved. As men were traditionally believed to be endowed with greater reason and valued for their moral leadership and adeptness for learning, their wardrobes well into the eighteenth century were typically valued higher than clothes owned by women. In the sixteenth and seventeenth centuries, men were seen as arbiters of taste perhaps even more than women, and certainly as much as women. Women also were more clearly targeted by sumptuary laws to limit their consumption.[109] But here, too, lay the roots of Monsieur Jourdain's constant question 'Do you think the dress suits me?', and the whole effort to try to look at themselves through the help of mirrors, paintings, or mediating others as social equals and superiors would look at them, to be sure about what they did look like.

Added to this, another hallmark of the Renaissance among elite men as much as women was a similarly unprecedented use of jewellery, further fuelled by the European expansion.[110] In 1453, the very first Italian text by a woman publicly defending women's rights was prompted by a Bolognese cardinal's new sumptuary legislation. Nicolosa Sanuti challenged this cardinal with a typically Renaissance kind of arrogance: 'Does not everyone know that gold and such adornments and all decoration are testimonies to virtue and heralds of a well-instructed mind?' Christian writers had frequently taken gemstones to symbolize virtuousness. The twelfth-century writer Marbod of Rennes in his *Liber de gemmis* had influentially fused this tradition with Arabic views on the magical and medicinal powers of stones.[111] Sanuti now appropriated these views cleverly to claim that they perfectly advertised female intellect. 'New Catos' were not to steal these tokens of high-born female virtue.[112] We know that by 1475, Sanuti owned a necklace of gold, stones, rubies, and diamonds worth over 300 ducats to stake her claims to virtuousness, learning, beauty, and standing.[113] In just this same year, margrave Anna of Brandenburg wittily reported following about the queen of Denmark's visit to her court. First they had hunted a stag, then the queen wished to see Anna's jewellery. Anna was not keen to show it, but had to hand over Italian jewels she wore on a band around her head to the queen, which, she explained to her female addressee, 'sparkle as you move'. The queen looked into a mirror. She thought herself so pretty that she called in all her entourage. Anna knew this effect of jewellery on old women: 'we think ourselves so beautiful that we don't see our wrinkles around the eyes'.[114] In the following decades, cross-cultural trade in gold, silver, and precious stones accelerated to advertise real or imagined beauty, virtue, wealth, connections, connoisseurship, and power. In 1532, Habsburg envoys turned pale as Süleyman the Magnificent received them in Istanbul in an extraordinary crown he had especially commissioned from Venetian jewellers to combine elements of the Holy Roman imperial crown, the papal tiara, and a military helmet.[115] Precious stones from Ceylon were sold to Italian and Portuguese merchants in Cochin from 1506. By the time the Nuremberg traveller Hieronymus Köler arrived in Lisbon in 1534, he was immediately offered a job as diamond cutter in a mill owned by a German nearby, which staggeringly cut 365 stones 'in one go'.[116] Black velvets and silks were valued not least for setting off jewellery so well, which explains why black was already favoured by Burgundian court culture; Jean de Berry already was an ardent collector of precious stones. Hat-wear largely served as a foil for jewellery, too. Paintings hardly ever catch how magically rubies, pearls, and gold fascinated contemporaries through their ever changing reflections of light at day and by candlelight. Cheap imitates of pearls and paste gems were increasingly available for a wider market.[117] The juxtaposition of glittering jewellery and uncleanliness meanwhile worked perfectly for literary fantasies of disgust, as when della Casa advised in his conduct book *Galateo* (published in 1558) not to look at the inside of one's handkerchief after blowing the nose 'as if pearls and rubies have descended from your brain'.[118] Within Europe, the dichotomy of the ragged and sewn, as well as the bejewelled, took hold of people's imagination of how social being manifested itself: 'I present myself as a king, adorned in diamonds and all sorts of precious stones, and then in a moment become a beggar, all my clothing in rags', Drebbel reported on his optical experiments.[119] Social standing could be related to a visual act of tremendous versatility, constructed through the sensory qualities of cloth, dyes, cut, fit, and accessories as media that structured the process of perceiving people in new ways and conditioned new modes of seeing.

VISUAL ACTS

This greater involvement with things was related to a new visual culture and mediality, a whole set of visual practices, and a greater status given to visual perception. Renaissance elites liked to display a lot of silver, or rugs, and they took pleasure in these goods which were patterned, crafted, luminous, exquisite, exotic, and to an extent stored value. This was as true for cultures within as outside Europe. The Ming dynasty was the first to draw attention to visual qualities in its very name: 'Empire of great brightness.' Not only did its elites value the famous blue and white porcelain vases and other aesthetic objects, but an official reporting from a famine stricken area in 1594, for instance, added thirteen pictures to his report as 'visual agents of political action'. Image-making thus also became a technique to render something real, to impress it vividly like news footage on the minds of beholders.[120] In Europe, artists aspired to make naturalistic likenesses of people, their dress, and accessories. There are many other examples of how important visual practices became for contemporaries to represent the world to themselves. And these visual practices not just recorded something existing, or represented preformed ideas, but shaped perceptions of reality as much as questions about deception. They could develop ideas by visual means and lend them particular force. Ernst Kantorowicz famously showed that royal effigies—in effect puppets of the king—began to be used at funerals from 1422 to visualize how royal majesty was enshrined in an office that never perished. This was long before writers articulated theoretical reflections on the dual nature of kingship.[121] No globe neutrally visualized space. It interpreted what cartographers and globe makers thought to be there, or thought ought to be there. At the same time, these objects lent an experiential dimension to the new knowledge that the world was circular, and also made such knowledge manageable through dynamic spatial interaction. You could walk around a globe, turn it, point at it. It is important to bear in mind that visual media were not just in the realm of elites, even though this remains ill explored.[122]

Visual displays therefore need to be addressed as cultural artefacts and agents in their own right. Since the notion that language is not a passive reflection of existing ideas but consists of speech 'acts' has been widely adopted, we might indeed equivalently speak sometimes about visual 'acts'. The cultural historian Aby Warburg introduced the notion that images can be deeds, are 'hitting images' (*Schlagbilder*), which forcefully capture emotions, pathos, or symbolize control over human anxieties. Warburg thought that such images shaped civilizations through subsequent reformulations. Building on Warburg's ideas, the art historian Horst Bredekamp rejects what he regards as a long tradition in Western thought that goes back to Plato's cave example and treats images as a mere reflection of something happening elsewhere, as epiphenomena. Bredekamp's new philosophy of the visual starts from the hypothesis that the visual can produce what it represents, that it is 'image active' (*bild-aktiv*).[123] One of his examples is van Eyck's famous small portrait of the man with a red turban from 1433. What a familiar, but utterly strange, painting! (Fig. 8) In what is very likely to have been a self-portrait, a critically looking older man with a tense mouth, irregularly drawn eyes, and many wrinkles around them looks at the spectator. The size of this face is matched by the size of an extraordinary, artfully made turban in a precious deep red dye. Despite its height the turban looks light, as a bit of its end comes out just over the right side of the forehead. Portraits began to be produced in Flanders at this time, prompting the new idea that a supreme gaze could capture onlookers standing at opposite angles and yet retain an intimate presence for each. This type of portrait was not just judged or designed as a more or less accurate depiction of a man. It appeared as an artefact that caused a particular sensation, on which spectators were prompted to reflect. But of particular interest to us is the centrality of the turban with its luxurious Eastern appeal. The red turban was painted for the first time as a real three-dimensional object, given volume and perspective, and dramatically set against a black background. Its play of shades in truly bold folds was central to the ingenious display attempted here. This certainly was a man from a commercialized courtly and urban environment 'attaching himself in a dynamic and creative way' to a thing, even if only for the purpose of the painting, rather than in everyday life.[124] 'Images … can help produce what will then be mirrored and reflected on', Bredekamp concludes.[125] Van Eyck wanted onlookers to be captivated by the immediate presence of his likeness, which would follow your eyes from wherever you looked. But if it had not been for the turban, nobody might have

8. Jan van Eyck, *Portrait of a Man in a Turban*, (possible self-portrait), 1433, oil on wood panel, 33.3 × 25.8 cm. © National Gallery, London

looked twice. As portraits became more common, they suggested new ways in which appearance could create a memorable social visibility.

In 1975, the art historian Anne Hollander began to work towards the idea that images actively intervene in 'reality' by positing that when people dress, they make 'pictures' of themselves 'to suit their own eyes, out of the completed combination of clothing and body'. Her book *Seeing through Clothes* dwelt on the argument that such mental pictures are 'directly connected to the pictures they [people] ordinarily see and accept as real'.[126] The advent of Renaissance naturalistic art, in her view, prompted a different visual self-awareness as clothes made the image of man in a steady 'accord with the way artists make, not lifeless effigies but vital representations'.[127] Hollander then over-aestheticized her approach, because she did not want dress to be reduced simply to a social or psychological phenomenon. She maintained that clothes must not be studied 'primarily as cultural by-products or personal expressions but as connected links in a creative tradition of image making', concluding therefore bizarrely that the study of clothes had 'no real substance other than in images of clothes'.[128] Yet silk fabrics, for instance, were very difficult to represent naturalistically. Artists, moreover, could decide to keep the value of portraits moderate, in order to attract more commissions. In Germany, the court artist Lucas Cranach the Elder prided himself on his quick speed. He used a large workshop in which he and his journeymen would intermittently work on paintings to help him maintain a large output and good living. Visiting Augsburg in 1552, Cranach produced several portraits of men and women in oil on canvas, which cost five florins, and a small size that cost merely one and a half florins.[129] By comparison, the 1530 imperial police ordinance prohibited common burghers and artisans to spend more than ten florins just on belts and girdles, and yet allowed women to wear golden rings valuing five and six florins.[130] This suggests that prosperous artisans could certainly afford portraits. Given the conditions of their production, artists therefore usually stuck to repeating the same patterns of dress or jewellery designs they had learned to do, rather than doing justice to a far wider and changing range of beautiful materials and objects that were on offer.[131]

Visual media undeniably played a greater role in framing the way in which particular groups of people made an image of themselves dressed. A Swiss chronicler in 1503 thus criticized 'artistic' painters for creating images of sumptuous fashions in churches that were even adopted in convents.[132] But people were equally influenced by mental images they formed of others whom they encountered in everyday life. Art and clothes both suggested socially emplaced identities that interrelated with aesthetic ideals; they gave expression to religious, political, gendered, or ethnic ideas, and could play with expectations. For Ibn Khaldûn, for instance, it was clear that Muslim Andalusians were subjecting themselves to Christians in Spain as they took over their 'dress, their emblems, and most of their customs and conditions. This goes so far that they even draw pictures on the walls and have them in buildings and houses.'[133] Moreover, objects and technological innovations really mattered in and of themselves, rather than being reflections of artistic trends. Hose, breeches, particular kinds of shoes, or the three-piece suit in Europe, newly shaped the body and what it felt like to be a man. And we certainly need to ask more precisely about who had access to what kind of representations of dress as we widen our inquiry from fine art paintings for elites to broader society and include cheaper media, such as broadsheets, or more publicly available painting, such as church decorations.

Art historians and historians thus have begun to locate the cultural meaning of particular imaging practices and visual displays relevant to particular people or communities in a given period and place. What was the role of woodcuts of dancing peasants or soldiers as 'cultural artefact within a social setting'?[134] What were the purposes of particular outfits, we can similarly ask, or their visual representation in a specific context? Growing attention to people's appearances must have had an impact on the very process of what people noticed when they looked at each other as well as on the sensation of being looked at.[135] Such questions make an inquiry into the 'life' of objects and images as well as historically specific practices of looking so fascinating. Art historians more frequently reconstruct how and where visual media were produced, how they were marketed and exchanged, displayed, seen, and their stylistic ideals described in contemporary terms. All this allows us to find out about their meanings in their own time. The most difficult part often is to know what forms of interaction gave them meaning, to understand them in their social aspects.[136]

Often we only get glimpses, but these can be striking. Consider the Swiss medical doctor Felix Platter's account of how his former neighbour was executed. This was a Protestant 'sectarian' called David Joris. Joris secretly spent the last twelve years of his life in Basle with a group of followers he had taken with him from the Netherlands in 1544 and for whom he had acquired splendid lodgings. He renamed himself John of Bruges. At last, the magistrate became suspicious of his heresies, and three years after his natural death Joris was exhumed. In life he had been known for his striking red beard and his face was still recognizable after death. His corpse had been dressed up with a velvet pointed cap lined with scarlet, and a sumptuous gown. Now the hangman tore all this off, in order to make Joris's dead body visible 'all over'. The corpse was burnt in front of

9. Netherlandish Master, Portrait of the Anabaptist David Joris, c.1550/1555, oil on panel, 78.9 × 68.5 cm (Inv. 561). © Kunstmuseum Basel, Photo: Martin P. Bühler

a large crowd alongside Joris's books and a portrait of himself that he had owned. The council retained a second portrait that had been confiscated in Joris's house in 1559, depicting him as an elegant man with velvet trims on his clothes, a codpiece, thin gloves, and a beautiful sword, not the look to be expected of a true prophet of God (Fig. 9). Hence, these portraits functioned as evidence: the first one demonstrated to everyone that this same man was burning, as it duplicated his former appearance. This ritual also heightened the impact of the shaming punishment. It visualized sumptuous pretence, and tore it away from a conceited man to reveal a bad, dead body.[137]

The other portrait could then be kept by the council as a monument to its preservation of honesty and orthodox belief among the Basle citizens. Its role was to provide evidence that this identical man had disappeared from the community. Today, this Renaissance portrait hangs on a museum wall, like so many others. And yet it uniquely leads us back to a world in which visual practices had become prominent in an exploration not just of the aesthetics, but also of the conceits and drama of existence, an exploration of processes of deception, unmasking, or attempts to make something real.

This book, in sum then, is about dress displays and their visual presentation. It examines them as part of cultural arguments about display and identity, which reveal the dynamic of early modern society in new ways. The act of dressing became a much more important 'signifying practice' for many in this period. We can think of it as part of the symbolic toolkit through which people could acquire and communicate attitudes towards life and construct visual realities in relation to others. Consumption remained contested. Nobody could escape debate about how much of it, for whom, and where it was appropriate. Some rejected how much appearances mattered, insisting that dress displays should not create the illusion of something 'real'. Humans seemed too vulnerable to the deceptive power of vision and too able to manipulate these symbolic toolkits for their own purposes. Therefore the notion that clothing did not actually represent something real and led to misidentification rather than the identification of a person was soon creatively explored.[138] One of the very first Spanish novels, published in 1554 and soon a bestseller translated across Europe, was the picaresque autobiography *The Life of Lazarillo de Tormes*. It narrated the fatal mistake of a boy looking for service who trusted the appearances of a nobleman only to find out that his house was completely empty and there was no food. The whole plot brought into question the relationship of dress to reality in a much larger and dynamic urban world where one could not trust appearances and yet had few means to gather secure knowledge about newcomers.[139] Or take the extraordinary story about how one day the painter Adriaen Brouwer (1605/6–1638) apparently arrived in Amsterdam naked after a pirate robbery. He cut some sack-cloth into a suit. Then he took out his paint and brushes to paint it into the 'best and most expensive material in the world'. He paraded with it on the streets, so much so that fashionable ladies began to search shops for this cloth. Finally, at the end of a comedy in the Amsterdam Academy, Brouwer climbed onto the stage holding a wet sponge. He dramatically exclaimed that the 'rare costliness of his clothing' was nothing but 'dirt, deception, and vanity', just as the world was 'deceptive and false'. At the end of this impassioned speech, Brouwer wiped off all the colour. Representation here became a moral act to disillusion rather than to serve illusion. This is why he needed to present the material itself, sack-cloth and paint. Another time, at a cousin's wedding, Brouwer smeared gravy on his velvet suit, just because his relatives had complimented him on looking smart for once![140]

There existed a tension then between those embracing the playful metamorphosis ever new materials allowed for and those who resisted the whole notion that dress should be there to objectively represent and produce a person's characteristics, while others defended that clothing should symbolize rank or constitute magnitude through splendour and beauty. A further group used artistic media, such as the emerging novel, to draw attention to the ambiguities any notion that status, masculinity, or femininity could be objectified created in real life. Finally there were those like Brouwer, endorsing the strict view that clothes were a deceptive 'outside' of fallen humankind, a mere fiction created by symbolic means: appearance not reality, *Schein* not *Sein*. This latter position endorsed that the spiritual needed to transcend the material. Others maintained that materiality could mediate between the human and the divine. Shrouds worn by a holy person, for instance, could be seen as imbued with the sacred through having touched a holy body and possessing healing power. Many oscillated between these poles, and resigned themselves to the fact that appearance and being, dressing up and identity might be interrelated.

These divergent attitudes towards how matter mattered have become further enshrined as a crucial part of our cultural heritage. Their understanding is essential even to analyse the symbolic universe of contemporary fashion statements about merchandising and mutability. At one end of a spectrum, fashion statements can celebrate the traditions of early modern luxury craftwork through intricate embroidery, lace, and beadwork. The designer Martin Margiela, by contrast, subverts the notion of dress magnificence by laying bare seams or even by growing moulds and bacteria on clothes to make apparent their future decay and our knowledge that most clothes will end up as discarded consumer goods.[141]

GERMANY

In order to explore how dress and images of clothing served to imagine identifications in the sixteenth century this book will mostly draw on German sources. This is because from a European and global perspective its profusion of visual practices engaging with everyday life and therefore with dress displays during this period stand out. Quite simply, if we wish to understand this particular society, we need to be able to analyse its visual production and the role it played in cultural arguments. John Hale perhaps did most to point to this specificity of the Northern Renaissance tradition from a comparative perspective and analyse its causes.[142] Hale found that whereas the depiction of soldiers became a prominent theme in sixteenth-century German art, Italians hardly ever cared about it, despite the equal prominence of warfare at the time. Why should this have been so? Italian artists were taught that any depiction of everyday subjects for their own sake was beneath their honour. Every subject needed to be part of a higher mythological, classical, historical, biblical, or otherwise moral theme. Portraits were stylized to represent the honour and civility of clients. Soldiers, peasants, or ordinary folk thus played the assigned parts subservient to these larger noble themes, rather than being freshly observed for their own sake. For Alberti, as Svetlana Alpers has similarly emphasized, Italian art was meant to open a window onto another, dignified world, rather than work from observing everyday life. There existed of course connections between the Italian and the Northern Renaissance, but by and large we can say that Netherlandish and German artists became more interested in humanizing rather than dignifying their subjects or presenting emotions in terms of emblematic states. 'Of course', Hale sums up, 'German art was selective, elaborative, personalizing as "art" must be, but it was less excluding of what was familiar, coarse, ugly than were the more self-consciously tuned antennae of art in the south.'[143] Jeffrey Chipps Smith agrees that Northern Renaissance visual practices particularly valued curiosity about people and the natural world.[144] Dürer built his whole theory on artists' special ability to create through being 'inwardly full of figures' they had observed from life.[145] This was a very different process from applying a universal ideal of beauty that could be measured out.

Add to this that leading artists were attracted by three centres of an emerging print culture, Strasbourg, Augsburg, and Nürnberg. Entrepreneurs repeatedly financed heavily illustrated projects with wholly innovative designs. These were a success in terms of their appeal, if not always in financial profit. From Strasbourg, Sebastian Brant's *Ship of Fools* with its copious woodcuts became not just a German, but European bestseller. In Nuremberg, Schedel's first world chronicle, published in 1493 with its 1,809 woodcuts, fascinated a broad elite audience. It was produced by Anton Koberger, who owned twenty-four printing presses and employed around one hundred workers.[146] Next, Emperor Maximilian I used Augsburg and Nuremberg expertise and the local coming together of humanists, artists, and printers in close collaboration to follow through his unprecedented use of woodblocks for mega-projects to propagate and memorialize his rule, the *Weisskunig*, *Triumph*, *Theuerdank*, and *Ehrenpforte*.[147] Then, as Germany was gripped by intense debate about religious reform straight after Maximilian's death, illustrated broadsheets in the early 1520s became a versatile vehicle to campaign for Protestant ideas, once more as in no other culture. These were often attractively coloured by specialized craftsmen.

A final example for the extent to which it had become possible in this society, and in this society alone, to believe in the importance of images is an Augsburg edition of the early Renaissance humanist Petrarch's book about the fortune and misfortune of happiness, *De remediis*. Well over 200 years after he had conceived it in manuscript, Petrarch's message still retained its meaning: it was far wiser to replace the hope of happiness or fear of unhappiness with stoic beliefs and Christian faith. This theme was brought out with reference to a plethora of everyday situations. A person who prided himself for smelling nicely and perfuming everything was foolish; those who thought they had many friends were misguided, and so on. Many editions of Petrarch's manuscript appeared all over Europe after the advent of print. Yet apart from a French edition with eleven woodcuts nobody had commissioned pictures.[148] In Augsburg, publishers decided to translate the text in 1518. They recruited Sebastian Brant as advisor, got a local councillor and later none less than Duke Frederick the Wise's humanist secretary, Georg Spalatin, to translate the text into the vernacular and add minor passages, for instance on the horrors of adopting foreign clothes. They paid for a full 261 woodcuts of outstanding quality, which were finished within two years. The publisher filed for bankruptcy before the book could be printed. But the manuscript and woodblocks were acquired by another printer, Heinrich Steiner, who finally published the work in 1532. *Von der Artzney* (Fig. 10) became another bestseller, with nine editions by 1620, a success which already enabled Steiner in his time to print a whole set of heavily illustrated classical or Renaissance books which popularized Greek and Roman ideas of civic morality rooted in communal responsibility.

The woodcuts in the Petrarch edition engaged vividly and often critically with the theme of how appearances communicated attitudes to life. We might contrast this keenness to give appearances a role in the drama of everyday life and cultural arguments about values with an earlier, rare depiction of an Italian urban scene, in which we do find something ugly. When Ambrogio Lorenzetti was instructed to paint his famous frescoes in the town hall of Siena (1338/40), he placed nine youthful male dancers in the centre of an image depicting 'good government' (Fig. 11). Seven of these dancers are elegantly dressed, but two others wear very strange cloaks indeed. One is moth-eaten. The other has appliqué worms on it. This depiction of decay, however, was only meant to manifest a Christian belief in the presence and power of pain and sadness in the middle of life. Lorenzetti's painting suggested that good civic government by the Sienese council of nine men overcame sadness.[149] Elegant dress was seen to display and engender virtue and beauty. Startlingly, it could now be regarded as integral to the symbolization and artistic legitimization of institutionalized political order, wealth, peace, a happy

10. Petrarch, *Von der Artzney bayder Glück*, Augsburg: Heinrich Steiner 1532, frontispiece, BL C39.h.25. © The British Library, London

community. From its beginnings, then, Renaissance Italian visual tradition and the particular genres in which it expressed itself primarily explored an ideal of beauty. German prints, album and even wall paintings engaged with the significance of appearances and meanings of display in far more varied and open ended ways.

This visual culture could invite the practice of looking as imaginative discovery of people in the streets, of what they did, in Germany and around the globe. Global interconnections became more present in the local, for everyone to see. From 1607 until

11.   Ambrogio Lorenzetti, detail of *The Dancers in the Allegory of Good Government*, Siena. Note the shoemaker in the right corner. © Su concessione del comune di Siena, Photo: Roberto Testi

the early twentieth century, for instance, the weavers' guild's house right in the centre of Augsburg was covered with murals of local wool and cotton traders in Venice striking deals with Italian and Asian men. There also were two painted windows. One side of each window was opened, revealing a neatly dressed woman with a small child beside her on a table inside. She looked as keenly out to people passing by as they would look at her.[150]

What does all this engagement with cloth and clothes and images of dress tell us about this culture and time? Dress was obviously experienced in dialogue with the body and its social meanings had to be lived with. So this book is curious about what this lived, and for us increasingly removed, reality of wearing hose, tight bodices, or even exotic bright feathers on hats might have been like. It asks how more competitive consumption influenced emotional lives. The dichotomy of the shaped and the shapeless, the whole and the torn, the simple and the refined in dress was becoming relevant not just as an experience, but as a symbolic categorization and form of metaphorical thinking in people's understanding of life. This dichotomy provided a particular language to express—often ambiguously—aspiration and anxiety. It fed into fantasies about beauty as equating perfection. A perfect fur coat, for instance, was taken as an achievement that bespoke endurance, skill, and a deeply sensuous appreciation of natural beauty. Yet, almost everyone in this period believed that life on earth was imperfect and marked by much dishonesty. Dishonesty in turn would graphically be equated to a badly made fur that was dyed in false colours and would lose its hair after four months.[151] Commodities became loaded with an emotional language of what was socially right or wrong. The most sophisticated dress displays, on the body or through art, in turn could create visual fictions attempting to comment on, resolve, or just state contradictions in life: Lorenzetti's contradiction of moths and elegance, sadness and joy, fictively resolved by the council of nine; van Eyck's contrast of an aged, wrinkled, startlingly unidealized face and an ingenious, sumptuous turban; Brouwer's pretend luxurious sack-cloth on a naked body. Images and dress displays in these ways provided a powerful language to explore what it meant to be human. Indeed, if these and the German album paintings and woodcuts we shall turn to now had any effect, then we might say that this was a period in which the social in part was produced by visual means.

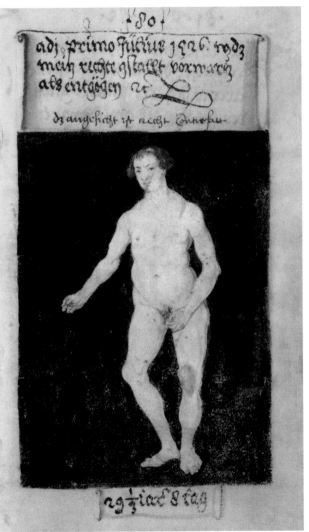

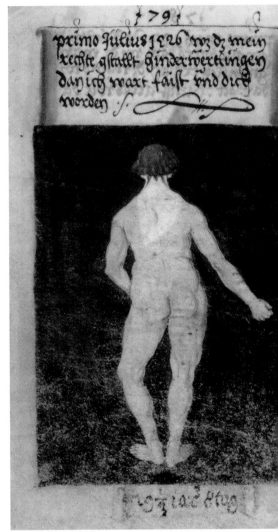

12. (*above left*) Matthäus Schwarz, Book of Clothes, Illustration 80, nude picture from the front, July 1526, 16 × 10 cm. © Herzog Anton Ulrich Museum, Braunschweig, Kunstmuseum des Landes Niedersachsens, Museumsphoto Bernd Peter Keiser

13. (*above right*) Matthäus Schwarz, Book of Clothes, Illustration 79, nude picture from the back, July 1526. © Herzog Anton Ulrich Museum, Braunschweig, Kunstmuseum des Landes Niedersachsens, Museumsphoto Bern Peter Keiser

CHAPTER TWO

Looking at the Self

MATTHÄUS SCHWARZ OF AUGSBURG

In 1526, the head accountant of the mighty Fugger merchant company in Augsburg was a man called Matthäus Schwarz. Schwarz was a successful 29-year-old. He had trained in Venice, written about double entry book-keeping, and had worked with Jakob Fugger, one of the most wealthy and influential people of his time. On the first of July Matthäus Schwarz took off his jewellery, weapons, and clothes. His doublet was unlaced, which held up his hose. He took off his shirt and his under-drawers, and posed for two small watercolour paintings. A 19-year-old aspiring miniaturist called Narziss Renner dipped his brushes into water and paint to depict Schwarz, first from the back, then from the front, on precious parchment paper (Figs. 12–13). No one had ever done this before. During his lifetime, Schwarz commissioned a further 135 watercolour images of himself dressed. This, too, nobody had ever done. The series retrospectively began with his infancy and ended when he was 63 years old. All these sheets were exquisitely bound around 1561 and turned into a book creating a unique record of how a sixteenth-century man displayed his body to successive Augsburg portraitists and added his own inscriptions. It survives as one of the most intriguing sources of his time.

The book of clothes is stored in a small German museum, but two more formal visual self-enactments of Schwarz are on open view in the Thyssen-Bornemisza collection in Madrid and the Louvre Northern Renaissance galleries. To find a book-keeper's portraits in two of the best museums of the world is in itself astonishing. It is testimony to his skilled used of new visual media to create a lasting presence. The Louvre half-length oil painting shows Schwarz earlier in the same year that he commissioned the nude images, on his birthday in February 1526. It now hangs prominently next to the first self-portrait that Albrecht Dürer painted of himself in 1493 as a 21-year-old. Both panels point to the different ways in which both sitters used the medium of portraiture at a

14.   Albrecht Dürer, *Self-portrait 1493*, oil on canvas, 56.0 × 44.0 cm,
Paris, Louvre. © RMN / Jean-Gilles Berizzi

particular point in time to communicate how they wished to be seen. Dürer depicted
himself with rough hands and entirely unkempt shoulder-length hair. He wore characteristically distinctive clothes, and an extremely strange and striking red headdress (Fig.
14). The left pupil of his eye, positioned in the far right corner, made him look unsettled
and questing. This was an image of daring and striking youthful originality. Set against a
black background, his figure confronted the onlooker directly—there simply was nothing else to look at. Dürer, as we saw in the Introduction, was the first artist to use self-
portraiture. He painted himself in oil three times during his twenties to demonstrate
his inventiveness and superiority over craftsmen. His self-portraits, it can be argued,
produced the 'possibility and rules of formation' for what subsequently became such an
important pictorial tradition in the West.[1]

15. Hans Maler (active from 1500–1529), *Matthäus Schwarz 1526*, oil on canvas, 41.0 × 33.0 cm, Paris, Louvre
© RMN / Jean-Gilles Berizzi

Schwarz's portrait, by contrast, was made by an artist who would have happily regarded himself as an artisan and accordingly was called Hans the Painter—Hans Maler (Fig. 15). Maler based himself in the booming Tyrolean silver mining town Schwaz near Innsbruck, its population of 20,000 inhabitants living in houses beautifully perched against snow-capped mountains.[2] Today the Schwaz mines can be visited but have long stopped working. But from here came some of the German cash flow that was essential for a more interconnected economy across the globe. Maler specialized in portrait commissions, and in this case delivered an accomplished and pleasing birthday picture of Schwarz. He looked like an outstandingly stylish young businessman with a lute, fine features and hands, exquisitely finished clothing, jewellery, armoury, and a tidy skull-cap under his Spanish beret. Maler had painted an understated portrait of Anton Fugger when he took over the Fugger company just the year before, dressed in a black gown and merely adorned with a golden toothpick, which the Louvre has rightly relegated to a side wall. The portrait of Schwarz, by contrast, exposed a new aesthetics of gracious civility and decorousness (*Zierlichkeit*) open to Renaissance men. Lively, harmonious colours underlined this effect.

Aged twenty-nine, Schwarz could aspire to adulthood. The progression from youth to adulthood was constructed as a surprisingly drawn-out process for early sixteenth century upper-class men, which could continue into their thirties.[3] Male youth, in fact, only ended properly with marriage, with being head of a household. Before this, men's sexual identity was not yet bound to clear-cut ideals of honourable virtue, as it was for women. In Schwarz's youth it still allowed for displays of sweet delicateness as well as hyper-masculinity, for courting different partners, and illicit sex. Dürer had likewise produced his final self-portrait in oil aged twenty-eight. But he by then was already a married man and a celebrated artist. He posed in that brown, fur-trimmed gown to claim his honour and visualize his masculine moral maturity (Fig. 4). Schwarz, by contrast, emphasized his capacity for judicious, chic refinement, his still clean-shaven youthfulness and sexual attractiveness.[4] In these ways, urban citizens below the nobility, whose status was more flexible, could value pictorial displays of dress, accessories, hairstyles, and their comportment to signal how they wished to be regarded by others. This was especially meaningful as they were about to end youth, when others had so much power to decide on their reputation, careers, marriages, and thus wealth and public influence. We hence need to think of such portraits as visual arguments and performance acts, which in Schwarz's and Dürer's cases were to have an astonishingly lasting exposure to different audiences across time. What would you think if you now saw Dürer's and Schwarz's portraits in Paris? Is it still possible for us, who are so used to the camera and a lifelong history of visual recording, to be in a room full of Renaissance portraits and yet to appreciate afresh that something quite new and curious was happening at the time, as more and more men and women of not just the aristocratic but upwardly mobile middling classes paid to prop themselves up at length in front of a man with an easel or a drawing pen?[5] For it was of course only with the Renaissance medal and portrait that subjects were considered worthy of a lifelike representation.

How did these changes in 'visuality', that is the way in which new visual media functioned, in turn affect peoples' perception of themselves and others? For the emergence of central perspective paintings in the Renaissance needs to be seen as a distinctive Western invention and symbolic practice. It centred on the eye of the beholder. Through her or his privileged position in front of the image, the world unfolded as a visually simulated three-dimensional field in representation. The new prominence of portrait paintings thus heightened the symbolic presence of an individual person, as looking from that privileged central viewpoint, or as centrally depicted. This was in contrast, for instance, to Arab art, which positively valued surfaces to mediate mathematically calculated geometrical and ornamental patterns as spiritually invested practice. The privileging of a directed gaze onto people who were depicted in seemingly lifelike ways was a specifically Western invention and now occasioned new ways of exploring personhood—in the West, and soon in other parts of the world.[6]

Yet we must not forget that these new visual practices continued to run alongside an interest in the ornamental, and rather than radically individuating the self also brought with them a new relationship: an intriguing dialogue between artists and sitters. Dürer's self-portraits, for all we know, were really painted by him without any workshop collaboration, whereas Schwarz was portrayed. This is an important difference, because it means that the visual artefacts displaying Schwarz's body emerged through this human relationship. It was likely to entail exchanges about what kind of display would be most effective, how it related to previous portrayals, what look a particular painter's skills allowed for, and how much it would cost. Putting in a lute and elegant fingers playing it, for instance, obviously added to the cost and value of a portrait. Lutes were a relatively new instrument, expensive, and difficult to play. They sounded soft and would be sung to with restrained voices. Hence, they signalled wealth and an embodied gentle, decorous civility, as well as intelligence and artistic sensibility. Schwarz would later send one of his sons at the age of ten to be taught by renowned local lute masters. Renaissance painters made considerable efforts to learn how to depict instruments naturalistically as three-dimensional objects. Dürer even included a lesson on how to correctly represent a lute in his writings on perspective. It is therefore helpful to think of painters with their specific experiences, modes of production, and skills as mediators for sitters to visualize their identities in particular ways.[7]

Schwarz, like some other sitters of Maler, next made the Louvre panel portrait his own through the same process of inscription as used in every one of the depictions in his *Klaidungsbüchlein*. He wrote on it 'I Matthäus Schwarz had this appearance at Schwaz [when] I was just 29 years old.' This shows that he identified with his representational self through an idiom of likeness, just as he repeatedly remarked on other images that he thought his face had been properly captured. But how did Schwarz know what he really looked like? This inscription presents us with a clue: either people he intimately knew looked at the paintings and verified whether it was a true likeness, or Schwarz used a mirror in the belief that it reflected his true likeness and systematically compared this reflection with his depicted self. The inscription is also significant because it alleged that he was neither interested in an ideal-typical depiction emphasizing his office or lineage, nor in the process of portraiture as performance, permitting subjects to 'come out better', or allowing for cultural reinvention. Such attitudes fuelled the great age of studio photography in Europe and India.[8] Schwarz even excluded his carnival masques from the book. His project was based on a commitment to authentic naturalism to endorse the idea that art should produce a 'deep' likeness drawn from life to record a particular person with distinctive characteristics at a particular point in time. The key purpose of such depictions seemed to be to objectively record information. On the nude pictures later that year he even noted 'that was my real figure from behind, because I had become fat and large', and again, this 'was my proper appearance from the front, the face is properly represented [*contrafat*]'. Below each picture he noted his precise age—'29⅓ Years 8 days'.

Looking at them more closely, we instantly see that these nude pictures remarkably did not follow Southern Renaissance artistic conventions to recover ancient traditions and present an idealized body of masculine beauty and perfect Vitruvian proportion. Neither did they mirror the splendour of Adam's divine creation. Schwarz's shoulders were sloping down and not particularly large. Only the legs and arms appeared to have some muscularity. His belly was portly, his bottom and thighs large and quite shapeless. His private parts were covered by his hand, even in the view from the back— this was no attempt to reveal Herculean *grandezza* either. The body furthermore was bound in a very soft, flowing manner, rather than through clear, strong lines which at the time typically conveyed a defined and enclosed sense of personhood against its environment. This ideal of a perfect, classical body complemented contemporary images of the grotesque body as luxuriating in flesh, laughter, fertility, excrement, exuberant in its constant exchange with the world through eating, drinking, sex, sociability, and defecation, its boundaries constantly extending and changing.[9] The French doctor and writer Rabelais is best known for creating the grotesque figure Gargantua, who needed twenty-four and a quarter yards of cloth just for his codpiece! Yet Schwarz presented his naked burgher body in a way that defied playful illusion, in a naturalistic mode as normal and changeable through weight and age, as deeply human, as well as an object of anxiety about the loss of shape.

What was the place of these startling images in a book of clothing? One historian, Valentin Groebner, has warned that we should not regard the nude pictures as 'authentic' representation of this burgher's body. Groebner argues that they need to be seen as self-conscious representations for a venue conceived as social as the weddings, funerals, and political events Schwarz visited. He suggests that it was commonly believed that people would arise from death with the body they had had around the age of thirty. Based on admittedly tentative evidence he argues that this was Schwarz's humble 'paradise or purgatory "look"'.[10] Groebner then extends this argument to claim that despite its naturalistic manner, nothing in the *Klaidungsbüchlein* promises us privileged insights into the intimate, private world, or 'real self' of a sixteenth-century man.[11] Rather, it presents to him a controlled recording of well-performed social roles, documenting Schwarz's successful navigation of a complicated urban world that often seemed incalculable. Seen from this perspective, Schwarz needs to be understood in the most literal sense as an expert in self-fashioning: a shrewd bookkeeper, whose self-perception was structured by the merchant world in which he lived, that is, a daily practice of accounting, registering, judging trust, manipulating, and being aware of others' manipulations, which was replicated in sartorial management.[12] Schwarz thereby is easily made to fit a story that sees the Renaissance as the beginning of an archetypal modern man. This is the emergence of 'economic man', who controls his actions through strategic reasoning to maximize professional achievement and capital gain. Gisela Mentges likewise contends that Schwarz followed a logic of commercial arithmetic in recording his garments in terms of quality, colour, and shape and was rooted in an 'economically determined cultural context'.[13] 'By orienting himself closely to the order of bookkeeping', she writes, Schwarz successfully transformed his lifetime into a linear structure and thereby developed a 'coherent' sense of masculine self-hood.[14]

In contrast to these views I seek to show that the *Klaidungsbüchlein* was not a controlled experiment, and not a 'picture chain' similar to a continuous account book registering business figures. Matthäus Schwarz's appearances were certainly highly staged and expressed a new kind of self-awareness among urban burghers. Yet what makes these images so fascinating is that they form a more complex visual myth which turned out to be as much about the loss of control as about the ability to control, about changing fortune, generationality, and thus mortality, and about the grip of social roles, and their limitations on the expression of desire. In contrast to historians and literary scholars who assume that elites succeeded in fashioning favourable impressions of themselves, I question whether the visual record of a lifetime that emerged through interaction with different painters could be managed rationally. Nor are historians right in assuming that the permanent practice of putting figures and balances in an accountancy book straightforwardly fostered a rational mind and self-assured mode of controlling masculinity. The *Klaidungsbüchlein* seems to have been treated as a private record, which Schwarz shared with people of his own choice; it was neither, as far as we know, publicly displayed, nor a completely 'secret' book, which only he looked at. This, however, could be just the same for panel portraits or medals. Portrait paintings were not usually hung up on walls, but put into chests and selectively displayed to onlookers so that they would take on much of their meaning from the precise setting in which they were revealed. The chief purpose of some of the watercolours in the *Klaidungsbüchlein* was to record information of how Schwarz had looked, and to convey a passionate aesthetic fascination for dress. Yet other depictions were invested with a more personal affective interest, and hence allow us to access the emotional as much as the rational dimensions of his life. Schwarz's book, moreover, strikingly changed in character during his late maturity, and as he had to change the artists with whom he worked. This is why we need to reconstruct, as far as possible, how visual sources were produced and whether they were exchanged, and integrate the results into our interpretation of their meaning and use. I take the increasing frequency of gaps in portraits of Schwarz towards the end of the book as a clue. It seems as if Schwarz was at pains to find a suitable end and a suitable painter for an increasingly awkward project he had embarked on forty years before as a young man. This chapter therefore seeks to show how Schwarz experimented with a representation of his self through the medium of dress displays and their visual recording in a way which had become thinkable in his time, but also how this project turned against any notion of a self and continuous self display that could easily be controlled. One might therefore formulate that if Dürer successfully showed the possibility of the genre of self-portraiture, Schwarz showed the psychological and practical impossibility of the genre he could have founded for his time: a continuous visual record of a bourgeois man's interaction with dress throughout personal life events, aiming to be 'true to life' and yet representing an ideal of virtue or successful masculinity. The book rather ran contrary to any heroic myth that true men controlled their environment, body, and emotions. This explains why it remains unique.

The fifteenth-century Florentine Leon Battista Alberti was a central figure in the invention of perspective as Western symbolic practice. When he commissioned a profile medal of himself, Alberti chose a winged eye as an emblem underneath his face. This device symbolized the way in which the Renaissance could now liberate the power of the mobile gaze as sovereign agent in the world, and conceive of the subject as a person who would gain knowledge principally through seeing and observing. Yet curiously the medal carried the motto 'What now?'[15] This ambivalence as to what these new visual practices would lead to is similarly present in Schwarz's experiment. It documents less a complex of coherent visual arguments than the problems Western individuals would now encounter in controlling the production of images, which alongside clothing mediated their sense of selfhood and the real.

BEGINNING THE BOOK

The year was 1520; a new king and future emperor of the Holy Roman Empire had just been elected; Martin Luther was under threat of excommunication and his roaring *Address to the German Nobility* had sold out in a fortnight. In it, he condemned not just the pope, but the new merchant capitalism fuelled by the Fugger firm, dividing Augsburg people ever more glaringly into the super rich and poor. Germany was a place of uncertainty and unease. Matthäus Schwarz of Augsburg would turn twenty-three in February. His father, a wine merchant, had died aged seventy in November. On his own birthday, which he always marked as important, Matthäus, in 1520, began his book of clothes in the following way: he held a paper scroll on which he announced how much he had always enjoyed talking to older people, not least about what they had worn decades ago (Fig. 16). He had looked at drawings of what some of them had worn thirty, forty, or fifty years ago, and now wished to record his own clothing to see 'what might become of it'.[16] Since the age of fourteen, Schwarz had started to make drawings of or entries about his clothes, and he remarked that the manner of clothing 'changed around daily'.[17] He knew that shoes would have been long and pointed when his father had been little, and that one of his own mourning gowns was already unfashionable. Aesthetic judgement evidently changed, while the historical contexts explaining changing fashions were not always clear. Schwarz therefore declared himself engaged at the very outset of his book with a sense of impermanence and the indeterminable. As his father died, he began to inscribe himself in time. What would become of his appearances and own life?

Schwarz first commissioned twenty-eight images of himself up to the age of twenty-three. The series began with an image of his aged father and, anachronistically, of his young mother as pregnant with Matthäus, recording a sense of lineage, as well as a fascination with his own physical origin as he noted 'I was hidden'. From underneath her clothes he emerged into baby-wear: 'this was my first dress in the world', he wrote next to the image of his mother rocking him in a cradle. His youth was largely narrated around amusing stories, rites of maturity, or important events. It was accompanied by a separate, short chronicle, entitled 'Course of the World', *Weltlauf*, to which the *Klaidungsbüchlein*'s inscriptions refer, but which Schwarz later destroyed. It is therefore only these images that now tell us what seemed relevant to Matthäus about his boyhood: for instance, how he had measles and was entertained with toy horsemen by his maid in the hot summer of 1500; how he received his first proper hose after being toilet trained; how he learned to write; how he accompanied Emperor Maximilian I's famous court fool Kunz von der Rosen at carnival for three weeks; was taken to be educated by a priest and his maid in Heidenheim; ran away; herded cows with village boys; returned to Augsburg aged eleven and wanted to become a monk as he loved to look at altar paintings and light candles at the Schwarzes' home altar; threw away his school bag aged thirteen and was apprenticed by his father (Figs. 17–20). Business trips on ever more beautiful horses took him to Munich and then, aged sixteen, still further away to the Lake Constance area, until he was off to Italy the year after, to learn the language and the art of accounting. It would take thirty months before he saw Augsburg again.

Matthäus's sense of independence had clearly risen immensely when he was away on business by himself aged fifteen. He nearly always wore adult weapons, could control

16. (*opposite*) Matthäus Schwarz, Book of Clothes, frontispiece. © Herzog Anton Ulrich-Museum Braunschweig, Kunstmuseum des Landes Niedersachsen, Museumsphoto Bernd Peter Keiser

1520

Auch heütt ·20· Februarto 1520. do ich
Matheus schwarcz von augspurg, krad·23·
Jar alt, in obgmelter gstalt: Da sprich ich
dz ich all mein tag gern vor bey den allten,
vnd ire antwurt meyner frag was mir ein
grose freüd zöhern: vnd ynder anderm ward
wir etwa auch forod der trachtüng vnd mo=
nier der klaydungen, wie sy sich also teglich
verkeret: vnd etwa zaigten sy mir ir trach=
ten controfatt so sy vor 30:40: in so iarn ge=
tragen hetten, dz mich fer wundert vnd

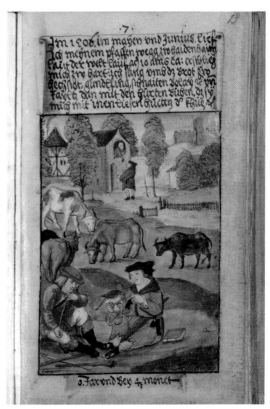

17. (*above left*)   Matthäus Schwarz, Book of Clothes, Ill. 4, aged 5 in 1502, learning the alphabet, his mother had just died. © Herzog Anton Ulrich-Museum Braunschweig, Kunstmuseum des Landes Niedersachsen, Museumsphoto Bernd Peter Keiser

18. (*above right*)   Matthäus Schwarz, Book of Clothes, Ill. 7, aged 9, having run away. © Herzog Anton Ulrich-Museum Braunschweig, Kunstmuseum des Landes Niedersachsen, Museumsphoto Bernd Peter Keiser

horses, and retrospectively thought of himself instantly as looking much older and taller. This was a period in which horse-riding embodied physical eloquence, male strength, and intelligent control. Schwarz's changing self-perception and his painters' mediation accentuates an extraordinarily striking feature of the book of clothing, right to the end: up to the point of teenage maturity most depictions involved other characters, maids and mates, told a 'story', and were thus set in specific domestic, urban, or rural scenery. Nonetheless, even as they depicted one or two other figures besides Schwarz, these images were surprisingly *empty*. This emptiness appears stranger yet once we realize that Schwarz belonged to one of the largest families in Augsburg at the time. When his father died, one chronicler duly noted under the heading 'About someone, whose name was Ulrich Schwarz, and left many children' that Ulrich Schwarz had had thirty-two children

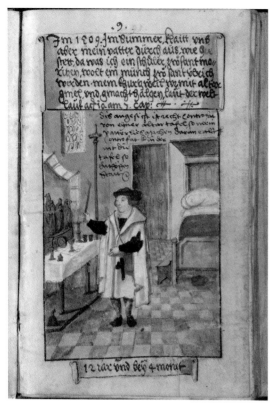 

19. (*above left*)   Matthäus Schwarz, Book of Clothes, Ill. 9, aged 12, engrossed in religious worship and on his way to becoming a monk. © Herzog Anton Ulrich-Museum Braunschweig, Kunstmuseum des Landes Niedersachsen, Museumsphoto Bernd Peter Keiser

20. (*above right*)   Matthäus Schwarz, Book of Clothes, Ill. 11, aged 14, trampling on his school books and finishing with school. © Herzog Anton Ulrich-Museum Braunschweig, Kunstmuseum des Landes Niedersachsen, Museumsphoto Bernd Peter Keiser

from three wives and five more illegitimate children as a widower. Twenty of these had been alive when he perished, thirteen of them boys.[18] Matthäus was part of this crowd, and his own mother had died when he was just five. The boys would have all worn the same, or similar outfits, or remade items from a sibling. St Moritz school, a Latin school he went to for one year, was also depicted empty except for Matthäus, and he even chose to imagine himself playing alone (or in duplicates) on the streets of Augsburg, a city that would have been teeming with children, as most of the urban population was made up of them. Animals—pigs, hens, house dogs and cats, stray dogs and cats—also participated in early modern urban street life. Slaughtering in Augsburg took place in the central square, until people got too squeamish about the odour of blood. Among the urban crowd were carters, sweepers, beggars, maids, artisans, peasants on their way to

the market or tavern, the clergy (a staggering ten per cent of the population), merchants, officers, foreign dignitaries, and printers. Spinners and the many weavers formed the dominant local craft; all life was present in this city of around 45,000 souls in 1540. Jörg Seld, a friend of Schwarz, produced a large aerial view of Augsburg and its environment in 1521, which visually represented how much the city had grown and how closely it interlinked with its environment (Figs. 21–23). Most people entering Augsburg would have first made their way through miles of bleaching grounds, on which hundreds of thousands of pieces of cloth dried every year, before being exported. These were mostly made from a mixture of local fibres and foreign cotton, traded via Venice. By 1536 the weavers' guild numbered around 1,450 members.[19]

Would any child in this city ever have played by itself, or anyone been in the streets alone? It is noteworthy that Schwarz and his artists were able to abstract from these experiences to such an extent, to focus just on him. This mode of depiction, of course, followed the representational conventions of single portraiture, which depicted a person in relationship to objects referencing their professional achievement, but not in intimate relation to other people. The genre thus projected a very particular sense of personhood, which by definition was more interesting to use for men and their almost exclusively male painters. Still, for his boyhood Schwarz's sense of self was seen to be emerging in relation to his rejection or acceptance of particular social expectations in his family. The

21. (*above left*) *Aerial view of Augsburg*, 1521, produced by the goldsmith Jörg Seld and the Petrarch Master, woodcut from twelve printing-blocks, 81.7 × 190.7 cm. © Städtische Kunstsammlungen, Augsburg

22. (*above right*) Matthäus Schwarz, Book of Clothes, Ill. 15, aged 15, as a flirtatious boy (*Gassenbuhler*), who nonetheless remains 'clean'. © Herzog Anton Ulrich-Museum Braunschweig, Kunstmuseum des Landes Niedersachsen, Museumsphoto Bernd Peter Keiser

23. (*right*) Matthäus Schwarz, Book of Clothes, Ill. 20, aged 17, riding to Milan. © Herzog Anton Ulrich-Museum Braunschweig, Kunstmuseum des Landes Niedersachsen, Museumsphoto Bernd Peter Keiser

tale of the prodigal son was one of the most popular stories of the time, ending with vows of virtue upon the return. But after his leap in autonomy, aged fifteen, and for the remaining 125 images of the book, other figures hardly ever appeared in the background and none, except one, in the foreground of a painting. Apart from Schwarz, only his first and decisive patron, Jakob Fugger the Rich, featured as a life-size adult figure.[20]

THE WORLD OF THE FUGGERS

Schwarz started to record his current appearance, in 1520, at the age of twenty-three with regular sittings. This first phase of his book project has an exuberant feel to it. By then, Matthäus had been employed by Jakob Fugger for over three years. The Fuggers were among the most important German merchant and banking firms, who frequently secured extraordinary profits of about 150 per cent, and continuously sought to extend their influence, especially by providing enormous loans.[21] They largely kept out of formal council politics, but firmly linked themselves to the papacy and house of Habsburg, helping the latter, in turn, to extend its own influence in politics and commerce. Most famously, in 1520 the Fuggers successfully lobbied and transferred sufficient sums of money to the electors of the Holy Roman Emperor of the German Nation to make them choose the young Habsburg descendant Charles V as successor of Maximilian I, with whom the Fuggers had already maintained particularly close personal relations and whom they supplied with money, sumptuous cloth, and jewels. In 1531, as Charles V's relationship with Augsburg had soured through the city's tolerance for Protestant ideas, Anton Fugger bought substantial quarters in which Charles now lodged every time he stayed in Augsburg, and where the Italian artist Titian finished six paintings for him in 1548.[22] Michel de Montaigne later judged this 'palatium' the 'richest rooms he had ever seen'. Marble abounded, Charles's name was chiselled into chimneys, and the imposing Fugger building facades in the centre of Augsburg were painted with the imperial eagle alongside elaborate classical scenes.[23] In 1547, when Charles triumphantly arrived in Augsburg after his defeat of the Protestant princes and a momentous look at Luther's grave, Anton Fugger was asked by the council to beg the emperor for forgiveness. The city could not have sent anyone else. Charles took revenge on the city and dramatically reinforced oligarchic patrician power by ordering the abolition of all guilds and selling their prized meeting houses. Especially for this fateful imperial visit the Fuggers' head office was further improved—despite the fact that between 1533 and 1539 the truly enormous sum of over 14,000 florins had already been invested in it.[24] In this magnificent office, traditionally called the 'golden' writing chamber, Matthäus Schwarz would preside alongside other accountants and scribes to review all transactions, receive political news from all over Europe, send stenographic instructions to managers from Lisbon to Antwerp and Cracow, and keep track of New World trade links (Fig. 24). In 1536, Anton Fugger instructed one of the best local artists to make a painting of these far away 'New Indies', which presumably would have prominently hung on the office walls.[25] Big business in credit, sumptuous brocades, damasks, silks and other cloth, gold, silver, copper, jewels, precious faience ceramics, Venetian mirrors, and other art was

24. Matthäus Schwarz, Book of Clothes, Ill. 28, aged 19, as Jacob Fugger's accountant in 1516. © Herzog Anton Ulrich-Museum Braunschweig, Kunstmuseum des Landes Niedersachsen, Museumsphoto Bernd Peter Keiser

managed from these Augsburg rooms, which manifested through their very architecture and interior beauty a new age of material wealth and sophistication for those able to afford it. When the Fuggers in 1511, for instance, lent the Emperor 10,000 florins, this sum was broken down into Hungarian gold, English cloth, velvet, silk and camelhair, as well as some direct payments for court officials and artisans.[26] Some of the most important people of the century ate at the Fugger table, or lodged in its employees' houses when the Fugger palaces overflowed. Thus, during the Imperial Diet of 1548, Charles V's confessor Pedro de Soto logged at Schwarz's house, for which he had received a long-term loan of

1,000 florins from the Fugger firm.[27] Personal loyalty to the Fuggers was vital for their most important employees, who were made to feel part of an extraordinarily hierarchical, patriarchal, and tightly monitored family firm, and its religious and political mission. For unusually so, only direct male relatives of the Fuggers were allowed into partnerships and there was one patriarch with superior power at its head. In the clothes book, Schwarz's patronage by Jakob Fugger, the funeral of Jakob Fugger in 1526, the wedding of his new patron, Anton Fugger, in the following year, and Anton Fugger's funeral in 1560, were recorded as among the most significant experiences of his life. Schwarz's sense of self merged with his service for the Fugger patriarchs.

Wide streets and squares in the centre of Augsburg, between the triangle of the Fugger houses, the Perlach square, and Golden Writing Chamber, provided public sites in which men such as Schwarz could effectively show off their wardrobes and armoury as they walked or even speeded about in elegant sledges when there was snow. A new sense of urban life as display manifested itself in a series of richly detailed paintings depicting architecture and crowds of Augsburg men and women from all walks of life throughout each season. These four monumental paintings measure 220 × 60 cm, and we do not know who commissioned or painted them. The Fuggers and other families owned copies.[28] The sheer number of things to discover in the paintings is astonishing, from the splendid little red bag carried by a woman day-labourer, who otherwise wears a simple white dress to do her harvesting, to the beggar asking for food on the margins of the April–June painting, or the fool baring his bottom at a finely dressed courting couple. You will find much more (Figs. 25–26). People began imagining how they looked being

25. (*opposite*)   Anonymous, *Augsburger Monatsbilder, October–December*, oil on canvas, 225 × 348 cm. © Deutsches Historisches Museum – Bildarchiv

26. (*above*)   Anonymous, *Augsburger Monatsbilder, July–September*, oil on canvas, 225.5 × 358 cm. © Deutsches Historisches Museum – Bildarchiv

looked at, as they paraded in public space. This public space was full of images itself—the town-hall facade was newly painted with murals in 1516, the houses of leading merchants likewise showed murals by Italian painters. There was a great fashion for window roundels with coloured glass, and much money had obviously been invested in different churches.[29] The mostly urban, outdoors, and socially diverse settings of the anonymous paintings of the seasons contrasted to another thriving local genre, the 'patricians' dance'. Over three-metre-wide panels depicted local patrician families in historically accurate dress at a dance in an impressively large town hall, looking at each other in this exclusive and confined space[30] (Fig. 27). New families were co-opted into the patriciate. The Fuggers, for instance, cleverly used visual techniques to create and broadly disseminate a public image of themselves as virtuous merchants, who rightly belonged to the nobility despite their humble origins. Broadsheets of Jakob Fugger wearing his distinctive merchant's cap made of gold-thread circulated and could be coloured in.

In the midst of this vivid visual culture, the bulk of the images in the *Klaidungs-büchlein*, a total of *seventy-one* (in addition to the thirty-six images capturing Matthäus before the age of twenty-three), were commissioned during the highpoint of his life as Fugger accountant, between 1519 and 1535, a mere sixteen years. In addition, he commissioned a prayer-book on parchment in 1521, and, one year later, an extremely ambitious parchment painting of a *Geschlechtertanz*, featuring thirty couples of Augsburg patricians dressed in clothes dating from the thirteenth century up to his time, framed by their coats of arms. Two years later, he worked out Christ's genealogy and had it illustrated on parchment, not, of course, forgetting to add a portrait of himself. *After* 1535, however, for the remaining twenty-five years during which he continued his project, he had merely twenty-nine pictures entered in his book of clothes. The book ended with Schwarz's dress at Anton Fugger's funeral, fourteen years before Matthäus himself died. In between the two last images was a gap of seven years. If we therefore wish to assess 'how a sixteen century man wanted himself to be seen'[31] through the *Klaidungsbüchlein*, we must take note of these distinct parts into which the book falls in its display of different modes of masculinity and interpret its curious ending.

27. *Augsburger Geschlechtertanz*, 1550, with sixteen participants and seven representatives of the old patriciate. © Städtische Kunstsammlungen, Augsburg

THE LANGUAGE OF CLOTHES

Headwear, doublets, hose, shoes, jewellery, weaponry, armoury, purses. The extended phase of Schwarz's adult youth, from the age of 23 up to the age 38, celebrated his fascination with all these items that attired his naked body and their production, with cloth as material and its myriad transformations through cuts and colours (Figs. 28–29). Just after his twenty-sixth birthday, for instance, he had himself depicted in a spectacular all white cotton doublet and hose; the doublet, he claimed, had 4,800 small slashes. To create a garment with so many small holes that still made up a whole, instead of fraying all over to dissolve, was superbly skilled. Slashed clothing had become a hallmark of German fashion at this time, and Schwarz perfected this look. Small black ribbons contrasting

28. (*above left*) Matthäus Schwarz, Book of Clothes, Ills. 37–40, aged 23, mourning his father in four different kinds of dress. © Herzog Anton Ulrich-Museum Braunschweig, Kunstmuseum des Landes Niedersachsen, Museumsphoto Bernd Peter Keiser

29. (*above right*) Matthäus Schwarz, Book of Clothes, Ill. 61, aged 26, wearing a doublet with 4,000 slashes (*Schnitz*). © Herzog Anton Ulrich-Museum Braunschweig, Kunstmuseum des Landes Niedersachsen, Museumsphoto Bernd Peter Keiser

with the white were used as a girdle, around the arms, and as trims. White velvet had been used under the thousands of tiny holes, each of which was individually sewn round the edges. Schwarz also wore a necklace, and carried a dagger on his right side, and a very long sword on his left. All his outdoor outfits were highly refined in this way. He used locally manufactured cloth only once, and preferred a range of especially shiny silk fabrics (*Atlas*), heavy silken damask, fabrics from camelhair and wool, a mixture of wool and silk (*Burschet*), velvet for trims, and a range of half-silken material (*Arras, Taftetta, Zindel*). All of these came in a wide range of colours.[32] He rarely specified where exactly these fabrics came from, but his references included Italy, Spain, and Flanders. In 1538 he had himself depicted in a violet coat with large black velvet trimmings and a white padded and patterned doublet and hose made from Turkish silk.[33] Schwarz would often comment with detail on how his clothes were made in order to underline their specific make: the inscription for a 1540 depiction of him, for instance, ran: '20. February 1540: a Spanish cape with two velvet trims and silken bands.'[34]

Customers such as Schwarz needed to find superior dyers, tailors, tanners, and furriers whose technical skills were constantly adapting to changing demands. In addition, such high-end consumers had to be prepared to make a long-term effort, invest time, use all their networks of information and diverse agents, exercise constant quality control, and push for the right pieces and prices at the right time. This is strikingly documented in Hans Fugger's correspondence later in the century. In March 1586, Fugger decided that he wanted a long Hungarian coat made from lynx fur, ideally for the following winter. He had already obtained information that beautiful lynx could be bought in Venice, but thought they were too expensive. He told his Nuremberg agent for most luxury items, Philipp Römer, that 'surely you get better and cheaper ones from Sweden'.[35] Römer in turn sent him twenty-four pieces, from which Fugger only picked the two best. He had a man in Prague whom he alerted to make every effort to find further pieces.[36] During the autumn Fugger tried to assemble sixty pieces of brown fur from Spain to line a long coat. He knew that the late Cardinal Granvelle (a busy traveller and connoisseur, who had visited Augsburg) had worn such a fur, and hoped that his belongings would be auctioned according to the Spanish custom. Genoese aristocrats, too, eagerly bought from an auction at the Spanish ambassadors' house in 1569.[37] Fugger wrote to his Madrid middleman Hans Frick in November 1586, to thank him for twenty-three pieces of fur, but also to remind him that he needed sixty. He had given up hope that he would have this coat made by winter.[38] On 13 December he told his Nuremberg agent that he had chosen six out of twelve pieces of lynx fur he had been given by yet another person, but if he were not offered similarly advantageous prices he would only take one of them.[39] Fugger next once more involved his Madrid agent. He still needed twelve to fourteen regular, beautiful pieces from the back of the lynx, rich in hair. His furrier had told him that he could best get them from Spain. If he were to get a whole fur that would be fine. But since all of this was too late for the current winter season the agent should push for a good price.[40] All of this effort makes clear why a splendid fur coat equalled an international financial transaction and event in this period among luxury consuming, competing male elites who were supremely 'dress-literate'. They were able to look at a garment or fur and work out from it how it had been made.⁴¹ These clients' relationships to the final product was extremely intimate. They might have chosen and skilfully bargained for every piece of it. Fine clothing registered as vestiary achievement in this world, and this made splendid or technically intricate clothing displays such a momentous visual act for others.

Up to his wedding day, Matthäus also regularly wore jewellery: for a long period from the age of seventeen he was not to be seen without a crucifix on a long necklace, then followed several pieces of gold, pearl, and coral jewellery (Fig. 30). Matthäus more rarely showed himself wearing rings, but prominently displayed three rings on the opening page of the book and in a later panel portrait of him in 1542. Schwarz's armoury was highly varied. As the *Klaidungsbüchlein* unfolded, he showed himself able to control almost the full range of contemporary weapons: swords of differing length, bow and arrow, a rapier, sword, and spear, we too know that he fenced. He nearly always carried a long sword at his side, and all of this armoury was exquisitely made. To constantly display weapons was a specifically German custom. Augsburg was famed for its gold- and silversmiths—and each of these items was meant to be for aesthetic display as much as to mark wealth and

a civic, virile adult masculinity that prided itself on the ability to defend its honour, freedom, and a 'fatherland', here understood in local terms.

Schwarz wore a good, but not excessive, range of shoes and boots, but never remarked on them. It is clear that the most commonly worn open shoe, the *Kuhmaulschuhe*, required care to maintain balance and forced the wearer to tread slowly. They had to be fitted with care to ensure that a man did not slip out of them.⁴² Yet they were generously cut, and hence must have seemed a liberation from narrow, pointed Gothic shoes, which had been in fashion for all of the previous century. Dürer nonetheless impatiently produced a detailed drawing for his shoemaker of a

30. Matthäus Schwarz, Book of Clothes, Ill. 42, aged 23, in love with a lady from the Netherlands. © Herzog Anton Ulrich-Museum Braunschweig, Kunstmuseum des Landes Niedersachsen, Museumsphoto Bernd Peter Keiser

shoe to be made for him with a string, to add stability and comfort. It had precise instructions written on every part and also told the shoemaker what decorative pattern to press into the wet leather at the upper front part of the shoe. Dürer's shoes seem to have been so distinctive that he was pictorially remembered wearing them.[43] Hose could be directly sewn onto shoes to add stability. Schwarz, once in 1530, even preferred comfortable slippers outdoors, which Turkish people typically wore. These covered the toes, but not the back of the foot, and hence were only suitable outdoors for dry weather.[44] Shoes, in other words, considerably influenced what postures men and women could adopt. Walking in them was a learnt bodily technique, as Hungarians, who were used to boots, could find to their cost when they travelled in Germany and slid down staircases in newly made shoes.

Schwarz's headwear characteristically was a much more important and versatile item. It gave attention to the head as the noblest part of the body, and would be used for an eloquent symbolic language of paying respect to and greeting others. Rules defined when to take one's cap or beret off, when to raise it or merely touch it, and these could be played with. Schwarz only depicted his hair shoulder-length in Venice, but otherwise consistently short, cut just over his ears, which gave his headwear a better and more stable fit. He nearly always wore a cap, and, from 1522 onwards, he often wore a skull-cap underneath his hats to tie his hair together. Headwear was seasonal. In 1524, Matthäus thus wore a warming beret with fur in January, while in May he had proudly obtained a red cap with gold-coloured dots which, as he noted, had belonged either to the duke of Milan (Massimiliano or Franceso II Maria Sforza), or the 'Duco de Bari' (Fig. 31). He sported this cap in an astonishing ensemble with a tight violet damask doublet with wide pomegranate patterns and two golden trims, violet hose, and a short trunk-hose with yellow panes and red points worn over it. He also wore a finely pleated white shirt, a green heart-shaped bag with a golden string, a rectangular piece of jewellery with his coat of arms, and his lute.[45] He had such fun with clothes! The approximate provenance of such vintage items mattered, because it underlined that Schwarz cultivated a lifestyle in exchange with Italian or Spanish high aristocrats. Wealthy urban elites in Augsburg or Nuremberg characteristically blurred the boundary between their burgher or patrician descent and noble living, and accessories such as headwear or gloves were an important tool to imagine a particular identity. By June, two of Schwarz's male friends had noticed his fascination with headwear so much so that they gave him a cap, and a well-located Augsburg friend working in Antwerp gave him a beautiful scarlet beret with golden threads, three gold buttons, and a black gem-stone set in gold—a sign that they clearly accepted his particular love of dress displays. Matthäus raved: 'it's scarlet red and from super fine (material) from Valencia in Spain, costs 8 florins and has gold threads, I went to Andre Schregl's wedding like this'.[46] Despite the fact that it had been a gift, then, he knew exactly how expensive the beret had been. It was the only time the accountant noted the value of an item of clothing, perhaps to avoid accusations of illegal over-spending. Variations were infinite. A further red beret had a brim sewn with alternating red velvet and silk fabric, to contrast their textures.[47] Another beret had ostrich feathers on its top that had been dyed black and dipped into gold at their ends.[48] Ostrich feathers were

31. Matthäus Schwarz, Book of Clothes, Ill. 66, aged 27 in 1524, with lute and a beret from an Italian duke. © Herzog Anton Ulrich-Museum Braunschweig, Kunstmuseum des Landes Niedersachsen, Museumsphoto Bernd Peter Keiser

particularly impressive because they were long, bushy, resisted vigorous movement, and came from far away. They were associated with dashing male courage; so mercenary soldiers would love them. Schwarz also wore them for a local tournament in their natural white colour.[49] Right up to his old age such headwear documented his interest in exploring the fashionable possibilities within a global market he skilfully accessed to make his wardrobe special.

The striking heart-shaped bags, which he wore in green and red, displayed a young man's search for love, and green clothes underlined this hopeful quest for luck. Matthäus's son, Veit, later wore a padded hose embroidered all over with hearts upside down and the right side up.[50] These displays were not about status, they were emotionally resonant and demonstrate how cleverly embroiderers as well as bag makers looked for marketing devices to cultivate new commodities that signalled new emotional styles. Their open sentimentality suggests that these courting young men hoped for flirtation and love, rather than an arranged marriage. And yet everyone in this culture thought that looking for love made you vulnerable to be fooled by passion and Lady Fortune. Schwarz only after his marriage wore his heart-shaped little bags in black.

Schwarz's clothes, in this phase up to 1535, were extremely colourful: there were purple, red, orange, yellow, blue, or green outfits, as well as many multicoloured ones, which stripes would frequently make particularly striking. Black was frequently used with multicoloured linings. In 1528, for example, he wore a mixture between a partlet and vest in an innovative cut, made from black damask, which opened at its top into one reverse side made from green velvet, and another from red velvet.[51] There was cunning finesse in a turn-around-coat he had had made when on business for the Fugger firm during the Peasants' War. It could be worn either red or green—and the green, he thought, disguised him and helped him to make necessary friends in the villages. Soon after, he sported a black riding coat, which had forty folds, and thus had taken a lot of material, money, and skill to make. He seemed almost proud when an item cost more to make than the materials themselves, a benchmark of unparalleled contemporary luxury, which moralists routinely condemned.[52] Some coats were openly worked, revealed beautiful fur lining, and were slightly altered or dyed in different colours over a number of years. Yet such luxury was not necessarily entirely wasteful. Apart from pinked items much could be reworked and handed on. No Augsburg clothes ordinance has been found for Schwarz's lifetime, but the second, more precise ordinance in 1582 allowed maidservants to wear velvet trims and hairbands, while male servants were forbidden to wear silk, velvet headdresses, pearls, gold threads, and costly weapons. Otherwise they were allowed to wear what their masters gave them.[53] In 1583, the first initiative to implement sumptuary laws exclusively focused on women and a few extravagant rich men. They specifically targeted sixty-five maidservants for wearing fur hoods. This led to sixty-two indictments in autumn 1584, before the initiative petered out with ten more cases until May 1585. This was a mere two years after anyone had got agitated enough to act.[54] During Schwarz's lifetime, imperial police ordinances stipulated guidelines for dress and jewellery appropriate for each rank, but urged that local regulations should adapt these.[55]

Up to the age of 38, Schwarz recorded particular care in dressing up when he was courting particular women (for a 'beautiful person', he once comments), for political and social occasions, as when he twice met Ferdinand of Austria and subsequently attended Ferdinand's wedding to Anne of Hungary, at other weddings, and male 'society' gatherings. In 1530, when Charles V was back in Germany after nine years for the Imperial Diet of Augsburg with his brother Ferdinand, Schwarz recorded six new and highly complicated outfits he had had tailored—one explicitly to 'please Ferdinand' (*Ferdinand zu lieb*) (Fig. 32). Charles and Ferdinand used this Imperial Diet for an extraordinary attempt to

32. Matthäus Schwarz, Book of Clothes, Ill. 102/3, aged 33 in 1530, dressed to please Ferdinand at the Imperial Diet of Augsburg. © Herzog Anton Ulrich-Museum Braunschweig, Kunstmuseum des Landes Niedersachsen, Museumsphoto Bernd Peter Keiser

demonstrate the magnificence and power of the Habsburg dynasty. Ferdinand had just convinced Charles that he should promote him, rather than his son Philip, to be elected as his successor. The emperor ennobled a person and gave permission to use coat of arms,[56] so for Matthäus there was a good reason to 'please Ferdinand' through sartorial magnificence if he aspired to gain nobility. Schwarz looked slimmer, and his hair was cut very short, just like the emperor's. He wore garters around the knee, tied into prominent bows just above it. There is no sense, then, that dressing up for Schwarz was just an art in itself. He did so to explore fashion, but always for specific different social or political occasions, for work, social promotion, or courtship, and it fused with his ambitions or feelings about these events and their memory. Funeral clothes clearly mattered in this society, and sports clothes were also carefully considered. Ball games, fencing, as well as shooting were seen as integral to ideals of elegant, athletic Renaissance men, for this era saw the 'sportification' of life.[57] Yet Schwarz's son, Veit Konrad, once noted that he had to fence in a hose filled with thirty Augsburg pounds of fabric! This surely made it difficult and hot to fence gracefully for long.[58] Other activities Schwarz recorded were his procession into Augsburg for the merchants' chamber, his travel clothes, the clothes he wore when recovering from strong headaches, and from fever at a spa another time.

As the book progressed, it was thus not his recording of clothes, but rather the context of Schwarz's social life that was beginning to look increasingly odd. For, after completing 112 images, on a number of which he showed himself attending weddings of male friends, Matthäus was 38 years old and still not married. And in this society, only a 'householder' who supported his family, and built up his own legitimate lineage, was considered a properly civil adult man. The Reformation debates that gripped Augsburg accentuated this view, dramatically insisting that sexuality was like a drive that needed to be expressed by every adult, and yet resolutely had to be confined within marriage.[59] Active sex was therefore turned into something that had to be central to everyone's identity from a young age onwards; yet prostitution was forbidden and pre-marital sex punished. This targeted the whole notion of a prolonged youth, marked by playful courtship and even sexually ambiguous behaviour. Respectable manhood was redefined by artisan guildsmen, whose youth had been somewhat shorter than was tolerable for elite men, and whose workshops were made profitable through everyone's work in the household. Except, of course, that wives and daughters never received formal training, pay in their own right, or political representation. But to be an honourable man now more than ever before meant to be sexually active and deal with the responsibility of a household as its head, affirming one's authority through both practices in the small commonweal, and thereby forming the basis of ordered society at large.

The miniaturist artisan Narziss Renner, with whom Schwarz had worked so intimately, had been married all this time. It seems highly likely that his wife Magdalena began to portray Schwarz for his book while Narziss suffered a long illness. Once, Schwarz was depicted with a sword on his right rather than his left side—a faux pas apparently unthinkable for any man.[60]

MARRIAGE

Schwarz seemed to experience the prospect of his marriage as momentous, and ambivalently so. A clue to recovering some of his attitudes is an image depicting him as a 26-year-old, dressed up and racing on a sledge through snowy Augsburg. The sledge was carefully decorated. On the front side of the sledge was an image of a woman pulling three small men with fool caps on strings through rings. Right in front of Schwarz was another image, of a couple with a child. This design therefore endorsed a ubiquitous image that men formed of gender relations during the early modern period: it was their pleasurable, but deeply ambivalent fantasy that women took the lead in turning men into folly by evoking their desire (Fig. 33). Marriage and children on the other hand locked a man into a steady relationship with a woman, as, in practice, Protestants as much as Catholics did not grant a divorce for unhappy couples. Women's nature stereotypically tended to be defined by extremes: deep down they were less clever, emotionally unbalanced, gossipy, sexually insatiable, out for money and power. Marriages across all classes could easily enact a battle for breeches. These everyday dramas of how couples devalued and shamed each other were rarely kept behind closed doors. Men typically attempted to control their anxieties about women through misogynous humour. But as the honour of the paterfamilias as steadfast, virile head of a controlled, pious household was ever more emphasized, men's increased anxiety about their own shameful denigration could easily turn into outward aggression.

One night in September 1535, for instance, Jeremias Ehem entered the public meeting room of local patricians, the so-called *Herrenstube*, to confess to a group of men that his wife had kicked him out. Later everyone joked about women, and he showed a phallic object that looked like a radish to another man, called Joachim Herwart. Ehem, presumably in a somewhat drunken state, told Herwart that 'his was useless, for he could not get it up anymore'. Herwart retorted: 'Let me over your Barbelein and she is going to feel it.' Ehem should look for 'another fool'. A fight erupted, and Ehem killed Herwart with his rapier. Schwarz would certainly have known the story by the next day. As intercourse could perform male authority in marriages, rather than a loving or even passionate union and sexual play, it easily unleashed a destructive emotional dynamic of anxiety and aggression, a ready-made script for tragedy instead of joy and intimate exchange. Manhood could be bound up with the idea of lifelong, regular sexual dominance in marriage. Impotence or failed potency sometimes loomed as large in the male psyche as codpieces bulked.

In that same year, 1535, Schwarz had himself depicted looking older, with the beard he had just started to grow, another sign that he now wished to assume greater maturity. His right arm was stretched out, as if signalling something, his eyes looked into the distance, his right foot stood on a fool's cap (Fig. 34). A wave of plague was sweeping through Augsburg, which would finally take Narziss Renner with it. The miniaturist, who otherwise had only ever enjoyed modest artistic success, had over all these years diligently collaborated in producing a particular vision of Schwarz, and in visualizing a

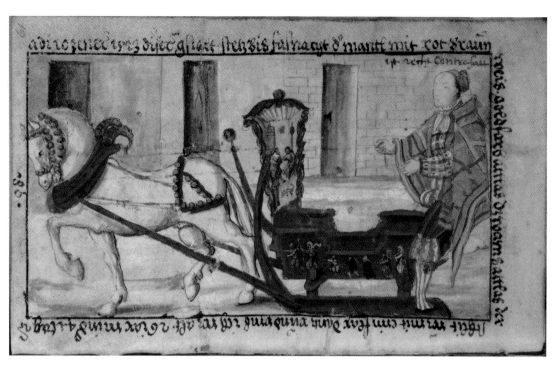

33. (*above*)   Matthäus Schwarz, Book of Clothes, Ill. 58, a sledge painted with couples dancing and a couple spinning. © Herzog Anton Ulrich-Museum Braunschweig, Kunstmuseum des Landes Niedersachsen, Museumsphoto Bernd Peter Keiser

34. (*left*)   Matthäus Schwarz, Book of Clothes, Ill. 111, aged 38, August 1535, ‚when the plague started in Augsburg', standing on a fool´s cap. © Herzog Anton Ulrich-Museum Braunschweig, Kunstmuseum des Landes Niedersachsen, Museumsphoto Bernd Peter Keiser

particular identity, one which Schwarz obviously had loved—hence the repeated commissions. On nearly every picture from his twenties and thirties, Renner and his wife had depicted Matthäus with the same very young, boyish face, not marked by time.

As we have seen, Schwarz was disconcerted when he put on weight. This intimate awareness of weight was connected to the new sensation of closely fitting clothes or armour. Weight here became not a positive idiom of being cared for by others, as it is in some cultures, nor a symbolization of wealth and plentiful access to food resources. Schwarz in this phase of his life saw weight as fatness, associated with age, excess, heaviness rather than the agility so crucial to the idea of civility, with flesh working against a tight fit. In one image, Schwarz even noted how much his waist measured; an astonishing 60 cm (Fig. 35). A slim, tall silhouette was also idealized in the many presentations of hyper-fashionable and sexually attractive Landsquenet soldiers, who were ubiquitous in Augsburg, or in woodcuts of Maximilian I in his armoury on horseback, his figure elongated through long peacock feathers on his helmet, which were printed in Augsburg (Fig. 75). The increasing importance of regularly practised sports, such as fencing, likewise bolstered the notion that a tall, slim, flexible body was ideal. Yet this ideal was not necessarily connected to Herculean muscular, military masculinity, broad straight shoulders, and a linear frame. Schwarz in many of the images, as we have already seen, cultivated a look that was far more androgynous and linked to Renaissance notions that positively allowed for softness (*dolcezza*) and delicacy (*delicatezza*) in young men rather than Herculean *grandezza*.[61] Men like Schwarz created this delicate look through sloping shoulders, which often connected with very widely cut sleeves for the arms, as well as through an emphasis on a very tight upper waist, just below the rib cage, to contrast with a widening around the lower body. The face was clean shaven. All this was not meant to be effeminate, as the weapons underlined, but more gracious and noble. But this delicate masculinity seemed impossible to maintain in a marriage, as a husband and father. Throughout his thirties, Schwarz was usually depicted by Renner wearing clothes emphasizing his slim waist and often with a gentle smile on his youthful face. It was as if part of him wished to physically as well as mentally resist generationality: the passing of time, which, on the other hand, he had exposed himself to—by recording his very own figure when setting out with the clothes project.

The next image by a new artist, on his thirty-ninth birthday in 1536, captured his face well: but he now looked his age, unsure in his comportment and facial expression. After this no image was added for two years. It seems as if Schwarz did not know anymore why and how he wished to be seen. The image that follows is one of the most startling in the whole book. It depicted Matthäus from behind, showing off the beauty of a new grey-brown coat trimmed with green half-silken taffeta in his home, posing with his right leg raised on a chair. The text simply commented '20 February 1538

35. Matthäus Schwarz, Book of Clothes, Ill. 43, aged 23, with a traditional Franconian embroidered shirt, his waist measuring 60 cm. © Herzog Anton Ulrich-Museum Braunschweig, Kunstmuseum des Landes Niedersachsen, Museumsphoto Bernd Peter Keiser

when I took a wife this coat…was made' (Fig. 36). Once again, this was his birthday. By now, Schwarz was 41 years old and had never lived with a woman before. It was not unusual to occasionally portray clothes from the back; but to do so to mark a wedding certainly was. Schwarz and Renner had used this format once before; when in 1529, they depicted Matthäus from the back as he walked down an Augsburg street. In the distance, a woman was looking out of the window. A much smaller figure of Schwarz used a long stick to write three words on the facade of her house that were meant to end a relationship: 'it is nothing anymore' (*ist nix mer*). Here he was emotionally in control, able to turn a woman down. The image announcing his wedding therefore appears to have had a manifest and a latent meaning: it manifestly documented his rank as well as his esteem of such a fine coat, but it also latently showed that he could now enter a marriage and turn his back on it at the same time, without fully involving his emotions, without losing himself in passion and deep love, and thus would be able to assume the conventional role of a husband. Barbara Mangolt never appeared in the *Klaidungsbüch-lein*. She was already 31 years old, in an age when well-off women married in their late teens or early twenties. Depictions made Mangolt look broadly framed. Her father had been a long-term local manager in the Fugger firm. This was an arranged, economically and politically sensible match, based on feelings that at best were supposed to grow rather than exist. Her advanced age would clearly make it impossible for the couple to have very many children—yet this was an age in which elites invested marriage with the hope to build up an honourable lineage. The phrasing 'I took a wife' documented

Schwarz's transition of a passive youth who could be fooled by women to a man assuming agency, it conveyed the security, but also the socially circumscribed rigidity of these settlements. Matthäus and Barbara married in April 1538. The wedding was a superior event to dress up for—it was here that the 'couple laid claim to the social prestige which the marriage contract and dowry level had already set out, by displaying their wealth—in giving, dressing, and in feasting'.[62] Schwarz displayed two further extremely precious outfits, as he went to his engagement administered by a priest (*Stuhlfest*) and as he went to church. Despite it being spring time, both were dark and looked heavy, one coat was made

36. Matthäus Schwarz, Book of Clothes, Ill. 113, aged 41, image on his birthday recording that as he had decided to marry this coat had been made. © Herzog Anton Ulrich-Museum Braunschweig, Kunstmuseum des Landes Niedersachsen, Museumsphoto Bernd Peter Keiser

37. Matthäus Schwarz, Book of Clothes, Ill. 116, Schwarz as a married man in August 1538. © Herzog Anton Ulrich-Museum Braunschweig, Kunstmuseum des Landes Niedersachsen, Museumsphoto Bernd Peter Keiser

from black velvet and lined with black fur. From now on, Schwarz consistently was depicted looking broad-shouldered and voluminous, hiding the contours of his body. This body posture, together with the beard he had only now grown and his much older-looking face, gave Schwarz the appearance of a settled, mature husband and father (Fig. 37). He kept a short book in which he noted his three children's pranks, and enjoyed having them around when he was ill at home, or taking his son to accompany him when he needed to go out in armoury. He also made sure that his sons both got connected with the Fugger firm. After the image depicting his wedding gown, Schwarz simply announced on a blank page that he had also thrown away the short autobiography he had simultaneously kept, now tellingly entitled *Bubenleben*, which in German denotes a loose life, but literally means 'a boy's life'. He noted down something else on that page, which he later erased. All this again marked the break he saw in his life, without any stable sense of himself, a life conducted partly through negating presentations of former selves. There had been no image for two years, no certain sense of how to continue, no linearity; here was a new start into full maturity.

Soon, there were his achievements to celebrate. In 1541, Schwarz was ennobled by Charles V for his services and promptly had himself depicted wearing a coat lined with beautiful fur taken from the back of marten-skin, which was restricted to the highest elites. Such fur was homogenously coloured dark brown and came in rectangular pieces measuring up to 60 centimetres[63] (Fig. 38). It materialized the rich man's coat in contrast to the beggar's fur, which would be made of lots of little minor pieces of fur, with lots of seams and shades of colour, and would easily disintegrate. Yet his ennoblement brought not just prestige, it further accentuated Schwarz's strange social position. He was wealthy and honoured by the emperor, and yet he was also a wine-merchant's son and not seriously rich, like the Fuggers themselves. He could have never married a noble

38. Matthäus Schwarz, Book of Clothes, Ill. 122, aged 44, 1541. © Herzog Anton Ulrich-Museum Braunschweig, Kunstmuseum des Landes Niedersachsen, Museumsphoto Bernd Peter Keiser

woman, as the Fuggers strategically did for large dowries, or a local patrician's wife. There presumably was one further, murkier reason for this, as we shall see in a moment. And although Schwarz never used his title, just like the Fuggers, he depicted his coat of arms in the image he had made for the *Klaidungsbüchlein* on his birthday that year.

Schwarz, it seems, now commissioned parchment paintings for his book of clothes from a new, sophisticated local artist called Christoph Amberger and his workshop. Amberger began to establish himself as the key portrait painter for Augsburg elites in 1530. His business thrived from the 1540s onwards, when the work of Ferdinand I's court painter Seissenegger and Titian's influences became more dominant in his paintings. Amberger got men to pose assertively in dynamic scenes, sometimes with interesting backgrounds, always with a beautiful weapon and harmonious, darker colour schemes, while his matching female portraits had far blander expressions.[64] Schwarz certainly used Amberger to execute a second, medium-sized panel portrait on pine-wood, with a complementary portrait of his wife. Now he could make use of this genre, the marriage portrait, for a public representation as 'senior civis', as the inscription stated. Contrary to our contemporary imaging practices, the Renaissance marriage portrait as a genre usually did not depict a couple together. It consisted of two entirely separate panels, which nowadays are often in different collections, as is the case with the Schwarzes'. The genre was adapted to a social class characterized by serial monogamy: wealthy women married early, had a long period of fertility and correspondingly ran a higher risk of dying in childbirth, so that men often remarried several times. Unusually for Amberger, Matthäus Schwarz's panel emphasized transitory elements and thus temporality, so that we must assume that Schwarz himself suggested their inclusion (Fig. 39). It revealed Matthäus's horoscope prominently in the right corner, and recorded minutely when he had been born (on 20 February 1497 at 6.30 pm), and when the portrait itself had been finished. None

39.   Christoph Amberger, *Portrait of Matthäus Schwarz*, 1542, oil on panel, 73.5 × 61 cm
© Museo Thyssen–Bornemisza, Madrid

of the figures related to each other symmetrically. Set against the background of tur-
bulent, rainy mountain scenery, where the sun was clouded over and thunder loomed,
the portrait had a troubling and questing atmosphere. Once more, it was important
for Schwarz to locate himself at a specific point in time. Anyone looking at the painting would therefore have been aware that time had moved on since the execution. This
painting, then, as Anette Kranz convincingly argues, served not to memorialize Schwarz
through an illusion of timelessness and an ideal of fixed gentlemanly comportment and
virtue. It was very different to the panel painting of him as a young man, for Schwarz
now played with the conventions of settledness the painting of a mature, respectable
man was designed to evoke.[65]

The mood of the *Klaidungsbüchlein*, too, had irreversibly changed. Matthäus now
typically wore Spanish fashion and clear, monochrome colours, mostly black and white.
The exuberant surprise of colourful variety and sophisticated, playful detail had gone.
The occasions for which Matthäus chose to have himself depicted continued to be his
birthday, illness, and, much more regularly than before, political events. From 1546
onwards, he no longer supplied detailed specifications of his clothes. Instead, he commented much more consistently than before on politics. It was as if at last he was no longer able to split off the dramatic changes surrounding him from the story he told about
himself. And at this time in Augsburg, politics was deeply intertwined with religion, for
these were the tumultuous decades of the Reformation years.

The Reformation

Augsburg was one of the most dynamic centres of Protestant preaching and printing in
early sixteenth-century Germany, and it was influenced by ideas right across the diverse
spectrum of Lutheranism, Zwinglianism, and Anabaptism. Its urban Reformation was
extremely protracted, and only politically settled by the Peace of Augsburg in 1555. For
two decades from the 1520s to the 1540s, thousands of men and of women gathered to
join Anabaptist meetings. The Anabaptist Hans Hut slowly died in an Augsburg prison,
and an anxious council repeatedly hired hundreds of mercenary soldiers to avoid riot-
ing. For much of the time, councillors looked for a middle way of selected reforms. They
feared the loss of favours from the emperor, to whom the council was subject, as well
as social criticism that came with the call to constitute a truly Christian society. They
were deeply nervous about the craft proletariat of weavers, on which the city's economic
prosperity depended.

As the Reformation movements divided Augsburg, stories of dressing and undressing vividly symbolized beliefs that were no longer shared across society or even among
couples. In 1526, a butcher who got wind that his wife had attended the Protestant
preacher's Urbanus Rhegius's lectures on the New Testament, tied her dress up and hit
her until she bled.[66] One year later, over a thousand people were said to secretly meet
in gardens and have themselves re-baptized, women and men naked except for their

underclothes.[67] In 1533, the council loaded two wagons full of precious vestments from the Barfüßer-convent and had them sold at a shop under the Perlach tower, to be used as people wished.[68] In the same year, the old clergy made its traditional procession without vestments, and at another occasion a clergyman who wanted to read morning mass in his vestment had it taken by the city guards.[69] In 1537, as the four remaining nuns of the St Niclaus convent were forced to move out by an assembly of councillors and police, an old prioress tore her veil and cap, and let out her short hair, resisting as much as she could. Later, all of them affirmed they wanted to burn rather than change their lives.[70] Four prostitutes had to be given proper clothes, as the city closed down its two brothels.[71] The Catholic chronicler Sender felt that the unity of communal spirit and thus well-being of Augsburg had been destroyed by constant 'floating dissonances' (*schwebenden widerwertigkeiten*), the metaphor suggesting that he found them so threatening because they had no clear location, but pervaded the atmosphere.[72]

Charles V himself sometimes was thought to under-dress, but in Augsburg he certainly always knew how to dress to impress. His majesty needed to be seen and performed through rituals in which jewellery and clothing were crucial symbolic tools.[73] The cloth of his entourage was black velvet, and the men wore golden chains like the emperor. In ceremonies, he would use crowns and clothes estimated to be worth a staggering 300,000 fl or more. They were adorned with precious stones, and thus a vocal element in the rituals of government conducted by an emperor who could speak no German. While Augsburg never forgot the ease of former times under Maximilian I, who requested dances and games in which a relatively wide selection of citizens would participate, and for which the Fuggers would settle enormous bills immediately after, the Imperial Diets under Charles and his brother Ferdinand were splendid international events. Representatives from Africa and Arabia would be present in their distinct clothes, and his massive entourage included noble men from 'all countries',[74] certainly from most of Europe, to create the fiction that Charles was within reach of a universal monarchy.

Religious reforms were hesitantly implemented from 1534 onwards, but Catholic worship was only forbidden as late as 1537 when two Zwinglian mayors were elected. 'Discipline Lords' were appointed and a marriage court was set up. Over the next decade, as we have seen, the guilds strengthened their influence against patricians, until Charles V's troops finally occupied the city in 1547. Now the emperor dramatically abolished guild government and reintroduced Catholicism. Then, during the Protestant Princes' War, everything changed again for two months, before Anton Fugger's money once more helped Charles V to mobilize troops and restore his and the patricians' power.

Schwarz, of course, was loyal to established hierarchies, to Catholicism, the Fuggers, the Habsburgs, and the idea of patrician and merchant superiority over craftsmen. To an important extent, his personal honour and success rested on this position. Here, too, in all likelihood lay buried a further reason why he found it so difficult to find a suitable wife. The skeleton in the cupboard was his grandfather, who had supported guildsmen's increased political participation in the late fifteenth century, and despite his non-patrician background had been elected as mayor.[75] Ulrich Schwarz had also stood out for his love of fine clothes. His velvet doublet and use of rare and precious marten-skin as well as pearls had left patricians reeling with disapproval.[76] They would have served him as a tool to demonstrate that status was impersonated as plausibly when it was gained as when it was inherited. Only, Ulrich was publicly executed for corruption. The city council even forbade the hangman to appropriate his clothing, so as not to perpetuate his memory. As the conflict over power between patricians and guilds kept flaring up during the sixteenth century, Ulrich Schwarz's example was vividly remembered. Matthäus Schwarz himself was already eleven when his paternal grandmother, Ulrich Schwarz's widow, died in 1508.[77] The city council's scribe Hektor Mair would draw gallows in the margins of manuscripts every time he referred to this dishonourable mayor (even though, or perhaps because, Mair himself became deeply involved in corruption to finance a sumptuous lifestyle).[78] As late as 1548, an anonymous document supported Charles V's abolition of any guild influence with reference to Ulrich Schwarz's execution in 1478, arguing that it was only to be expected that those who were not wealthy would become corrupt if they were given the right to politically participate.[79] Now, Augsburg men with egalitarian ideas were Protestants, who were mainly influenced by the Zurich reformer Zwingli. No wonder that Matthäus never aspired to any significant political office and distanced himself from his grandfather's ideas as much as he could. No wonder either, that he did not commission a genealogy, as Raymund Fugger, for instance, spectacularly did in 1545, with historicized costume illuminations for the Fugger book of honour, the *Ehrenbuch*. It formed part of the extensive effort to argue that this family had gained nobility through their virtuous behaviour, stature, and extensive charity.[80] Such illustrated genealogies became much more common in sixteenth-century Germany to further document the nobility of one's ancestry. The first German illustrated genealogies with figures in historical costumes had been produced in Nuremberg for Lazarus Holzschuher in 1509 and Bartholomäus Haller von Hallerstein in 1530.[81] Schwarz could neither honourably represent his grandfather, nor avoid his memory. He had to live in his shadow.

ENDING THE BOOK

Schwarz loyally defended his city against Charles V in 1546, but commemorated the Imperial Diet in 1547, the abolition of the guild regiment and the final emperor's presence at the Imperial Diet in 1550, as well as Charles's departure in 1551 (Fig. 40). He noted especially that the Protestant preachers were now expelled from the town. In July 1553, Matthäus celebrated his fully restored health after a stroke, as well as the death of Moritz of Saxony, who had championed the Protestant princes and cunningly undermined Charles V, while siding with Charles's brother Ferdinand of Austria (Fig. 41).

If we look in detail at the last series of images of Schwarz, after his stroke, we can describe them as follows: in July 1550 an image commemorated Charles V's entry into

Augsburg, for which Schwarz was again largely able to move freely by himself. His left arm was still lame, and he never again depicted himself after 1547 carrying weapons. He wore a black beret, robe, and shoes, which contrasted with a white doublet with a small collar, and an equally brilliant white hose. The next image followed in October 1551, when Charles rode to Innsbruck and Protestant preachers had already left Augsburg: Schwarz wore mostly black, except for light brown boots and brown fur lining in his coat. Next followed an image for his birthday in 1552, again all in black and

40. (*left*) Matthäus Schwarz, Book of Clothes, Ill. 127, in armour to defend his city. © Herzog Anton Ulrich-Museum Braunschweig, Kunstmuseum des Landes Niedersachsen, Museumsphoto Bernd Peter Keiser

41. (*right*) Matthäus Schwarz, Book of Clothes, Ill. 131, aged 52, at home after suffering a stroke. © Herzog Anton Ulrich-Museum Braunschweig, Kunstmuseum des Landes Niedersachsen, Museumsphoto Bernd Peter Keiser

white, and after that, in July 1553, another black and white outfit to celebrate Moritz of Saxony's death and his own fully restored health (Fig. 42). A wreath of white roses in his hair, it is probably fair to assume, underlined that he regarded Moritz's death as a victory for Catholicism. Schwarz had thus integrated the dictate of black clothing following the Habsburg influence since the mid-1530s, but still mixed it with white items. White and black corresponded to his different view of life and his age, after his 'fool's life'. Change could no longer be taken easily and played with, in the manner that he had tricked the Tyrolean peasants during the Peasants' War. It was as if for him this had become a world that forced people into consistency and appearances signal-ling principle and clarity. In the first treatises on colour symbolism, several of which by now had been published in Europe, black denoted constancy and sombreness; white symbolized faith and humility. Parti-coloured clothes could now be connected with an 'unsound' mind and the humanist Erasmus straightforwardly told boys and their parents in 1530: 'Slashed garments are for fools; embroidered and multi-coloured ones for idiots and apes.'[82] Tellingly, when all of the six Augsburg Protestant preachers were instructed by the council in 1528 to preach the same message, they were told they should not speak 'white, the other black'.[83] The contrast of what Newton would later describe as non-colours could identify parameters of honourable existence in a society that had utterly changed.

After this, Schwarz did not know how to continue. In 1555, the Catholic defeat was sealed as the Augsburg Confession stipulated the right for every German prince to regulate whether his territory should follow Lutheran or Catholic beliefs. Augsburg be-came a city of mixed confessions. Charles V had abdicated, and retreated to Spain. He had bitterly accepted a deep division among Christians, a rupture in the way in which European society and its history from now on would have to be imagined. At around the same time, the Fuggers' trade became more difficult to manage—Anton Fugger's initiative slowed down.[84] Spain, Portugal, and France successively stopped their interest payments; a crisis which the Fuggers only overcame in 1562.[85] Several other merchant firms crashed and never survived the crisis. Interest in alchemy abounded among the Fuggers and other leading merchant families for the next generation. Intriguingly, after Anton Fugger had died, the council interrogated a healing woman, who surprisingly disclosed that she and Fugger had engaged in crystal gazing in his headquarters. He had wanted to see his far away factors, one of whom at least had become impossible to control and made considerable losses. Fugger wanted to see how they were housed and what they wore. According to the woman, he had once exclaimed: 'my servants are better dressed than I'.[86] We also know that he commented on one factor who worked for him in the Netherlands that he was 'too luxurious, too rich in his things'.[87] Fugger, who was to be addressed as 'his majesty' (*seine Herrlichkeit*), in these years of crisis also began to actively support the militant Catholic renewal. He stopped his support for humanist projects in Protestant printing houses, helped Jesuits to take root in Augs-burg, and invested in Catholic churches elsewhere. When Fugger added to his will in 1560 before he died, he darkly assumed that all trade likewise was to 'cut itself down and die out'.[88]

42.   Matthäus Schwarz, Book of Clothes, Ill. 136, aged 56, when Moritz of Saxony was shot. © Herzog Anton Ulrich-Museum Braunschweig, Kunstmuseum des Landes Niedersachsen, Museumsphoto Bernd Peter Keiser

As these years passed by, Schwarz would not fill a single page of his book. And yet he *needed* to end it: anyone looking at the book would have judged it a failure if it closed with a picture of him triumphing over Protestantism, celebrating Moritz of Saxony's death. And so Schwarz decided to end his project in September 1560, this time to commemorate deep sadness. Two days ago, he wrote, 'my gracious lord, Herr Anthoni Fugger, in holy memory, died the 14th at eight o'clock in the morning' (Fig. 43). He depicted his black funeral dress, a vast robe that hung heavily on his shoulders and down to his feet. He did not comment on his clothes or appearances, as if they finally did not matter much any more. Underneath the picture, as always, he noted his age with exactitude, 'I was 63½ years and 25 days old.' But this time he added laconically: 'this 137th image is unlike the 86th image'. The 86th image had depicted him more than thirty years earlier, dressed in the most splendid red silks and velvets for Anton Fugger's wedding in 1527, in his prime (Fig. 44).

43. (*opposite*) Matthäus Schwarz, Book of Clothes, Ill. 137, final image aged 63 in 1560, at Anton Fugger's funeral. © Herzog Anton Ulrich-Museum Braunschweig, Kunstmuseum des Landes Niedersachsen, Museumsphoto Bernd Peter Keiser

44. (*above*) Matthäus Schwarz, Book of Clothes, Ill. 86, aged 30 in 1527, at Anton Fugger's wedding. © Herzog Anton Ulrich-Museum Braunschweig, Kunstmuseum des Landes Niedersachsen, Museumsphoto Bernd Peter Keiser

MEANINGS

Who was the *Klaidungsbüchlein* for? Despite the age of printing, sixteenth-century Europe still abounded with richly illustrated manuscripts, which were valued for their originality and idiosyncrasy. They would typically be shown to others to exhibit an artist's work and the manuscript's unique features and ideas, to entertain, or assemble knowledge. If they were precious, they would be shown to foreign dignitaries when they visited. Some of them then led to printed books.[89] It is therefore problematic to assume right away that Schwarz would have continuously thought of the *Klaidungsbüchlein* as a secret book he did not wish to circulate. For a start, of course, he shared the project with successive painters, one of them presumably female. Next, he himself referred to his discussions with older people about their clothes, and to images of them, and regarded his record partly as a historical venture. He constantly invested money, time, and ideas in it, and motivated his eldest son to start a similar book in 1561. So his son, Veit Konrad, it seems safe to assume, would have known the pages which Schwartz had only bound around 1564; perhaps all of his family and friends during particular periods knew several as well. From off the pages, moreover, Matthäus vividly communicated, gestured, and postured in so many variations towards an onlooker and wanted, it seems, not merely to memorialize for himself, but very much to show off to others, the clothes he had worn when he had dressed like a young Venetian gentleman on his Italian journey, when he had been away on business trips for the Fuggers, worn the costume Anton Fugger himself had given Schwarz to attend Fugger's wedding in, or defended the city in beautiful, expensive armoury inscribed with his monogram. To look at refined appearances was certainly thought of as something intensely pleasurable by contemporary male elites. In addition, his gestures and postures as well as the settings usually seemed to want to communicate something about his personal experiences—about illnesses, his work for the Fuggers, his youth. All of this makes it unlikely that the *Klaidungsbüchlein* was a private record or even an instrument for self-control. It rather draws our attention to the narrative framework Schwarz created, particularly at the beginning and the end of the project, when he connected more consistently with stories and events that would have been familiar to many people. Indeed, Schwarz himself may not necessarily have always known what he wanted the book to be for, or even been aware that his views about this changed. He had started it aged twenty-one, out of a fascination for recording stages of his life so far and a sense of impermanence after his father's death. But how could he have envisaged that a project of this kind would take on a life of its own as it grew, and as life took its course? What kind of memory had he in effect created for himself? Could he have envisaged that the book would force him one day to confront his picture as a happy man, in a world that had shifted? For sure, this self presentation still related to one of the stories this society told itself about age: that men were 'old' from their late forties onwards and became more melancholic in temperament as their blood turned stale and darker, as they became colder and less potent, in a final and very different experience of male gender, after youth and a relatively brief phase of full masculine maturity.[90] These 'stages of man' were visualized by broadsheets and engravings. But this clearly was not the only story he told about his age—still surrounded by young and maturing children—or as he showed off his controlled, responsible, and mighty military service for his city, his delight in Moritz of Saxony's death, and his retreat from vanity. It is important to note then that his became also the story of a life that he could neither control nor manipulate easily. Girls failed to fall in love with him, despite his amazing efforts to dress to impress them, or the match was somehow not right. His grandfather's story loomed over the family's name. Even so he was hired as bookkeeper by the most powerful merchant firm. He needed to marry, because that was what society demanded. He had escaped the plague, but suffered a stroke, nonetheless regaining much of his health after one year. Despite all their money and shrewd manipulations, the Fuggers were unable to ensure the dominance of Catholicism in Augsburg, or even in their closest family. The Fuggers and Schwarz needed to live through the upheavals of their time. Could they manipulate business figures and be in control of trade? Florentine account books too were not at all an instrument inducing a logic of order and calculation in a new generation of assured Renaissance men, but rather turned out to become an 'often fragile and almost always doomed attempt to control a shifting world of material possessions'.[91]

Gains and losses mingled in the experience of these lives and had to be *lived* within the course of the world, the *Weltlauf*, as Schwarz entitled his autobiography. Schwarz seems to have felt that life was a *Gauggelsack*, a 'bag' of laughter, full of incongruities. We have seen that he also believed in the influence of astrology on a person's life. The Renaissance quest for astrology to explain individual differences accelerated in the sixteenth century. Schwarz might well have identified with the 'children' of planet Mercury, as depicted in a contemporary Augsburg woodcut series by Georg Pencz, for instance (Fig. 45). Mercury's children were subtle and quick-witted, fast and artful people, whose element was fire, and who evidently loved fine calculations, music, art, and scientific investigation. Schwarz could easily identify with all these attributes, and had even written an account of double-entry bookkeeping when he was young. Children of Mercury clearly dressed with corresponding refinement and taste, but would naturally be curious to adapt to change.[92] Schwarz's chosen motto was wholly pragmatic in spirit: 'Every "why" has its cause.' Yet what seems significant is that these ideas about the human condition ran alongside each other. For early modern people, as much as nowadays, held different ideas simultaneously and applied them to different contexts at different times. In turn, they cannot be easily pinned down to one mindset arising from one dominant context connected to their life—as the self-fashioning approach tends to suggest.[93] It is too limited, therefore, to understand Schwarz's narrative solely through the prism of an ideal-typical, calculating bookkeeping mentality, which controlled and manipulated, and captured a static male self beyond fear, age, belief, sexuality, and other forms of embodied emotion.

Finally, in order to understand the identity of a man like Schwarz, we have to remember how seriously sixteenth-century people in the south of Germany took the

45. Georg Pencz, *Mercury and his Children*, broadsheet, Inv. No. H155 Kaps 46a. © Germanisches Nationalmuseum, Nünberg

paradoxical notion of the fool, who could be wise, and the wise, who could be foolish. This was a 'deep' paradox, which was never neatly untangled. But it certainly stood in contrast to any safe notion that self-knowledge might cumulatively be gathered and finally turn you into a wise man. The fool was still given a marked cultural significance in this society. Maximilian I had several 'natural' fools at his court and also a prominent jester, whom Schwarz accompanied for a full three weeks during carnival as a 7 year old boy, and whose fearless, unconventional image was popularized through a portrait woodcut.[94] Afterwards, Matthäus wrote about how Cuntz had morally corrupted him, and his parents had sent him away from home to be educated by a priest. He nonetheless later had four full size images of local fools (and of no one else, except for himself, of course) entered into his prayer book, and wrote short descriptions of what they did. He depicted himself with a fool's cap under his feet when he decided to change his life and marry. The *Klaidungs-büchlein* excluded all of his carnival outfits as an adult man. The fool could therefore be externalized to some extent, but this took tremendous effort. Foolishness, moreover, was associated with sinfulness, as in Sebastian Brant's bestselling moralizing and intensely visual publication *Ship of Fools*, but also with relief from rigorous social conventions and straight morals. Without foolishness, seriousness and melancholy threatened to overtake; life became lifeless. To follow fashion would prove one to be foolish; yet this is what had given Matthäus's life rhythm, colour, excitement, amusement, and surprise.

CONCLUSION

This chapter has explored the intricate mental and political shifts that could inform attitudes towards clothing and the question of how clothing and portrait images interacted with the identity of a particular sixteenth-century man. Matthäus Schwarz's example clearly shows that he shaped his self-perception at different points of his life in dialogue with visual representations of that self. He balanced his desire to stand out and express his real fascination with clothing and accessories, and a notion of personhood which related to different groups—to young men, marriageable girls, the Fugger firm, the Catholic elite, and, later, mature men. We can see why this balance had to be managed carefully. Far from encouraging individualism, powerful men like the Fuggers were anxious to maintain hierarchies and not to be outdone by those in their service. It seems equally problematic to suggest that Schwarz's record of his appearance was determined by the economic environment in which he lived. Rather, we need to write the history of the Renaissance self in a way that allows for people's interior complexities and relationship with their bodies.[95] The *Klaiderbüchlein* can not be properly understood if we do not take notice of all the elements that played a part in Schwarz's life—the early loss of his mother, his many siblings, the importance he accorded every year to his birthday, his enjoyment of self-display in the centre of spaces, in the centre of a parchment book, in dialogue with the artists depicting him, recomposing scenes of his life, insisting so long on an image of elite youthfulness. Schwarz's book provides us with a sense of how one man represented not just the high points of his life, but his life-cycle. Changes such as becoming a head of a family and ageing seem to have been experienced by him in strongly physical terms, and his appearances accentuated a new heaviness and slowness, but also gravity and pride. His mature identity hinged on his place in local society, on his professional acceptance and the trust of the Fugger patriarchs for their servant, as well as on his ability to be sexually active in a marriage and build his own family. It was also shaped by his adaptation of elements from contemporary ideas and beliefs, such as astrology, religion, and notions of foolishness. Yet Schwarz never set an example to others, because he did not narrate his life from his marriage onwards, which would have invited identification as a model of a path towards virtue. Who wanted to look at himself recovering from a stroke, or as sardonic old man? His was not a heroic tale, but as close an account of an early modern man in the jumble of life as we are likely to get, with its phases of grandeur, crisis, doubts, and compromises. If one is to understand the concept of identity as centring on the notion that a person forms an image of her- or himself that she or he identifies with, then Schwarz's visual and textual practices to relate his life reveal the impossibility of a fixed and immutable identity without question marks, revisions, lacunae, or the notion that memory could haunt. Schwarz's imaging practices interrelated with the understanding of himself he formed as a series of visual acts that played their part in temporarily constituting images of himself he wished to be identified with.

'I propose', Arjun Appadurai writes in his pioneering collection of essays on the 'social life of things', 'that we regard luxury goods not so much in contrast to necessities (. . .), but as goods whose principal use is *rhetorical* and *social*, goods that are simply *incarnated signs*. The necessity to which *they* respond is fundamentally political.' Luxury goods were not only expensive, but often difficult to resource, and one needed to constantly renew one's knowledge of how to use them in sophisticated ways.[96] These points are essential to analyse how Matthäus Schwarz used luxury appearances, as did other men in his time. There can be few more telling examples of the rhetorical and social use of clothes as 'incarnated' signs of esteem in this period as Dürer triumphantly writing from Venice to his Nuremberg humanist friend Willibald Pirckheimer 'my French mantle...and brown coat send you best wishes'.[97] Clothes could thus be imagined to literally speak their own language; they made the most immediate and powerful statement about social status to contemporaries: in an extremely hierarchical society, which was by definition a politicized process. They embodied regard by others, and the social capital of *savoir-vivre*. But if we look at the book of clothes as a project that represented Matthäus Schwarz's use of appearances, another, more intricate, dimension becomes visible as well. His display of luxury appearances responded to a further necessity, an emotional and historical one. Clothes, for Matthäus Schwarz, were incarnated signs, and their recording and doubling was bound up with his inscription in time.

His son knew better, or he knew better for his son. If Matthäus had started his project open-endedly to 'see what might become of it', Veit clearly delineated what the purpose of such an undertaking might be: Germans had always been like monkeys in their clothing, he declared, and had imitated many nations, as well as sometimes bastardizing their manners. 'This', he went on pithily, 'is witnessed abundantly in my dear father's little book, which he calls his book of clothes, which he has had made from 1520...until now.' He had clearly looked at it, but could only laugh about his father as a young man. The world, Veit continued, was getting 'more and more foolish and there is still no end to the new strange modes of dress until nowadays'. Veit's book of clothing was a contained undertaking. It involved one year of collaborative work with one artist. Forty-one images were produced, starting with his infancy, finishing in March 1561. Veit Konrad was nineteen years old, confidently entering his prime. He proudly went to his wealthy peers' wedding feasts, and, as customary, had them pay for much of his outfit. In one of the last images, Veit recorded how he had been unable to bear wearing mourning clothes for Anton Fugger any longer. He had attended a wedding and neatly calculated that the total cost of his appearance amounted to the enormous sum of 290 florins, which included a fine sword and an even more valuable golden ring with his coat of arms, a ruby, and a diamond worth 50 ducats (Fig. 46). The riches of these East Indian stones glowed on his little finger. He highlighted its precise market value, rather than masking it. Yet despite all his splendour and sociability, Veit would die a single man aged forty-seven, still living in the family home. His mother had perished in 1580, six years after Matthäus himself had died.[98] Somewhere in that house, the Schwarzes' books of clothes were stored.

46. (*opposite*) Veit Konrad Schwarz, Book of Clothes, Ill. 39, aged 19, 1561, for Hans Herwart's wedding, 23.5 × 16 cm. © Herzog Anton Ulrich-Museum Braunschweig

Nobilium pueri commendantur benedicto *
sacris firmantur nobilium pueri

CHAPTER 3

The Look of Religion

GOD'S LIVERY

In 1505, Martin Luther entered the Augustinian convent in Erfurt as a twenty-two year old. His prior put a hooded cowl over him, which was not yet consecrated, and prayed: 'May God clothe you with the new man, who is created after God in justice and the sanctity of truth'.[1] Clothing mattered deeply to the Renaissance clergy: it could mediate the divine.[2] Simple monks' and nuns' cowls were regarded as imbued with the power to morally transform the wearer; they were God's livery. Cowls were usually consecrated before they were ceremonially put on to help effect and signal the devoted life of a person who had left behind worldly temptations. This act of investiture was beautifully conveyed in a north-German panel painting from 1495, which was displayed to the pious in a Lüneburg church (Fig. 47). It depicted two aristocratic fathers leading their sons to join St Benedict. One father looked just like a pilgrim, with short hair, a long coat, a large bag hanging from his belt, and a walking cane. The other nobleman wore refined, colourful clothes, spectacular hose, beautiful boots made from the finest leather, and curled long hair. Both displayed an amulet with Christ's face on Veronica's cloth on their right shoulder. One boy was freshly tonsured as a sign of penance and humility and wore a black cowl over a white tunic. The other prepared himself in prayer to hand over his fur-trimmed robe and have his golden hair shaved off. The fathers clearly had carefully considered and invested in their own attire, yet they idealized poverty as sacred. Nothing suggests that the painter regarded this as a contradiction. Only the space left in the painting for the coat of arms of a family who wished to be associated with the painting would never be filled.

47. (*opposite*) Panel from the Benedict-cycle, Lüneburg, 1495, 123.5 × 81 cm, WM XXXVII 17b. © Niedersächsisches Landesmuseum Hannover

The painting takes us back into a world that religious reformers would vigorously fight. Soon, Luther argued that poverty was nothing to be idealized; it was a policy problem of how to get lazy, able-bodied people to work and organize welfare for respectable citizens who were needy. Luther also demystified Catholic clerical appearances as a secular sign system that the church had used to deceive the laity. It was not imbued with divine power. Clergymen were to be like other citizens: marry, pay tax, be liable to secular courts for their wrongdoings, and in dress. But: dress how? This turned out to be a complicated question. Reform-minded men and women had surprisingly conflicting expectations about the meaning of clothing as signs. These ideas corresponded to different views on an unexpected range of subjects to do with status, belief, and emotions, such as how Lutheran clergymen as a new professional group should mark their rank and honour, the laity query the learned, or Lutheran men bring joy, laughter, and manliness into their lives. They also reveal how Luther could eventually use clothes to assert his claim for charismatic leadership through red clothing, despite the fact that he had declared that clothes did not matter. These varied and far from stable reflections document fascinating ambivalences in Protestant views about whether and how the visual display of clothing bore meaning. There was nothing homogenous about 'Protestant' culture. Clothing practices and their symbolization can reveal specific 'taste communities', which not everyone or even all Protestants approached the same way and rigorously followed through. Lutheranism itself continued to be marked by a plurality of ideas rather than a mere continuation of Luther's views.[3] Its bourgeois urban mainstream even founded a Protestant material culture. This chapter seeks to show that rather than preaching austere simplicity, it endorsed a notion of civil decorousness and hence adapted Renaissance ideals.

THE COMING OF THE REFORMATION

'Catholic' looks were a natural target for those campaigning for religious reforms. While monks and nuns at least looked humble, the church had since the Carolingian period used elaborate appearances as a vital tool in a symbolic system to claim particular esteem and majesty for its clerical elite and popes in solemn rituals. 'Those constituted in positions of dignity and the ministers of the altar more than others are decked out in costly robes', Thomas Aquinas's *Summa* set out, 'not for their own glory, but to signify the nobility of their office and of divine worship; therefore for them it is not wrongful.'[4] Elites at this time always performed functions before others through physical signs. This visibility and precise control of a culture of appearances underlay medieval and early modern politics in both church and secular government.[5] Distinguished royal habits, for instance, could be used as a communicative tool to evoke a sense of the marvellous and thereby manipulate an audience into acclamation.[6] High clerical vestments, too, were used to represent their wearers' interior moral qualities and authority, as well as the strength and wealth of the church. They embodied the treasure-like magnificence bestowed on them by God and sacred rituals. Magnificent, shiny dress reflected the glory of God on earth in the interplay of sumptuous fabric and luminosity. It drew the supernatural into the material, allowing precious matter to be celebrated as a splendid and sensational event, as enlightening epiphany.[7] *Decor* and *splendor* were frequently acknowledged as aesthetic categories, which mediated the divine and touched the spirit of others. It would therefore still be entirely plausible for the sixteenth-century Lateran canon Tommaso Garzoni to praise the qualities of silk and its enhancement of courtly, military, and church life:

> Is it not clear that silk adorns everything? Is it not silk that adorns the coaches, the carriages, the litters, the maritime gondolas, the horses of the Princes, with trappings, with outfits, with tassels, with fringes, with cords, with cushions, with cloths, and a thousand other beautiful things? Does not silk adorn the banners, the standards, the insignia, the halberds trimmed with brocaded velvet and fringes, the sheathed pikes, the bandoleers, the trumpets, the uniforms of soldiers at war? Does not silk adorn the umbrellas, the canopies, the chasubles, the copes, the pictures, the palliums, the sandals, the cassocks, the dalmatics, the gloves, the maniples, the stoles, the burses, the veils for chalices, the lining for tabernacles, the cushions, the pulpits, and all other things of the Church?[8]

Many extant vestments invite us to imagine how the laity might have feasted their eyes on the warm reds of brocade or shining silks of a deacon's dalmatic robe.[9] Precious Chinese silk fabrics, folded up and shipped in wooden barrels, found their way into Hanseatic ports like Bruges and Nowgorod from the fourteenth century onwards. One dalmatic from the first half of the fourteenth century was tailored from five different green and blue Lampas silk fabrics, which must have been produced in northern or eastern central Asia (Fig. 48). Patterns showed lotus flowers, phoenixes, and glorious peacocks. The dalmatic was lined with purple silk and generously trimmed with a turquoise Lampas silk fabric with peacocks.[10] The visual effect of the gold and finely shaded colours in their extraordinary luminosity must have been dazzling, especially in their constant interplay with light and movement, which defied normal experiences of colour constancy.[11] Another vestment used a fabric for the end of the sleeve that had a golden leopard with pink flames on it, holding a band with the woven Latin motto 'Love is the reward of restraint.'[12]

As Italian and Spanish silk fabrication expanded during the fourteenth century, it adapted many of the lively Oriental animal and plant motives. One red fifteenth-century silk dalmatic dramatically displayed golden lions fighting with dragons.[13] Another late fifteenth-century German dalmatic was made from one piece of the best Florentine brocaded velvet, woven to display a pomegranate, small leaves, a pineapple, and artichokes. It was perfectly possible for vestments to be sewn together from different parts, which could even contrast in colour and differ in their age. The fifteenth-century Brunswig tunicella worn by a deacon used many small parts of a hundred-years-older Egyptian red-golden silk for its one part, while the other part was made from contemporary blue half-silks.[14] In addition to such vestments, pontifical gloves were delicately knitted to

perfection with fine silk and metal threads, and helped to cover all of a high cleric's body apart from the face. Such gloves were either white or red, and were consciously used to enact purification on their wearer.[15] As early as 1389, one French royal advisor took it for granted that the laity would lose 'half or more of its faith' if a bishop were to celebrate mass dressed like a poor chaplain.[16]

Jewellery likewise helped to radiate papal majesty, just as a king could now be metaphorically described as a precious, highly visible jewel.[17] A famous report of the coronation of Pope Felix V in 1440 dwelt on the visual and emotional effect of his crown with an abundance of precious stones, which had received its third coronet in 1334. It was estimated to be worth the staggering sum of 30,000 florins. People held their breath when this tiara was brought in at the height of ceremonies; almost cathartically the coronation was followed by immediate shouts of acclamation.[18] This triple-crown became an emblem for the way in which splendour had become successively more important to manifest and legitimize Roman curial, secular, and spiritual majesty through these forms of symbolic communication in competition with secular rulers in a court society of its own making. 'Our popes', Enea Silvio Piccolomini thus affirmed against German critics in 1467/8, 'need to be rich and mighty'. He explained that everyone would just laugh at a priest who celebrated the mass wearing a gold-decorated robe in the morning, but then walked about shabbily dressed for the rest of the day. Dignity manifested itself in clothes, jewellery, and an entourage. Christ had not been poor to show that Christians should be poor, but because he knew he had to be crucified to redeem mankind.[19]

The Middle Ages in turn greatly furthered a debate about whether precious matter in art, architecture, clerical, or papal appearances helped or hindered true devotion. In the early twelfth century, the Cistercian Bernard of Clairvaux certainly set out that his order 'regarded as dung all things shining in beauty . . . in order that we may win Christ'.[20] His order wore simple white habits, which for him was a colour of 'purity, innocence and all the virtues'. Peter the Venerable, abbot of Cluny, nonetheless told him that white was a colour of pride, glory, feast days, and the resurrection. Only black could effect penitence and humility.[21] Martin Luther revered Bernhard's decided stance for purity, but as he began to question monastic life found that he could no longer agree with this position either. His lectures on Romans in winter 1515/1516 told students that 'all clothing is allowed', as long as it was decided upon in a general spirit of modesty and love.[22] After his *Ninety-Five Theses* against the indulgence trade had gained such attention in 1517, and the Roman church had set out to excommunicate him, Luther began to argue that neither a humble habit nor splendid clerical clothing should mark anyone out as holy. Luther's 1520 treatise *The Freedom of a Christian* declared that priesthood was simply an office assumed by someone in the community. God had granted grace through the death of Christ to all believers. Nothing other than belief in this truth of scripture was necessary to gain salvation. In Luther's view, God had never suggested that he would sanctify special communities of men and women living apart under vows of chastity and

48. (*opposite*) North-German (Stralsund?) dalmatic, fourteenth century, Stralsund Kaland KHM, Inv.Nr. 1862:16. © Kunsthistorisches Museum Stralsund, Photo: Volkmar Herre

doing good works. Neither had any Roman emperor ever entitled the papacy to a role equal to or superior to secular power. This argument naturally was of great interest to German rulers, and Luther used familiar themes developed by anti-courtier literature to vent his criticism against the immoral life, flattery, and self-interested advice given to weak popes. In his view, they made Rome a den of sin rather than a New Jerusalem.

SATIRIZING APPEARANCES

In May 1521, a carefully timed initial Wittenberg image-campaign of twenty-six wood-cuts pointedly followed Luther's official excommunication by the Roman church. In response, the Saxon court lobbied for Luther to be heard before the newly elected Emperor Charles V at the Diet of Worms. Luther explicitly described this series as 'beneficial for the laity', and the laity crowded the streets of Worms as Luther arrived. Many had already bought cheap woodcuts of Luther depicted with a halo above his head.[23] Thirteen pairs of images contrasted Christ's simple life with the papacy's satanic pretensions. One woodcut showed the pope in splendid vestments on a throne, receiving his triple-crown: 'Emperor Constantine', the Roman church was represented as announcing below this image, 'has given us this imperial crown, precious adornment, and all other jewellery, and just as the emperor, a scarlet dress and all other dress and the sceptre to use'.[24] By then it had become widely known that a document legitimizing the church's ambitious grip on power had been forged, the so-called *Donation of the Roman Emperor Constantine*. The satire encouraged people to see through the pretence of adornments. It emphasized that Christ himself, of course, had only ever worn a simple cloak. This contrast was to generate a further push for those who had already distanced themselves from the church to look for religion that truly followed Christ. The final woodcut showed that those following the pope would end in damnation, and true followers of Christ be saved. The Passional was immensely successful: one Latin and ten German editions were published within a few years, and many later adaptations appeared, not least in the Calvinist reformed tradition.

Did Luther think of his image propaganda as a success? Writing to Archbishop Albrecht von Mainz in 1525, he declared himself content that 'the common man is now so broadly informed and advanced in understanding that the clergy are worthless, as has been shown all too well in numerous songs, sayings, and satires which one paints on all walls, on many sheets, and not least through monks and priests on playing cards, that one is nauseous whenever one sees or hears a cleric'.[25]

Reformed ideas circulated through hundreds of thousands of people's minds through preaching, singing, performances, and discussions. This was fuelled by print. We know that twenty-five per cent of book-owners in Strasbourg, for example, were artisans or working people, including women such as one Salome Schmid, whose husband was a cloth worker. Alongside books, small printed pamphlets and cheap broadsheets with woodcut images were produced for a popular market and made up pedlars' wares (Fig. 49). Broadsheets cost around four Pfennig, which roughly equated to two sausages and eighteen eggs, while Luther's *New Testament* in 1522 cost 1½ florins, or 360

49. Workshop of Lucas Cranach the Elder, *Satirical Coat of Arms for the Pope*, Wittenberg, 1538, text by Martin Luther, hand-coloured woodcut 21.2 × 21.4 cm, AN248829001. © The Trustees of the British Museum

Pfennig, and his small catechism in 1537 five Pfennig.[26] Heavily illustrated books, once again most famously Sebastian Brant's *Ship of Fools*, had sought to cultivate a broader audience for print media through images. Brant explicitly announced that even the wholly illiterate should see themselves reflected in the copious woodcuts illustrating foolish sinfulness.[27] Yet nobody half-literate or illiterate would write down that she or he had seen an image or heard about one. So there will never be conclusive evidence to settle the question of how broadly such images were distributed.[28] But this makes it just as problematic to sustain that they remained the preserve of the highly literate as it is to argue with complete confidence that they communicated with a wide and socially mixed audience, as Luther himself nonetheless firmly believed. As the Reformation matured, moreover, broadsheet images certainly were adapted for a broadly accessible art of instruction through altar images and paintings on church walls and ceilings. German Lutheranism hence was not iconorexic. It pushed visual culture on to develop its themes.[29]

One year after he had written to Albrecht, in 1526, Luther therefore launched the most heavily illustrated satirical attack on the Roman church of the entire Reformation movement.[30] This forty-page pamphlet entitled *The Papacy with its Parts* contained no less than sixty-five woodcuts. A previous version of *The Papacy* had presumably been sent to Luther by a prominent Nuremberg preacher called Andreas Osiander, and the verses accompanying the pictures were penned by the famous shoemaker-poet, Hans Sachs. Luther added a preface and afterword, and the Wittenberg court painter Lucas Cranach may have contributed new woodcuts. This teamwork of German scholars, artists, and artisans stretched across cities, and created innovative formats to communicate ideas. Three editions appeared in Wittenberg; four revised editions from Nuremberg further ensured the pamphlets' distribution over decades. Woodcut after woodcut depicted pope, cardinals, and the numerous male religious orders who sought to make themselves recognizable through particular appearances (Figs. 50–51). For the very first time in European history, a printed work systematically focused on the dress of a particular group of society in order to describe and characterize it, and to show through the plurality of dress codes that all these were human customs, not divinely imbued practices. Hans Sachs's verses specified what was distinctive about these clothes as deceptive outer signs of an evil clergy. Because it treated costumes as custom, *The Papacy* was a costume pamphlet before the later age of the costume book.

The Papacy was a popularist pamphlet designed to unite people just after the Peasants' War. When Luther had negotiated his release from the Wartburg, where Prince Frederick the Wise had taken him into protection after the imposition of the imperial ban on Luther in 1521, Luther's strongest argument had been that he would be able to ward off any rebellion among common people, which rulers of this time so feared. Since 1524, unrest had swollen not only among many peasant communities, but also among rural artisans and parts of the urban population. The 'radi-

50. (*left*) Martin Luther/Hans Sachs, *Das Papsthum mit seinen Gliedern*, 1526: Pope, BL 555.A.47. © The British Library, London

51. (*opposite*) Martin Luther/Hans Sachs, *Das Papsthum mit seinen Gliedern*, 1526: Benedictine. © The British Library, London

cal' reform movement had begun to set out what they regarded as a more egalitarian, biblically-justified ethics. Many of Luther's supporters were shocked by the licence he gave princes to kill rebels. They were now unsure about the movement's ideals and Luther's leading role within it. After these years of upheaval one Catholic Nuremberg chronicler interrupted his narrative of annual events to vent his complete incredulity:

> everybody thinks they are free, so that we don't need preachers, everybody's a preacher, no sacrament is worth anything, and you are not allowed to confess or fast, in sum do any good work, but only believe, so everyone believes what suits him, the lowest as the highest.[31]

Hence *The Papacy*'s message repeated three familiar elements of Lutheran reform propaganda: the clergy was hypocritical, corrupt, and greedily drained Germany of all financial resources; it belonged to the order made by the Antichrist and the end of this world was near; and Martin Luther had been sent to Germany as divine prophet. In Nuremberg, two further and equally extensive pictorial histories authored by Osiander in the following year similarly drew on this established apocalyptic mood to reveal Luther as biblical man incarnate of age-old prophecies against papal tyranny, which were now brought to light.[32] Luther was presented as a freedom fighter and symbol of hope for a different life in eternity. As usual, his own words matched the challenge. 'I beg you for God's sake, look at them [the clergy] properly!' Luther's preamble to *The Papacy* urged: 'You will find no one who fames himself for faith and love; these two they do not respect.' Rather, he ridiculed, 'this one wears something flat, that one a cap…'.[33] Medieval reformers had long been criticizing too diverse and arbitrary clothing practices. As Nicolas of Cusa put it: 'There is only one college of cardinals; why are there so many types of capes?'[34] The humanist Agrippa of Nettesheim in 1526 wittily reported to have looked at all historical depictions of monks to see when the hood on the cowl had been invented, only to find out that the first depicted the devil in disguise tempting Christ.[35] Luther likened this diversified clergy to swarming insects of the plague, who had eaten up and destroyed the land. It was a fear-inspiring vision. The images, he concluded, served to better reflect on these figures and

Der Benedicter Orden.

Der Orden zu Kaſſyn anfieng
Darnach in die gantze Welt gieng
Gros ſchwartz Kutten tragen ſie an
Auch ein Biſchoffs ſtab müſſens han
Jn gros reichthumb ſtetz geſeſſen
Darbey ſie Gottes han vergeſſen
Das die Schrifft ſie nicht verfüre
Dorffe jr keiner nicht ſtudire.

give thanks to God for revealing this order and to redeem believers. Of course the series began with the pope. In line with all evangelical propaganda it did not attack any specific pope but the 'Bapsts stand', all those belonging to this rank. Sachs's verses expressed the hope that this Antichrist and all those hanging on him would be destroyed, while commenting reassuringly that God supported only 'his', i.e. the evangelicals. Many of the following verses reiterated the message that clerical vestments were mere appearances, 'Schein', to disguise the devil's sect. The characteristically simple and memorable rhyme on a cardinal ran: 'This sect is all dressed in red, on its skin not one good hair is to be had.'[36] The rhetorical strategy throughout the pamphlet was to apply the term 'sect' to the Roman church itself, which had argued that once popular bible reading was allowed, Christianity fell apart into small divisive parts. Already the third verse emphasized that the pope's main goal was to get money, and that he had therefore sent his fishers of souls around the world to impress through good appearances and pious pretence.[37] For this reason almost all of the physiognomies in the woodcuts were made to look dismal and hypocritical rather than holy. A deacon was depicted with beautifully embroidered vestments carrying a big sacred book, but the verse simply remarked that 'there is no one pious under these clothes'.[38] Other verses ridiculed Benedictines, who were not allowed to read the bible, or the white dress of Praemonstrants to signal their chastity, which, however, was only in existence when they slept. Many rallied that after everyone had been blinded, there was now hope for an end (Fig. 52). The fourteenth woodcut presented Luther himself, drawing on a by now iconic image of him as a holy Augustinian monk (Fig. 53). Hans Sachs celebrated Luther as a hero, who had taught God's word since 1519 and damaged papal dominion. Hermits were the only ones credited with integrity, but characterized as sadly deceived by the devil.[39] Virtually all the other orders had greedily taken German money and were disguising their feasting and whoring with vestments. This served to undermine any respect for particular reform orders or the

Der Thumbherrn stand.

Canonici / der Bischofftnecht
Auch aus des Lucifers geschlecht
Ein weissen Rorock trugens an
Auch Peltzkappen sie musten han
Jr Horas betten sie allzeit
Das hertz jn war daruon gar weit
Nur schlemmen leben in dem saus
Jch hoff es sey nu mit jn aus.

Der

52. (*right*) Martin Luther/Hans Sachs, *Das Papsthum mit seinen Gliedern*, 1526: Thumbherrn. © The British Library, London

53. (*opposite*) Martin Luther/Hans Sachs, *Das Papsthum mit seinen Gliedern*, 1526: Luther as Augustinian. © The British Library, London

Der Auguſtiner Orden.

Auguſtiner gantz ſchwartz gekleidt
Jr Ord helt nicht viel vnterſcheid
Als man tauſent fünffhundert Jar
Dazu neunzehen zelt furwar
Aldo aus jrer Sect erſtand
Martin Luther in Saxer Land
Gottes wort er vns wider lert
Des Bapſts Reich hat er gar verhert.
                    B iij   preſ

hope that another order might be the solution to the church's failings. Sachs finally wished that God would grant peace and quiet from all of them.[40]

Luther's afterword referred to St Paul in adding that all laws restricting what and when to eat, drink, touch, or what to wear were man-made, and that good works contributed nothing to a person's grace or wisdom. In and of themselves good works merely created 'puffed-up hearts' and the illusion of holiness. Next followed Luther's own post-war rallying cry: many said that the papacy and clergy had now been denounced through so many means that one knew them well, but was unable to overcome them. However, as had been written in the biblical book of Revelation, the force of God's enemies had to be countered again and again with pain and suffering, until they were trodden down like excrement on the streets. Now these enemies and Catholic princes were triumphing about the defeat of the peasants and waiting to be reborn. That is why polemics were needed, to stir the dirt that liked to stink, until they had 'their mouth and nose full of it'. 'Therefore', Luther energetically proclaimed, 'dear friends, let us start again to write, rhyme, sing, paint and point.' He exhorted the lazy to participate in these activities, since God had started to gnaw the enemies on earth and turn them to ashes. Tongues, voices, and pens were the only weapons in the service of God. *The Papacy* was not even a defaming pamphlet (this implied that it should not be subject to censorship). It was a 'public punishment of the public, disgraceful horror and devil's game, which God wishes to be punished'.[41] The aim of *The Papacy*, then, was to involve audiences in the humorous and hateful sensation of unmasking those who pretended to be more holy than other people and to inspire a sense that everyone's action was needed and was effective.[42]

As a piece of popular propaganda *The Papacy* was exceptionally well targeted against its enemies, and certainly not visually complex. It was less clear, however, in addressing the question of how Protestants themselves should think about clothes. It was paradoxical to posit that there was meaning in a simple habit while at the same time insisting that it had no meaning. Yet, was this not implied by continuing to depict Luther as monk as late as 1526, when, as we shall see, he had in fact already stopped wearing his Augustinian habit and was a married man?

Before returning to the question of what Luther thought about appearances and which dress could successfully symbolize distinctly Lutheran beliefs, it is important to note once again the extent to which conflicts over religious ideas could involve undressing or re-clothing in these years. One particularly articulate pamphlet, *To the Assembly of the Common Peasantry*, printed in Nuremberg in 1525, spoke for the 'poor' and sarcastically vented its anger about the absurdities of life in servitude to landlords:

> May God, in his justice, not tolerate the terrible Babylonian captivity in which we poor people are driven to mow the lords' meadows, to make hay, to cultivate the fields, to sow flax in them, to cut it, comb it, heat it, wash it, pound it, and spin it—yes, even to sew their drawers on their arses.[43]

An Augsburg chronicle writer recorded how a common man helped to punish a count during the Peasants' War, and then took his heavy silk damask jacket, slipped into it and asked the count's wife: 'well, woman, how do I please you?'[44] In March 1525, peasant women indulged in similar fantasies of role reversal when they told nuns of the Heggbach convent that it was their turn to 'go out and milk the cows and wear rough jerkins', while the peasant women 'would come in and wear clean fur'.[45] In the summer of 1524, meanwhile, peasants near Frauenfeld in Switzerland had undressed a Carthusian monk, who cried while he had to watch them cutting and tearing apart his habit and cloak. This social drama of profaning divestiture took away the robe's sacred substance and integrity. The peasants insisted that the monk should be equal to them.[46] The Catholic church, for its part, derobed at least one 'heretical' Lutheran monk and led him to the executioner in a simple tunic and a black, cut-up beret.[47] The Peasant Oath of the Nobility in Franconia in 1525 meanwhile simply stipulated: 'If any count or noble has under their protection in their territory any convent, whether for monks or nuns, they shall see to it that these same persons shall dress in secular clothing, and that no further persons be admitted to those same orders, and the inmates be allowed to die out.'[48]

Artists and readers could create images that revealed their criticism of the church through the idiom of dress. One anonymous reader of the most popular contemporary book of prophecies thus took a close look at a woodcut depicting the pope and clergymen enforcing the rule that young men cut long hair and get rid of pointed shoes. He quickly drew a sausage on top of the papal staff, a fool's bells on the triple-crown, a Jewish mark on his robe, to characterize him as Pharisee, and a devil swarming next to his head.[49] If papal splendour could be shown to have been 'invented', then papal preaching against lay splendour seemed mere hypocrisy. The Petrarch Master illustrated a passage on the trappings of false glory with an image of the pope, bishops, and cardinals. They wore rich clothing as a disguise for a false spectacle of power (Fig. 54). He then chose an extraordinarily inventive view from the back of the papal throne to illustrate a passage on the papacy. This perspective unmasked a ritual as mere spectacle, orchestrated

54. (*opposite top*) Petrarch Master, *Von der Artzney beyder Glück*, Augsburg: Heinrich Steiner 1532, BL C39.h.25. © The British Library, London
55. (*opposite bottom*) Petrarch Master, *Von der Artzney beyder Glück*, Augsburg: Heinrich Steiner 1532, BL C39.h.25. © The British Library, London

by an assault on the senses and pomp, as the heavy tiara was lifted onto the pope's head among waves of incense. The woodcut fascinatingly shows how images could aim to provide critical role-models for readers. It depicted a man swearing against loyalty to the pope and two critical bourgeois laymen, one of them with his arms folded, as the sole audience of this pathetic ceremony (Fig. 55). This was a radical visual act. It is clear that this heavily illustrated and hence more expensive book publication of Petrarch's *De Remediis* would have mostly reached a bourgeois audience, well-off artisans, and their

households. Once more we naturally have no reports of cooks, journeymen, or maids looking at these images. Yet it is important to stress that images could travel across media, and that cheap images painted on pieces of cloth were sold by illuminists in a city like Nuremberg, though obviously none of them have survived.

We know, on the other hand, that one broadsheet image created in 1531 by the Nuremberg civic painter Georg Pencz was adopted for an elaborate media of tapestries no less than sixteen years later. It depicted Charles V kissing the pope's feet. Pencz's broadsheet probably drew on a magnificent woodcut by Hans Holbein, which depicted Charles's anticipated coronation as Holy Roman Emperor by the pope through the same act of submission, and showed the pope surrounded by devils and skeletons. The Wittenberg Passional woodcut series in 1521 had likewise contrasted this very scene to Christ humbly washing his disciples' feet; and the Passional itself referred back to a tradition imported by Wycliffite students through anti-papal wall-paintings in their Prague flat.

Such simple scenes of papal pomp and tyrannical dominance hence became icons of Protestant self-definition by negation. Given the extent of lay involvement in the Reformation, we can, however, assume with relative certainty that they did not exclusively remain in learned circles.[50] In 1535, for instance, a court joiner was granted possession of a former Franciscan chapel to live in when the Reformation was introduced in Silesia. He dressed up as the pope, and told a crowd of supporters to dress up as Catholic clerics. Next he demanded of the Franciscans that they should kiss his feet, then forced them to dress up as devils, and rallied for all his people to throw them out of town.[51] A whole group of people, then, had been involved in this enactment. The symbolism of appearances in these ways lay at the heart of much religious satire.

DRESSING THE CLERGY

A further important example of the impact of reformed ideas on dress displays concerns Nuremberg nuns, counterpart to the male orders tackled in *The Papacy*. While Osiander, Sachs, and Luther in their publications spared nuns from similar scorn and 'public punishment', Nuremberg nuns in reality had a far greater share than their male counterparts. This is particularly well documented in the correspondence between the Nuremberg humanist Willibald Pirckheimer and his six sisters and three daughters in different convents. The best known was his most resilient and vocal sister, the abbess Caritas.[52] Pirckheimer sympathized with Luther's cause early on. Hence his gifts to the nuns included Luther's writings, as well as conventional images of saints, mass vestments to be embroidered, and even indulgences until 1520. His growing criticism of monastic life first expressed itself jokingly. He offered some of his sisters two rusty pieces of armoury to wear. They declined likewise in jest by saying that they were really terribly spoilt and soft, and would only take them to clean pans.[53] At the end of 1524 the Nuremberg council wanted to deprive the nuns of the Klara convent of their male confessors. Pirckheimer's relatives in the convent asked for his help in writing a petition to the magistrates. He agreed, but only on condition that Caritas would eat a basket of meat and other food during the period of fasting in front of a niece who acted as go-between to make this humiliating scene happen. He wanted to show that castigating the flesh was not essential for faith and to use this moment to exert some control before he surrendered to what he saw as their stubbornness.[54] In the summer of 1526, when *The Papacy* was published, the Nuremberg council demanded that the nuns would change the cut of their habit and dye them. They refused.[55] Several mothers of patrician nuns entered the convent and had their daughters measured for new clothes before they were later violently dragged home. Katharina—one of Pirckheimer's daughters, who had decided to enter the convent aged fifteen—begged her father in writing to let her stay. Her response to her father's following letter once more highlights how significant attitudes towards clothing had become: 'I have never thought to be sanctified in my habit', she defended herself, 'but I still think I please my bridegroom [Jesus] better in it than in a pearl-dress.' A biblical quotation was entered in support. She told her father that his permission to stay pleased her more than if he had sent her a 'velvet gown'.[56] This implies her awareness that female beauty was to be defined in relation to men. If it was not for Christ as bridegroom, then elite women needed to be principally adorned to secure a marriage alliance. Certainly no monks were ever forcefully and publicly reclothed by their families in colourful hose. Women moreover were expected to display their virtue and beauty to honour a civic community, which explains why travellers' reports stereotypically commented on the beauty of women in particular localities. When the 1526 *Papacy with its Parts* was put together in Nuremberg by Andreas Osiander, who had repeatedly preached to the nuns and well knew their iron will, it thus related to this campaign to 'communalize' spirituality, and to make manifest through ordinary clothing that dress did not sanctify and legitimately set one apart. Any woman's true office was to marry, be sanctified through the pain of childbirth, and cultivate a virtuous, productive household alongside her husband.

Yet could piety go together with material luxury? Sumptuous velvet, silk, brocade, expensive, vibrant dyes, and pearls were familiar enough to nuns. They had sewn and embroidered ever more precious vestments for some of the clergy, adorned statues of Mary and child, or made precious little bags for small relics. Yet to them this seemed different: it was not done to seek personal vainglory, but once more to express divine glory and the importance of an ecclesiastical office. As late as 1519, for instance, the Nuremberg humanist Scheurl sent to Luther a consecrated mass vestment from the nuns of the patrician Ebner family for holding services. He even promised Luther 'larger gifts' if they were welcome.[57]

So how could or should Protestant preachers dress? Was it true to argue that clothes did not have any spiritual significance at all, that they really only mattered as a sign to demarcate secular meanings? Did clothes, just as particular gestures, not in the end become powerful embodied markers of confessional belonging, 'incarnated' signs once again?[58] Osiander, a striking figure with determined eyes, prominent folds that ran from his nose to the edges of his mouth and a sharply cut black beard, was himself bitterly attacked for his love of sumptuous clothing and jewellery. The humanist Pirckheimer, despite his initial support for reform, had already had enough of Osiander by 1524. He privately rhymed that this 'haughty scribe' and 'vain cleric' with his golden necklace should be slain.[59] In 1525 he publicly challenged Osiander for allegedly and outrageously telling the Klara sisters that the worst whore was better than a good nun. Allegedly he had also feasted with nuns who had abandoned the convent. Pirckheimer commented disparagingly on the luxury in Osiander's house, on silver tableware, and precious furnishings. By 1527, the Zurich reformer Zwingli was well-informed about Osiander's love of dress and precious stones, and used this to provoke him in a letter. Osiander sniped back that it looked as though Zwingli wanted to erect a new order of monks.[60] In 1544, a pamphlet entitled *Speculum Osiandri* attacked his meanness and greed for money. The Swiss reformer Vadian reported soon after that everybody in Nuremberg hated Osiander for his expensive lifestyle and thirst for money. This charge was to be retained in local memory—'Osiander thet Hoffahrt treiben' commented a portrait engraving in 1565.[61] Our Nuremberg chronicler criticized: 'evangelical preachers, I think they preach Christ, if a preacher used to have sixty or seventy florin he now needs to have two- or three-hundred'.[62] Osiander's own position is well documented in his extensive negotiations for a salary rise. He detailed why living expenses in a city like Nuremberg were higher than elsewhere.[63] For his own living expenses even 200 florins were a tight budget; he thus asked for a salary of twice the sum. Not least, he argued, because the council would find not ten men in Germany of such God-given abilities as his. Osiander was ashamed that, despite his considerable God-given talents, he should be unable to conduct his household adequately and respectably (*ziemlich*) in Nuremberg. Why should his studying not put him at an advantage over adept artisans? Many people would be wary of sending their child to study if they saw him so poor despite all his art.[64] Osiander, who came from humble origins, became the best-paid Protestant preacher in Germany, belonged to the wealthiest circles in town, and married well-off women.[65] Luther, who himself had married an impoverished noble-woman, also looked at him critically. And yet Osiander's case brought to the fore questions that were not easy to resolve. What was the social rank of the new clergy and their families, and how was it to be assumed symbolically in and outside the household? What, moreover, about leading figures in leading towns, such as Osiander? Should they be allowed to visually stand out? Osiander clearly retained Aquinas's sense that the nobility of the office expressed itself materially, but claimed that his God-given gifts and political services needed to be honoured too. Asserting the importance of recognition, he confidently renounced any link between asceticism and holiness. In this sense, his battle was truly directed foremost against the nun. The annual income of top cardinals ranked in the tens of thousands—Matthäus Lang, for instance, commanded an income of over 50,000 florins. Compared to them, Osiander's demands doubtless remained moderate.[66]

LUTHER IN RED

Luther himself chose to dress up when he wore secular dress rather than dress down. This was in marked difference to his prolific senior colleague in Wittenberg, Andres Karlstadt. Karlstadt was of aristocratic descent, but dressed like a peasant for a period after 1523 to emphasize his brotherhood with the common man. By contrast, in that same year, the Polish humanist Dantiscus von Hofen reported after visiting Wittenberg that Luther wore 'clothes which are indistinguishable from those of a courtier. But when he returns to where he lives (the former Augustinian monastery), so I have been told, he puts on his friar's habit.'[67] Cranach painted him in these years with the Augustinian garb, but outgrown tonsure.[68] In the Wartburg, Luther had been given a doublet, hose, a red beret, and sword, an outfit which he described as that of a 'horseman' in his secret life as 'nobleman Jörg'[69] (Fig. 56). This transformation was spectacularly exhibited in a Cranach woodcut, based on a drawing from life in the Wartburg. Luther was depicted with full hair and a mature, curly beard. Then the picture almost turned into a sketch, merely hinting at the existence of simple clothing; Cranach's panel painting of the same year represented Luther with tamed hair and in an ill-defined black upper garment.[70] Cranach, as has been mentioned before, worked exceedingly fast with his workshop on an astonishing range of tasks. He usually created types or templates, with details that could easily be copied and were often repeated.[71] Yet it was also as if Cranach shied away from representing Luther in secular dress, even though he wore it at the time. This again suggests that the image built up of him as a divine prophet depended on his continued association with 'pious' clothing, and dress was clearly not regarded as an indifferent matter. Meanwhile in Wittenberg, the dukes would include precious cloth amongst their gifts to Luther. Most intriguingly, in 1526, the city council paid for a gown or coat (*Rock*) of 'purpur', a scarlet red material, to honour him.[72] In Cranach's representation of the elderly Luther, he consistently depicted him as wearing a white shirt with a decorous black ribbon sewn onto the collar and opening into a bow of strings. Over this, Cranach depicted him as wearing a bright red doublet or woollen overshirt, over which he finally wore a black, generously cut, long gown. In contrast to his former monk's habit, Luther might now have required help to lace up a doublet and presumably hose, and he would perhaps have smelt sweetly, as fine, scarlet materials were usually not washed, but perfumed. The council's gift suggests that Luther might have used his red coat at least for his best dress, just as his favourite biblical prophet Daniel had been dressed in scarlet and with a golden chain when he had been honoured by King Belsazer (Dan. 5, 29). This kind of red moreover was related to Christ's blood in the Christian tradition, as well as being a sign of divine justice that could be transmitted to secular rulers. The churchfather Cyprian's treatise *De habitu virginum*, meanwhile, had told laypeople that God would have created red sheep had he wished them to wear red.[73] For Luther, this perfect scarlet, 'purpur' red, in part must have symbolized his prophetic status and connection with secular power. It also marked his professional standing as a doctor of divinity, which in turn legitimized his prophetic status in a historically unprecedented way.

Luther's authority above all resided in the fact that he was a man of sound biblical learning in contrast to popes, cardinals, bishops, and lower Catholic clergymen who usually had no such training. His choice of scarlet clothing also reflects the increasing sartorial distinction that scholars had begun to use to raise their status during the past two centuries and their appeal to many clerics. The learned bishop of Rochester, for instance, had himself been painted in 1500 in the red robe of a doctor of theology.[74] Around 1516, Nicolaus Manuel painted a doctor of theology for his extraordinary dance of death on the walls of the Dominican convent in Berne. This theologian was clad in a red doublet and hose as well as a light blue gown.[75] It was hence entirely plausible to imagine doctors, and even doctors of theology, in red. When around 1550 the Nuremberg silk-embroiderer Hans Plock pasted woodcut images of Luther and Melanchthon into his bible, he had them coloured as wearing red gowns and Luther in addition a red cap.[76] Just after his death, a woodcut printed in the Lutheran bastion Magdeburg commemorated 'Martinus Lutherus Doctor of the Holy Bible' and depicted the reformer full-size (Fig. 57). His clothes underneath a fur-lined gown with short sleeves were highly visible, and bright red. While Cranach successfully framed our contemporary image of Luther in black, which for many has become emblematic of Protestant austerity, it turns out that we might have to reimagine a Luther more frequently dressed in red. Because Cranach and his workshop created types in multiple, uncommissioned copies and marketed these effectively, Cranach is not a reliable guide to ascertain the range of clothes Luther really wore. Luther nearly always signed 'Dr Martin Luther' and had himself addressed as Dr, even by his wife. His degree legitimized some of his claim that he, rather than all the other clergymen and scholars who had met in Church Councils in previous centuries, should know the one and only truth about grace, scripture, and faith. Contrary to his exceedingly liberal views in 1520, Luther soon held that any man could in principle still become a clergyman, but not without a theology degree, and preferably from Wittenberg. The degree and the mode of address it implied had become central to his identity throughout the contests of the radical Reformation.

One of the little known key scenes of the Reformation thus was the day when, in August 1524, Luther furiously went to debate with a cobbler and other locals in Karlstadt's rebellious rural parish of Orlamünde. The people of Orlamünde defended their right to elect pastors and interpret the bible. The council and commune had jointly sent a letter to Luther in which they had addressed him as 'our spiritual teacher Martin Luther our brother in Christ'.[77] Luther could only see this as an attack on his superior scholarly authority. He aggressively accused them: 'You have written a letter to me like an enemy, for you have not given me my title, which many princes and lords, who are my enemies, give and do not break away [abbrechen].'[78] The mayor justified this mode of address by saying that this had been a secret letter from them to him in a brotherly spirit. Luther now threw a tantrum. He kept shouting to his servant 'Get the horses ready, Get the horses ready'

56. (oppposite) Lucas Cranach the Elder, *Portrait of Martin Luther as Junker Jörg*, second edition woodcut 1522, 31.2 × 20.8 cm, AN 49473001. © The Trustees of the British Museum

Quæsitus toties, toties tibi Roma petitus,
En ego per Chriſtum uiuo Lutherus adhuc.
Vna mihi ſpes eſt, quo non fraudabor, Ieſus,
Hunc mihi dum teneam, perfida Roma uale.

ANNVS CONFESSIONIS VVOR- ANNVS PATHMI ANNVS REDITVS EX
MACIÆ 1521. 1521. PATHMO 1522.

Cæſaris ante peDes , proCeres ſtetit ante potentes A Rheno properans CapItVr , benè ConſCIa PathMI CarLſtaDII ob ſVrIas aD SaXona teCta reCVrrIt,
ACCoLa qVà RhenI VangIo LIttVs aDIt. TeCta , PApæ ſVgIens retIa ſtrVCta, petIt. FaVCIbVs ex IæVIs rVrſVs oVesqVe raDIt.

57.   Johann Daniel Müller, *Martinus Lutherus*, coloured broadsheet, Magdeburg: Johann Daniel Müller (1546/7), Sign. grfl IId 583. © Luthergedenkstätten in Sachsen-Anhalt

(*Span an, Span an*), and insisted that Karlstadt had to leave. The mayor could only save the situation by formally addressing Luther as 'honourable highly-learned *günstiger* Herr Doctor'. Luther accepted to stay. Yet he refused to take his doctoral beret off to honour anyone. The beret was red.[79] It had become his visual mode of address, a dramatic prop to perform his authority and command instant respect.

Wittenberg students by contrast seem to have taken over a completely black academic look as a livery of devoted and dignified learning. Dress, or the way in which hair and beard were cut, once more symbolized and affected a particular state in life. In 1527, Luther's closest colleague, Melanchthon, fiercely lectured against the 'new affectation' in dress, with its medley of thousands of peacock colours.[80] The Nuremberg son of a tailor, Hieronymus Köler, described his figure in such a way before he went to study in Wittenberg. One leg of his breeches was light-blue, the other striped yellow and pink. He wore armour on his upper body and arms because he served a military man. His hair was shorn, and he had dyed his cropped beard black, which until now he had described as 'yellow'.[81] In 1531, Köler arrived as student in Wittenberg. There he often heard, as well as ate and drank with, the 'highly learned, divinely blessed' Martin Luther, while lodging in the house of a 'well learned' man. He now wore a 'big, long, black gown, with long arms, the cap of a student, on a shorn head, a big, cropped beard, black breeches, in my hands a writing board and paper, a feather quilt behind my ear, a kalema [writing instrument] on my belt, black high shoes'.[82] Academic dress in Wittenberg minimized signs of status differences and was used to integrate students of burgher and aristocratic descent as well as many former monks into a special community of honourable learning. It focused on Martin Luther as cult professor. Writing instruments and books were displayed like insignia to signal belonging and the distinct purpose of this existence.[83] In 1538, the duke himself announced that those wearing 'short gowns, which do not cover the knees' as well as slashed clothing, and silk and velvet trimmings would be expelled from university.[84] Appearances had become integral to a way of seeing, knowing, and belonging in this community.

SPIRITUAL MATERIAL

Parishioners could certainly insist on sartorial distinctions between clergy and laymen in order to see a special connection with the divine manifested. Clerical appearances remained symbols that embodied the church as a legitimate institution. They needed to be agreed on between clergymen and parishioners as part of a shared idea of order.[85] Yet in the early decades of the Reformation such agreements, too, were often in flux. When, at the very beginning of evangelical reforms, a service in Riga was conducted without any Latin liturgy or clerical vestment, critics objected that 'one now dealt with the holy sacrament on the altar as if it was ham or a piece of beef (and) the clergyman stood before the altar where he was to give the Eucharist like a smith's servant or shoe-maker'.[86] Even radicals were not united in their views of whether the formerly sacred should now be profaned. Thus, in the nearby city of Dorpat, the mayor had taken the golden Eucharist chalices to make necklaces for his wife and daughter. When the mayor once arrived slightly late at a service conducted by the radical preacher Melchior Hoffman, Hoffman sarcastically commanded everyone to kneel, for 'just now the golden dress of our Lord Jesus Christ was being carried in'. Hoffman was expelled from the city.[87] In Zwinglian Zurich, clerical vestments were given to the poor, statues were used for warming fires, and tombs for building work. Christ was seen to be among the needy and in the middle of communal life, but never contained in and conveyed through gold.[88] 'The ministers', one Catholic chronicler noted, 'baptised the children without liturgical vestments, and married couples and proclaimed the Word of God from the pulpit dressed the same as laymen, and most of them grew long beards like ascetics.'[89] Long beards indeed were sometimes regarded as a necessary masculine distinguishing mark, and here could associate clergymen with the patriarchs and provide gravity, especially for many of the young, newly trained clergy.[90] It also distinguished them from the old clergy, who were forbidden to wear beards, and in this sense affirmed particular understandings of manhood against Catholics, who were often portrayed as morally feeble and effeminate. But the fashion was far from being uniformly adopted, because if they were not grey and long, and unless they were groomed, flourishing beards could also be associated with disruptive masculine virility, or with Jewish practices. Agrippa of Nettesheim thought that women were superior to men not least because their hair grew in the right place; beards often made male faces ugly and made men similar to wild animals.[91] Some Lutherans rejected beards because the radical Thomas Müntzer had worn one; Brandenburg pastors were forbidden to wear beards. Even so, long beards became a hallmark of Lutheran theologians from the 1570s onwards, when the Palatinate was re-Lutheranized.[92] Perfectly groomed beards obviously needed to be kept in shape through frequent visits to barbers, and could appear overly decorous and effeminate. Medical writers and theologians throughout Europe moreover continued to discuss whether male facial hair should be regarded as a natural divine gift and part of a properly masculine body, or whether it was to be shaved off as a mere superfluous growth, devoid of life, and even as dirty.[93]

All of these questions were far from straightforward then, and in many places debates about the look of the new clergy turned on whether there were to be any differences at all in dress between preachers and their laity. A wandering evangelical preacher in Schleswig, nicknamed 'mad Frederick', for instance, proclaimed that he followed the example of St Paul in living from voluntary donations and his own craft work. He dressed in a simple robe of coarse blue cloth to show that he was no different from the 'common man'.[94] In 1524/5 in Sommersfeld, by contrast, an ex-monk turned evangelical preacher attacked clerical dress from a pulpit, sporting a long red coat, fashionable shoes, and a red beret.[95] At the other end of the spectrum, the Zurich synod in 1533 criticized the widely respected theologian Laurentius Agricola for using 'rough, warrior like gestures, and carrying a long sword; he dresses like a horseman and indecently. All of this he shall stop, because everybody otherwise enjoys his teaching and life.'[96] Given the social and stylistic differentiations that were sartorially expressed at this period, it was nonetheless impossible to dress like 'the' laity; the question was like which laity one dressed. The notion that fashionable appearances could be deeply sinful, on the other hand, was well ingrained among the laity—wandering preachers, like the widely remembered Franconian 'drummer of Niklashausen', had found it easy to stimulate collective catharsis around the mass slashing of long pointed gothic shoes and cutting of long male hair.

THE STRIPED

Cultural arguments relating to dress thus were strikingly dynamic and open-ended in these early Reformation years. This is further substantiated if we analyse how contemporary pamphlets used the verb 'striped'.[97] Stripes, especially in multi-coloured hose that clung tightly to men's lower bodies, had aroused comment since the Middle Ages. On the one hand, they symbolized the height of fashion and sophistication, because they followed northern Italian models and were difficult and costly to make. For upper-class men, to be 'striped' could therefore positively denote being 'up with the times' and clever.[98] On the other hand, as Michel Pastoureau has argued, moralizers insistently contrasted the unified, simple, and the mono-coloured with anything displaying variedness, spots, stripes, different colours, materials, and slashes.[99] Hangmen, in particular, were often forced to wear striped or strangely cut clothing, and are frequently represented in this manner in crucifixion scenes or martyrological scenes to emphasize their daring and thoroughly immoral force. In addition, moralistic literature began to specifically attack the lower social orders who were overstepping status boundaries by wearing expensive, slashed, and striped clothing, 'with all colour wild / over wild', as Sebastian Brant's best-seller *The Ship of Fools* emphasized in 1494.[100] Such dress, moreover, was associated with mercenary Landsquenets and Swiss soldiers, who took money to fight from whoever wished them to, were fearless of death, and dissolute in comportment.

Since the late fifteenth century, a thoroughly intriguing new term gained currency: people spoke of the 'striped layman' (*gestreifter Laie*). This designation was used to specifically denote those who had received little formal education, but were able to read. They preferred their independently gained knowledge to what they heard from preachers and scholars.[101] 'Striped' or 'stripy' (*gestreiflet*) people began to be associated by clergymen such as the Strasbourg preacher Geiler von Kaysersberg and Luther's vocal and visually eloquent opponent Thomas Murner with laymen who based their partial knowledge on readings in the vernacular. They asked sharp, 'clever clever' questions about the church and theology. This new figure was therefore linked to sinful curiosity, vainglory, and a disobedient attack on rightful hierarchies of knowledge, morality, and status.[102] They were 'striped' because they were unable to build up the whole picture of a subject—the nearest equivalent English designation might be 'patchy' laymen.

Reform scholars, by contrast, could explicitly address 'striped laymen' as their audience in positive terms, because they valued the broad dissemination of knowledge that was epistemologically seen as linked to experience rather than scholarly abstraction. They could explicitly value the ability of the striped to criticize the status quo.[103] In 1522, one anonymous pamphlet, *The Striped Swiss Peasant*, was published by a renowned printer of vernacular books, probably in response to Murner's criticism, and represents another turn in the argument.[104] Its title page provocatively rhymed that it had been made by a peasant in the Entlibuch region, and those who did not like it could kiss him on the 'bruch', i.e. the region around his genitals (Fig. 58). The woodcut depicted a tall and imposing peasant of provocative comportment. His head was held up high and with pointed defiance against a superior clergyman. He was clad with laced boots, which had become the hallmark of peasant rebellions since the late fifteenth century, a good shirt, a long sword, and a threateningly long rake.[105] The author challenged the preaching monk for alleging that 'striped laymen' read German books. They seduced others with issues they were unable to understand.[106] Yet Jesus himself had regarded Jewish biblical scholars and Pharisees as 'striped'. Monks and clergymen knew that Jesus was 'God', but told the simple folk differently. 'Our scholars now', the author scathingly noted,

> if they know the true way of the sacred scripture can not stop there but show us blue and white, green and yellow, and make many stripes over the words of holy scripture, here with Aristotelian and Platonic teaching, there with poems and philosophical arguments, here with man-made laws, there with invented examples and fables, and thus evangelical teaching becomes striped with this sumptuous doctrine.[107]

Pious laymen, by contrast, could understand the truth of the bible without these additions, stripes, spots, and many colours, simply in its undivided and mono-coloured form if they read the text through true faith.[108]

In the same year, 1522, the influential Franciscan friar Johann Eberlin von Günzburg published a pamphlet about *Seven pious, but desperate clergymen lamenting their pain* in Basel. One of these unhappy clergymen decided that it was better to preach scripture in a clear, direct way, and in German, to escape disrespect from the common, 'striped' laymen. To be 'striped' in this pamphlet therefore signalled a positive path towards knowledge rather than misleading half-knowledge.[109] Meanwhile the author of a further Basel publication, entitled *Wolfsong* (1521/2), even asserted the daringness associated with stripes in this debate. False prophets were like wolves. They always answered lay people's biblical quotes with a contrary quote from scripture. Only the 'striped layman' with his courage, profound knowledge of scripture and clever use of it might be able to corner the old clergy.[110] These metaphorical usages of the 'striped' disappeared after the defeat of the peasants in the Peasants' War.

Protestant reformers were therefore left with the task of how to create images of the pious laity that different sections of society could identify with, but which avoided contested associations of this kind. 'Haughty' peasants certainly did not belong. Thus the title page of one south-German edition of Luther's 1525 pamphlet against the 'murdering and robbing hordes of peasants' tellingly contrasted with the Basel depiction of the striped peasant (Fig. 59). The banner ridiculously professed 'I luv God', while the image detailed the stupid simplicity and hypocrisy of rebellious peasants who were anything but poor. The peasant sported feathers in his hat, jewellery, and an overly long sword, used just as adornment. There was a sack precariously overflowing with unsold eggs and a goose producing them. No tools indicated hard work, and the peasant's body signalled no masculine strength. The boots hung down untidily, and, rather unseemly, no hose was worn. The shirt looked ridiculously short and effeminate. He gazed at the ground immediately in front of him. The peasant's appearance, in short, revealed him to be a laughable, inconsistent, limited figure, who just wanted to look fashionable. Luther had peasants exclaim in his writing that they just wanted 'marten gowns and golden necklaces' and to eat partridge, the very symbols of elite belonging.[111] The visual strategy

58. *Der gestryfft Schwitzer Baur*, frontispiece, Universität Bern, Universitätsbibliothek Bern, Zentralbibliothek, AD 15:12
© Universitätsbibliothek Bern

Widder die Mordischen
vnd Reubischen Rotten der
Bawren.

hab got

lieb

Psalm: vij.
Seyne tück werden jn selbs treffen/
Vnd seyn mütwill/ wirdt vber jn außgeen.
1 5 2 5.

Martinus Luther. Wittemberg.

59. (*left*) Martin Luther, *Wider die Mordischen vnd Reubischen Rotten der Bawren*, Landshut: Weissenburger 1525, frontispiece, Resl Germ. sp. 671n. © Bayerische Staatsbibliothek, München

60. (*opposite*) Martin Luther, *Eyn Sermon von dem Wucher*, Wittenberg: Rau-Grunenberg 1519, HAB 129 Theol. (16). © Herzog August Bibliothek Wolfenbüttel

deployed in this simple woodcut similarly dismissed any notion that the peasants' egalitarian claims for society might need to be taken seriously or have to be feared. Two lines from Psalm 7 clarified in support that evil action would only harm aggressors. Vestiary codes, in other words, which everyone in this society understood, here clearly added up to present a visual argument to those looking at the pamphlet. Unsurprisingly, no heroic figure of an 'evangelical peasant' was ever disseminated from Wittenberg itself either, with the questionable exception of a burlesque peasant group in a 1545 image campaign pointing their bottoms towards the pope on his throne in Rome to inundate him with smells. Peasants in the Black Forest uprisings meanwhile had cleverly adopted a term which probably first had been used to make fun of them: *Zierheld*, meaning decorous, beautiful heroes. It turned into one of their calls to arms, and these Black Forest *Zierhelden* were soon feared. They rejected any identification with poor or silly tastes.[112]

CAPITALISM AND CREED

Luther and several of his printers also insisted that Jews should be singled out visually as unbelievers through their dress, comportment, and physiognomy.[113] Luther's pamphlets of 1519 and 1520 against usury helped to establish him as a popular reform writer. Several editions carried one of four different representations of Jews[114] (Fig. 60).

The woodcuts strengthened the image of Luther as a Christian author who would stop Jews taking away Christian property. In each woodcut the Jew demanded to be paid, or he would take away everything ('Pay or give'—*Bezal oder gib*'). These title pages were visually innovative and easy for laypeople to understand.

The populist campaign against usury connected with the theme that Germany was 'sucked dry' of resources through capitalist trade as well as Roman greed and luxury generally that had loomed large in reform writing since the fifteenth century. It was starkly expressed in Luther's *Address to the German Nobility* in 1520, followed by calls that it was the duty of evangelical Christians to resist these evil forces. This rhetoric implied that German Christians were under existential attack from a clearly identified, satanic enemy who needed to, and could be, resisted to reach salvation. In his limited thoughts on actual political reforms, Luther's *Address* prominently targeted Germans' taste for sumptuous imported textiles, arguing that laws against costly clothing were urgently needed. God had given this land, as other lands, enough natural fibres for decent, honest dress. Vel-

vet and silk were traded by 'secret robbers', who created jealousy and the desire for everyone to look the same.[115] The Lutheran attack on merchants, as we have already seen, now specifically targeted the Fuggers, who dealt with precious materials, were deeply involved themselves in papal and Imperial politics, and had been ennobled in turn. In 1524, Luther's treatise on trade and usury lamented the effects of global expansion:

> but foreign trade, which brings goods from Calicut and India and the like, such as precious silk and golden objects and spices, which serve no use other than splendour and suck money from land and people, should not be allowed where we have a government and prince.[116]

Gold and silver currencies went to England to buy cloth, or to Portugal to acquire spices. The Frankfurt fair was a 'silver and gold hole'. Germans, in this vision of doom, became beggars.

In 1520, the former Franciscan friar Johann Eberlin von Günzburg, who was close to Luther, wrote one of the most extended discussions of dress as a key political issue in his popular pamphlet *I Wonder why there is no Money in this Land*, composed during his various stays in Wittenberg.[117] In it, three beggars set out what they thought had caused their state. The first one blamed warfare and the spread of bad habits through the Landsquenets and the Swiss soldiers. As his counterpart remarked, the French had bribed them with beautiful clothes.[118] The second beggar blamed merchants and directly voiced many of Günzburg's concerns. Germany, he reiterated a widely shared view, had plenty of natural resources of all kinds to look after everyone's basic needs. Moreover, it was unique in having enough gifted artisans to process them. But this was not enough for people. So they had brought 'too many precious unknown cloths, precious stones, spices, wine' from 'the end of the world', and with it 'artisans who invent all sorts of cunning clever ways how they can refine them for sumptuousness, so that we are tempted like monkeys to give away all our sweat, labour, and money'. When the money was gone, it led to all possible violent behaviour. Nobody worked honestly anymore. Instead, people wanted to trade and sell silk skirts, robes, or caps to steal people's 'eyes and hearts'. The money went to faraway port cities. Yet previous generations had enjoyed themselves, even though nobody's clothes had been worth as much as a beret cost now. Clothes were no longer useful, just bad and assuming (*muthwillig*). Poverty among the common folk, usury, and the infiltration of merchants into the patrician caste followed. 'Rotten' people simply decided on their Lutheran or Catholic belief according to where they calculated the most material gain.[119] Simple clothing, made from German natural materials and by German hands, thus had important political meanings, which the following chapter will further explore. For Luther and other reformers it exhibited an aesthetic directed against new luxury consumption and refinement, which in this early phase of the movement still linked simplicity with honesty, happiness, utility, and the indigenous.

Carnival

An important further consequence of emerging commitments to honourable dress among contemporaries was unease about masquerading. Disguise became associated with the immoral, and only the 'real' with the sincere. Osiander clamped down on the Nuremberg carnival, which was organized by the butchers' guild and young patrician men. Its disappearance produced an extraordinary tradition of visual memory in the Schempart books.[120] In the second half of the century, a particularly disastrous event for Lutherans was prominently retold and re-envisaged, the so called 'Waldenburg carnival'. In 1569 the counts of the small south-west German Lutheran principalities Waldenburg and Hohenlohe had visited the count of Tübingen during carnival, but the count of Tübingen turned out to be extremely depressed. 'We have no fun amongst us', the exasperated count of Hohenlohe exclaimed one night. He proposed a mummery—a fancy dress party—in which they would be wild men. The count of Tübingen, of course, had been wary of joining in, but did so nonetheless. When the fun started, however, a big black cat jumped out of a box. Now the men were not to be stopped. They carried torches and, unfortunately, a torch fell and all the animal skin and green leaves around their genitals caught fire. The men were burnt alive and the fire could not be put out: even the count of Hohenlohe's heart could be seen in the burnt aftermath.[121] The episode shows how masquerading was ambivalently associated with the power to provide fun and a good, courageous spirit (*guten mut*) to fight sadness, as well as with disdainful *Über-mut* (haughtiness).

We therefore see once more that dress in this period was not just regarded as marking status. It engendered strong emotional experiences, for instance of playfulness, enjoyment, or masculine energy. These were thought to overcome anxiety by affirming the 'wild' and providing 'courage' (*muoth*) to affirm life. 'Mut' was a central idiom in sixteenth-century Germany to describe what other cultures understand to be 'spiritedness'. For us now it is perhaps most familiar in the French use of 'esprit'. People wished each other good, *guten, Mut*. This was related to a sense of survival against the hardship of life. *Mut* was a dynamic quality, which pointed forwards, but could spill over into unreasonable *Über-mut*.[122] Nonetheless, people usually saw themselves as needing *Mut* to bring joy into their lives by engaging with each other playfully with emotional aliveness and with the material world. High medieval courtly literature had similarly seen splendid clothes as an emotional expression and conduit of self-confidence and joy, *vreude*. Careless, bad clothing, in turn, was associated by Walther von der Vogelweide with an immersion in worries and a lack of energy to assume social distinction when he lamented: 'Wheresoever we turn, nobody is cheerful any more. Dancing and singing are overcome by worries. Never before has a Christian seen such a miserable bunch. Just look how the ladies are wearing their headdresses! The proud knights are wearing peasant clothes.'[123] Some Protestants could now see fancy dress as too tainted with immorality and too playful to be decorous. Principles restricted and kept everything in well-defined limits; consequently, emotional transformation spread danger. The 'Waldenburg carnival' revisited the imaginary boundary between the playful and licentious, and involved every reader in a gruelling tale of death, skilfully dramatizing that it was pointless to revel in worldly remedies. True hope and joy in this strand of Protestantism was increasingly confined to the spiritual. The Nuremberg humanist Pirckheimer, when aged and miserable, already had turned away the fool that Katharina the nun had sent to cheer him up.[124]

DEVIL BOOKS

Since 1555, a particularly Lutheran condemnation of lay sumptuousness and playful experimentation with clothes gained enormous publicity through a new genre of print: the so called 'devil books' (*Teufelbücher*). This literature documents particularly well how increasing Protestant concerns about measured civility in comportment led to a fascination with excess.[125] The genre took off with a divinity professor's pamphlet about a type of fashionable baggy hose, *Pluderhosen*. These were ankle-long, very wide, and also consumed much more cloth than any previous type of hose because its panes were sewn over silk or similar light tissues and hung out in large, untidy scalings. They were associated with Ottoman warriors and Landsquenets, and used with large codpieces.[126] For *Pluderhosen*, large stripes of light tissue were also sewn onto the codpiece in flourishing bows. Andreas Musculus (1514–1581) had been close to Luther in Wittenberg and then became preacher and professor in the eastern city of Frankfurt-on-the-Oder.[127] In 1555, one of his deacons preached against baggy *Pluderhosen* and told the congregation to fight them. Maddeningly, on the next Sunday, a pair of *Pluderhosen* had been nailed on a pillar that ran across the pulpit![128] Musculus believed in the complete depravity of humans and imminent apocalypse, but resolved to angrily preach against this provocation. The sermon was printed the same year, and went through ten editions until 1563. It was translated into lower German, and even into Danish by the bishop Palladius.[129] The first edition of the pamphlet carried a striking woodcut of a middle-aged man clad in such hose, its slashes made to look like small flames, which symbolically linked it to a lurking devil awaiting the man's death.[130] A further edition turned the man himself into a devil with baggy breeches (Fig. 61). Musculus asserted the role of the Lutheran clergy to prompt secular authorities to provide effective discipline to avoid divine punishment.[131] His political argument reiterated that luxury consumption in dress swept all German money away to foreign nations and left the country poor and defenceless.[132] He particularly criticized the taste of young men for *Pluderhosen*, and thus generational change in spending on luxury. Everyone wearing them was repeatedly equalled to a 'sea-monster', and Musculus surprisingly suggested that authorities who were unsure about formal punishments would do well to dress up 'bad boys' as sea-monsters and carnival fools to run after men with baggy breeches![133] He praised Duke Joachim of Brandenburg for imprisoning three Landsquenets dressed in this manner and exhibiting them in a cage for three days. Everyone was urged to shame such people on the streets.[134] Why, however, asked Musculus straightforwardly, was this fashion only to be found among Christians, and mostly among Lutherans? He had no trouble in providing an answer: the devil did not dwell in the desert, but most liked attacking the clean and decorated house of true believers. Now the devil had made Lutherans look like himself, so that scripture and sacraments were defiled and enemies of Christ could easily question their faith.[135] 'Clothes', Musculus summed up,

> do not damn you / That is true / neither do they sanctify you / that is also true so that remains true as well / as the proverb says / the feathers show you what bird it is / As a white pagan has written about / how you can understand about man's heart / nature and characteristics / from his body / speech / manner of walking and dress / so if your slashed hose does not damn you / so your own heart still does / which you have revealed through such clothing / your clothes show what sense / thoughts and spirit [*mut*] you have.

61. Andreas Musculus, *Hosenteufel*, frontispiece, Frankfurt-on-Main: 1563, BL 4374.de.29. © The British Library

Slashed breeches clearly showed that anyone wearing them was possessed by the devil.[136] In fact, they originated in the filth associated with Satan. For it was only through the excrement of worms that silk and 'all dirt' had come about in matters of dress.[137] Musculus's successful production was followed by several books of the same kind and a series of broadsheets on monstrous births allegedly caused by God's punishment of extravagant fashions. These publications now also attacked female sumptuousness.

Musculus's writings developed a specific type of theological reasoning for the later age of Lutheranism. Appearances did not constitute good or bad 'works'. Yet they were no meaningless outer signs either. They revealed whether a person was pious or taken by the devil. In other words, even though one did not dress in order to be sanctified, appearances and all aspects of comportment showed whether one was among those who could be sanctified. This in fact lent them particular importance. Yet Musculus focused only on the full length version of baggy breeches commonly used among wealthy men, which continued to be fashionable until the end of the century. The most splendid church of the town in which he preached, the Marienkirche in Frankfurt-on-the-Oder, indeed contained an epitaph of a couple from 1585, in which the husband was dressed with a shorter *Pluderhose*. It was held together by just two panes, stripes of upper material revealing rich fabrics underneath, and crowned by a lavishly adorned codpiece[138] (Fig. 62). This was acceptable. Musculus himself meanwhile rose in prominence through his publications and successfully gained Joachim of Brandenburg's patronage. He received a 'beautiful court dress' for his stays in Berlin and large amounts of money for daily expenses. In Frankfurt-on-the-Oder he was given a house and furnishings. Later he entered into long negotiations with the magistrate about whether or not he needed to pay taxes on his income from all four houses he had successively acquired.[139]

62. Epitaph of a fashionable Lutheran couple, detail, late sixteenth century, Marienkirche, Frankfurt (Oder). © Evangelische Kirchengemeinde Frankfurt (Oder), Photo: Susanne Seehaus

There was considerable room for tension among Protestants, then, between a renewed emphasis on the importance of comportment and standing, which positively stressed the ideals of being decorous, civil, gracious, and respectable ('*zierlich*', '*ziemlich*', and '*ehrbar*') as a basis of civic morality for clergy and laymen, and increasingly muted appeals to an ethics of simplicity, frugality, and an undecorous kind of masculinity. The second 'devil book' against sumptuousness written by a Protestant pastor attacked any excessive use of silk, velvet, or gold, especially if someone had to borrow money to pay for them. But it carefully set out that different things would be right for different people and ranks, while applauding that 'fine bourgeois cloaks in winter and summer/ Especially a fine, long and honourable mantle/ with or without arms/ dress and *zier* well old and young people'.[140] Pastor Johann Strauss confirmed that clothes should clearly indicate whether one was addressing a miller or a lord, and, above all, that one should not use any foreign dress. But his principal intent was to demarcate the difference between excessive pomp and fine, commendable decorousness, rather than mere plainness. And while the Nuremberg moralist Hans Sachs would predictably warn young couples against marrying too young because of all the household necessities they would need to pay for, a late sixteenth-century Strasbourg poem on household goods could even relish in rhymes about all the money that should be spent on 'fur robes, shirts and doublets', all manner of veils, silk, or precious animal skins, encouraging the addressee: 'you don't worry about the sermons' waffle'.[141] It ended with exuberant good wishes for the New Year and God's protection for a well-equipped household, 'ein recht wol versorget huß/ Et cetera Buntschuch es ist nun uß', that is, 'laced boot it is over now'. This prominent reference to the peasant rebellions in this region, which had taken as their symbol the simple, Germanic laced boot, shows how well-off Strasbourg Protestants could assert that they did not limit their own consumption in view of now distant egalitarian claims.

VISUALIZING BELIEF

Reformation art, for its part, detailed with much precision that enemies of the faith could be identified through their extravagant dress and immoral behaviour. Yet pious appearances were not always depicted as strictly plain or common, but visually proposed an understanding of appropriate bourgeois Protestant civility and decorousness. The precise manner in which preachers and audiences were depicted tells us much about different visions of reform. Two leading artists of the day, Lukas Cranach the Elder and the lesser known Matthias Gerung, are of particular interest. Gerung created fifty-four propagandistic woodcuts for the Protestant count of the Palatinate Ottheinrich across two decades, between 1536–1556, to illustrate a recent Zurich commentary on the apocalypse.[142] He illustrated Revelations 7, 1–3, contrasting the papal trade of indulgences with a church service of evangelically minded people in heaven (Fig. 63). The scene below shows a slender pope decked out in his costly robe and partly immobilized by his heavy triple crown. He is surrounded by a flurry of activity from his satanic helpers who are selling the indulgences promising the remission of sins in purgatory. In the left corner, a Swiss soldier turns his back to onlookers, clad in expensively made slashed clothing, which licentiously emphasizes his buttocks, next to which hangs a highly ornamented rapier. A hat with large feathers as well as a long lancet rounds off his appearance. Next to him, in the far left corner, stands an ill-clad laman who does not appropriately cover his arms or legs. Close to him we find a woman with uncovered hair and a low-cut gown. The many evangelical women in the upper half of the picture, by contrast, have all completely covered their heads and bodies, revealing only their faces and hands. All the men, on the other hand, have taken off their headwear. Apart from two men in more costly coats next to the pulpit, their dress is depicted as simple and decent to mark out the evangelicals as honest, sincere, and true believers. They are bound up in worship, and made to look removed from flirtations with worldly pleasures.[143] Another image made to illustrate the Zurich commentary of Revelations 11, 1–14, set out how two men who prophesize that there will be 1260 days before the end of the world are killed by a terrible beast. It followed the Wittenberg tradition of equating this beast with the papal Antichrist carrying the tiara.[144] Gerung's illustration shows the prophets, surrounded by clouds that already seem to be moving them into Heaven, preaching about the sins of the Roman church (Fig. 64). All the laity once more wear modest dress, which appropriately covers their heads and bodies. In the back, Karsthans, the evangelical peasant wielding his flail in defence of the Gospel makes a final appearance in Reformation propaganda. But he no longer carries a sword, and the flail flops over his shoulder as a tool, rather than a weapon. The coming of the apocalypse was certain, and did not need to be brought about militarily. The pious laity in this depiction are identified mostly, though not exclusively, as men of simpler standing, who do not display any interest in fashion, but wear decent clothing, appropriate to their standing. The preachers are clad in a sack-cloth, to display extra humility, as the bible

suggested, and as the Zurich commentary itself had emphasized: 'Clad with sacks. That is, provided with a bad and love-less dress.'[145] Simple clothing of this kind was associated with a particular moment of repentance and spiritual preparation, with an absence of caring about anything other than the end of the world. Any loving, creative human crafting, and embellishment of objects had become meaningless. Loveless dress clothed those ready for the end of the world.

63. (*opposite*) Matthias Gerung, *Apocalypse and Satirical Allegories on the Church, Allegory on Indulgences*, 1546, 23.3 × 16.2 cm, 158.1. © The Trustees of the British Museum

64. (*above*) *Matthias Gerung, Apocalypse and Satirical Allegories of the Church, The heavenly Protestant and earthly Church*, 1548, 23.3 × 16.2 cm. © The Trustees of the British Museum

It is hard to imagine a greater contrast to these woodcuts than the celebratory Witten-berg altar-piece by Lucas Cranach the Elder, placed in Wittenberg's civic church in 1547, which has remained there ever since (Fig. 65). Luther had died the year before. Hence the task was to create an image which would aid onlookers to identify with Luther's legacy,

65.   Lucas Cranach, *Wittenberg Altar Piece*, 1547, oil on panels, Baptism, Lord's Supper, Confession, and Luther preaching to the Congregation (Predella). © Ev. Stadtkirchengemeinde Wittenberg, Photo: Jürgen M. Pietsch, edition Akanthus

to memorialize him.[146] Wittenberg had been advertised as the New Jerusalem, a cultic place, and students and visitors came from afar to see this otherwise marginal town away from any of the major trade routes.[147] The laity in this monumental oil triptych are beautifully and richly clad, with just one exception. This is the tall, wildly bearded man in the right panel, running away from confession. This sinful man wears deeply yellow hose, a short deeply red doublet and jerkin, both of which have yellow trimmings. He carries a small sword in a sheath of richly ornamental silver work on his right side that is simply for display rather than fighting. The vestiary and gestural codes that characterizes this sinner serves as a foil against which the dress of all the other laity needs to be understood. He is extravagant, immoral, and unable to suppress his desires to fit into a moral, civic community. The deep yellow marks him out as a liar and ally of Judas, depicted in yellow in the central panel. Almost all the pious laity wear precious long, black gowns, which show off different kinds of fur, embroideries, or reveal brighter colours worn underneath. Child-bearing women are prominently depicted. And here is Luther in the predella with his white shirt and red doublet, partlet, or red woollen over-shirt underneath a black gown. Most amazingly, Cranach managed to create an image in which this bourgeois, decorous, and honourable church dress did not provide a disturbing contrast with Christ's nudity on the cross (Fig. 66). Luther's red and white colours underneath the gown connects with his son's charming white shirt and red doublet on the other side, and also with the dark robes worn by the adults and Abraham on the back of the panel. Christ's loincloth was given swirling flourishes that visually link with the traditional tight-white veils bound around the chin by several of the women sitting immediately in the front. Not a single common man or woman, peasant, or poor person, is brought into view. The image thus affirmed that Lutheranism could not be an inner religion based on an individual's relationship with the divine. At its core were its remaining three sacraments, infant baptism, holy communion, and penitence, as well as the act of listening to the message of salvation through biblical preaching. The Word was not a dead letter; it led to a visualization of Christ on the cross. The ritual act of attending church for these occasions constituted belonging. Parish and preachers publicly materialized their sense of moral integrity, honour, dignity, and reliability through their comportment. Comportment was to generate

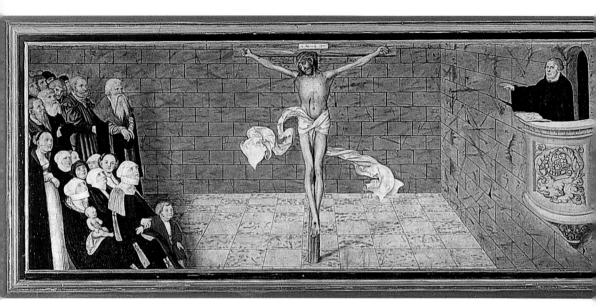

66. Lucas Cranach, *Wittenberg Altar Piece*, Predella. © Ev. Stadtkirchengemeinde Wittenberg, Photo: Jürgen M. Pietsch, edition Akanthus

trust in this new church and communicate itself through an embodied relation with the senses: who and what one touched, how one ate or drank, how one listened and spoke, how one looked. Spirituality was communalized and related to civic morality.

Cranach's altar piece thus presented a striking visual act. No altar painting before had set out the sacraments within an actual community of those holding an office and administering them and those receiving them. Neither had any altar painting shown that listening to a particular man preaching about the crucified should underpin all belief and salvation. The painting enshrined Luther as the central figure for the Reformation and created a visual fiction of an ordered, consensual hierarchy among the reformers. Its language of dress provided Lutherans first with a negative identity. They belonged by not looking like their enemies. In addition, it helped to develop an aesthetic of honourable dress that was not 'plain', but largely at ease with particular expressions of neat and refined dress[148] (Fig. 67). By targeting those who favoured the most extreme fashionable dress and did not observe particular codes of decency at church, Lutherans identifying with Cranach's proposition could feel justified in their own choice of appearance. This view was also part of a bourgeois political conviction. It contrasted an aesthetic that highlighted unitary, durable elements, at least on an outward layer, covering all of the body, to an aesthetic that only matched different small pieces of fabric, in varying bold colours, was short, fitted, and showed more seams and fastenings. This symbolic valence of dress strikingly corresponds to other ways in which Luther made sense of the world. Luther's commentary on Psalm 101 was his most influential writing on secular authority. In it, he metaphorically described all secular government as the permanent mending of a 'beggar's bad fur'. It would keep breaking, and always show new holes on an ill body. No clever

67.   Andreas Herrneisen, *Historia der Augspurgischen Confession* (1530), with fashionably dressed Lutherans attending the Eucharist, 1602, Kasendorf church. © Photo: Dieter Schmudlach

reform plans or particular rank of better people would ever help to change this. The work of mending and re-mending, rather than renewing, secular government through advice was all the clergy could hope for.[149] Hence Cranach's Wittenberg burghers were displayed in their long, engulfing robes as a community who knew, through Luther's preaching and the Eucharist, of the grace of salvation in eternal life. In contrast to Lorenzetti's Sienese frescoes discussed in this book's Introduction, sadness in life, according to Luther's vision, would never be overcome by a secular magistrate. It was overcome by faith alone.

Civility and the Reformation

Such decorous displays additionally mattered because Luther's popular Catholic opponents, Thomas Murner and Johannes Cochläus, had attacked Lutherans for their lack of stylistic civility. Murner's woodcut campaign likened Lutherans to fashionable Landsquenet soldiers enthusiastically waving the banner of evangelical freedom. Cochläus produced a powerful parody in the form of a dialogue between Rome and Wittenberg, which first appeared translated into the vernacular in 1524. If people were to follow Luther's calls for the

'freedom' of all believers, then all of Germany would soon look like Wittenberg and simply
return to barbarity. There would be no proper learning any more, only 'clumsy folk of half-
learned, striped laymen'.[150] According to Cochläus, Wittenberg was a cold, dirty place. Nobody had even known about it until twenty years ago. No wine or any fruit grew there, and
everyone drank beer. It was no real city, but 'a miserable, poor, shitty little town, not worth
three pounds against Prague, yes, unworthy of being called a city in the German lands'.[151]
There were only Lutheran, that is 'shitty' houses, 'unclean alleys, ways, paths and streets
full of filth, a barbarian people', and merchants who handled no value and wealth. The
marketplace was empty; it was, Cochläus scolded, a 'town without burghers'. Its citizens,
who did not deserve the designation 'burgher', were explicitly characterized by 'petit bourgeois clothing (*kleinbürgerliche kleidung*), and much want and poverty among all who live
there'.[152] There was no joy (*Freid*) to be had in this place. Cochläus thus endorsed a view
that informed Lorenzetti's paintings and was typically cultivated by Italian humanists—that
dress signified the advance of a civilization and the positive effects of wealth, beauty, and
worldly pleasure made possible by a temperate climate, ingenuity, skill, commercial activity, and good government. Germans, as the next chapter will more fully explore, were often
derided as barbarians, and yet had a chance of benefiting from Italian civilization through
an endorsement of their commerce and culture. In response, the reformers needed to stress
that they could establish a different culture and cultivate the earth. Luther therefore asked
for different kinds of seeds to be sent from Nuremberg, and got no one less than the local
humanist Lazarus Spengler to resource them. Soon, melons and pumpkins grew in Wittenberg during the summer, just as in Italy. Luther also asked for seeds of a miraculous Erfurt
giant radish, and all such plants were seen to bring the magnitude of God's creation to local
soil.[153] Luther is still famous today for his love of the apple tree—which connected heavenly
horticulture to the German homeland. Luther and his wife, Katherine of Bora, also cultivated grapes for wine-making.[154] Gardening, clothing, or architecture could become central
practices with political and spiritual meanings with which to build a culture and make it
visually manifest through sensual involvement. Given Cochläus's biting remarks, it is no
surprise either that the Wittenberg council paid to build Melanchthon's beautiful house
with a Renaissance gable and water pipes for cleanliness and sweet smells.

In all these aspects, then, it is impossible to separate the Reformation from a Renaissance
spirit in which 'man embarked on the adventure of creating that dynamic world of goods
in which he has found his characteristic identity'.[155] Many Lutherans, too, created a sense
of identity and belonging through a creative exchange with the material world. Contrary
to what Greek philosophers such as Seneca had advised, they did not cultivate a rigorously austere policy of sustenance, nor were they necessarily nervous of variety as pleasure
leading to vice and an immoral end. Lutheranism developed its own material culture and
world of goods. They did not stand around in loveless sack-cloths, or multicoloured coats,
inspiring envy like Joseph, or dress up sumptuously for an eternal kingdom as did the Anabaptist Jan van Leiden in Münster in 1534. Bourgeois Lutherans typically cultivated an
aesthetic of appropriate, whole, and monochrome cover, a layering effect that allowed for
honourable decorousness underneath a robe. This corresponded to another important element within the symbolic system used by Lutherans to create meaning: linguistic clarity.

Contemporary rhetoric always talked metaphorically about the use of 'dressing up', or colouring arguments. Luther thought that there needed to be a single, basic meaning—a single colour, as it were—of a text. All images or metaphors needed to relate back to this clear and accessible meaning. This would avoid 'patchiness' as much as affected decorous over-elaboration. But Luther did not deny the richness of language and advocate plain, colourless speech at the cost of variety. He marvelled at its richness.[156]

These wider symbolic associations with dress were keenly kept alive. Around 1618, for instance, a Protestant broadsheet would depict the church as a person who had been violently stabbed. Her hair was wild, her cloak completely made of patches in different colours. This still symbolized the profusion of mendicant orders the church had allowed to exist. She begged a reformer to wrest the sword out of her chest and restore her glory in red and white.[157] Image and text together presented an appeal that was likely to make the reader identify with the reformer and reiterated the principles of an aesthetic style based on larger, homogenous monochrome fields. No stripes, no patches, no mixture, no messiness. Protestants across Europe, moreover, routinely derided relics as meaningless remains in rags.

CONCLUSION

Religion can be described as a historically specific way of investigating and representing whatever a culture takes to be the supernatural. This is why the sociologist Emile Durkheim treated religion as a 'social fact', rather than a set of ideas. What is interesting to find out about is not whether cultures get their religious truth right or wrong, but how ideals of interacting with and knowing the divine function in their practices. So the question becomes one about acts, about how one shows that one is a prophet or clergyman, or draws the supernatural into the natural world, and how these acts are connected with beliefs which form a wider sense of religious identity. Religious truth therefore cannot be adequately studied just through an engagement with doctrinal beliefs. Beliefs also resolve into gestures and habits and temperament ingrained by a religious upbringing or further theological training and daily repetition.[158] Acts embody and build up specific ideals about the way in which a community of believers locate themselves on earth in relation to the divine. They implicate the religious self physically as well as intellectually.

So, even though Luther drew on St Paul to argue that all laws restricting what and when to eat, drink, touch, or what to wear were man-made and contributed nothing to a person's grace or wisdom, powerful strands within Lutheranism developed vestiary codes that displayed who was on the side of salvation or damnation by encoding what kind of dress legitimately formed part of a spiritualized civic morality. This position firmly asserted that everyone's dress possessed a spiritual dimension all the time, thus further emphasizing the meaning of dress displays.

The same was true for Calvinism. When the Calvinist preacher Nicolas Pithou of Troyes wished to ridicule a rare visit by an Italian bishop to Geneva to further ecumenical ideas in 1556, he simply dwelt on Carraciolo's habits. These spoke the mind just as much as his theological practices:

The bishop resolves to be there in the best array he could muster...a long silk
robe and four-cornered bonnet...in this gear he went to the auditorium where
Calvin was giving the lesson. But this sort of outfit so strongly displeased the
audience that they took little account of him, which he found very strange...he
was enlightened by some people who told him frankly that it was none other
than his outfit that had been so improper.[159]

The bishop, according to this account, then changed his clothes before he went to speak to
Calvin in private. Calvin reprimanded him sharply for still chanting the mass, in response
to which Carraciolo looked for excuses 'thinking he could dazzle Calvin...by clever words
and a big show'. Calvin, of course, saw through this futile wordiness. He cut him short and
went away. From a Calvinist viewpoint, values and behaviour were all part of one piece:
the Catholic mass was a vain show to maintain the clergy's elevated position rather than
to relate the biblical word and the centrality of Christ to a community of moral believers.
These vain elites practiced deception and changed clothes as needed. They used seemingly
clever, over-decorated rhetoric, but were incapable of uttering the truth. All Catholicism
was a big puppet-show to hide the lascivious, indulgent lifestyle that principally secular
elites financed through lay-people's pockets. Clothing was a key manifestation of this evil
state, which is why Calvin insisted that all mass vestments should be abandoned. Lutherans were less consistent here, because Luther had declared that they did not matter, as long
as they were not treated like cultic objects. From the 1550s onwards there was also a stream
of Genevan civic regulations against extravagant dress. By and large, few men and women
were actually prosecuted in a city that had a strong mercantile elite and ironically thrived
on silk production.[160] However, one unlucky young man was imprisoned to sew together
his slashed hose—a punishment nearby Berne had introduced in 1521.[161]

Protestant clergymen and theologians themselves frequently used appearances as tools
to create an impression of wisdom, dignity, and rank. Long beards, as we have seen,
could play such a role, while from the early eighteenth century onwards wigs became
widely used. The German enlightenment author Friedrich Nicolai was probably the first
to survey portraits of university professors of divinity and clergymen across a hundred
years for his ingenious 1801 treatise *On the use of false hair and wigs in former and recent
times. A historical survey.* Nicolai reported that if a clergyman nowadays wanted to abandon his wig, parishioners in many places thought he also shed the dignity of his office.
They had forgotten that this custom had been a new invention that had spread only
gradually since the late seventeenth century.[162] Appearances continued to create socially
meaningful fictions of how an office was to be adequately materialized and respected—
to Nicolai this explained why judges were so fond of false hair.

Lutheran clergymen, too, used sartorial distinctions to mark out common country
parsons from, say, the proud pastors of burgeoning mercantile Hamburg, who later in
the seventeenth century (and until today) began to wear ruffs with their black robes. Yet
not even a Lutheran court preacher would have ever come close to owning 400 items of
clothing, like the twenty-six-year-old archbishop of Milan. Ippolito d'Este had become
archbishop aged nine. By 1535 he was twenty-six, but only forty-three of his items of

apparel were religious. He owned 'eleven archiepiscopal cloaks and capes, five white linen rochets and twenty-seven hats. Sixty-one items were identified as clothes he used for hunting, jousting or dressing up for Carnival and other activities. Judging by the relative quantities', Mary Hollingsworth concludes, 'Ippolito clearly preferred partying to performing his religious duties.'[163] Two years after this inventory was drawn up, Ippolito d'Este became a cardinal in Rome. Here he would be used, with his own ceremonial assistants, as retinue for the pope, and be part of a complex set of meticulously specified hierarchical interactions.[164] At the masses, all the cardinals would enter with their own entourage. A *caudatario* had the important office of holding the end of the cardinal's long soutane, and at times his beret, in particular ways depending on whether he was sitting down, honouring the pope or the holy sacrament, or celebrating the sanctus. These insignia of sovereignty achieved their special effects through this ceremonial 'concert' of subservient officeholders who all acted around all the cardinals' and the pope's figure with exactitude. The coming together of graceful movement, splendid sounds, scents, and sights ideally worked towards a synaesthetic experience, which was to occasion a sensation that all this superseded human nature. Spectacles, which were likewise elaborated in secular courts for rulers claiming to be directly sanctified by God, more than ever performed an alleged supernatural presence in counter-Reformation Rome through inventions and extraordinary expense on clothes and accessories.

The difference between Protestant and Catholic clergy, or Moravian Hutterites, could be seen, felt, and smelt, rather than just be read about. And in this, Protestants had to acknowledge that the material never could become immaterial nor easily be separated from spiritual meanings. A divinely blessed reformer did not dress in stripes. The dominant black clerical gown, similar to doctoral gowns and councillors' robes, gradually replaced precious vestments in church and effaced any enchanted cultic worship. It slowly came to be policed to ensure institutional stability and a homogenous professional Protestant 'look' which clearly distinguished Protestant and Catholic confessions. The same was true for Catholic clergy after the Catholic Renewal. The church now insisted that clergymen should never wear secular dress and thus always embody their office. The laity—especially women, it seems—were exposed to vehement criticisms of extravagancy in sermons. In seventeenth-century Germany, many narrative examples and devices to attack excessiveness were shared by Protestants and Catholics alike, and popular Catholic preachers like the indefatigable Abraham a Sancta Clara heavily illustrated their moralistic works with engravings.[165] These theological commentators left no doubt that since clothing was principally created by man after the Fall, the right kind of customs needed to be identified on which civic morality, national honour, and God's protection could be built.

Alas, when an Italian priest called Locatelli travelled to Lyon in 1664, he was dismayed to realize that he needed to adjust to the French manner. Boys harassed him on the streets. He took off his coloured stockings as well as his high hat with a broad brim, called 'sugar bread'. Then he dressed with a large collar, a black soutane reaching half way over his thighs, black stockings, slim shoes, and silver-buckles. Now, poor Locatelli recorded, he 'no longer believed he was a priest'.[166]

CHAPTER 4

Nationhood

DOCUMENTS OF NATIONAL STYLE

Previous chapters have already suggested that everyone in the Renaissance was increasingly confronted with questions about the national styles her or his dress adhered to. Castiglione for one chided Italian courtiers in 1528 for adopting French, Spanish, and German, as well as Turkish manners of dress.[1] Clothes were seen to manifest and even impart the customs and morals of cultures. The naturalistic art of the period reflects this stance. Most prominent among the Germans once more was the Nuremberg artist Albrecht Dürer, who twice travelled to Venice and had closely copied Gentile Bellini's path-breaking studies of Orientals, drawn 'from life' in Istanbul.[2] Dürer in his youth was a close friend of a great promoter of patriotic ideas, a humanist called Conrad Celtis. Celtis lauded Dürer as the new German Apelles, the naturalistic master artist described by Pliny, whose affectionate dog mistook his portrait for the real man. Celtis had known Dürer from his boyhood. He lodged in the same street as the Dürers when he stayed in Nuremberg, and Dürer soon produced bookplates and broadsheets for Celtis's publications. In Celtis's vision, Dürer played a central role in a cultural campaign for what they called a *translatio studii*, to bring the height of education from Italy to Germany. Celtis saw Dürer's destined place next to the emperor, to point towards a new way for peace, harmony, and reconciliation with God.[3] Did Celtis know that Dürer was a second generation immigrant, whose father was a Hungarian of rural descent? Dürer therefore was not straightforwardly 'of the German nation', and his father's cultural heritage and adaptations would have been integral to life at home. It is very likely that it informed Dürer's great curiosity about other cultures. Yet in a retable on the Martyrdom of the Ten Thousand completed in 1508, just after Celtis's death, Dürer represented himself and Celtis intimately side by side in the centre of the panel.

68. (*opposite*) Albrecht Dürer, *Nürnberg woman and Venetian woman*, c.1495, pen and ink drawing, 24.5 × 15.9 cm. © U. Edelmann – Städel Museum/ARTOTHEK

On the basis of this friendship and Celtis's patriotic ideals, one of Dürer's most interesting early costume studies deserves particular comment (Fig. 68). It directly contrasted a middle-aged Venetian and a Nuremberg woman, and thus was highly unusual for the period. Erwin Panofsky drew particular attention to it in his discussion of Dürer's interest in costume. Since Panofsky's interpretation has remained canonical, it is worth quoting in full:

> in one truly remarkable drawing he [Dürer] illustrated the fundamental difference between the Southern and the Northern fashion by representing a Venetian *gentildonna* side by side with a Nuremberg *Hausfrau*. Everything wide and loose in the Italian dress is narrow and tight in the German one, the bodice as well as the sleeves and shoes. The Venetian skirt is cut on what may be called architectural lines; the figure seems to rise from a solid horizontal base, and the simple parallel folds give an effect not unlike that of a fluted column. The German skirt is arranged so as to create a picturesque contrast between crumpled and flattened areas, and the figure seems to taper from the waist downward. The Italian costume accentuates the horizontals (note the belt and the very form of the necklace), uncovers the shoulder joints and emphasizes the elbows by little puffs. The German costume does precisely the opposite. The very idea of this juxtaposition might have been suggested by Heinrich Wölfflin. Dürer contrasted the two figures as a modern art historian would contrast a Renaissance palazzo with a Late Gothic town house ... in sum, the costumes are interpreted, not only as curiosities but also as documents of style.[4]

Hausfrau and *Gentildonna*, late Gothic townhouse and Renaissance palazzo: these oppositions gain further meaning if we consider that Panofsky thought that Dürer was seriously (and not just jokingly) delighted by Venetian female costume and by the women themselves. Indeed, Panofsky equated Dürer's Nuremberg wife Agnes with a workman-like, limited Gothic aesthetic, pitted against an Italian expansiveness, pleasure-loving culture, Renaissance learning, and sophistication.[5] Panofsky wrote during the Third Reich, and attempted to 'internationalize' Dürer against current nationalistic appropriations of him by those loyal to the fascist regime.[6] This meant that his book had nothing to say about Dürer's friendship with Celtis, or his possible influence on the artist.

But if we pay more attention to the physiognomy and comportment of the figures as well as dress, the point of the contrast becomes clear. It seems that Dürer first drew the Nuremberg woman and then the Venetian, who is positioned in the foreground and takes up more space. The Nuremberg dress is extremely neat, defined, and modest, as it fully covers the head, arms, and much of the shoulders and chest. Covered hair in this period affirmed a husband's sexual control. This depiction reflected the grip of a good government that ensured modesty, as sumptuary legislation indeed forbade Nuremberg women, as much as Venetian women, to wear low-cut bodices. The Venetian woman, by contrast, is far more loosely drawn in the upper part of the body. Fewer shading effects are used, so that her whole appearance lacks structure. The sleeves have many more decorative elements, but appear slovenly; a piece of cloth hangs messily over the right arm, and half her breasts are openly revealed by a low-cut bodice. Some of her hair is loose, escaping the veiling. A large left hand hangs down without any apparent purpose. The shoes are broad and placed clumsily next to each other, whereas the Nuremberg wife has pointed shoes placed in an artful step. The Venetian woman gazes vaguely from large eyes directed upwards while the Nuremberg wife could be said to regard the Venetian rather critically, as she places her elbows determinedly on one hip. Cesare Vecellio's late sixteenth century costume book depicted several Venetian women from this earlier period, but never in such a negligent pose.[7] No wonder then that Dürer modelled his Babylonian whore of the Apocalypse on a similar type of Venetian woman, who was more elaborately dressed and is likely to have been a prostitute. All this suggests that, as in his other costume studies of neatly dressed Nuremberg women, Dürer had Celtis's ideal of a cultivated indigenous urban aesthetic in mind to represent Nuremberg as the most glorious and promising city of the empire. Female dress had political significance, for it symbolized not just civic morality, but also national virtue or vice. In this, Panofsky was right. Dürer's drawing was not a comparative study of clothing as curiosity, but a document of national styles.

Barbarians

In 98 AD, the republican historian Tacitus wrote a brief ethnographic treatise entitled *Germania* to warn Roman leaders that Germans were dangerous if left unconquered.[8] Tacitus contrasted German simple resilience with the dangers of conspicuous consumption that cosmopolitan Romans of his time indulged in. Chapter seventeen was devoted to clothing. All Germans, it set out, wore a cloak held together by a pin, or, even simpler, a thorn. Animal skins were also frequently worn, and wealthier men displayed more of their bodies. Women might embroider clothes with purple, leave their arms uncovered and one breast exposed, but generally they wore the same as men. Germans living inland were unable to obtain finery through trade, but even those closest to the riverbanks had no concern for style. Tacitus later added that 'Suebi', living in the greater part of Germany, tied their bristling hair back and on the top of their heads. This was not, Tacitus hastened to add, 'to love or be loved', but to appear taller and strike terror in their enemy, the 'shock and awe' look, as it were[9] (Fig. 69).

Tacitus's treatise was rediscovered by German humanists at the end of the fifteenth century. He was hugely exciting to them in their quest to further the love of their mother- and fatherland. This was notoriously difficult in the absence of a monarchical dynasty to which notions of a heroic past and future could be securely linked, and in a country that was part of an empire whose boundaries were not easily defined, and shifted constantly through wars and negotiations. The Holy Roman Empire always encompassed several cultural 'nations': Bohemia, Austria, Burgundy, parts of upper Italy, 'lower' Germans in the north and upper Germans in the south, as well as the Swiss. The emperor over these 'nations' was elected in Germany, and, as was seen in the succession from Maximilian I to Charles V, emperors' involvement and identification with German domains could vary dramatically. Calls for religious and political renewal had resounded in the German lands

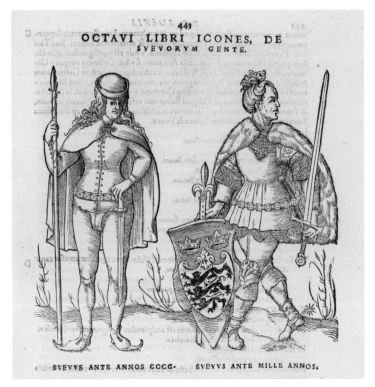

69. Wolfgang Lazius, *De aliquot gentium migrationibus...*, Basle: Oporiniana 1572, T.1.14, p. 443, Swabians. © By kind permission of the Syndics of Cambridge University Library

since the fifteenth century. Concurrent notions of 'Germanness' soon were strongly connected to anti-Roman and hence Italian sentiments, for 'Germans' regarded themselves as humiliated and exploited by the papacy. Perhaps the most poignant and to us amusing episode which circulated in the Reformation years, calculated to arouse shame and in turn defiance against Italians, was a description of Cardinal Jerome Aleander, of whom it was said that 'he considers a German name contemptible and those of that nation in his service he summons in a feigned barbaric accent: "Come barbarian, go barbarian, do this and that barbarian."'[10] Intense anti-German stereotyping was marked in the classical literature humanists discovered, and travellers still encountered it.[11] In 1495, for example, the Strasbourg humanist Wimpfeling disdainfully recalled how Italian fathers would insult little boys as 'German pig' (*porcum dedischo*), if they did something wrong.[12] Unsurprisingly then, after Maximilian I had appointed the painter and print-maker Jacopo de Barberi as court artist in 1500, fellow Venetians nicknamed him 'Jacopo of the Barbarians' when he duly took up residence in Nuremberg.[13] Whereas Tacitus had at least highlighted the virtuousness of German simplicity, many self-aggrandizing Renaissance Italians seemed to know only arrogant contempt for uncultured, rough, and temperamentally choleric people environmentally exposed to too much cold and rain.

Already in the mid-fifteenth century, the Sienese humanist Enea Silvio Piccolomini, later Pope Pius II (1458–1464), had composed an ironic verbal portrait of one of the most significant German representatives at the Roman curia, Gregor von Heimburg. It applied Seneca's environmentally based conception of Germans in his treatise *On Anger*.[14] Enea first described Gregor's extraordinary beauty, height, and vividness, only to set out how badly it was matched by his lack of controlling his conduct, his lack of shame, and total rudeness. After dinner, Enea concluded, Gregor would walk at the foot of Monte Giordano, overcome by heated anger as if full of contempt for Romans and his own office. He marched up and down with hanging boot legs, bared chest and head, rolled-up sleeves, and would neither stop blaspheming Rome, Eugen, and the curia, nor stop being 'very cross about how hot this land was'.[15] This pointedly indicated that Gregor's problem clearly lay in the heat he himself generated through his choleric anger, which in turn was generated by his inability to make agreements and thus enter politics and society proper. And at the root of this was his inflexible and primitive German love of liberty alongside his uncontrolled, and in the final instance, self-destructive, nature. Line by line, this portrait insinuated that in a more complex, interdependent political world, Germans needed to be ruled to exist. Enea's description of Gregor's dress underlined that the temperament of northern German people made it physically impossible for them to cope with warmer countries, as their anger in conjunction with the climate caused them to overheat, even if they already dressed over-casually with a shirt. Everyone familiar with the iconographic visualization of anger (*ira*) in that society— everyone, for instance, who had seen Giotto's stunning depiction in the Arena chapel in Padua—knew that a man who let himself be overcome by such uncontrollable anger would in no time tear off his shirt from his already bared chest. For their own good, Germans seemed best off confined to their own lands.

Enea used the newly invented printing press to full effect to publish politically incisive portraits of this kind as well as topographical descriptions. One of the most prominent humanists and politicians of his generation, he was similarly cunning when he refuted German claims of decline as a result of papal rule. In an influential open letter entitled 'Germania', published in 1457, Enea praised the wealth, urban, and technological development that Germany had evidently seen since classical times, which clearly resulted from Christian and Roman influences. There was no rational cause for antagonism between Germans and Italians; rather, it would have followed, room for optimism, if Germans accepted Italian superiority and rule, instead of each of its many rulers defending their own freedom.[16]

IDEOLOGIES OF DRESS

By the end of the fifteenth century, defiant 'anti-barbarian' and 'anti-Roman' voices multiplied in the German lands, as a politically active core within the empire agreed on reforms or grievances against Rome. For the first time, a German nationalistic ideology took shape. This ideology—and we need to term it such because of its coherence as a thoroughly invented way of thinking about the origin and future of the German nation—was developed by the second-generation humanist Conrad Celtis, whom we have already learnt about as Dürer's friend. Celtis, in 1487, had been crowned by Frederick III in Nuremberg as first Imperial poet laureate after Petrarch and Enea Silvio. Celtis made Tacitus widely available in print for elites, and used him foremost as evidence that Germans were an indigenous race. He stated that Germans had been directly created by a God called Demogorgon. Enea's 1458 treatise on Europe, by contrast, had set out how migration from different regions had made up the people now known as Germans, while the Habsburg emperor Maximilian I soon built on the more established myth that Germans were direct descendants of Trojans, who had escaped to the German region of Franconia after their city's fall (Fig. 75).[17] Celtis's indigenous race had instead been endowed directly with the German lands. It had three important sociopsychological characteristics: Germans took all hardship, hated laziness (in direct contrast to what Tacitus had written), and lived like brothers. Demogorgon generously had made them huge, and, as the Greek geographer Strabo had described, they were well proportioned, with white bodies, light eyes, and blonde hair. They had thoroughly male voices, their rough 'palate' evidence of their fearless warrior spirit. This new nationalist ideology, in other words, was patriarchal to the core: it took men, male roughness, hardness, and even violence to be the model of the German race. These men, whom Celtis praised in his *Germania generalis* of 1498, were ready for a bloody revenge when any injustice harmed them; and ready, too, to spill their pink blood for their fatherland.[18] As for Tacitus, these mythical Germans were hence primarily distinguished by their warrior spirit, and, Celtis added, by their willingness for sacrifice—a concept that equated male revenge and sacrifice with the noblest qualities of a people. So important was it to masculinize this political ideal of liberty from outside rule and defence of the fatherland that women were not mentioned once in Celtis's *Germania generalis*, as if men did not live in connection with them. Rather, he especially emphasized that these men's voices were not like women's; a comment which introduced the feminine as something that would weaken the violent male, whose self-image and success depended on his ability to inspire fear in all those men who were not his racial brothers.[19] Celtis next followed Enea in arguing that Germany had developed from barbarism to a civilized nation, of which its cities and technological inventions were foremost testimony. The reason for this, however, was not the exogenous influence of the Roman church, but cosmic change: Germany was now much closer to the sun and had become a fertile country.[20] Moreover, it had been druids and their descendants who had acted as a cast of philosopher-priests throughout German history. They had brought barbarians out of the woods into cities, and had disseminated rules for living together and education.[21] Under Charlemagne they had become Christianized. This had furthered the development of civilization, but the church had not been its cause. Charlemagne had gained the highest political power—that of an empire—for Germans, and Celtis regarded himself as following the traditions of druids who showed the necessity of complementing political strength with learning. Druid-humanists achieved the highest ideals of greatness until the end of that empire.[22] Germany had succeeded Greece and Rome as leading empire, and had turned any residues of its barbarian nature into virtues. 'Wild brutishness' had been expelled to make way for a 'softer nature', ready to absorb laws, religion, language, and philosophy.[23] Celtis's most ambitious plan was to work out a *Germania illustrata*, a description of German geography, ancient history, customs, religion, language, emotional makeup, and bodily characteristics, based on fieldwork, the study of literary sources, and scholarly teamwork. It never substantially progressed in writing, but Celtis was at the node of a large network of people whom he inspired with his interest and vision.

The patriotic aim of refuting Italian allegations of primitivism or cultural dependency created the framework for much German thought about the meaning of clothing and appearances throughout the fifteenth and well into sixteenth centuries. It closely connected a political ideal of Germanness with social ideals of comportment. As in any myth of nation, regeneration for some was easiest to think of as a return to past values. Tacitus was popularized through a vernacular translation by the former Franciscan friar Johann Eberlin von Günzburg in 1526, who we have already encountered in his Reformation campaign against foreign influences. Unsurprisingly, then, he added comments such as 'Count Frantz of Nirandula scolds the Germans for wearing such wide clothes and not tight ones like their elders', or, with palpable reproach, 'just as nowadays furs for children are sleeveless, so was the old German dress of the common man'![24] Yet inventing the necessarily tight boundaries of an indigenous identity nonetheless proved tricky. For if Germans were to aspire to return to the material simplicity practised by their forefathers, then how could they avoid appearing as primitive barbarians again, as 'pellitus' with their animal skins and long hair, which Romans had made the very stereotype of Northern barbarians?[25] Was more sophisticated clothing a desirable sign of civilization within Germany, or was it evidence that this culture had been corrupted and effeminized from outside, through trade and luxury, which, as in Rome, surely precipitated its fall? Celtis's speech to the students of Ingolstadt University in 1492 blamed Italian greed and commerce with luxury goods for draining Germany of its resources, trying out the simplest 'us versus them' rhetoric in elegant Latin on this audience of aspiring young men:

> But from the south we are oppressed by a sort of distinguished slavery, and under the impulse of greed, that old and accursed aid to the acquirement of comfort and luxury, new commercial ventures are continually established, by which our country is drained of its wonderful natural wealth while we pay to others what we need for ourselves.[26]

The ironic key phrase here is 'distinguished slavery': if Germans fell for luxury they betrayed their political heritage as free men and were reduced to smart-looking slaves. This told youths, who were thought to be most susceptible to fashion, that choosing one's dress was not an attribute of freedom. Hence Celtis later rhetorically admonished students that Italian sensuality had so corrupted Germans that it would be better if they practised again the 'rude and rustic life of old, living within the bounds of self-control, than to have imported the paraphernalia of sensuality and greed which are never sated, and to have adopted foreign customs'.[27] This was intended to make clear to them that indigenous utilitarian dress constituted them as Germans. Nationhood, in short, was tied to matter and its relation to the body rather than merely to abstract ideas in its making and unmaking. Even if students chose sensuous luxury just once, it would engulf them in the spiralling dynamics of greed and effect the nation's fall. Celtis, in other words, constructed the cultural and political ideals of Germanness as interdependent and grounded them in matters of appearance. In addition (and in contrast to the ideological praise of the *Germania generalis*) Celtis's elegies used the genre in the tradition of Roman satirists, in particular the blazing Juvenal, to lambaste women: these were the men who held that women exhibited expensive dress, lasciviousness, and general moral decadence in particular starkness. Old Germans had been a cabbage-eating 'casta simplicitas', new Germans had diseased bodies.[28] This contrast between old and new Germans mirrored the opposition between old and new Romans in Juvenal's satires as well as his comments on clothes, which he merely praised for their functional use against cold. Otherwise, Juvenal's fantasy, if anything, had been to 'escape the toga' when the sun allowed, and he supplied old men with the role to admonish the young: 'The person who is not embarrassed at wearing high rawhide boots in the ice, who dispels the east winds with skins turned inside out, will have no wish to do anything forbidden.' Juvenal predicted, as previously mentioned, that 'it's purple cloth, whatever it is, foreign and new fangled, that leads people to crime and wickedness'.[29] In this way, Juvenal provided one influential model for the dramatic portrayal of clothing as the foundation— or destruction—of morality and why therefore it should be of fundamental cultural and political importance (Fig. 70).

70. Wolfgang Lazius, *De aliquot gentium migrationibus...*, Basle: Oporiniana 1572, T.1.14, p.785, Scottish and Irish warriors. © By kind permission of the Syndics of Cambridge University Library

Celtis's visionary sense of German history, as developed in the *Germania generalis*, nonetheless implied that a return to skins and pins could not take place. If Germany had developed into a warmer and cultivated land but maintained indigenous virtues of simplicity, then dress must reflect this process as well. The main rule to observe was to stick to indigenous fabrics and tailoring, and to be frugal in expenses; but the whole point of this new German aesthetics was to craft simple elegance onto body, mind, and senses (just as the elegance in speech Celtis admired in ancient languages). Out of this would result a simple yet cultivated and appropriately decorous style to exhibit that the German empire was at its height, autonomous in its values, and with its eyes on defending or extending its borders.

Celtis made this politically motivated aesthetics of appearance concrete in two principal ways: in his discussions of Nuremberg women and of Lapps. In a poem in praise of the city of Nuremberg, the *Norimberga*, Celtis applauded women for their frugality and modest appearance, but also their 'cultus'.[30] He took the negative figure of a corrupted woman named Elsa in his elegies *Amores*, published in 1502. Celtis followed Juvenal's attack on female decadence and described a lascivious, unfaithful, heavy drinking woman as emblematic of contemporary German decadence. Elsa used artificial beauty products, and dressed luxuriously and erotically. Elsa was not the lover any German was to lust after. Ideas about good and bad femininity and masculinity, as we have already seen, figured prominently in nationalist ideology. Tacitus had admired the warrior nature of German men, but also emphasized the sexual virtuousness of Germans, who practised monogamy, punished adultery harshly, did not abandon children and—all in obvious contrast to his contemporary Romans—had mothers who nursed their children and looked after them closely.[31] This meant that German women were less forced to compete for attention, and instead could be modest and domesticated. Celtis's adaptation of Tacitus's conception of Germans as an indigenous race, moreover, potentially implied that sexual virtue was a cornerstone not only of national honour, but of a national future: any intermarriage with foreigners would corrupt a race by weakening inborn virtues. The marriage of a modest, but cultivated German woman who saw her place in the household, rather than at parties, and as dutiful mother, could be lent political significance. Thus, as the Renaissance stimulated once more the idea that cities were emblematic of civilized achievement based on legal order and peaceful political rule, so the visual performance of sexual difference through make-up, dress, and comportment could be taken to exhibit a people's virtue or vice. Though Celtis, Pirckheimer, and other humanists might brag about their love affairs in their correspondence, Celtis's poetic praise of Nuremberg women served to show that women after all were able to attain political praise if they behaved in these ways and not like Elsa (Fig. 71). As men understood women to be naturally inconstant and morally weak, this would also demonstrate the success of patriarchal institutions governing them—from magistrates and courts to fathers and husbands. Gender, in these ways, was central to early nationalist ideas. Such views in turn endorsed the staging of sexual difference through distinct appearances;

71. Melchior Lorck/Hans Sachs, *Honour and praise of a beautifully decorated woman...* Nuremberg: 1551, broadsheet, 24.6 × 32.7 cm . © The Trustees of the British Museum

Tacitus's assertion that German men and women had largely dressed the same was not usually taken up to demand more gender-neutral dress practices. In some contexts, nonetheless, a unisex look based on male dress could interestingly serve to publicly and politically display a notion of honour based on traditional virtue and generational continuity. The 'book of honour' of the Augsburg Herwart family from 1544, for instance, showed the patron couple of the beautiful folio volume both dressed in the long black gowns worn by governing men. Herwart was mayor, and his wife, too, represented this position in her dress. This minimized any sense of sexual difference and fashionable change[32] (Figs. 72–73).

Lapps, too, were repeatedly discussed by Celtis in the light of the classical tradition to argue who were the real 'barbarians'. Lapps figured as poor, squalid, uncultured inhabitants of the extreme North, whom Tacitus had named 'Fenni'. They were simply and carelessly dressed with skins, did not settle, and indeed were unable to converse with anyone who approached them. Celtis falsely claimed to have visited Lapps in their deserted and hardly human existence, to which their freezing climate and nature condemned them until there was cosmic change.[33] They had no political culture. The significance of this construction is obvious: these truly were the contemporary barbarians and there was no point of comparison with Germans. To dress merely for protection from the elements—in the way Juvenal had positively envisaged—was therefore associated with carelessly bordering on neglect, which in the Christian tradition was associated with sinful, slovenly behaviour, and had been discussed by Aquinas, for instance, alongside immoral overdressing. At the same time, Celtis followed Tacitus's sudden final thought on the Lapps, where at the end of the discussion of these primitive people he ambivalently added that 'without concern in their relations with men as well as with gods, they have attained a most difficult thing, not to have the need to express a wish'.[34] In this specific respect, Lapps and other Northern ethnic groups could still serve to identify serenity through a positive Nordic lack of desire.[35]

Such discussions of civic morality based on ethnic stereotyping were by no means confined to humanist elites. Nor was the link between a patriotic discourse and reflections on clothing—Brant's *Ship of Fools* already declared short upper garments and codpieces as a 'shame for the German nation'.[36] Most remarkably, in 1534, a Nuremberg broadsheet presented a woodcut of a bizarre looking 'wild Lapplander', which Hans Sachs's verses

72. (*left*)   Georg Herwart, mayor, in a *Schaube*, 1544, from the Herwart's family *Book of Honour*, Schätze 018. © Stadtarchiv Augsburg

73. (*right*)   Veronica Bimlin, Georg Herwart's wife in the female equivalent of a *Schaube*, from the Herwart's family *Book of Honour*, Schätze 019. © Stadtarchiv Augsburg

set out to explain (Fig. 74). His uncombed hair immediately showed his contra-political existence—Heinz Widerporst had strange ideas of his own, his own will, and detested any laws or common concerns. The verses transported him into the social institutions that constituted Nuremberg life—magistrate, crafts' guild, sociable gatherings, neighbourhood, household, and parish—where he would only use spiky words and cause conflicts. As nobody liked having anything to do with him, Widerporst disappeared back into the woods to an isolated life. His example served Sachs to show that it was necessary to distinguish between good and bad, but with the will to turn everything to its best, and conduct oneself in an easy-going way with people, quietly, and peacefully. In response

74. Hans Sachs/Eberhard Schön, *Hans Widerporst*, coloured broadsheet 1534, 16.6 × 12.5 cm. © Stiftung Schloss Friedenstein Gotha, photo: Lutz Ebhardt

to this figure of the real barbarian, the German development into a culture with 'varied cults' in many cities for Celtis and his followers now needed to be studied and preserved in its genuinely German development towards greater civilization.

In the wake of Celtis's influence on German elites, urban communal dress with regional peculiarities—and not courtly or clerical or rural dress—became most interesting to anyone seeking to consolidate a patriotic and German imperial identity. This of course perfectly overlapped with the largest audience humanists addressed. For the most vibrant centres of fifteenth- and sixteenth-century German technical, economic, and creative production were seen to be the sixty-five 'free' Imperial cities, which were subject to the emperor and thus had no princely court. The most important, as we have seen, were Nuremberg, Augsburg, and Strasbourg. Particularly in Nuremberg, the coming together of different forms of highly specialized knowledge and skill with capital and an interest in visions for that society enabled innovative teamwork and ambitious undertakings. The most famous of these, as has been mentioned, was the voluminous World chronicle by the Nuremberg physician Hartmann Schedel, published in 1493. It showed the progress of time through six ages of the world, which would be concluded with the Days of Judgement. Copious woodcuts for the final, sixth age detailed the sheer number of more recent German cities, and thus made visually manifest that this nation stood at the height of civilization and power in the world.[37]

But the nation needed to affirm German and urban values, as Celtis once more critically remarked in a further description of Nuremberg, now explicitly attacking courts alongside trade as conduits of corruption:

> The citizens of Nuremberg mostly dress in black, but the form of their dress varies frequently. For they have taken over bad manners from the foreign peoples with which they trade and let themselves be influenced by different nations. Perhaps our dukes contribute most to this, for they have already renounced the old German ways in many other respects, and now betray their fathers' morals and their fatherland, take on a new way of speaking and a new look and feel displeased when thinking of their home country and the way life used to be, when peace still ruled and there was loyalty and constancy in all things.[38]

Black naturally materialized politicized values such as constancy and loyalty because it could not be dyed in any other colour: black is black, only its shades differ. Self-denigration became fashionable: Wimpfeling, for one, admitted in 1495 that Italians had some justification for calling naughty boys German pigs, since 'most of our people are rude, "porci et inurbani", shallow people in pompous clothes, with effeminate headdresses and shoes, furious and inconsiderate, addicted to drink, despising learning etc'.[39] A popular song book entailed the following reflection on the old question of why there seemed to be no money in the German lands: 'it is a question and great lament/ how money disappears from the land/ from the land/ but there is no question really/ one gives it away for silken dress/ Worldly pomp is all powerful/ vanity breaks out/ without measure or meaning/ without measure and meaning/ one dresses over costly over costly'.[40]

The influential Bavarian sixteenth-century historian and chronicler Aventin, in response to these dilemmas, busily constructed an ideal of political personhood by writing extensively about Charlemagne's attitude to dress, so as to provide a role model for contemporary rulers. Charlemagne's biographer Einhard had set out in detail that this mighty Christian ruler had worn simple hose and a tunic trimmed at the border with silk. In winter, he used common animal skins and fur for vests and a blue cloak. He always carried a sword at his side. Most importantly, Einhard wrote, 'he disliked foreign clothes no matter how beautiful they were, and would never allow himself to be dressed in them'. Charlemagne only used precious jewellery or foreign dress on a very few ceremonious occasions, in accordance with specific protocol. On the whole, however, 'his dress was not much different from that of the common people'.⁴¹ When Germans and Franks had fought in Italy and France they had already adapted their fashion for 'short slashed coats and frocks'. Charlemagne had seen this, Aventin vividly related, and had shouted at them furiously:

> 'oh you Germans and free Franks, how inconsiderate and inconstant you are! That you take over the clothing of those you have conquered, whose lords you are, is not a good sign, means nothing good: if you take their clothes, they will take your hearts. What are these Italian patches...good for? They don't cover all of the body, but leave half of it naked, are neither good for cold nor heat, rain or wind; and if someone needs to pee in a field (I beg your pardon) it doesn't cover one, your legs freeze.' Then he sent out a law for all the country that French clothes were neither to be bought nor sold in Germany.⁴²

It was difficult to put this more strongly: foreign clothes *will take your heart*. This was the message by humanist scribal elites repeated after Celtis. Once more we see here that clothing continued to be understood not as something external to the body, that could be simply put on and taken off, or that could function as an abstract sign: rather, it was seen to mould a person and materialize identity. Consequentially the German heart could only remain pure and strong and (as such organic metaphors always suggested) maintain a healthy body politic, if a practical aesthetics of the 'whole' was followed and guaranteed integrity. Patches were to be avoided. Only one unified cloth worked as protection from the elements, and this, after all, was the main function of clothing. For the robber-knight von Hutten, imported silk and clothing was infectious for the body politic: it took away manly strength. Whereas Celtis had proposed that Germans might have become softer as a result of civilization, this positive 'softness' was only sometimes gradually related to refined masculinity. Hutten valued masculinity most for its toughness and violent affirmation of what he understood as independence. As Hutten developed his ethos of Germans as robbers in their fight for political liberty, he even excluded merchants from the nation on such grounds. His 'School of Tyranny' set out that

> it is hardly credible that things which do not originate here are good for those born here. If this was the case, then nature would ensure that they were grown here. This is why one desires them not for everyday usage, but for pleasure. Not to keep up the body, but to indulge it, you (merchants) circulate these tempting

75. (*right*) Hans Burgkmair the Elder, *Maximilian I on horseback*, in armour with peacock feathers, 1518, woodcut from two blocks, 32.3 × 22.6 cm, AN56092. © The Trustees of the British Museum

things. Thus it is no surprise that health is endangered and that one is prone to suffer every illness. Also you have imported silk and every kind of foreign dress, through which the inborn German strength is softened up and the best morals are corrupted, because through you a female obsessiveness about looks and awful effeminacy spreads in the life of man.[43]

For Hutten, any pleasure in appearances diseased the nation. Manliness and the political future were dependent on the right attitude to material things: as if tough men needed rough cloth to prickle their skin. Such views lent support to the idea that secular authorities needed to police their subjects' dress to maintain the nation.[44] But such discussions did not resolve the question of whether Germans should dress retro-simple, or adapt refined clothing to their advancing civilization.

SYMBOLIZING GENDER

Yet, as Dürer's drawing showed (Fig. 68), the basic representation of female virtuous dress in Germany had been given clear parameters: it was closed instead of low-cut, it fitted tightly around the waist, projecting an ideal of controlled eating and drinking, it was designed for labour rather than idle leisure, and it was decorous, but not overtly showy. It was *teutsch*, not *welsch* (Italian), and the one thing to remember about this time is that '*welschen*' for Germans was synonymous with men delighting in homosexual 'arse-fucking'.[45] German dress ideally displayed women and elite men in an iconic way as honourable, heterosexual, and differently sexed, suggesting a binary distinction between 'man' and 'woman', rather than a spectrum of shifting sexual identities to be experimented with. Civic respectable male dress, as we have seen, was most clearly represented through the outer layer of a long, black, fur-trimmed silk gown (*Schaube*) (Fig. 72, 73). It was exclusive to elites, who almost by definition were also governing elites in communal politics. Imperial cities were especially proud of such political autonomy from princes. The *Schaube* hence resembled the black toga Venetian councillors wore. Franceso Sansovino in 1581 indeed endorsed that such constancy in modest customs made Venice the least corrupt and most stable of all Italian republics. Most Italians, he thought, had been corrupted by 'northern' fashions—which to him meant that they had taken over French and Spanish (!) clothes.[46] Yet the German *Schaube* still permitted a greater display in colours and cut of doublet and hose that would be worn underneath.[47]

For the first half of the sixteenth century there moreover remained greater ambivalence about what constituted male dress as symbolic of not just civic but also imperial honour. This was because ideas of civil restraint had to be related to ideals of manly virility, boldness, power, and pride. The figure of the Landsquenet soldier clearly revealed this contemporary ambivalence and consequently was an extremely prominent subject of contemporary woodcuts on broadsheets, title pages, as well as in books.[48] Landsquenets were mercenary soldiers who were first recruited to make up a 'German army' by Maximilian I from 1500 onwards, to defend as well as to extend his territories. This drew common men into prolonged, though still temporary, military service and de-emphasized the status of noble-born knights as a supreme warrior class. A prestigious Augsburg 1529 edition of Venegati's classical treatise on military affairs, for instance, was filled with no less than 125 large woodcuts by skilled artists such as Jörg Breu the Elder, and depicted glorious Landsquenets as contemporary knights.[49] Visual media spread new beauty ideals (Fig. 76). Soon, broadsheets depicted Landsquenets as inhabiting a world with concubines, which was diametrically opposed to the ideal of the 'holy household' for which craftsmen so successfully lobbied during the Reformation movements. Herein lay much of the Landsquenets' appeal. Several series of Nuremberg broadsheets produced around 1530 with their representations of strikingly fashionable Landsquenets thus constituted deliberate visual interventions in rallying for men to defy advancing Ottomans. They specifically depicted the attractions of this military life for tailors, bakers, shoemakers— the same group of artisans whose civic life had during the Reformation movements been so firmly founded on an ideal of sensible marriages and a well governed household, on careful spending and investment in a generational future, on respectable, controlled masculinity as part of a communal sense of urban morality for the sake of the common weal. Landsquenets were imagined through them as new German warriors, out to fight and win or fearlessly die; they served their fatherland and mighty emperor; went from place to place, with wayward women in tow, receiving big bounties and salaries; they were tall, strong, and slim, erotic, and, last but not least, exempt from sumptuary legislation.

By all accounts, military service hence counted on its attractiveness to keen dressers. Landsquenet displays partly related to their rank within the army. But all depictions advertised that even a poor tailor could instantly aspire to an appearance impossible in ordinary civic life. Mercenaries were always depicted with striking amounts of exotic ostrich or peacock feathers on their heads, which must have been sourced from Southern Europe and the Middle East, and an abundance of ribbons on doublets. They seem to have worn body-clinging hose, vivid colours, bold, and sometimes experimentally patterned slashes as well as the large, diagonal slits of the Burgundian St Andrew's cross, and their clothes apparently were made from costly, sensuous materials like silk and velvets. Proudly they carried long, heavy swords, spears, or pikes, and were often represented with elaborate beards or long hair. Most importantly, perhaps, the Landsquenet 'look' was achieved through an elongated, erect silhouette, but could also tolerate rough sloppiness, which manifested itself in a slightly bent walking style and disintegrating, torn hose, revealing straps linking it to drawers or the doublet (Fig. 77). This was a display of dress and undress, of finery and squalor in these potentially overdressed bodies, a style to which contemporaries simply were not accustomed. Critics could depict all this as effeminate frippery that got in the way of proper fighting, as luxury motivated by greed, lasciviousness, and vainglory, rather than traditional chivalric values, and sometimes represented Landsquenets as old men with grey beards but little wisdom. Other observers drew attention to the miseries of real war, depicting how these splendid clothes would turn into rags, becoming a sign of lost honour, barely covering lost limbs, or how they would be torn straight off dead bodies before they became too cold, bloody, and stiff on the field. The depictions from the first half of the sixteenth century, by contrast, slanted towards the hyper-masculinity of these athletic, bold, and aesthetically attractive bodies, who would deservedly gain praise and money. Contemporary lewd songs described how women, even married women, tempted these men into their homes for play. Arnold von Bruck, esteemed Kapellmeister for Ferdinand I in Vienna between 1527 and 1546, merrily composed a song of a

76. Lucas Cranach the Elder, *Landsquenet decorated with feathers*, c.1506, woodcut, 24.2 × 9.0 cm, AN49476001. © The Trustees of the British Museum

77.   Jost Amman, illustration to Leonhard Fronsperger, *Order of War*, Frankfurt: Feyerabend & Hüter 1563, soldier with a lance and a canteen woman carrying poultry, AN76419001. © The Trustees of the British Museum

Landsquenet out of money passing by a tavern where 'the ale-wife looked out of the window, and then a little more, as so many times before'. At this point the bleating song in a consciously ill-refined *teutsch*, non-*Welsch* musical fashion developed into a long list of aphrodisiac plants, some of which directly evoked the image of an erect penis and intercourse—a device followed by other songs. There was no moralistic commentary.[50] Landsquenet soldiers, in sum, were a distinct social group licensed to exhibit a whole new spectre of fashionable, sexually attractive, and valiant male dress, entirely at odds with notions of civic morality and the honourable simplicity and sexually domesticated life of ancient German warriors. Landsquenets had a strong urban and rural presence— they were hired to protect Imperial events in the cities, marched into battle, or returned waiting for new assignments. Their distinct comportment through dress, as much as gestures and speech, was critically discussed by some as much as supported by others, and thus allowed for identification and to some extent imitation from men and women across society. Women depicted as Landsquenets' concubines would have busily worked as seamstresses for them to care for their special clothes.[51]

After 1550, however, this particular visual cult of the young, audacious Landsquenet patriot used for recruitment purposes was coming to an end. They now tended to be represented as older, battle-hardened men. In 1555, Hans Glaser, a prominent Nuremberg illuminator, still attempted to provide a distinctive, but respectable, image of a sturdy, steadfast soldier with a long beard, valiant posture, and voluminous dress, a giant in the landscape.[52] This image sought to create confidence in and support for the figure of the 'good', God-fearing patriotic soldier, who knew that his 'beginning and end/ stood in God's hand', and that God's help and protection in turn depended on his moral comportment in everyday life. Far more typical, however, were critical depictions of mature Landsquenets in exceedingly long, overly sumptuous, and unpractical baggy breeches, which easily ripped and tore. As in the Lutheran preacher Musculus's discussion, it was the length of the breeches, and hence their excessive use of fabric, which distinguished them from appropriate decorousness in civilian dress.[53] Their depiction as torn revealed that young soldiers had to learn how to steal and escape without making a mess of their dress, and that real mercenary life was about robbery and conceit[54] (Fig. 78). Little honour was left; and it seems that Protestants, who were the prime movers in public discourses about German values at this time, now withdrew their support for the contested ideal of Landsquenets as

78.   Albrecht Altdorfer, detail of the *Triumph of Maximilian I, Utrecht Campaign* (Inv. 25208). © Albertina, Wien

the embodiment of German masculine patriotic honour, which had been so crucially projected through dress displays.

The absence of consensus in the second half of the sixteenth century about how to display heroic masculinity could in turn further fears of cultural instability. This is strikingly revealed by a very large embroidery, which dates from 1571 and adorned a fireplace in Leipzig's town hall (Fig. 79). It displays nine figures. Starting on the left is a half-naked 'white Moor', followed by a Hungarian, a Gypsy, an Italian, a nude 'black Moor', a Frenchman, a Swiss, and a Turk slaughtering a Christian child. The series ends with a nude but bearded German, balancing several pieces of cloth on his left arm. The inscription declares that he likes the clothing of all nations and does not know which to choose. This German is going to a tailor to allow him to decide on the style that would make him look like a hero.[55] The verse below all these figures reads laconically without any of the usual rhymes: 'So look at this depiction / How strange a matter clothing is throughout this world in all countries, And nobody now keeps to their ran / And it was not like this in the past As one reads in old histories.'[56] The Italian and French men wear elegantly fitted clothes, giving them a refined look of wealthy civility. The Moor, Hungarian, and the Swiss soldier all emphasize their masculine pride in their physical prowess at fighting or hunting. Six figures carry carefully-made and eye-catching weapons of wood and metal. Remarkably, only four other Christians are represented, making the German seem equally attracted to non-Christian and Christian dress and culture, and mostly to those outside central Europe. The embroidery thus offered Leipzig's town-councillors and their visitors a picture of a world where identities and masculine firmness in Germany were unmade through cultural exchange. Fixed traditions had been eroded by experiencing diversity, and history could seem unpredictable and uncontrollable. The hanging suggested a distinction between the 'natural' nudity of savages—or what Montaigne would call 'natural apparel'—and what we might call 'cultural' nudity, resulting from a loss of identity. The fear was that Europeans had to acknowledge such cultural nudity, or to face their own diversity, whereas non-European cultures in fact were positively rooted in clear customs and stable societies.

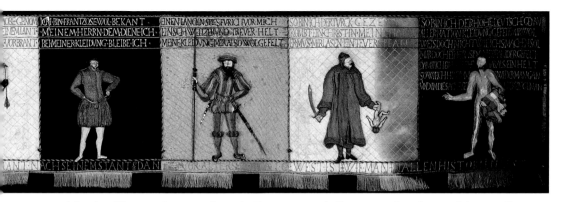

79. (*above*) Chimney-hanging from the Leipzig town-hall, 1571, embroidery with linen, silk, metal threads, wood, paper and metal pieces, 40 × 285 cm, Inv. No. V 466. © Grassi Museum, Leipzig

80. (*right*) The naked German, at the close of Wilhelm IV of Bavaria's *Book of Court Costumes* (Hofkleiderbuch), Cgm 1951, 460r. © Bayerische Staatsbibliothek, München

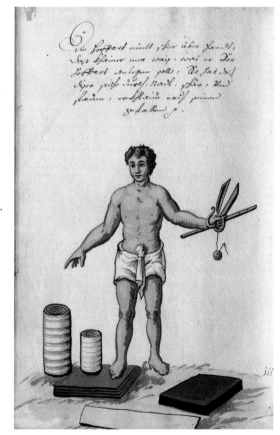

Fashion was the very materialization of inconstancy. The image of the naked man on his way to a tailor hence quickly turned into an icon across Europe, which made the experience of accelerated change in this period concrete. We have already heard of Andrew Boorde, who in a woodcut created such a naked Englishman in his *Book Of Knowledge*.[57] In the early sixteenth century, the French preacher Michel Menot alarmingly told his audience about a Venetian palace in which there were wall paintings of people of all nations. Only the French man was represented naked with cloth and scissors in hand.[58] A book that recorded many of the clothes Duke Wilhelm IV of Bavaria wore and handed out to his court surprisingly ended with another depiction of the naked man with his scissors in hand surrounded by cloth, lamenting the ever growing vanity in dress (Fig. 80).

Moral Geographies

One available political response to this troubling experience of cultural exchange and dislocation in the age of state formation was to successfully cultivate what Gábor Klaniczay has identified as defiant 'ostentatious barbarism'. This in part happened in Hungary and Poland, where the substantial gentry used oriental clothes, weapons, and hairstyles to emphasize its closeness to Asian rather than Western European aesthetic ideals, as well as male valour and hardiness. Italy, France, and Spain mattered far less than Ottoman, Russian, and Tartar styles, so that French observers of Polish ceremonies routinely felt as though they were back in periods of ancient Persian glory.[59] But for Germany, as we have seen, this was no real possibility, as its elites mostly wished to document its successive indigenous civilization, to claim national superiority.

Another possible response was to create moral geographies in print, which would then orient people's dress styles. It is in this context that the first book that visually set out what it regarded as the various 'cults' of dress in the German lands was devised.[60] This comparative moral geography in a global context was created by the woodcut artist Hans Weigel in Nuremberg, with help from his better known colleague Jost Amman. The *Trachtenbuch* was printed in 1577 by one of the leading entrepreneurial publishers of the day, Sigmund Feyerabend, in Frankfurt, which was already home to the bustling book fair. Weigel's book was the most comprehensive and lavishly printed costume book that had appeared in Europe so far, and stood right at the beginning of a successful new genre, of which the best known examples have remained the Venetian Cesare Vecellio's two even more comprehensive costume books, published in 1590 and 1598 (Fig. 81). Many of Vecellio's (and his Nuremberg cutter Chrieger's) depictions would be based on Weigel's book. Before Weigel's publication, as we have seen, artists like Bellini, Pisanello, and Dürer had been interested in costume studies, and some ambitious collections of watercolour studies of dress had been compiled. The Venetian artist Enea Vico had begun to pioneer costume engravings in 1545, and several specific studies on Turks had been printed, most strikingly the Frenchman Nicolas de Nicolay's emphatically empirical and sumptuously illustrated report of his voyages to Eastern Europe and the Ottoman Empire in 1562. Nicolay and his artist praised themselves on their diligent observations from nature in contrast to ancient Romans. The point of their work was as much to present instructive, useful knowledge as delectable variety for the eye and spirit in a 'pleasant spectacle' of different people.[61] Nicolay was almost immediately translated into German. A preciously illuminated edition from Nuremberg is among the holdings of the British Library, documenting how patrons valued images of other cultures created by travellers (Figs. 82–83). In 1562, too, the first 'costume book' proper appeared in Paris, a small French book revelling in the *'diversité'* of world clothing, published by Richard Breton, which incorporated Europe, Asia, Africa, and the *'isles sauvages'*, mixing 107 simple woodcuts on 56 sheets with guest appearances of monsters and marvels.[62] A Venetian called Fernando Bertelli next published a Latin book of costume in 1563 with

81.   Silk-embroidery with costume scenes of men and Italian women as in Bertelli and Vecellio, south-German, late sixteenth century, Inv. No. D 193. © Badisches Landesmuseum, Karlsruhe

60 sheets, which was reprinted in 1569, while from 1572 onwards the German team Franz Hogenberg and Georg Braun successfully sold their beautiful, extraordinarily ambitious tomes depicting cities of the world, which included detailed vignettes of people. In 1577, the same year as Weigel's book, there appeared a final significant publication by an Antwerp etcher, Abraham de Bruyn, who published his Latin work with 206 figures on fifty sheets in Cologne and included a preface by a humanist.[63] The genre thus had quickly established itself not just as an entertaining one, but also a serious one.

Weigel's book comprised 219 single-page woodcuts in full quarto format, with captions and verses in German as well as in Latin. Its lavish format invited owners to customize the book by investing in splendid colouring, making it a prize piece in their collection. It boasted a six-page historical introduction in German and a programmatic cover- and end-page. Weigel's production therefore was the first ambitious costume book in Europe directed at a broad European audience.

Costume books are often treated as a genre. More recently it has been proposed that this genre should be seen as 'equivalent to contemporary efforts in cartography to

82. (*above left*) Nicolas de Nicolay, *Von der Schiffart unnd Raiisz in die Türckey...*, Nuremberg 1572: designed by C. Saldoerffer, noble Turkish woman at home, BL C55.i.4, 10r (1). © The British Library, London

83. (*above right*) Nicolas de Nicolay, *Von der Schiffart unnd Raiisz in die Türckey...*, Nuremberg 1572: designed by C. Saldoerffer, Janissary, BL C55.i.4 (1), 231. © The British Library, London

publish an atlas of the whole world'. Even the earliest books, Ulrike Ilg argues, followed the 'historiographic approach' proposed by the French scholar Louis Le Roy, who wrote the first universal history in 1567. Le Roy declared that peaceful exchanges manifested a 'New European spirit to live "in the same city and a world republic".'[64] This would have been an extraordinary political aim for this period in books encompassing the Americas, and it is difficult to see how costume books indicated that they shared Le Roy's thoughts. Instead, it makes more sense to analyse these predominantly visual sources in the same way as one situates texts. Rather than seeking to find one underlying idea typical of a genre, it is of greater interest to reconstruct what particular intervention an author was trying to make in a specific political and social context. What is interesting about costume books therefore is less what they have in common than how they differed and sought to use the visualization of clothing customs to impart political and social ideals to particular audiences. Hence our primary question has to be what kind of visual acts they constituted. Even less, of course, should we treat such productions as a reliable index of what people actually wore, without consulting other evidence.

Such an approach means that we need to spend more time looking at the contents of a heavily illustrated book like Weigel's than has hitherto been the case. Weigel's depiction of clothing thus turns out to have been a renewed attempt to picture an ideal of comportment in order to construct a positively patriotic sense of civilized urban German behaviour, especially for women. He contrasted this ideal above all with Italian and French luxury as well as with male 'incivility' anywhere. This visually captivating global moral geography identified a series of national types in a single volume, from which an ideal of Germanness could emerge and serve as a model for its readers. Weigel's introduction explicitly stated that a nation's future depended on the success of its habits. Costume once again was given meaning as a political subject.

Two remarkable images by the artist Jost Amman opened and closed Weigel's book (Fig. 84). Amman was the son of a Zurich professor of classics, rhetoric, and logic, and had received a distinguished humanist education. He had moved to Nuremberg in 1561, and after just one year took over the workshop of Virgilius Solis the Elder, the foremost Nuremberg woodcut artist of his time. Amman worked in partnership with the Frankfurt publisher Sigmund Feyerabend on a large number of illustrated book projects, of which his *Book of Trades* (1568) with verses by Hans Sachs is now the best known. He was also involved in genealogical projects for Nuremberg patrician families, on which he worked with the best illuminators. His prolific activities document the extent to which Nuremberg in the age after Dürer remained a focus of supreme artistic education and skill, teamwork and patronage, which the next chapter will further explore. Dürer's successor as 'genius' was the goldsmith Wenzel Jamnitzer, who also closely cooperated with Amman, illustrating his theoretical writings.[65] Weigel's *Trachtenbuch* reflects the sense of innovation, scale, and ambition these networks sustained. Amman's frontispiece provided the first programmatic engraving among the costume books. It was a humanist tradition to present the argument in visual summary, in order to ensure its emotional impact and memorability. This frontispiece depicts the expulsion of Adam and Eve from Paradise in its upper part, satirically setting out its consequences in its lower part. While Asia, America, and Africa are identifiable through men in distinctive costume and armour, no such figure can be found to represent Europe. Like an imperfect Adam, Europe covers himself with a large roll of fabric, scissors in hand. He, too, is on the way to a tailor, wondering how to dress, and eager to follow the latest style. This made the visual argument that even America with its elaborate feather cloak could not be termed naked; Europe alone was denuded and without any identifiable identity as a continent. For the first time, the topical figure of the 'naked European' was put directly in a comparative context with the other continents in print. Yet this naked personification of Europe is also depicted as strong and confidently moving forward in his predicament. He is open to change.[66] Amman on the other hand closed the book visually with a depiction of John the Baptist, illustrating the third chapter of Matthew. It presents John wearing a cloak of camel hair with a simple belt around his loins, admonishing people to be truly penitent. Amman's depictions therefore made it clear that the moral framework of the work was biblical and important, while the title announced that these costumes of 'many and the most noble nations' were also 'very funny and entertaining' to watch. The naked European satirically set out the larger problem: at the very worst, political ideals could no longer be matched by enduring social ideals of comportment. Europe advanced through its move away from traditions and awareness of other cultures. This would not make it vulnerable to outside rule as long as it retained its judiciousness. Did man's passions allow for judiciousness to be retained?

Weigel dedicated the work to the ruler of his native Amerbach, Ludwig, duke of Bavaria and *Churfürst*, in order to gain patronage, but also to introduce his work as patriotic. He then set out a brief moral history of dress. First, humans had tried to cover their shame with figleaves, then God had given them animal skins. Next, they had elaborated clothing, to protect themselves from the elements, but soon also in accordance with their 'inner senses'. Thus they had started to abuse clothing, adding superfluous elements and taking on foreign customs. The consequences had been disastrous: Romans had been drawn into sumptuousness and *Übermuth*, and all their thoughts had been directed at how they could outdo one another. They had forgotten about welfare and the common good. Hatred, envy, anger, and contempt had spread. Such ill feeling had culminated in civil wars, and brought about the destruction of a beautiful and constitutionally well-defined government, which had then been finally ruined by foreign nations.[67] This presented the fall of Rome as the final consequence of a precise sequence of a causal chain that had begun with creative dressmaking and sartorial cultural exchange. Weigel's next historical example was provided by Alexander the Great. Alexander famously had taken on luxurious and sensuous Persian dress, demanding to be worshipped as a god. His native Macedonians regarded him as foreign and treacherous, and rebelled against him. Weigel, too, therefore ascribed to clothes an extraordinary psychological force as they affected Alexander's sense of self and rule. 'Everyone's way', Weigel stated, 'is made known through clothing.'[68]

He now addressed the 'strange wondrous change which foreign and strange clothing' had introduced in 'our common fatherland'.[69] These developments, he confessed, made it difficult to find any steady German dress, and Orientals were ridiculing this changeability of mind. But some of the 'old honourable' and more comfortable clothing had not fallen out of use completely. It was much more decorous and pleasing to see than many of the new fashions. This kind of old fashioned civil honourable clothing, Weigel concluded, was laudable, as long as 'utility, morals and civility' prevailed over luxury and sumptuousness. The Roman 'wise men' had advocated abstaining from gold, precious jewels, and scarlets, modest, and gracious dress.[70] Weigel ended by presenting his innovative compilation as a toolkit for morally upright readers to enjoy looking at all the different manners of clothing, but then to 'grab and take' whatever was reasonable,

84. (*opposite*) Hans Weigel, *Trachtenbuch (Book of Costumes)*, frontispiece, L.11.33. © The Master and Fellows of Trinity College, Cambridge

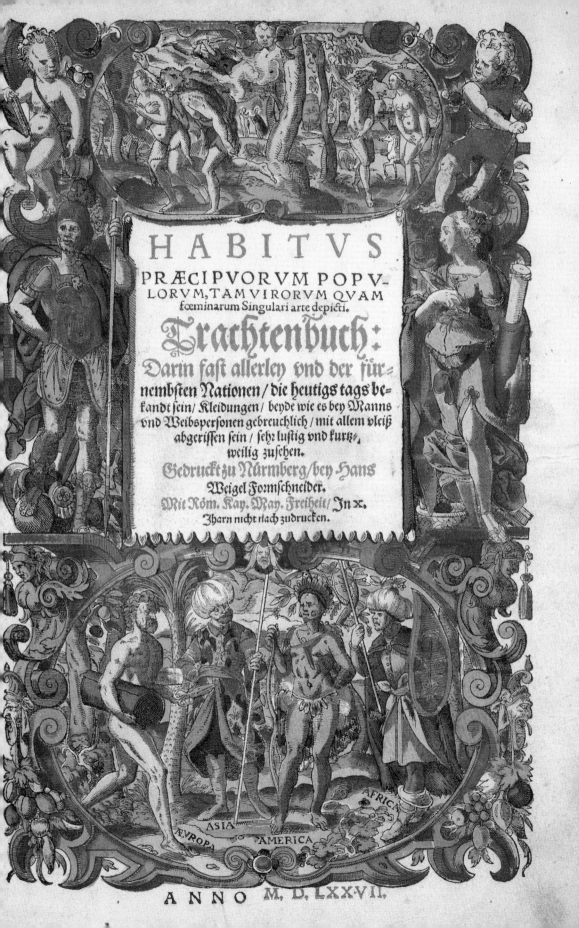

HABITVS

PRÆCIPVORVM POPV-
LORVM, TAM VIRORVM QVAM
fœminarum Singulari arte depicti.

Trachtenbuch:
Darin fast allerley vnd der fürnembsten Nationen/ die heutigs tags bekandt sein/ Kleidungen/ beyde wie es bey Manns
vnd Weibspersonen gebreuchlich/ mit allem vleiß
abgerissen sein/ sehr lustig vnd kurtz-
weilig zusehen.
Gedruckt zu Nürmberg/ bey Hans
Weigel Formschneider.
Mit Röm. Kay. May. Freiheit/ Jn x.
Jharn nicht nach zudrucken.

ASIA

AFRICA

ÆVROPA   AMERICA

ANNO M.D.LXXVII.

honourable, and suitable, while escaping from everything extravagant or low.[71] Weigel's volume thus described its value in the following way: it helped Germans to remind themselves of the few examples left of old honourable clothing and encouraged them to develop this ideal in civilized ways. Hence, unlike Vecellio's later books, none of the plates contrasted old and new looks. Appearances thus emerged as a form of active political commitment, through which citizens could morally sustain their fatherland. This was applied and popularized humanism. Weigel referred throughout to the Roman ethics of civic virtue, which were built on a rejection of luxury and an endorsement of useful and comfortable clothing.[72] This type of active moral patriotism was predominantly advocated by Protestants. After 1550, 'readers' of early humanist nationalist texts as well as patriotic plays published by Protestants became the staple of a broadening elite school education.[73]

The function of clothing to regulate gender was once more lent particular importance. Weigel immediately emphasized that God had ordained men to wear male dress and females to wear only female dress, and this had been subsequently endorsed in Christian councils and Roman law. He provided several historical examples of abuse, referencing the recent case of a wealthy, but reckless Roman woman during the (non-Italian) Adrian VI's papacy. She had dressed and acted like a man, and even though this was not a punishable offence in Italy, the reform pope Adrian had commanded that she be shamed and led across the city dressed merely in a shirt.[74] God had created women as women and men as men; women who rejected this notion challenged patriarchal hierarchies. Disguise could not be a matter of play, and boundary crossing was dangerous. This paragraph, in other words, emphasized that political order was visualized through the separateness of male and female dress, while Weigel's woodcuts would subsequently always represent men and women on different pages. He thus visually ordered gender to represent an ideal of assumed sexual difference. This projected a specifically honourable 'German' conduct, which Weigel's Roman anecdote had already contrasted to Italian permissiveness.

Weigel's illustrations for the German lands, which formed the first part of his book, were overwhelmingly urban. He spent no more than six pages honouring the political hierarchy to which his patron Ludwig belonged—from the Holy Roman Emperor, elected by 'autonomous' Germans who thereby avoided arbitrary foreign rule, to a German prince, and sumptuously dressed noble courtier (Fig. 85). Rapidly he moved on to an extensive section on Nuremberg, which began with images of patrician weddings. Its prominence documented the great esteem in which 'honourable' marriage was held; monogamy and rank-specific intermarriage were the basis of social order. The sequence of illustrations moreover observed distinction of rank, progressing from high to lower members of society, while predominantly focusing on women (Figs. 86–87). Almost all of them were shown as covering all of their body with clothing, and Weigel's verses under each illustration frequently used the attribute 'honourable' to reinforce the visual argument that such public enclosure made urban woman respectable. Gowns in unexciting brown and white colours underlined this appearance, and contrasted with later images of non-Germans whose brightly pastel coloured dress demarcated immorality, especially, for example, the disastrous Persian king,[75] or, exceptionally, a young unmarried Spanish couple together on the same page, to illustrate how those 'outside marriage' practised 'vanity and sumptuousness'[76] (Figs. 88–89). At the same time, Weigel made it clear that clothes worn below German gowns exhibited more decorousness through colourful trims. Even a Strasbourg peasant woman was depicted with a rustic face, but well and decently clad. The dress of maids was depicted as related to their mistresses' status and task: if a wealthy urban woman went shopping, her servant displayed the household's standing alongside her. Weigel also conveyed a sense of civic pride linked to

85. Hans Weigel, *Trachtenbuch*, a German *Landtsfürst* (territorial ruler). © The Master and Fellows of Trinity College, Cambridge

imperial privileges. Catholic cities were not morally inferior: 'This is how the women in the famous imperial city of Aachen go / Were many an imperial coronation happened. / The women go in this decent (*züchtig*) way / And take care to adorn themselves in this manner.'[77] Even so, Genevan women earned themselves particular praise, as Calvinist consistories ensured moral conformity. Their depiction served to make the general comment that 'honour, virtue and piety / is a woman's greatest ornament'—this, Weigel instructed the reader, 'is what we can see looking at Genevan women/ who are always fine (*züchtig*)'.[78] These rudimentary rhymes thus repeatedly enshrined the same values of female virtuousness, above all honourable and disciplined conduct (*ehrbar and*

86. (*above left*) Hans Weigel, *Trachtenbuch*, Nuremberg woman. © The Master and Fellows of Trinity College, Cambridge

87. (*above right*) Hans Weigel, *Trachtenbuch*, Nuremberg woman attending an invitation to a meal. © The Master and Fellows of Trinity College, Cambridge

88. (*opposite*) Hans Weigel, *Trachtenbuch*, Persian lord. © The Master and Fellows of Trinity College, Cambridge

CLXXIII.
Ein Perſier Herr.

Ein Perſier in dem Gwandt /   Daß der groſſe König Alexander /
Auß Perſia dem verheerten Land.   Mit Krieg verderbet alleſander.
                                                 X f

züchtig), while also positively emphasizing the industriousness (*fleiss*) that would go into the making of such an honourably decorous but not extravagant appearance. Hair was always either braided in unmarried girls, or covered, whereas, as we shall see, German urban women had long started to display their hair underneath small berets and caps[79] (Fig. 90).

In France, the Lorraine city of Metz stood out because it had formerly belonged to the Empire. Weigel stated this in his book, and the fact that Charles V had beleaguered the city, and depicted another neat woman. This insinuated that women's clothes reflected that Metz was legitimately German rather than French, or at least documented how much their morals had benefited from German rule[80] (Fig. 91). French women otherwise gained praise if they were depicted appropriately covered,

IVVENIS ET VIRGO PISCAIENSIS
siue Cantabrica,

CLV.
Ein Junckfraw vnd Junger Gesell auß Pischtaia.
JUng Gsellen vnd Junckfrawen eben/ Gehen daher in solcher Tracht/
Die noch ausser dem Ehstand leben. Wenn sie treiben hoffart vnd pracht.
Qq iij

ANCILLA COLONIENSIS.

LXXXIII.
Ein Haußmagdt von Cölln.
WEnn du wilt wissen fein/ Die Haußmdagdt einher gahn/
Wie zu Cölln an dem Rein. So sich nur dise Figur an.
X iij

89. (*above left*)   Hans Weigel, *Trachtenbuch*, a Biscay couple. © The Master and Fellows of Trinity College, Cambridge

90. (*above right*)   Hans Weigel, *Trachtenbuch*, Cologne maidservant. © The Master and Fellows of Trinity College, Cambridge

but were usually depicted in much more refined clothing than Germans, which Weigel clearly regarded ambivalently as partly 'magnificent' and partly too much finery (Fig. 92). Several Italian ladies were depicted with luxury accessories, which affected their comportment: whereas German women carried baskets or folded their hands, these women held large exotic feather fans or huge pairs of leather gloves, which would have been perfumed. This engulfed them in decorous sensuousness and removed them from the ordinary tasks of market shopping, which German urban women of rank were depicted as taking seriously enough to do themselves in order to govern households well. Italian dress was mostly presented as far more elaborate and low cut, even though Weigel also drew attention to a considerable degree of variety within Italian towns, and to the fact that according to their cultural values such clothing could be

91. (*above left*) Hans Weigel, *Trachtenbuch*, French lady. © The Master and Fellows of Trinity College, Cambridge

92. (*above right*) Hans Weigel, *Trachtenbuch*, Lorraine woman of Metz. © The Master and Fellows of Trinity College, Cambridge

CXLVIII.
Also gehen die Frawen zu Neaples.

ZV Neaples in Welschem Landt/   Die schönen Adelichen Frawen/
Gehen daher in solchem Gwandt.   Daran mancher sein lust thut schawen.

'*züchtig*' (Fig. 93). His comments on Indians or a woman from Fez likewise made clear that they thought of themselves as beautiful and fine, whereas he took it that his European audience would be dismissive of them. There were nonetheless glimpses of an ethnographic interest, which was pedagogically evoked to prevent instant moral judgements. An Indian woman, for instance, was depicted holding an object, which Weigel explained was a stone casket with a particular name, which she worshipped as God, as he noted apologetically, 'they do not know otherwise'.[81]

German urban men were presented as respectable in ways that would have bored Matthäus Schwarz. Civic magistrates gained praise for their 'long, honest' dark gowns, and both forms of apparel contrasted with padded out and puffed up aristocrats and courtiers (Fig. 94). Open abjection, however, was reserved for a few interspersed male labourers from different cultural backgrounds, who represented a primitive roughness of people who would be unable to act in accordance with communal values and oblige to leadership: a horse-carter from the Allgäu, the mountainous south-German region, with large, rude features, and equally large unstructured clothing, a big sword and big, sloppy, thoroughly ill-fitting boots (duly copied by Chrieger for Vecellio as an image of a rough 'German', shouting obscenities); a French peasant was introduced as a 'wild' and 'sour' rebel, and evidently lazy, because he went to market with hardly anything to sell, had scraggy hair, torn shoes, and untidy rags for clothes (Figs. 95–96);[82] a gypsy represented a people 'despised'.[83] Landsquenet soldiers were only represented through a reckless Turk, risking 'life and soul' for little gain.[84] A sailor from Zeeland appeared outlandish in his widely cut, simple clothes,[85] while another man from a mountainous region in Spain looked exotically rustic.[86] Swiss men, conversely, were overtly applauded for their more elaborate civilized dress, because it never changed[87] (Fig. 97).

93. (*opposite*) Hans Weigel, *Trachtenbuch*, Neapolitan woman. © The Master and Fellows of Trinity College, Cambridge

94. (*right*) Hans Weigel, *Trachtenbuch*, Saxon courtier. © The Master and Fellows of Trinity College, Cambridge

95. (*above left*) Hans Weigel, *Trachtenbuch*, French peasant. © The Master and Fellows of Trinity College, Cambridge

96. (*above right*) Hans Weigel, *Trachtenbuch*, horse-carter from Flammerspach and the Allgäu-region. © The Master and Fellows of Trinity College, Cambridge

97. (*opposite left*) Hans Weigel, *Trachtenbuch*, Swiss man. © The Master and Fellows of Trinity College, Cambridge

98. (*opposite right*) Hans Weigel, *Trachtenbuch*, a Spanish priest's concubine. © The Master and Fellows of Trinity College, Cambridge

Weigel's moral geography was thus built on selection. It privileged urban German bourgeois or patrician men and women, but also depicted other realms of the Empire—Switzerland, the Netherlands, Bohemia, Burgundy—as marked by decent respectability among the upper classes. It limited the variety of types associated with Germany—no Landsquenet was shown; no prostitute, as for Italy; no priest with concubine and son in tow, as for Spain (Fig. 98); no ethnic or religious minorities, except for the gypsy. This variety was a variety of sorts, and it principally served to project the 'varied customs' of civilized civic Germans on which a healthy Empire could rest. Weigel could emphasize such healthy regional diversity because he likewise constructed a unifying ideal of a patriotic commitment to decency among burghers. His costume book thus presented precise visual arguments in a political culture marked by debate about patriotic ideals.

Italian costume prints, too, fostered an identification of readers with people of the same status and time in cities such as Venice, obliterating differences of parish, confraternity, or occupation. Venice, in fact, was the only other European city apart from Nuremberg that from the late sixteenth century onwards published a host of books of costume and created a set of iconic images of the city. Bronwen Wilson argues that

> new formats and uses for printed visual imagery shaped the ways in which individuals interpreted the world and negotiated their place within it. Because the content and conventions deployed by printmakers overlapped with social practices, printed imagery may have helped to secure ideological values that were

HELVETII ALICVIVS AVTORITATIS
quando in publicum prodit.

LXVI.
Schweitzer in ihrer Tracht.
Ein Schweitzer wann er prangt vnd pracht/ Vnd ist an jn ein löblicher sitt/
Geht er in seiner alten Tracht.   Daß sie jr kleidung verendern nit.
X ij

SACERDOTIS HISPANICI
concubinæ vestitus.

CLX.
Also gehen die Hispanischen Priesters Weiber gekleidt.
Jn Spanien eins Priesters Weib/   Wann sie geht in jrer andacht/
Ist also klaidt an jrem Leib.   Vnd acht sich keiner andern Tracht.

central to Venetian cultural life, such as noble status, masculine virtù, religious identity, and appropriate forms of female comportment. Print was central to this claim, for it would have been the repeated identifications of sixteenth-century viewers with representations that cemented and regulated identities.[88]

Such publications were therefore more likely to affirm local, national, gender- and rank-specific identities than cosmopolitanism and universal values.[89]

Visual representations of regional peculiarities, which did not fit national stereotypes, in turn could be recategorized to avoid confusion. A most interesting example for the German lands is provided by its marginal northern province, East Frisia, which granted special privileges to its 'free' peasants and still upheld a constitution based on chieftains. From the fourteenth-century onwards, several sources commented on the distinct appearance of East Frisian men and women. They used copious silver or gold jewellery to braid the hair, for belts and other decorations, and for fastening their bright red or green clothes. This elaborate form of dress clearly informed a sense of regional pride in wealth and its more equal distribution. The reformed, highly educated, and well-travelled chieftain, Unico Manninga, chronicled this tradition in 1571 in his house-book through striking images of men and women of different rank.[90] Manninga's contacts with Heidelberg as the German centre of Calvinism ensured that the reformed collector of images, Marcus zum Lamm (1544–1606), copied several of Manninga's astonishing depictions into the costume section of his thirty-two-volume compilation of images, the *Thesaurus Picturarum*. Yet zum Lamm needed to recategorize East Frisian as Turkish:

> The people of Phrygia minor inhabit part of Asia, opposite Carthea, where Ilium lies, which is now called Troy. Today they are subject to the Turkish empire. This landscape is famous for and distinguished by its amount of gold and silver. But the people there have a wild mind and enslaving stupidity. This is why already Terence said that the Phrygian will only become wise through misfortune. Their gods are the stars, which they worship. This is why they tend to decorate their clothes with figures of cosmic signs, which they artfully engrave in gold.[91]

Each female figure was presented through the attribute 'orientalis phrygiae habitus' (Fig. 99). Manninga had represented two peasant women as particularly imposing, one with a large pitch-fork and the other far taller than a man. Zum Lamm eliminated this association with strong Amazonian women on the margins of Germany by reducing women to a standard size and look. Such visual strategies once more served to make sexual difference imaginable only in very limited ways. They instantiated gender through these acts, which for instance would make a woman recognizable as 'normal' only through a shorter body size in relation to the man she was with.

99. (*opposite*) Marcus zum Lamm, *Thesaurus Picturarum*, Frisian woman, Hs 1971, vol. 15, 179r. © Universitäts– und Landesbibliothek Darmstadt

Phrÿgiæ Orientalis foeminarum 179
habitus à ~~tergo~~. Fronte.

THE IMPACT OF FRENCH FASHION

Despite efforts to endorse patriotic commitment through everyday practices such as dress, one dilemma typically persisted for German humanists. They wanted to establish patriotic values and stereotype cultural enemies. Yet they also retained a marked taste for national self-deprecation. We might wish them to have been coherent in their views, but they simply were not. Take the Tübingen professor Nicodemus Frischlin (1547–1590) who created the intriguing figure of a French pedlar of luxury wares in his historical comedy *Julius Redivivus*. The play was first performed at the Lutheran Württemberg court at a ducal wedding in 1585. It did not relate to any specific contemporary historical event, but far more ambitiously created a historical comparison to actively revise ideas about the course of history in order to support German patriotic ideals.[92] The plot turns on Caesar's and Cicero's imagined return to sixteenth-century Germany. They are introduced to the beneficial changes that have taken place since Roman times through their contemporary equivalents. Caesar's equivalent as military leader is Hermann, and Cicero's a humanist called Eobanus. A lewd chimney sweep represents contemporary Italians, whose barbarian language Caesar and Cicero no longer understand. Instead of handling weapons, he only knows how to handle a brush. Moreover he is so black that Cicero thinks he has to be a black man from Sicily rather than a north-Italian from Milan! The chimney sweep nonetheless credibly claims to be a citizen of Milan, adding that his family comes from Bergamo and have done nothing other than sweep chimneys for generations. 'Oh dear, with what rags he is clad', Cicero exclaims.[93]

The French character is called Allobrox. Like many real pedlars of the time, he comes from the Savoy. In Frischlin's play he even is apt enough to speak Latin. French, the play explains, was no pure language, but a mixture of foreign influences, which the inhabitants of France imitated. This showed the French were masters of dissimulation and cunning. The pedlar immediately sets out to target Hermann's soldiers with his wares as they receive their pay. Allobrox praises the grace and beauty of his products, such as rapiers with silver sheaths. Hermann has asked him to provide solid, useful, and cheap iron weapons and armoury. Allobrox has none. Instead of helmets, he offers only silken head-covers to conquer beautiful women. Hermann announces that these little sensuous, immoral luxuries extinguish the wealth, warrior spirit, and manliness of Germans. When Allobrox keeps enticing him to buy one of his cloaks, Herman reiterates exactly what Tacitus had written: that Germans had only used to wear skins often tied together with merely a thorn. 'But that was a rough age', Allobrox objects, 'and the Germans had no civilisation as trade brings it.'[94] Yet Hermann maintains that Germans have only avoided becoming effeminate through their distance from Gallia and its pedlars. Allobrox now tries to market a concoction of sugar and pepper to spice up meals, only to hear Hermann explain that Asian pleasures and refinement in cooking and musical entertainment have been a further reason why German virility has declined. When Allobrox seeks to attract customers for his saffron and ginger, and promises ten nights with a whore in exchange for his bangles or fine muslin dresses, Hermann despairingly asks where great German Imperial leaders of former times found their equivalent nowadays. He orders his soldiers to beat this pedlar to death with club sticks for ruining German youth and being a pest to old Germans, corrupting their spirit for battle. Now, however, Allobrox calls upon Mercury—the despicable God of trade, who has already been introduced to the audience through his love of elaborate meals and leisurely trips to barbershops. Mercury endorses the idea that the fault lies not with the seller, but with the people who buy such fine foreign things. 'Nein', Hermann retorts, nobody would be corrupted if sellers did not enter the country. Mercury quickly counters with the longstanding argument that German men first needed to overcome their chronic insatiability for drink. Here lay the real reason for their decline.[95]

Frischlin's plays were widely used at Protestant schools and universities, as well as being performed at court. *Julius Redivivus* demonstrates how central the theme of foreign corruption through trade remained in reflections on Germany's history and future. It also shows how powerful the ideal of placing a rough warrior spirit at the centre of German identity remained. This was coupled, nonetheless, with a positive image of a successful transfer of civilized education from Italy to Germany, which had begun to rule the world with Charlemagne's accession. The play, for instance, praised the German art of making fine paper through strong, fast, and clever workmanship, and the invention of book printing, which it had taught other nations. It lauded its humanists' superior skill to truthfully translate classical literature and produce orators who were truly learned, wise, and knew how to lend weight to their words without being wordy. The chimney sweep not only served to show that Italians were the new barbarians, but also to denote the cleanliness and racial purity of Germans through their whiteness and abstinence from ethnical, non-Christian mixing in history. A whole aesthetics of German integrity unfolded once more, endorsing its preference for honest, 'weighty' speech, musical instruments, worthy entertainment, indigenous spices, sex in honourable, indigenous marriages, solid rather than precious metal, functional weapons, the courage to kill through manly strength rather than through poison or even weapons at times, to remain in a rigid hierarchy in battles and instantly repair mistakes. Finally, of course, in Hermann's view, there should be no sensuous, seductive jewellery or clothes, no grace and adornment. And yet, this play left open how exactly Germans were to manifest greater indigenous civilization in their dress. It found no reply to counter the old truth and well-honed joke that Germans were drunkards. It produced image after image of women and soldiers alike being open to seduction; and finally admitted through its very construction that their French neighbours were seeping through all imperial boundaries and easily passed through the lands of their Swiss allies to further destroy an already perilous state of German rule.

CAVALIERS

Alongside the Italians, the French had frequently been depicted as 'natural' enemies of the Germans in the early humanist writings on German liberty and had been charged with tyranny.[96] They were stereotypically criticized because they thought of Germans as simple barbarians, lacked constancy in religion and everyday morals, and were greedy for fame.[97] Aventin, as we have seen, lauded Charlemagne for his attack on Germans who took over French clothing. Yet, as Frischlin's play reflects, French influence on German elite culture grew during the later sixteenth and early seventeenth centuries. Noblemen travelled across France. Courts employed French dancing masters, the language competed with its rival Latin, and in the later sixteenth century French fashion took over from Spanish influences.

Critics during the early decades of the next century continued to criticize French fashion as pompous and at the same time ill-disciplined. Formal, high, stiff Spanish hats now turned into a fashion for broad, soft, and flat felt hats, decorated with a large display of ostrich feathers. Men grew their hair longer, and individual longer locks, *cadenettes*, fell over the face. A range of beard-styles seemed to disfigure the face. Ruffs were no longer stiff, but floppy, or could be replaced by laced collars. Casual capes and cloaks hid any clear contours, and widely cut, long breeches were often depicted tucked into equally wide galoshes. Postures thus lacked rigidity and did little to inspire fear or authority, while walking sticks for idle promenading could now seem a more important accessory than even the smallest weapon.

Across Europe, anti-French fashion satires were vigorously developed during the Thirty Years' War (1618–1648).[98] English Civil War rhetoric would likewise pit the pious Roundhead, a freeborn Englishman who demonstrated his capacity for self-control through closely cropped haircuts and simple clothing, against the royalist Cavalier with his long locks and effeminate French manners, who had clearly succumbed to Catholic tyranny.[99] The Restoration King Charles II in 1666 might well have invented the three-piece suit to boost his legitimacy when, as the diarist John Evelyn recorded, he changed 'doublet, stiff collar, and cloak, etc: into a comely vest,...resolving never to alter it, and to leave the French mode, which had hitherto obtained to our great expense and reproach'.[100]

In German broadsheets, Frenchified cavaliers and women now contrasted with the new heroic representations of simple Nordic warrior cultures fighting for the Swedish Protestant Gustav Adolf. Right at the beginning of the war, for instance, one sheet lampooned Frederick V. He had been a fashionable man with long hair and a small beard, but now sought refuge in rags. His weaver from Zeeland (in the Low Countries) brought him tender white linen to dry his tears and anxious sweat about his kingdom, as well as durable linen for a pair of fisherman's trousers. He just asked for Frederick's rags in return, to make more paper and write on his behalf.[101] Prolific printing and political opinion could thus be explicitly seen as materially dependent on fashion, the constant renewal of clothes.

From the 1620s onwards a whole series of broadsheets based on Abraham Bosse's bestselling depiction of French noblemen would satirize fashionable aristocrats as 'à la mode Monsieurs'. They introduced the term 'fashion' into the German language as 'Mode' and its images were adapted in different European countries. A broadsheet

100. *A la modo monsiers* and ladies who reject traditional German
values, 1628, broadsheet, 41.9 × 33.5 cm HAB IE 155. © Herzog
August Bibliothek Wolfenbüttel

with a copperplate engraving of four of these men from around 1628 is representative
of the genre (Fig. 100). Wolfgang Harms has argued that these broadsheets are essentially ambivalent in that they provide detailed descriptions of the clothing without
caricaturing its wearers, so that moral satire served to cover a fascination with French
fashion.[102] But it would have been difficult not to see the faces at least as increasingly
disfigured as one looked from left to right. This is particularly interesting, as the far
right figure was meant to represent the most military of all these types, and the man
next to him the most decorous, with his fine ornamental shoes and lavish garters. The
text also describes the figures from left to right, so that the figures might also appear

as a progression of increasingly degenerated personae, who had lost what, for a culture intensely interested in physiognomy, defined personhood; they visually lost face. The second line of the text describes them as wondrous animals (*Wunderthier*), and soon they turn out to follow female preferences for artificially curled locks as hairpieces. The feathers on the hat are described as foxtails, which symbolized dissimulation, and the chief advantage of the broad hat is correspondingly described as a tool to disguise changeable dispositions. Throughout the twenty verses the 'monsiers' are presented as silly fools, who refuted tradition until 'not a little drop of German blood remains/ and in all of the country neither virtue nor gentility'. A further broadsheet from around 1629 explained that the wondrous animal fashion had been born from the union of *luxus* and *superbia*, so that Germania had lost its old liberty, courage, heart, and warrior spirit, and its men had been enslaved in their language, gestures, and appearance so as to look like sumptuous women. It was now on its way to hell.[103] During the same early period of the war, another broadsheet presented 'Matresen' as the female equivalent of the monsieurs, and as whores and latter day followers of Celtis's Elsa. They copied male fashion, as it was anyway effeminate, did not care about hierarchies of rank, wore silk gowns but possessed no undergarments, and had the worst manners. They heaped so much shame on the German nation that the author only wished that German steadiness, *Redlichkeit*, might be reimplanted in youth.[104] Meanwhile, the naked Germans reappeared in a series of broadsheets, sometimes surrounded by over-decorous Frenchmen and a ready-to-wear assortment of items in shops, as consumers would increasingly have found (Fig. 101). One of them presented the most heavily effeminized man of all à-la-mode broadsheets, whose curly hairpiece reached down to his elbow. This corresponded to the softness of his hat, as well as the large fur trimmings on his sleeves and coat. His whole silhouette was so broad that he looked as if he was wearing a gown.[105] The 1630s next produced the topical figure of the *Aufschneider*, the bragging, lying man represented with a huge knife and fitted out with puffed up sleeves and breeches, and his huge exaggerated hat in boastful French fashion.[106]

Most interestingly, as we have already mentioned, all these types were now brought into contrast with a series of sheets from the 1630s onwards depicting Irish and Finnish warriors as well as Lapps fighting for Gustav Adolf. Several broadsheets deliberately used crude woodblocks to visually reinforce the warrior's simple traditional appearance. The Irish were said to wear black wool from their sheep, which were made 'in a wholly barbarian way and with caps'. They were also described as black 'like gypsies'. Their difficult climate made them hard warriors with stamina, men who needed little to subsist, happily ate roots, and could walk twenty miles a day. They were positively described as politically subservient, as they paid taxes to the English king, and equally positively as obedient to strong hierarchies. Two types of broadsheet thus depicted their leaders in colourful, heavily patterned silk clothes. Straw shoes, big beards, and shoulder-length hair in older men nonetheless supported the conventional image of self-sufficient, manly, and courageous Northerners[107] (Fig. 102). A 1632 anti-Catholic

Alla modo Meßieurs.

Der Winter ift nur bald vergangn,
Ich will wieder was news anfangn.

Wie ein Teutscher Meßieurs will gekleidt fein. Er will haben.

Immagination	Haar.	Guarderobbe	Lang fpitzige	Occafion	Stieffel.
Favorit	Zöpff.	nägel, wie der Teuffel.		Refonant	Sporen.
Patient	Bahrt.	Verficolores	Haarhauben	Necefitet	Strümpf.
Refpondent	hut.	Malcontent	Wammes.	Aggoblato	Schuch.
Colorent	Hutfchnür	Ligato	Hemmätslin.	Refpect	Schurofen.
Legation	feder.	Accordant	Lamifol.	Poenitent	Degen.
Variat	Krägen.	Al' modo	Hofen.	Commendant	Stäblin.
Multiplicat	Kragenneftl.	Reputation	Hofenbänder.	Accommodant	Gurtel.
Inter medijs	Handfchuch.	Nervofo	Hembt.	Stultifsimo	Deheroen.

101. *Alla modo Meßieurs*, with the naked German in the middle of winter and summer clothing and a parody of the German Messieurs who affected French speech, broadsheet, 1628, 26.2 × 17.1 cm HAB IE 159. © Herzog August Bibliothek Wolfenbüttel

broadsheet thus represented a Fin, Lapp, and Irish mercenary in conversation. It set out the positive potential inherent in all discussions of extreme Northern people from Tacitus through to Celtis. The Lapp first declared that everyone thought of them as insolent. But in fact they had never been so wild as to bring shame and ridicule upon their fatherland and enslave their children. He then announced that the Spanish and Italians had wanted to change German loyalty and courage and had wanted the country to become a monarchy as well. The Spanish and Italians drew on Jesuit help, and the Irishmen affirmed that their roughness could win against Tilly's cavaliers. Protestant hopes to defend German liberty against a Southern monarchical, Catholic tyranny were now linked to the original spirit of simple, rough, but steadily moral Northern cultures, led by manly warriors strong enough to resist the imposition of foreign rule.[108] A further broadsheet of 1632 similarly presented primitive Scotts and Lapps as fighters for peace and unity.[109]

Kurße
Beschreibung/ deß auß Irrland/Königl. Ma
jeſtat in Schweden ankommenten Volcks/von dero Lands
Art / Natur / Waffen vnnd Eigenschafft.

In ſolchem Habit Gehen die 800 In Stettin angekommen Irrländer
oder Irren.

Es iſt ein Starckes dauerhafftigs Volck behilfft ſich mit geringer ſpeiß hatt es nicht brodt ſo Eſſen ſie
Würtzeln, Wans auch die Notturfft erfordert Können ſie des Tages Uber die 20 Teütſcher
meilweges lauffen, haben neben Muſqueden Jhre Bogen vnd Köcher vnd lange Meſſer.

102.   Irish soldiers as true warrior tribe, contracted for the Protestant
cause by Gustav Adolf of Sweden during the Thirty Years' War,
Nuremberg 1632, 34.9 × 25.9 cm, HAB IH 225. © Herzog August
Bibliothek Wolfenbüttel

Subsequent publications returned to satires discussing the status of fashion. In 1640 a
successful broadsheet satirized the many different styles of small artful beards that men
cared about and bought as detachable parts, among them even an 'Ethiopian' one.[110] It
therefore displayed a wrong kind of prosthetic masculinity, which did not come from
true bodily virility. The moralist writer Moscherosch next created the long standing
trope of the 'German Michel', who had no identity of his own and mixed up all sorts
of foreign languages and manners, as a result of which he was hardly recognizable. The
engraving correspondingly presented such a mixture of appearances, from the baggy
Pluderhosen to a large stiff Spanish ruff and French locks.[111] Others emphasized one
extremely long ostrich feather as ridiculous ornament. A further sheet with the most extensive text part in this series yet again told the story of the naked European who could
not be painted in his costume.[112]

The last series of broadsheets from the late 1640s chose the format of a conversation between a father and his fashionable son, Ernst Teutschmann and Wendel Frantzmann. 'Frenchman' had just returned from extensive travel to try to convince his father, 'Germanman', that any serious pedagogue had to keep his child at home. Instead of any education, he had picked up no other French word than 'mossier'. All the clothing just served to attract female attention. It had effeminized him and destroyed German braveness. Wide sleeves, Frenchman explained, covered the stinking flesh of idle people. Breeches now had become far too tight and made for ridiculous displays in front of ladies. The French habit of wearing several pairs of stockings in different colours likened illustrious men to Dutch peasant maids.[113] The broadsheet therefore formed part of a wider contemporary literature warning about the negative effects of gentlemanly travel. Men might return with a mixture of diverse cultural habits rather than any useful knowledge. This conversation between Teutschmann and Frantzmann, however, soon elicited a further broadsheet, in which the comfort, utility, and relatively low expense of French male clothing was defended against the late-sixteenth-century German fashions, in which baggy breeches, for instance, used up large amounts of fabric. Frenchman was now transformed into a dashing, confident young man with a proper sword, short hair and no hat, a proper ruff, half-length mantle, and short breeches displaying elegant legs in flat shoes. 'Germanman', by contrast, was now represented as an older man wholly consumed by elaborate and artificial exaggerated Spanish fashion—a long thin Dalí-like beard, wide ruffs, enormous sleeves, and a padded peas-body belly (Fig. 103). He nonetheless stereotypically argues that his concern had been that foreign fashion had brought in all these foreign nations and caused German ruin; to which Frenchman equally stereotypically replies that Germans had caused God's anger through their permanent sins. He likes comfortable French clothing and dismisses criticism of the younger generation as merely envious.[114] This meant that he was indeed a German Frenchman.

Because so few contemporary clothes survive it is difficult to reconstruct how exactly aristocrats positioned themselves in the debate about French fashion. The Bavarian National Museum possesses clothes found in the tombs of a minor ruling Protestant family—the Lauinger Fürstengruft. Lauingen was a small residential town between Ulm and Donauwörth.[115] Here we find an exceptionally preserved broadly brimmed, dark brown felt hat with several original ostrich feathers, likewise dyed brown, which belonged to the Count Palatinate August (1582–1632) (Fig. 104). Count Palatinate Johann Friedrich (1587–1644) had been buried in a relatively simple, and at that time typically more generously cut, doublet and still relatively tightly fitted breeches (Fig. 105). Both were made of brown velvet, with some decorous borders of precious fabric, but no silk ribbons, gold buttons, or any other kind of flamboyant detail. The whole family tradition for men, as well as for women, therefore apparently was to choose brown fabrics for official daywear, which funerary clothes were meant to draw on. Other garments that survive from seventeenth-century courts tend to be the most precious ones, from significant ruling men and women in *majesté*. Most paintings commemorated high political events. Yet there

103. *Revanche*, broadsheet, 1641, sheet: 27.4 × 34.8 cm, Gü 8045, fol.73. © Universitäts-und
Landesbibliothek Darmstadt

104. (*opposite top*)   Felt-hat of Pfalzgraf August (1582–1632) with several layers of dyed ostrich
feathers, width of hat: 15cm, Inv. No. T 4107. © Bayerisches Nationalmuseum, München

105. (*opposite bottom*)   Doublet and breeches of brown velvet, Pfalzgraf Johann Friedrich
(1587–1644), Inv. No. NN 1313,1314. © Bayerisches Nationalmuseum, München

are occasional paintings of a more informal kind, which do portray Charles II in less
decorous brown daywear, talking to his gardener, or the elderly Louis XIV with his
family, though he still wore his famous red heels.[116] And all courts were under pressure to show that they were not sumptuous when there was no particular need. As in
Weigel's book, the Count Palatinate's brown presumably stood for decency, and for
an appropriate balance of approving some of contemporary fashion, in order not to
be behind the times, and yet to signal that one did not belong to the group of over-
decorous, wasteful cavaliers who did everything just to be at the height of fashion.
Here was the choice of a characteristically minor Protestant ruling dynasty, to affirm
an aesthetic of courtly civility.[117]

Conclusion

There had only ever been one type of fashion that across Europe had been associated with German men—the heavily slashed clothing 'almain' style, which Landsquenets so elaborated, but many other social groups had also adopted. When the English traveller Thomas Coryat reported on his journeys to Germany at the beginning of the seventeenth century, he mused on the etymological origins of the name Alemannia. Some said it was the surname of Hercules, who had reigned here, others that it related to Tuisco's son. Coryat himself judged that 'the best and most elegant etymology of all' derived from the words 'All man', and he explained:

> So that they which deduce the name Alemannia from All man (as Münster
> [Sebastian Münster] doth) give this reason for it, because the auncient
> Alemannes were very courageous and valiant men, yea they were All men:
> as when we in our English idiome doe commend a man for his valour, we
> sometimes say such a man is all courage, all spirit: so the Aleman quasi All
> man, he is all valour, euery part of him is viril, manly, and courageous, no jot
> effeminate, which indeed was verified by their fortitude and manly carriage in
> their warres against the Romans. Though this etymologie be passing good and
> deserueth (in my opinion) to be most approued aboue all the rest, yet I perceiue
> that Philip Melancthon speaking according to the opinion of other writers,
> affirmeth that the Aleman is so called quasi Allerleyman a Dutch word, which
> signifieth a promiscuous multitude, which heretofore conioyned themselues
> together to recouer their liberty, by reason of the tyrannical insolencies of the
> Roman Captaines.[118]

So were Germans 'all man' or 'all sorts of men'? At least to other countries, the slashed almain style had the capacity to project a sense of German men as part of a thoroughly male warrior-nation, which Celtis and others had sought to revive. However, the Irish and Lapps were increasingly regarded as the new, hardy warrior-race. The fact that it proved too difficult for Protestant elites to unambiguously identify with the Landsquenet style meant that clothing was often developed through a more or less careful adaptation of foreign customs and use of materials. The horrifying image of a composite body politic made up of 'all sorts of men' rather than an indigenous race in turn would fatally remain at the heart of moralistic German self-perceptions for centuries to come. This body politic was nude, disorientated, and divided; corrupted, it lacked form and was unable to endorse civic morality. Yet such fantasies of demise were by no means unique to Germany. By 1606, for instance, the London playwright Thomas Dekker imagined an English patriotic body politic violently dismembered by foreign dress:

An English-mans suit is like a traitors bodie that hath beene hanged, drawne, and quartered, and set up in seuerall places: the collar of his doublet and the belly in France; the wing and narrow sleeue in Italy; the short waist hangs over a Dutch botchers stalls in Utrich; his huge slopes speakes Spanish; Polonia gives him his bootes; the blocke for his head alters faster than the feltmaker can fit him.[119]

German humanists distinctly emphasized that Germany had had a great past, and nonetheless was exposed to tyranny. Smaller rulers, it seems, such as the Neuenburger Pfalzgrafen, as well as part of the elites represented in territorial estates and civic elites, as we have seen on the other hand could positively try to endorse bourgeois notions of German moral decorousness (*sittliche Zier*) as an author like Weigel advocated.[120] One simple reason for this was that they did not have the means to properly emulate the magnificence of French aristocracy, something that the Protestant Dresden court, by comparison, was often desperate to achieve. Restrained clothing, which was not at the height of foreign fashion, also strengthened a political claim for liberty as absence of foreign rule. The Prussian court under Frederick Wilhelm I in the early eighteenth century therefore rigorously rejected French fashion and endorsed old ideals of rough male militarism. At the same time—through the Renaissance and the endorsement of Celtis—the notion that civilization expressed itself through education and appropriate expressions of aesthetic refinement gradually became central to German bourgeois ideals of nationhood. This framework, as we shall later see, fitted with the new aesthetics of a softer masculinity, characterized by discerning taste rather than boldness. Herein, too, lay the invention of Weigel's book of costume with its argument that discernment could only be trained through comparison and by looking at customs across the globe. Hence patriotism did not necessarily remain insular, or merely discuss ancient literature. It looked at customs abroad.

106.   After Hans Burgkmair the Elder, *Inhabitants of the West Coast of Africa, South-East Coast of Africa and Arabia*: Augsburg: Georg Glockendon 1511, 26.0 × 188.3 cm, a procession printed from a total of five blocks, AN552924001. © The Trustees of the British Museum

CHAPTER 5

Looking at Others

The King of Cochin

In 1508, a broadsheet appeared with an account of the first German New World venture to India. The text was written by Balthasar Springer, an employee of the Welser company. Springer had accompanied the first Portuguese viceroy of India, Francisco de Almeida, in one of three German merchant ships. The broadsheet was illustrated by the prominent Augsburg artist Hans Burgkmair and afterwards copied numerous times[1] (Fig. 106). Burgkmair's original woodcuts were fittingly monumental, an almost two-metre long frieze of eight blocks, still in the possession of the Welser family. The woodcuts illustrated people of West Africa, 'Hottentots' from Algoa Bay, and people from Cochin, on the south-west coast of India.[2] They depicted people so exactly that Burgkmair probably relied on sketches made during the voyage as well as on 'Indian' artefacts owned by the Augsburg humanist Peutinger. Peutinger was full of excitement about the 'first Germans in search of India'.[3] A more extensive account of Springer's voyage was published in a twenty-eight page long booklet, printed in 1509, entitled *The Sea voyage and experience of new ships and ways to many unknown Islands and Kingdoms, which the mighty Portuguese King Emanuel has . . . conquered*.[4] It stands out among early publications of newly discovered lands for the equal weight it gives to text and images. There are thirteen woodcut illustrations by the cutter Wolfgang Traut, which accompany the text on a full page each or stretched over two pages as a pair (Fig. 107). Almost like a visual crescendo at the end, pages can be pulled out to look at a procession of the king of Cochin. One woodcut shows a distinctly European-looking tree and is repeated identically several pages later; all the other woodcuts depict human beings. The publisher therefore did not excite his audience with a sense of the exotic fauna that might be found in these lands or other natural riches that might be exploited, even though the ships had mostly been sent to bring back spices. This pamphlet rather made visually

107. Hans Burgkmair the Elder, *Inhabitants of the South-East Coast of Africa*, 1508, 22.9 × 15.4 cm, AN57103. © The Trustees of the British Museum

prominent the excitement about the depiction of people as they were described by its author as traveller. It no longer sought its market by resorting to stereotypes of far away people as pygmies or cannibals. Natives were categorized as more or less civilized, and clothing was an index of their advancement from a state of nature to human refinement. Springer thus described the 'Moors' of West Africa as wild animals, some of whom had no sense of shame and were stark naked, while others covered their intimate parts. Whereas Burgkmair's original woodcut had represented a nude black from the back, the later 1509 booklet showed him totally uncovered from the front. This, as it were, visually repeated the shamelessness described. But it curiously obscured the blackness, so that the unintended visual effect might have been to suggest the existence of white 'wild', shameless men in Africa. Otherwise, as Springer's text described, Hottentots and Indians were represented with covered genitals; some with robes and headwear. Women were portrayed as caring mothers and each one as attached to only one man, as if monogamy was a global phenomenon. Analogies made different customs intelligible: 'many', Springer explained, referring to the Bijagós islanders of Guinea in West Africa, 'have their clothes made of animal skins and hang it around themselves *in the same manner as in our lands we use short robes*'.[5]

Almost ten years after he had first depicted natives, Burgkmair returned to his drawings and woodcuts for a very different project: Emperor Maximilian I's planned 'Triumph'. This was modelled on the idea of the Roman triumph, of course, but now worked as printed visual display through an enormous quantity of woodcuts that were to be distributed to other rulers and noble families to affirm Maximilian's rule and impress audiences with his magnitude.[6] Here, Africans, Americans, and Indians were mixed together as the people from 'Calicut', all newly discovered lands. But now they were likened to animals. Children looked like monkeys, and men and women were given the same facial expressions as beasts instead of classicizing postures and expression. They were rendered in uniform apparel—simply feathers or animal skin (Fig. 108). There was no sense of their skills as warriors, or even danger as cannibals: these people of the newly discovered lands were depicted as easy to subjugate, without pride. Maximilian himself was presented as proud warrior, successfully extending his dominions across the globe, as the accompanying verses make clear:

> The Emperor in his warlike pride.
> Conquering nations far and wide,
> Has brought beneath our Empire's yoke,
> The far-off Calicuttish folk.
> Therefore we pledge him with our oath
> Lasting obedience and troth.[7]

108.   Hans Burgkmair the Elder, *Kaiser Maximilians I Triumph*, 1522, AN 19007100I. © The Trustees of the British Museum

Thus Burgkmair now created ethnic stereotypes to serve imperial propaganda. The emperor himself had given precise instructions on how he wished these far away natives to be depicted as subjected to his illustrious crown. Burgkmair's naturalistic approach and collaboration with merchants and collectors gave these exotic depictions a new authentic artistic authority.

GLOBAL WORLDS

Connections between German urban and global experiences during the sixteenth century are interesting to chart. They need to be integrated into our sense of early modern Germany.[8] Of course there were no major sustained colonizing ventures in Germany. Yet we should not underestimate the considerable interest in an expanding world to which Germans were politically connected through their emperors.[9] Maximilian I certainly entertained the vision that the Habsburgs would be emperors of a united Christian world and closely connected his dynasty to the Portuguese; Charles V was married to a Portuguese wife and was the first Old World emperor of a New World empire. He brought an entourage with 'people from almost every country' to Imperial Diets to indicate the reach of his majesty, who stayed with him in Augsburg and Nuremberg for months. Merchants, above all the Holzschuher, Paumgartner, Imhoff, Höchstätter, Gossenbrot, Fugger, and Welser companies, actively developed new trading possibilities through their representatives in Lisbon and Antwerp. It has even been argued recently that the New World typically 'functioned as a territory for the application of German expertise' rather than a place that signalled a culture that was radically different.[10] From Lisbon, a well-connected Bohemian resident called Valentim Fernandes provided accounts of new voyages for the Augsburg humanist Konrad Peutinger. Peutinger was related to the Welser family and became an early defender of the value of profit-seeking selfishness for the commonweal rather than economic state policies against monopolies.[11] Fernandes also sent exotic artefacts and the drawing of a rhinoceros with enchained front legs, which Dürer cleverly turned into a bestselling woodcut in 1515. Around the years 1491–1494, the Nuremberg humanist, physician, and cosmographer Hieronymus Münzer had supported Martin Behaim in the production of the first ever globe. It took the Nuremberg expert illuminist Georg Glockenden fifteen weeks to lovingly cover the globe with richly detailed drawings of mineral resources, animals, nomads in tents, and small Indian city views.[12] Münzer had travelled to Portugal and Spain, where he saw African goods and Moors, and was overwhelmed by the beauty of the Alhambra. Behaim passed on to him written accounts of the discovery of Guinea.[13] Whereas reports about pilgrimages to the Holy Land dominated the emerging print market literature on foreign lands during the fifteenth century, and like the celebrated book of the Nuremberg pilgrim Bernhard von Breydenbach (1486) even began to include large fold-out woodcuts of cities as well as insert depictions of Arabs and Greeks, sixteenth-century Germans soon proved to be most interested in reports about Africa and America.[14] Such manuscripts, books, globes, maps, exotic objects, and small animals, such as Peutinger's talking parrot from India, commonly became part of sixteenth-century scholarly and merchant households. In Nuremberg, the humanist Willibald Pirckheimer as early as 1508 encouraged the publication in his city of the Italian compilation of different accounts of 'newly discovered lands' by Francesco da Montalboddo, first published in 1507. There was more interest in these subjects than in literature about the advance of the Turks. Throughout the century, new travel reports were quickly published in German, and found their place in the libraries of the elites.

The discoveries, travelling, and an adaptable print market in these ways reinvigorated the Renaissance fascination with cultures and their customs. Some scholars at first remained sceptical about travellers' 'rumours' of uncivilized overseas people. A German ethnographic author of enduring European significance was Johannes Boemus, a humanist from Franconia, who from 1508 had lived as a priest and member of the *Deutschherren* order in Ulm.[15] He wrote his encompassing treatise about the 'manners, laws and customs of all people, collected from many illustrious authors and divided into three books; Africa, Asia and Europe' between 1517–1520. This summed up all printed ethnographical knowledge up to Pius II, and was inspired by a humanist ethos of observant description in the tradition of Herodotus. It proved a publishing success: up to 1620 there were at least forty-two European editions. Boemus's publisher was Sigismund Grimm, an Augsburg medical doctor and printer, who had caught his attention through the recent publication of two further ethnographic treatises. One was the first contemporary description of people and customs in north-eastern Europe and Russia, published in Latin and German, and prepared for publication by the Dominican Johann Eck. The other was an edition of the first curious, rather than self-interested, world traveller Varthema, which had first been published in Rome in 1510. In Basle, the prominent reformer Simon Grynaeus soon published his compilation of Latin texts on new discoveries in 1532, which appeared in a German translation shortly after.[16] In 1534, the radical Protestant humanist Sebastian Franck published his *Weltbuch* or *Book of the World: Mirror and Image of the whole Earth*. It described for the first time all continents of the world in the German vernacular, and positively evaluated all diversity as part of divine creation. The cosmographer Sebastian Münster was in constant touch with south German humanists and city councillors all over Europe to produce and constantly update his cosmographic writings, first published in 1544, and also tried to get sent correct city maps.[17] Sigismund von Herberstein's monumental description of Moscovy followed in 1549. By 1550, a total of 146 German vernacular print items had appeared on the subject of America and thirty-eight on Brazil.[18]

All these activities document that a far more developed interest in local cultures, as well as the description of human customs in their global variety, entered the horizon of many German intellectuals, merchants, officials, doctors and pharmacists, publishers, map- and instrument-makers, as well as artists. Elite libraries in merchant cities were designed to facilitate the coming together of different kinds of knowledge and ideas from local people and foreign visitors, travellers to distant lands, academics, publishers, artists, or specialized instrument makers, such as decorative clock- as well as compass-makers, herbalists, pharmacists, and cooks, not least to attract prospective patrons. Elite men and women, moreover, were interested in the medical properties of exotic plants and in their beauty, as patrician town and courtly gardens were enriched with exotic fauna that seemed to implant more paradisiacal splendour than German radishes could muster. Knowledge about these plants was collected in a series of pioneering publications as well as in private alba. Yet there were also explicit defences of German home-grown common flowers, simple herbs, spices, and the particular benefits of herbal medicines made from indigenous plants.[19] New discoveries hence further stimulated debates about the qualities of the *teutsch*, no longer in contrast just to the *welsch*, but to everywhere else. Cooking changed, as spices became more widely available. Splendid stones and pearls were traded from Goa via Lisbon to Venice and from Venice to Frankfurt and Leipzig fairs. They were more extensively incorporated into jewellery worn by men and women. Collections of exotic objects were cultivated through correspondence and contacts reaching across Europe, and might include the finest white cotton shirts with delicate folds and embroideries from Ceylon. How could the European expansion further influence ways in which appearances were registered as socio-cultural phenomenon at this time? To what extent did people change their sense of the world they lived in?

Dürer in Antwerp

The elder Dürer provides a fascinating case study. Aged 49, Dürer chose to travel to Flanders many years after his friend Celtis had died, and just as Martin Luther rose to the peak of his prominence before the Diet of Worms in 1521. These were changing times. Flanders—or Belgium, as we know it today—was the central European node of an emerging world system, dominated by Iberia rather than the Mediterranean world of trade. It belonged to the Holy Roman Empire, while Bruges was the seat of the Habsburg House of Burgundy. Antwerp was burgeoning with business possibilities. German merchants from the 1510s onwards keenly took copper and cloth to Antwerp to receive sugar, spice, and dye-stuff from India, São Tomé, Madeira, or Brazil, as well as English wool and cloth. They made up 'the vast majority' of foreigners operating here, loading up impressive wooden carts and shipping most of the overseas luxury products traded by the Portuguese and Spanish as well as the English cloth on to Germany, and from there onto other central European locations.[20] Even if Germans did not have their own ships engaged in colonial trade, its merchants were absolutely crucial to new colonial ventures in bringing in copper and silver currencies from mining areas under their control as well as selling on these global wares. By the early 1540s the highest value of shipments went to Leipzig, followed by Nuremberg, Frankfurt, and Augsburg. Taken together, the most highly valued goods went to the close south-German cities Nuremberg and Augsburg, despite the fact that neither of these had fairs. Here, local merchants had quickly established themselves to distribute Atlantic goods regionally, say to the Franconian Nördlingen fair, as well as supra-regionally.[21]

Dürer went to Antwerp in 1520/1 as all this was happening. He wanted to be in this exciting and cosmopolitan commercial city of about 55,000 inhabitants, secure his financial affairs after Maximilian's death, find other wealthy patrons, see spectacles, all sorts of people, houses, go out for meals, taste delicatessen, such as marinated lemons, pistachios, sugary sweets, drink with journeymen, go to dinners and feasts, gamble a few times, see things, travel around, and observe others (Fig. 109). A unique art market established itself in this city; since 1460 you could go to galleries at the market of the Church of Our Lady and shop for paintings alongside frames, tapestries, books, and a whole range of further decorative items. This two-storey structure was known as the *pand*. Such new merchandising techniques helped the rise of independent artists, who did not work for one particular court, but cultivated a range of clients as well as producing uncommissioned work, which they cleverly marketed. By the 1560s, around 300 painters and sculptors alone had settled here, and much of their output supplied trans-atlantic markets.[22] Paintings, etchings, and woodcuts as we have seen, were modestly priced in comparison to luxury commodities, something wealthier clients could easily pick up in passing. Dürer recorded making a very large number of portraits during his trip, including one of a goldsmith's journeyman, and these typically cost one florin,

109.   Albrecht Dürer, *Irish warriors and peasants*, 1521, pen and watercolour drawing, 21.0 × 28.2 cm. © bpk – Kupferstichkabinett, Berlin

whereas he asked eight florins for a portrait of a wealthy client, sold a good St Veronica face in oil for twelve florins, and asked ten florins for complete architectural drawings of a private house a client wanted to build. Pirckheimer's grandson, Willibald Imhoff, in 1573 owned paintings by Dürer that valued four florins at the most. One of Lucas Cranach Lucretias's was worth a mere two and a half florins. By contrast, one of Imhoff's gowns (*Schaube*) lined with good marten fur was worth eighty-one florins; while two pairs of woollen and one pair of leather hose still valued five florins.[23]

Luckily, Dürer kept a diary from his Antwerp stay. He sought pigments to make his colours, and bought a mere ounce of good ultramarine blue through the sale of artwork valuing twelve ducats. He also knew where to get red dye from bricks for a woollen shirt he had bought. Meanwhile, he received gifts or payments in kind of the many luxury cloths that were traded in Antwerp—velvet, 'printed Turkish cloth', 'two cloths from Calcutta, one of them silk', 'the best Brabantian black Atlas'.[24] Dürer evidently loved to shop for luxury gifts when he could afford to do so, just like Matthäus Schwarz's friends did. Thus in March 1521, we find Dürer shopping in Antwerp and spending over three florins on five silk girdles, as well as more than five florins on precious silk cloth, and further money on trimmings and several pairs of 'good' gloves for women. The list goes on: there was a large beret for his close friend, the humanist Pirckheimer, a partlet in deep red dye for another male friend and civic councillor, and two bags for two further women. Finally he bought a decorated scarlet beret for a three-year-old son of friends of his; and we will find further evidence in a following chapter that boys were cultivated to turn into fashion consumers through items of this kind surprisingly early on in their lives.[25] The women he chose gifts for were female kin of his male friends—their wives, sisters, or daughters. Luxury clothes and accessories in these ways could make for central relational gifts, helping friends to decorate and display themselves as esteemed, beautiful, and special. They infused exchanges with emotion.

Dürer was deeply fascinated by everything that came from the newly discovered Atlantic worlds.[26] In one famous passage of his diary he reported on how at Brussels he saw what the 'king', Charles V (who was only crowned as emperor by the pope in 1530), had received from the 'new golden land' of Mexico, which Cortès had just conquered (1519–1521). The passage commented on a large golden sun, a silver moon, much armoury, 'strange clothing', and bedlinen,

> and all sorts of wonderful things for different kinds of use, which is much nicer
> to see than objects of mere wonder (*wunderding*). These things were all precious,
> for one valued them around one hundred thousand florins. And I have not
> seen anything in my whole life which pleased my heart as much. Because I saw
> in them wonderful artificial things (*wunderlich künstlich ding*) and have been
> amazed by the subtle ingenuity of the people in foreign lands.[27]

There was no sense of natural Western, let alone German, supremacy in this. To see these amazing objects seemed to subvert rather than create a sense of mastery over the world. Dürer moreover clearly distinguished between curious objects and objects of use.

By choosing the word *Staunen* he purposefully articulated his response as knowledgeable, awesome wonder and informed esteem, rather than credulous curiosity. This, too, affirms how much he valued subtlety and ingenuity in the making of beautiful things, the decorative interacting with the practical needs of life lived. Equally importantly, he saw the royal animal garden in Brussels, with lions and baboons. One of Dürer's closest acquaintances in Antwerp was the Portuguese factor Rui Fernandes d'Almada, who supplied him and his wife with precious exotic gifts, such as coral, Indian nuts, parrots, Brazilian feathers, the shield of a turtle, or parts of a fish. Dürer built up his own small cabinet of curiosities.[28] Precious natural objects for him were testimony to the marvellous artistry of an encompassing nature crafted by God, which humans of outstanding talent could observe and gain knowledge of through imitation.[29] Human variety could then be regarded as part of natural variety that could only be understood if it was well observed and visualized. For this, an artist had to be in a bodily relationship with a person or object, instead of using descriptions and attributes, as Burgkmair had done. This implied encountering people from other lands and making it plausible to them or their patrons that they should be depicted. In Antwerp, Dürer produced the first European drawing of a female black slave who had received the name Katherina and was servant of another Portuguese factor (Fig. 110). His format was a close up portrait drawing of her face and exotic headdress. It revealed his particular interest in indigenous dress and physiognomy. This makes it even more remarkable that despite his obvious commanding power Dürer did not force the twenty-two-year-old woman to look at him and position her head upright, thereby respecting and rendering her sense of exposure to the artist's eye. For contemporaries, this would have conveyed a positive sense of natural female modesty, which was not usually associated with women, let alone 'savage' ones. Dürer also never used the drawing in any other way, reworking it into mythological or biblical scenery, or making a woodcut of it, as with the rhinoceros. He left it as a dignified rendering of an enslaved woman uncomfortable to look at him, and perhaps at herself through Dürer's eyes.

Dürer also continued his interest in costume studies during this period. These, as the previous chapter mentioned, had initially been sparked off during his Venetian stay by the local master painter Giovanni Bellini's naturalistic drawings of people he had met during his extended stay in Ottoman Istanbul, most of which Dürer faithfully copied.[30] John Elliott has argued that Europeans either assimilated American artistic creations into pre-existing patterns, or categorized them simply as 'curious'. But Dürer's drawings, as much as the objects he collected, were never destined to become 'mute witnesses to the alien customs of non-European man'.[31] The objects vigorously made him and others cherish the diversity of God's creation. Dürer's call for a reform of German society after his experiences in Flanders were even articulated through lamenting the impossibility of living together in a Christian world globally conceived, rather than through criticisms of Rome and a concurrent praise of indigenous Germanness. For him, all people on earth had been created by God and could be united in their diversity. This unity was not to be achieved through Crusade, conquest, and conversion. There needed to be institutional

110. Albrecht Dürer, *Katherina aged 20*, drawing 1521, Dis. 1060 E. © Florence, Gabinetto Disegni e Stampe degli Uffizi (Su concessione del Ministerio per i beni e le Attività Culturali)

change in the church and in the moral conduct of Europeans. Thus, when Dürer heard a false rumour that Luther had died, he broke out into intense lament. Then his writing turned into a prayer. It beseeched God to bring together Roman Christians, Indians, people from Muscovy, Russians, and Greeks, who had been torn apart through papal meanness and lies. If only we lived in a Christian manner, Dürer pleaded, then 'Turks, pagans and people from Calicut would want to belong to us and become Christian'.[32] His awareness of non-European societies and his respect for their craftwork thus reinforced Dürer's criticism of his own society. It led to an inclusive view of humankind. This stood in marked difference to the humanist patriotic concerns, which had been so vital more than a decade ago for Celtis, and had sought to invent Germans as an indigenous race to which non-Germans could not in any sense belong. Protestant ideas were just about to emerge as a major force within the community Dürer was now part of. The Nuremberg city scribe Lazarus Spengler was at the forefront of the Reformation, a nearby neighbour of Dürer's and among his very closest friends.

There is one further dimension that gives us a sense of how an awareness of human variedness influenced Dürer's religious ideas and was important in his thought. Dürer's *Lesson in Measurement* was first published in 1525, and his *Four Books on Human Proportion* posthumously in 1528. These writings dealt with the representation of the human body, which Dürer did not seek to capture through an idealized abstract construction of beauty, as in Italian art, but once more through a greater respect for the variedness God had created:

> Once and for all the Creator has made men as they should be, and I hold that
> the true shapeliness and beauty is inherent in the mass of all men; to him who
> can properly extract this I will give more credence than to him who wants
> to establish a newly thought-up proportion in which human beings have had
> no share.[33]

Beauty depended on the harmony of parts of the body, but was also conceived as contextual—it depended on the individual person and his or her milieu, or the theme to be illustrated. For Dürer, Pamela Smith sums up, art as such came to 'rest on a knowledge of the variety and particularity of matter and nature'.[34] Around 1512, Dürer had already chosen to illustrate Psalm 24.1 'The earth is the Lord's and the fullness thereof; the world and they that dwell therein' for Maximilian's Book of Hours with a strikingly naturalistic Brazilian Tupinamba warrior.[35] After Maximilian's death it became harder for Protestants to laud the Catholic Charles V as emperor over this diverse universe created by God. An appreciation of diversity in some people could further an impulse towards naturalistic and ethnographic observation, rather than any judgemental representation of people and their practices. We know that Dürer's drawings were collected, or copied in the sixteenth century. They could be key diplomatic gifts and showpieces, some travelling as far away as Goa, while Nuremberg citizens frequently copied them into alba. They intensely informed local artistic memory.

CHRISTOPH WEIDITZ

When Dürer's treatise on the principles of proportion was published, just after he had died, a religious settlement was not yet in sight. Just one year later, in 1529, an artist in his late twenties set off from Augsburg to see the Holy Roman Emperor, Charles V. His name was Christoph Weiditz (1500–1559). Weiditz had been trained as a form-cutter and sculptor. Having arrived from his native Strasbourg in 1526, Weiditz had met Augsburg artists like Narziss Renner, who, we remember, worked for Matthäus Schwarz. They shared an interest in providing a vivid sense of people through portraiture. Weiditz started making portrait medals. This was reasonably lucrative business. Within two years, he executed more than twenty medals of Augsburg burghers, not least of new Protestant leaders seeking to make an impression. Weiditz himself called them masterpieces, and they were.[36] Augsburg goldsmiths then seem to have challenged Weiditz's right to make medals, because he had not been formally trained. To safeguard his position, Weiditz travelled all the way to Castile to obtain the emperor's patronage and from there accompanied Charles V back to the momentous 1530 Diet of Augsburg and to the Netherlands. During the years of his voyage he continued making medals of important or wealthy figures. But, more surprisingly, he also produced no less than 154 exceptional watercoloured pen-drawings of ordinary people he saw, which he executed on heavy, cardboard-like paper. They were put into a sequence, as well as cropped and bound together by a later owner.[37] This manuscript is known as the Weiditz Book of Costumes, his *Trachtenbuch*, even though he did not give it that title. These sheets were no sketchbook to prepare for a celebration of Charles's ambition as a new Caesar. They are an unparalleled example of early European ethnographic observation. Weiditz depicted Indians recently brought back by Hernan Cortès, as well as black slaves and slaves of Muslim origin; he pictured female criminals and Christianized Moorish inhabitants of Granada. He seems to have mostly stayed in Castile. Hence we can not be sure that he drew his numerous plates of Moriscos from life, as well as his vivid series of Basque people. But no other model for these drawings has been identified, and they clearly cohere with his uniquely observant interest in people across society.

Detailed interest in the naturalistic depiction of those who were not able to commission portraits had begun in the late thirteenth century. Well-known examples are depictions of peasants and harvest workers in the Books of Hours, especially those by the Limburg brothers for the duc de Berry. This naturalism evidently had to focus much on appearances. So the Limburg brothers, for instance, would depict a peasant ploughing in March with a patched up and worn grey working shift to protect the nice blue one he wore underneath. In these works, however, there still operated a clear framework of who could be represented. Peasants and other types of labourers, such as woodcutters, typically played their part in a feudal story about the land or the forests which belonged to a lord and were well-managed. This story essentially cohered with a patron's interest and taste. It was a political iconography in a 'political landscape'.[38]

Weiditz's undertaking by contrast stood in the tradition of Dürer's ethnographic costume studies. It was most likely intended as a personal manuscript he could show to others who were interested, and certainly was not commissioned by a patron. All images measured 15 × 20 cm, were carefully executed, but followed his own fascinations as traveller. At the end he set out some comparisons of some New World appearances with former German fashion, and current Viennese, English, Irish, Italian, and Portuguese. In his images of Spanish society, Weiditz did not attempt to be systematic in coverage or to depict the orders of society in terms of a taxonomy relating to hierarchies of rank. Startlingly there appeared only two clerics. Both of them were rich prelates shown almost critically—with the servant boy they required to hold their robe when they walked and to hold their slippers when they rode! Religious orders did not figure. Two penitents were drawn, as were those going to church. Above all, it seems that Weiditz was fascinated by costume as part of a practice of life. Weiditz's gaze was not judgemental and looked for no narrative. As an artisan artist, Weiditz seems to have observed and copied, above all, how people 'did' things and 'were' in particular situations and environments, the physical and material expression of their social being and life tasks. It was this ability to observe and imitate that would give one a sense of a society, rather than abstract reasoning about its alleged orders and institutions. He particularly sought out and delighted in skilful inventiveness. Weiditz's plates uniquely show what it could mean 500 years ago to respectfully look at others. This is all the more interesting since he depicted an ethnically mixed society, which the Muslim conquest of Spain and the Spanish conquest of the Americas had produced, as well as different regional environments across the Spanish lands.

There are three sections that most clearly bear this out. First, and most famously, thirteen images depicted American 'Indians'; second, another thirteen plates depicted Moriscos; and finally twenty sheets represented Basque people. Taken together, these parts presented nearly a third of all the images Weiditz made. What impressed Weiditz about the 'Indians', first of all, was the way in which they skilfully used their bodies to play, and that the manner in which they used their hands when they played with small pieces of stone and wood was identical to Italians. Rather than trying to see them as different, he was therefore intent to point out similarities with European 'civilized' people. He depicted a performer's skill in using his feet to throw a wooden block in the air and catch it—and this process was shown in three stages, so as to convey it fully and facilitate an appreciation of how this was done, rather than for mere amusement (Fig. 111). This proto-cinematic sequencing of the movement helped onlookers to imagine the scene. An Indian woman was depicted in an elaborate feather dress, which covered most of her body (Fig. 112). He showed several Aztec men in feather dress and with precious stones in their faces. A man wearing a shift of feathers and jewellery was described as noble; he also held a parrot and an elaborate sunshade/sign. Another man held a wooden drinking jug brought from the Americas—this represented their skill of woodturning. Finally, Weiditz represented an Indian warrior, to emphasize the physical muscularity, endurance, and skill of those who 'walk for two thousand miles, where one finds gold in the water'.

111. (*left*)   Christoph Weiditz, *Indian performance with a wooden block (second phase)*, 15 × 20 cm, Inv.No. HS 22474, 6v. © Germanisches Nationalmuseum, Nürnberg

112. (*right*)   Christoph Weiditz, *Manner of Dress of Indian women*, Inv.No. HS 22474, 1e . © Germanisches Nationalmuseum, Nürnberg

In Granada, we see how Morisco men picked up bread loaves from local houses to be baked in communal ovens; how a woman with the customary breeches and loose shirt, swept in front of her house, went spinning, walked about with her daughter, and travelled with her child on a horse (Figs. 113–114). Different types of dresses worn at home and on the streets were drawn—one that covered a woman except for her eyes, and another style where the face was revealed. Finally, a Morisco dance was depicted with different instruments. Morisco people were thus rendered in thoroughly human terms—in their amusements and occupations, the women with their children. Weiditz did not depict an exotic culture in one homogenous outfit, but in various clothes: those worn indoors and outdoors, those of different classes, ordinary and noble (*edel*). This view was not attempting to stereotype—it provided an insight into the cultural varied-ness of ways-of-doing-things within the ethnically mixed cultures of Europe. It soon was to be historical, since Spanish kings and bishops first insisted that Moriscos abandon all their customs before undertaking the ethnic cleansing of Spain in 1609. Weiditz docu-mented the existence of a distinctive Muslim culture within the Habsburg Empire, but nonetheless viewed them as one group among others.

The third extensive section, on Basque people, depicted a differentiation in dress ac-cording to occupation (i.e. warrior and peasant), age (i.e. young and old woman going to church), marital status, wealth (i.e. the rich), dress at festivities and amusements, locale

113. (*left*) Christoph Weiditz, *Morisco woman sweeping*, Inv.No. HS 22474, 102r. © Germanisches Nationalmuseum, Nürnberg

114. (*right*) Christoph Weiditz, *Morisco man*, Inv.No. HS 22474, 104r. © Germanisches Nationalmuseum, Nürnberg

and region (in the mountains, in Santa Maria, at the frontier to France) and, most interesting of all, according to individual manner and imagination. It was women's stimulating and pleasing manner and 'fantasy' that was explicitly honoured.[39] One might wonder whether there was a political message buried in this, as Basque people conducted their political lives free from any overlord. German travellers typically remarked on the ways in which women arranged their hair and the sheer diversity of local customs invented in every village. The Spanish kings allegedly had given women the right to dress in lots of ways as they pleased. 'There is no village so small', Count Friedrich II of the Palatinate would comment later in the century, 'that they don't think of something bizarre'.[40] Yet Weiditz thought this was fascinating. So equally, rather than stereotyping or ridiculing rustic people as uncivilized, Weiditz once more portrayed people ecologically—as part of a place, and a situation in life, customs, and thus as cultural creators. Those living on the Franco–Spanish border looked different from women in the mountains. Such seemingly minute observations had potentially large implications for those looking at his drawings and deducing some sense of Europe's inhabitants from them. Weiditz's remarkable message was that if they were allowed to develop, dress as well as hairstyles became part of individual fashion and human expression, and would renew themselves even within one cultural group (Figs. 115–116). You did not have to be wealthy to do this. Everyone had creative potential through engaging with matter. A free society did have the option

115. (*left*)   Christoph Weiditz, *Galician woman going to the spinning-bee*, Inv.No. HS 22474, 18v. © Germanisches Nationalmuseum, Nürnberg

116. (*right*)   Christoph Weiditz, *Castilian peasant going to the market*, Inv.No. HS 22474, 19v. © Germanisches Nationalmuseum, Nürnberg

to cherish and constantly develop this creative diversity. Villagers thus for once were not thought to be at the end of a civilizing process defined by learning, elite teaching, or even guilded artisanal craft competence. Apparently intrigued by the mundane everyday world of the women and men that he observed, Weiditz could even become intensely interested in everyday embodied practices like threshing corn or ploughing fields in Castile with particular tools, or how two Dutch maids mixed dough.

'Sold Moors' were not treated in a separate section, but once more it is noteworthy that Weiditz was attentive to different possibilities of their service. He depicted an African army drummer employed for Imperial entries, in a splendid livery and with a large gold earring and white feather on a blue hat, as well as a black man in torn breeches. As Weiditz noted, he had once tried to escape, and was now bent over by the weight of the wine-sacks he had to carry. He further depicted a couple of black slaves putting drinking water into barrels for ships, with distinctive caps and simple clothes (Fig. 117). Weiditz's captions once more bear out that he was interested in how different types of labour were performed and, in this case, how the use of labour through the ownership of a person was politically embedded. There is no sense that Weiditz depicted blacks so as to 'define whiteness', or to 'stereotype blacks in opposition to Renaissance standards and ideals'.[41]

While Weiditz was on his voyages, his well-known brother, Hans, in whose Strasbourg workshop he had partly grown up, busily produced watercolours and woodcuts for the first naturalistic herbal, which depicted plants drawn from life in a perfect imitation of nature, as its title proclaimed: *Herbarum vivae eicones ad naturae imitationem*.[42] Hans noted details

117. *Slaves in Barcelona taking in water for ships*, Inv. No. HS 22474, 74rv. © Germanisches Nationalmuseum, Nürnberg

about the most common local plants and precisely when the image had been made. This mode of observation from real life was inspired by the initial Protestant questioning of established ideas of the high and the low, the mundane and the elevated, social hierarchies. For the Weiditz brothers it could lead to an emphasis on context over myth or rigid classifications, as well as reinforce detailed curiosity about the mundane.

HIERONYMUS KÖLER

Luther, as we have already seen, thought of merchant firms as fatally motivated by greed. There was little curiosity in Luther himself about non-European encounters. After Charles V in 1521 had mandated the Imperial ban against him, Luther would never again be able to participate at splendid international Imperial diets for fear of his life, or travel outside Saxony and Thuringia. Yet the first generation of young Protestants in the dynamic urban trading centres of Germany could explore these new worlds. Luther, we remind ourselves, had contributed to an interest in appearances as a cultural phenomenon through attacking the powerful symbolic fictions the Catholic church established through dress.

Hieronymus Köler provides a fascinating example of such a young Lutheran man. As we have seen, this Nuremberg tailor's son had studied in Wittenberg, but then went to Lisbon, Seville, and across the seas in the late 1530s. Köler went despite the fact that he was unable to speak Latin and hence chiefly relied on building up networks of German contacts during his travels. It proved a daunting, adventurous time. He later produced a richly illuminated manuscript of his experiences. Clothes for a long time provided an important part of his account of himself and even of the temptations of travels to unknown lands.

'While I was young I had lovely long yellow hair, longer than my shoulders', Köler's first entry on his appearance ran, as he proudly described his 'Hungarian'-style outfit with a black robe and a red beret with a feather as well as a red leather schoolbag worn on his back.[43] When he was a little older, he served a local juryman of the chamber-court, carrying his books in a sack behind him in high-heeled shoes. So in Köler's one hand there would be this big, black sack, in the other a grey hat with a nice cord; his hair now looking merely 'common, bad, yellow'. He wore red hose and a long grey riding gown with tight arms and brightly painted Burgundian emblems of the Habsburg dynasty—flames and the diagonally slashed Andrews-cross.[44] Köler next walked to Rome on his Italian travels with shorn hair and a Spanish look: black hose and doublet, a short Spanish mantle, and cut leather shoes.[45] When he returned to Nuremberg in 1529, he worked for a merchant. On ordinary weekdays he would wear green hose, high shoes, and a woollen grey robe with some velvet trims, and a shorn head. Yet on feast-days, Köler strikingly revealed, he would be seen with a 'large, broad yellow beard, a dark brown woollen coat with velvet trimming, white hose, and fine shoes'.[46] So the beard clearly continued to be an accessory he put on in a particular colour at particular times during his youth to create a distinct public visibility.[47] Many recipes for colouring hair black, grey, white, or blond circulated in this period as in the Middle Ages. These would even be printed in seventeenth-century Protestant manuals for good house-fathers and -mothers, without specifying that it might be more obvious for women to use them. There were further recipes about how to make hair shine like jewellery, make it grow, wash it, and keep it clean. The most important question was how one might prevent it from falling out, which was regarded as dishonouring and dangerous, as it took off the hair's natural protective shield from vapours and the like. All these recipes formed part of a practice of domestic 'medicine'.[48] Köler, meanwhile, in his next position wore his beard black and cropped, at Wittenberg large and black, as we have seen. Afterwards, back again in Nuremberg as a twenty-four-year-old 'honourable citizen's son', he would return to his 'yellow' beard, but this time cropped rather than large.[49] His family was now thinking about arranging his marriage. But Köler wished to travel once again. Just like Dürer, he went to the new hub of Antwerp, but then crossed the Atlantic to Lisbon. He revelled in the richness of plants and animals created by God for the sea, which sailors knew to be indescribable.[50]

Lisbon ranked among the largest European cities during this time. Its chief humanist, Damião de Góis, set out the unbelievable opulence gained from the Atlantic expansion during preceding decades in a brief treatise published in 1554. Near the fish- and sweet-market with its fishmongers, confectioners, greengrocers, butchers, bakers, candymakers, innkeepers, and fowl-sellers stood the 'house of India', 'executed in marvellous style and replete with the abundant spoils and plunderings from many nations and peoples', de Góis wrote.[51] In his opinion, *Casa da India* was too literal a name,

> it might sooner be called an opulent emporium, due to its aromas, pearls, rubies, emeralds, and other precious stones brought to us from India year after year; or perhaps a grand depository of gold and silver, whether in bars or in fashioned forms.[52]

This rhetoric was meant to provide a sensory experience of these new treasures one could not only look at, but touch:

> There stand patent, for whoever wishes to admire them, innumerable compartments arranged with an artful cleverness, overflowing with such a great abundance of those treasures that—word of honour!—it would surpass one's capacity to believe, if they did not leap before the eyes of all, and if we could not touch them with our own hands.[53]

Apart from precious metals, stones, and spices there were the new human possessions. De Góis did describe the slaves who marched up from their ships through the port; this was an enchained abundance. Köler saw 'Moors' from St Tomé being led through the streets and being sold, 'in this city of more than three times hundred thousand people', he recorded, 'are two thirds of Moors'.[54] He did not feel like offering his services to anyone here after a while, not even to the king. Instead, he walked on to Seville, to meet 'Segnor' Lazerus Nürnberger, a German merchant who had first traded with India via Lisbon but now had moved his base to the Spanish Atlantic. Nürnberger treated Köler like his own son, only to make it clear that he wished him to go to the newly discovered lands, 3,000 miles from Seville. Nürnberger obviously knew about Pizzaro's men who had conquered Peru just a few years earlier, between 1531 and 1533. In 1528, Charles V had made the Welser merchants governors of Venezuela, and their representatives were in Seville desperately trying to find reliable officeholders to conscientiously govern that land.[55] Over a meal, two members of the Welser company got Köler to agree to be among the 600 men on their Armada to Venezuela for twice the usual salary. They promised that he would be a judge 'in their India', which Charles V had granted to them. He need only serve them just on this trip, and thereafter would not be indebted to them in any way.[56] Köler agreed and helped to oversee the preparations for this journey over several months. Yet he later uneasily noted in his account how priests and different kinds of monks had come on board with their 'deceptive things', such as candles or vestments, to convert the 'poor, naked people and increase Christianity, yes, to get their gold and silver'.[57]

Hundreds of men were now fitted out in an awesome uniform, their helmets reminiscent of ancient Romans, of solid make and with beautiful tying laces ('points'). Köler described that he, of course, was at the front: 'with a shaved head, a broad black beard, a black beret with a beautiful big white feather, a red, brave warrior robe from Milan, with a broad, round facing and two black trims, which helped against the big waves and sea water, but also against the heat of the sun'. He wore black slashed hose and pointed slashed shoes.[58] Köler, the Protestant, took pride in the procession of all the men in the red and white colours of the Welser company, and the red, white, and blue colours with Burgundian crosses of Charles V, as they marched to a convent where they were consecrated (Fig. 118). This visual display attracted his most enthusiastic comments, replete with a sense of the grandeur of valiant, brave, conquering clothes and of extending an empire as the Romans had sought to do. There were a number of young Germans on board—a printer and a barber from Augsburg, others who were experienced in the mining trade, and a diamond cutter too. A strong-bodied 'Turk' from Fez who admirably controlled his bow and arrow entertained everyone.

Even so, Köler's doubts soon prevailed. There were too many languages spoken on board. Nobody understood each other when they needed to. He heard of the illnesses that befell people who had settled in these countries, of poor food and dirty water. Moreover, 'poor people are surprised, strangled and what is theirs is taken, just because of some ludicrous gold and silver. Afterwards one wants to say that one needed to convert these people with the force of the sword and make them obedient before the Emperor to spread Christianity, but I think that there will be a far more difficult way to account for everything before God.' Köler had decided to return to Europe before the ship had even landed in Venezuela. 'Only money rules the world', he now noted with total disaffection, concluding that those who were rich and wanted still more would only end their lives in misery.[59] He returned to Nuremberg in 1536, married, had children and held several significant offices, most notably as a civic judge. Up to the end of his life in 1573, Köler never again described how he dressed or what he looked like.

The Welser company, meanwhile, would invest 100,000 ducats and travel 20,000 kilometres inland to find the legendary 'El Dorado' as well as hunt for slaves, rather than investing in any sustainable economic and efficient administrative structures. They stopped their initiatives after Bartholomew Welser's oldest son was murdered in 1546. Ten years later, the province was formally taken away from them.[60]

118.   Hieronymus Koeler, *Order of the escort*, Bl Add.Ms. 15,217, 35v. © The British Library, London

NUREMBERG

Köler provides us with the human story and the face of a man who would have moved back from these encounters into a Nuremberg world in which an interest in other cultures was still vigorously mediated by printers, collectors, businessmen, and artists. Nuremberg remained a significant centre of artistic production in this period.[61] The genius artist of the second half of the sixteenth century was the goldsmith Wenzel Jamnitzer. As with Dürer, the Lutheran city council knew how to use his work in Imperial diplomacy, and likewise graced him with the status of a member of the great council. Jamnitzer specialized in life casts from plants and animals, which blurred rigid distinction between the natural and artificial. His work drew attention even to thin weeds as natural, divinely created, delicate, artful, and worthy of an artist's keenest observation and skill to recreate it in precious metals and glass. In 1549, the Nuremberg city council obtained a fruit-bowl, which celebrated the abundance of an exotically dressed Mother Earth with a multitude of life casts on every part of this table centrepiece—it is intriguing to wonder for what kinds of fruit it would have been used. This intimate experience of nature in its diversity still lay at the basis of a claim that the knowledge of how to make things was superior to simply reading about things.[62]

Hans Sachs, the moralist *Meistersänger* and prolific publisher, who did so much to translate humanist and Protestant ideals into the vernacular, died in 1576. Sachs had disseminated countless popular woodcuts depicting people from all walks of life, as well as Turks, Russians and other Eastern Europeans, ancient Romans, and biblical figures, all in naturalistic representations of what they wore. In 1568, Sachs had also engraved a large book of Jamnitzer's drawings of the five natural solids and their infinite variations, once more proof of how densely different scientific, artistic, and artisanal skills were networked in this city rather than neatly divided between popular and elite spheres.

Nuremberg, then, saw more continuity than decline after the age of Dürer, and new departures. The seriously rich part of the new and old merchant elite continued to invest in the kind of conspicuous consumption one would expect: they built and rebuilt houses, facades, courtyards, gardens, and invested in highly decorative interiors. Altogether, between 1589 and 1610, twenty-seven major new houses were erected in Nuremberg. The most spectacular examples were the Topler-, Peller-, Viatis-, and Fembohouses, while the Tucher- and Hirschvogelhouses dated from the first half of the century. Viatis was the richest of around twenty Italian merchants who settled in Nuremberg until the beginning of the Thirty Years' War.[63] Willibald Imhoff (1519–1580) and Paulus Praun (1548–1616) owned enormous art, book, and object collections, which rivalled princely collections, and Praun's collection remained in Nuremberg for centuries after his death. Imhoff in 1570 even commissioned a terracotta bust of himself gazing at a gemstone-ring delicately held by two fingers, rather than folding his hands in prayer. It was a monument to how time spent in material contemplation of commodities had become a meaningful pursuit in such circles, part of the practice and pleasure of aesthetic connoisseurship attuned to the particularity of matter.[64] Here was a person defined by the very act of looking at a thing he attached himself to.

Several enterprises were highly specialized: the Ayrer family, for instance, amassed about twenty-thousand woodcuts and engravings in one of the most important and earliest print cabinets.[65] At least four pharmacists and doctors ran major projects of plant and animal studies. There were outstanding calligraphers and illuminists of woodcuts or family genealogies as well. One of the most splendid and startling manifestations of this was the Nuremberg edition of Nicolas de Nicolay's travels to Eastern Europe and Turkey, which we have already referred to, brilliantly illuminated by the best of the Nuremberg illuminators, Georg Mack. Mack himself also published Jost Amman's pioneering 1574 etching *Costumes of the Nations of the World*, and re-published it in 1577. This sheet measures 34.7 × 45.2 cm and despite this small size claimed to represent 'all' dress of the four parts of the world, 'Asia Europa Africa and India or America'. Europe was depicted through no less than twenty-two figures in the upper part, whereas images in the lower part showed 'Moors', an Ethiopian, an Arab, a Gypsy, an Indian, a Brazilian, a Tartar, a man from Moscow, a Persian, and a Turk.[66] This was the first ever depiction then of costumes and a variety of people from all four parts of the world. It was a summary presentation, which would often have been hand-coloured and very possibly been pinned up on a wall. It testifies to the interest in such visualizations just as the comprehensive costume book proper was about to come on the market. Nuremberg prized itself on this ability for artistic innovation and perfection.

In the 1570s, moreover, a book genre of the art of travelling, the 'ars apodemica', was pioneered by authors in German-speaking lands. This new departure was marked by three works of European influence by a Saxon jurist called Hieronymus Turler, the Bavarian physician Hilarius Pyrckmair, and the Basle professor of medicine Theodor Zwinger. These men were all part of a generation born between 1520–1533 that had studied in Venice and Padua, despite the fact that Turler held Lutheran and Zwinglian reformed beliefs.[67] They encouraged travellers to diligently accumulate, and rigorously evaluate and present knowledge, just as merchants accumulated goods and money. This was so as to studiously compare the characteristics of different people, meet illustrious men, and hence further inform debates in the literary republic across confessional divides.

AN URBAN EHTNOGRAPHY

Just how the mix of contemporary interests in looking at the world with its predilection for direct observation and collecting could influence one Nuremberg man's outlook on local customs is demonstrated by a unique album, now in the Berlin costume library of the Freiherr zu Lipperheide. This vast volume presents the largest compilation of clothing anyone had put together anywhere in the world until then. It was assembled by a Nuremberg official called Sigmund Heldt, between 1560–1580. These decades were just the time when more ambitious printed costume books like Weigel's and de Bruyn's were beginning to be published. They also coincided with the first concerted effort by the Nuremberg council to enforce sumptuary legislation. A new sumptuary ordinance in 1560 was the first to distinguish ranks by profession rather than birth. Further, increasingly differentiated versions of the ordinance were publicized in 1562, 1568, and 1583.[68] Heldt's large quarto volume became a vast undertaking—a full 867 watercolour depictions were bound together on 506 sheets in expensive and artfully stamped leather.[69] It was larger even than Cesare Vecellio's famous final edition of the costumes of the world would be at the end of the sixteenth century. Yet it was never printed. Heldt incorporated earlier ethnographic depictions of Africans, Indians, Americans, Christianized Muslims, and Turks, while his project culminated in an extensive depiction of Nuremberg dress and customs. Heldt's album, which has never been discussed in the scholarly literature and only rarely ever been referred to, provides us with a strong sense of the kind of self-reflection on familiar traditions and society made possible by the awareness of cultural diversity across the globe. This is what scholars call 'transculturation'—when your experience of another culture changes the way you think of your own. The manuscript evinced a conservative view, which affirmed that local customs should be preserved, but nonetheless was informed by a sense of Nuremberg's cultural peculiarity. This perspective resulted from ethnographic knowledge (Fig. 119).

It might be best to first provide a brief catalogue of the distinct parts into which this massive manuscript falls. A first section of fifty-four sheets depicts clerical dress, including one 'evangelical' and two Wittenberg preachers as well as the pope and different orders. A mere ten further sheets depicts secular dignitaries. Roman costume briefly features as a reference on three further pages. A longer section on sheets 75–96 displays tournament costumes; ten further sheets, Nuremberg carnival displays. Sheets 112–159 memorialize the elites' dances at Nuremberg's town hall; 164–169 once more the Nuremberg carnival. The following 132 sheets form an extensive section of German female costumes, while only six following ones are dedicated to Venetian dress. After this, eighty-seven pages present Turkish, Polish, Russian, Greek, Moorish, African, and Spanish dress. German emperors are depicted in their coronation apparel on one double page. The final hundred sheets (388–499) return to Nuremberg dress, and within this section the last forty-three sheets are devoted to peasant clothing. Thus, local Nuremberg dress, rendered from personal recollection or direct observation rather than copied, form the largest part of this collection. It follows no strict order, and certainly suggests no hierarchy among ethnic groups. The only observable ordering principle relates to social hierarchies: Heldt's manuscript begins with dignitaries and ends with a sequence on peasants in Nuremberg's extensive environs. Its only texts are cursory inscriptions and a two-page prologue in which Heldt describes his project. This manuscript was a substantial investment if he did pay an illuminist rather than painting himself—we know that Marcus zum Lamm paid one florin each for similar illustrations in his *Thesaurus Picturarum*, although Heldt's images are more roughly executed.

What motivated Heldt? A brief prologue declares that he wished to make traditions accessible so that their good aspects might be preserved and recovered. His moral views were conservative. He sought to show how simple clothes used to be, so that young people would stop spending on such costly items as slashed hose of velvet and silk, 'which belong to high Lords and potentates'. Heldt was responsible for Nuremberg's books of debt, giving him some insight into people's finances. He maintained that artisans and servants needed to save money for their weddings and for tools to set up a household workshop according to their means. Instead, he lamented, they often contracted debts that they were unable to repay, and therefore had to leave or sell a house. He prayed to God to make everyone realistic about their social station and not overreach.[70]

Heldt's extraordinary project took a society of ranks and static, unequal wealth as God-given, but also *honoured* each rank in terms of its work, manners, and customs, giving it its proper dignity within society. He depicted peasants' clothing and honoured

119.   Sigmund Heldt, *Natives after Burgkmair*, Lipp Aa2, 362v. © Staatliche Museen zu Berlin, Kunstbibliothek, Photo: Dietmar Katz

them for 'their great work (*grosse arbait*) and amusements', rendering them as full human beings—humorous, sociable, and inventive. Similarly, he not only depicted noble tournaments, but also tournaments for children and ordinary people. The high and the low had their fixed places, but each were worthy in their own right. Yet what changed this traditional message and makes the volume so uniquely interesting in ethnographic terms was the fact that Heldt had Burgkmair's 1508 depictions of Indians, many of Weiditz's depictions, and Nicolas de Nicolay's woodcuts copied. His artist was not highly skilled, but he was also certainly not interested in racist stereotyping in the way Burgkmair had later introduced, or the widely circulating accounts of the German Hans von Staden's encounters with Brazilian cannibals.[71] So we find Weiditz's Morisco women and Moors; and Burgkmair's men and women from Cochin at the heart of the volume, just before the extensive final section on Nuremberg.

It therefore seems that in the course of his project Heldt not only copied many of these plates, he also assimilated Weiditz's ethnographic perspective and applied it to Nuremberg. Thus, besides replicating the Morisco woman sweeping in front of her house, the Heldt album also shows Nuremberg sweepers of houses and streets. This was not done to deliver the message that these were low subjects, but once more with an evocation of visual pleasure, such as in the depiction of a street sweeper taking cobwebs from the corner of the page. Heldt even depicted the manner in which Nuremberg peasants ploughed their fields or different stages of harvesting grain. He seems to have absorbed the message that if a Castilian peasant ploughing his field had interested Weiditz, there was nothing inherently obvious about German ploughing, that the familiar might seem equally strange to a different culture, or perhaps both were similar. It was a hybrid account, in which knowledge of other cultures shifted Heldt's sense of his own, rather than assuming that the indigenous was plain familiar and unshifting, while other cultures were the sole site of strangeness, difference, and change. Many humble activities became worth recording: people emptying wells and carrying away excrement;

a day-labouring boy with torn hose, but a little hat with dyed black and white feathers; different trades; women preparing flax; lying-in maids with babies; cart-men bringing fruit into the city. Women were not represented as mothers, but through various types of paid work. The manuscript in this last part on the people and civitas took on a dynamic of its own. It revealed the city as human association rather than as mere urbs, a physical unit of buildings and walls (Figs. 120–122). Classical as well as medieval writers were clear about this distinction between urbs and civitas, as when Isidore of Seville (c.560–636) defined the city as 'a number of men joined by a social bond. It takes its name from the citizens who dwell in it. As an urbs, it is only a walled structure…'. It would soon become commonplace to summarize that inhabitants, not stones, made a city.[72] Some writers in turn emphasized that magnificent cities depended on firm laws, clear boundaries between citizens embodying their civility and non-citizens threatening it, and growing populations. Others saw the city as a space in which social bonds were affirmed through customs, feasts, empathy, contact with a diverse range of people, and fun. Heldt evidently held an in-between position. He emphasized the importance of rank in his prologue, but in terms of the depictions he increasingly endorsed the importance of civitas. As with Schwarz's book of clothes, this visual project had begun in an open-ended way and was lived with over many years. As in Weiditz, appearances in themselves now only formed part of the picture, which was about a larger human story embedded, once more, not in scholarly learning, but in localized everyday life. His book unfolded as a pictorial discovery allowing the reader to appreciate life in these terms. His sense of amusement as part of the story of people joined together by inhabiting the same space and creating a social bond is particularly noteworthy. The album, for instance, depicted a cart full of apples that have tumbled, the mishaps of everyday life that provided stories to tell, eliciting humour and compassion stretching out to someone unknown. The unusual ethnographic interest in common people in Heldt's album likewise conveyed a sense that his world was alive, genuinely human, interesting and, once more as with Weiditz, surprisingly diverse. For example, there was not just one type of sweeper, but three, all dressed differently and quite strangely, and sometimes with holes in their clothes (Figs. 123–124). Patches or holes in someone's clothing were not pointed out so as to attract moral judgement—they simply were part of what people who had fewer means looked like. A carter was depicted with simple clothes, but also with a green felt hat and an elaborate bag. This perspective challenged bourgeois ideas that honour rigidly rested on neatness. Here it rested on honest work, humaneness, and humour within a community. There was a man just wearing his drawers being treated in

120. (*top left*) Sigmund Heldt, *Nuremberg bathing master*, Lipp Aa2, 435r. © Staatliche Museen zu Berlin, Kunstbibliothek, Photo: Dietmar Katz

121. (*top right*) Sigmund Heldt, *Ordinary Nuremberg craftsman*, Lipp Aa2, 440v. © Staatliche Museen zu Berlin, Kunstbibliothek, Photo: Dietmar Katz

122. (*bottom left*) Sigmund Heldt, *Peasant women bringing onions and carrots to the Nuremberg market*, Lipp Aa2 473r. © Staatliche Museen zu Berlin, Kunstbibliothek, Photo: Dietmar Katz

123. (*bottom right*) Sigmund Heldt, *Nuremberg captain of the foot-servants*, Lipp Aa2, 443v. © Staatliche Museen zu Berlin, Kunstbibliothek, Photo: Dietmar Katz

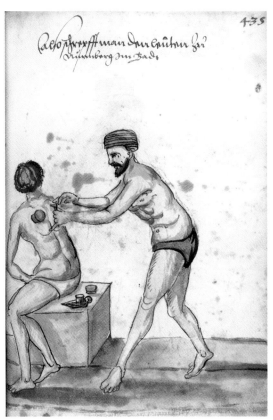

435

Ein schrepffman der bruter zu
Nürnberg im Bad

Ein Haubtmann in Ao 1550
ist gangen

453

Ein tragen die Neuen Braut kirchen
mittel sand fribalgen zu Nürnberg her
marckt

Ein Haubtman uber die fußknecht in Ao 1555
ist gangen

Ein Hauszknecht zu
Nürnberg

a bath, which showed that almost complete nudity was still an accepted part of people's display to each other in one particular social context, and not just a practice to be solely associated with savages.[73] Heldt depicted men and women of all classes in vivid colours for some parts of their dress. A chief man-servant in charge of other servants was shown in a lined coat, slashed red and black breeches, and a high black hat. Like many others, this image was dated—the caption recorded that this was what a man who had this occupation looked like in 1560. Inserting a date communicated that this was certain to change. Chronicling would therefore be an ongoing task. German regional and occupational dress could not be frozen in time (Figs. 125–127).

Heldt's project thus became an exercise in honouring local people and recording the passing look of community figures through representations on pages in his big leather-bound book. Any previous models he must have had in mind apart from Weiditz had set much more specific tasks for themselves. His father, for instance, belonged to the *Mendelsche Zwölfbrüderstiftung*, a small foundation for old and needy male craftsmen. Since about 1425/26 it kept an astounding record of beautiful successive alba respectfully memorializing its deceased members and their craft trades up unto the early nineteenth century—a total of 857 images (Fig. 128). So did another Nuremberg foundation since 1511, the *Landauer Stiftung*, with another 439 images.[74] Here too, then, and uniquely so

in Nuremberg, it had become an acknowledged way to honour and remember common people visually through what they looked like in everyday life, when engaged in their work, rather than in their best Sunday dress. In this view, what people did and hence knew about made them distinctive. The production of the famous Nuremberg *Schempartbücher* likewise flourished at this time, after the carnival had been abolished. They created a rich memory of this festive tradition with its licence to create imaginary appearances by depicting the butchers and noblemen in their carnival costumes and floats. But these records almost exclusively recorded men, and mostly skilled artisans.

124. (*opposite*) Sigmund Heldt, *Nuremberg house-servant*, Lipp Aa2 444v. © Staatliche Museen zu Berlin, Kunstbibliothek, Photo: Dietmar Katz

125. (*right*) Sigmund Heldt, *Berlin maid-servant*, Lipp Aa2 196r. © Staatliche Museen zu Berlin, Kunstbibliothek, Photo: Dietmar Katz

126. (*left*) Sigmund Heldt, *Man making Sauerkraut*, Lipp Aa2 488r. © Staatliche Museen zu Berlin, Kunstbibliothek, Photo: Dietmar Katz

127. (*opposite left*) Sigmund Heldt, *German carter*, Lipp Aa2 457v. © Staatliche Museen zu Berlin, Kunstbibliothek, Photo: Dietmar Katz

128. (*opposite right*) *Hausbuch der Mendelschen Zwölfbrüder-stiftung*, the hat-maker Hanns Eckel, 27.0 × 18.7 cm, Amb. 279.2º, 22r. © Stadtbibliothek Nürnberg

Even so, unlike Weiditz's Spanish pictures, and in tune with his traditional ethics, Heldt presented a culture without any ethnic diversity or cultural mixing, although many Italians, as we shall see in the next chapter, lived and vigorously traded in Nuremberg. Nor did he depict punishments, social discipline, or harshness. His book depicted a fictitious society and formed yet a further visual myth, in which different orders had their place, respected each other on those conditions and lived their lives with hardship as well as joy, an ideal civitas within a world globally conceived. Its message was not about conquering these new worlds. It was about how to preserve pleasure in local traditions and relationships across social hierarchies.

CONCLUSION

Michel de Montaigne's famous essay 'On the Cannibals' right at its end imagines a person objecting: 'Ah! But they wear no breeches...'. In Montaigne's view it was ridiculous to take clothing customs as an inflexible yardstick of civilization. He himself had spoken to the Brazilian Indians in Rouen. What mattered to Montaigne was whether a society seemed to practice justice, what they used violence for and why, whether men were determined in war and loving to women. Whether or not they covered their legs was irrelevant.[75] Montaigne's essay therefore justly stands as a monument to the early ethnographic tradition developed during the sixteenth century as an art of observation, which this chapter has explored in terms of one strand of German responses to dress. To ask about clothing for Montaigne meant that you needed to ask why particular customs made sense to particular people and what they thought of European society in turn. It exposed Europeans to a self reflective dialogue, which we have witnessed taking place in Dürer's, Köler's, and Heldt's minds as well. 'Combien d'hommes, et en Turquie surtout', Montaigne asked another time, 'vont nus par devotion?' He had gathered from Guillaume Postel's travel writing that it was customary for Turks to worship without clothes.[76] He had learned through Lopez de Gomara's *General History of the Indies* that 'the king of Mexico changed four times a day and never wore the same clothes twice; his cast-off garments were constantly used for gifts and rewards'.[77] Montaigne drafted a whole essay 'on the custom of wearing clothing' through information on ancient and contemporary global clothing he extracted from books and travellers. Yet he frankly admitted to his own formality. He could not bear to go out unlaced, and only wore black and white like his father rather than the medley of clothes every other French person wore. He knew, on the other hand, that the 'farm-labourers in my neighbourhood would feel shackled if they walked about all laced and buttoned up'.[78] Montaigne added all these observations and in this essay on clothing customs looked for no argument to order them. You could think about appearances just to observe and represent variety inside your society, among the ancients, and globally now. To relativize your own customs and morals could be just the point of thinking through clothes, even if it undermined easy certainties.

Sustained visual explorations of a truly ethnographic nature which were drawn from life without any explicit moralizing commentary such as those of Dürer, Weiditz, and Heldt were rare. They document some of the possibilities inherent in the encounter with global diversity which permeated their society. Many Germans and Europeans in the sixteenth century undoubtedly had become far more curious about other cultures and sought to gather more knowledge about them. Hans Weigel's costume book made clear that he thought that some extra-European people looked ridiculous but, as we have seen in the previous chapter, he would also enter some basic ethnographic commentary among a few depictions. So did Vecellio, who whole-heartedly admired particular features of New World clothing, and showed how, rather than being stagnant, 'Indian' dress was mixed with Old World accessories, such as mirrors brought by the Spaniards to Mexico.[79] The message of these pioneering and popular costume books was that different cultures had different customs, and these could either be dismissed, or alternatively be an inspiration.

By the end of the century, John White would produce a whole series of strikingly naturalistic drawings of native people in Virginia, first published in 1590 alongside a Latin edition of Thomas Harriot's 'Briefe and True Report' on this 'New Found Land'. These had the clear political purpose of selling the idea of English exploration and settlement to the crown, but also compared these natives to ancient Picts with their tattooed bodies, thus suggesting that civilization everywhere evolved gradually. One image showed nude Indians being handed a prettily dressed European girl doll—as an educative, a civilizing tool.[80] In 1596, Jan Huygen van Linschoten, former secretary to the archbishop of Goa, who had become Calvinist when returning to the Dutch Republic, published his *Voyages to the East Indies*, with an unparalleled amount of information on India, the Far East, and the lives of Portuguese and Moors in these lands. The text was provided in two narrow columns under thirty-six large engravings. The illustrations can be termed proto-ethnographic to the extent that they assumed that 'reality consists of an overwhelming plethora of phenomena, whose coherence and meaning can only be discovered by systematic observation and classification'.[81] Only such certain taxonomies would render visual knowledge useful by depicting general characteristics rather than local and thus intensely particular detail, in order to then categorize what one had observed in terms of likeness to a pre-established category, rather than on its own terms.

Yet, parallel to such a quest for taxonomies or the revived rigid Roman insistence that clothes made the man, a faint, but far more qualified argument had developed on the margins of European cultural life, which this chapter has tried to chart. It posited, as we have just seen with Montaigne, that if you wanted to know about what people wore, you needed to carefully observe them and explain their localized and historically specific practices. Heldt's heading above each image explained how one did things, made, crafted, laboured and looked. Heldt dialogically asked 'How do they do things' and 'How do we do things in Nuremberg'? Clothes could be seen not just in narrowly moralistic terms, but at least sometimes as part of the diversity and creative ingenuity of humankind, even an enjoyment of life, a diversity to be respected rather than regarded as deficient, to be homogenized, or to be rooted out.

From the second half of the sixteenth century, more Germans than ever before began to spend time abroad. They studied in famous universities, travelled through cities, or worked as merchants of luxury wares. Italians set up trade in major German cities, such as Nuremberg and Dresden. English theatre companies would come and play there. Fairs and spas were an international meeting place. Foreign travellers—Montaigne was one of them—would be received in German towns. Germans would soon join the ships of the Dutch East India Company in particularly high numbers. This reality of cultural exchange alongside books and prints underpinned a more global horizon that could be drawn into local worlds and needs to be set against the commonplace that confessional Germany became a more uniform, narrow-minded, and regulated society at this time.

1 5 ⁊ 5.

Omnia Vendunt Labor

Vna Gentildon,
na Fiorentina.

CHAPTER 6

Clothes and Consumers

RELATING TO THINGS

This chapter returns to the question of how early modern people gave meaning to clothing as consumers and in dialogue with visual practices, which underlay the chapter on
the Fugger company employee, Matthäus Schwarz. Excellent inventories provide an
understanding of what kinds of goods were administratively registered according to
specific rules as a person's property when he or she married and died. But they do not
easily provide a sense of how objects were used and became part of relationships. In
order to glimpse how goods were socially embedded and what they meant to people at
specific points in their lives, it is best to consult qualitative evidence. Letters, not lists
of things, then, are the principal sources used in this chapter.[1] Letters also relate to the
focus of this book because they tell us about the way in which clothing became part of
cultural arguments. Decisions about how much was to be spent on what kinds of dress
and fabric were rarely a matter of individual choice, or self-evident. The more there
was to buy, the more likely they became a theme of household discussions. Matthäus
Schwarz, as a single man in steady lucrative employment over many years, was unusual
in his capacity to decide with a great deal of liberty on how he wanted to dress. Normally, parents or guardians had a say. Married couples needed to agree on expenditure
and taste. Household discussions and hierarchies mediated an engagement with matter
and thus, to some extent, what kind of person you could become. Personhood, as this
book has argued, was not a pre-defined entity. It evolved through a series of relations
people entered into with others, institutions, with what they regarded as supernatural
and natural, as well as with things.[2]

129. (*opposite*)   Album Amicorum of Paul Behaim, entry Gienger 1575, Florentine lady, Eg.1192,
4r. © The British Library, London

This chapter focuses on Renaissance students, whom contemporaries already perceived as valuable concentrated consumer groups in many European university towns. Students had a wide range of needs, and parents who steadily provided for them. 'If there are a thousand students in one town', one pamphleteer calculated in 1524, 'they need throughout the year, which is long, much in terms of living-places, bedding, linen, clothes, coats, hose, doublets, berets, caps, hats, gloves, shoes, wine, beer, bread, cheese, milk', until his long list duly ended with 'books, paper, ink and quills'.[3] Concurrently, anxieties about spendthriftness also focused on young people. Students had no money of their own and hence wrote to their parents or guardians to negotiate their needs. Parents in turn had no absolute authority to decide on what their children wore. They had to spend considerable time controlling their spending and arguing with them in ways that sometimes became so emotionally involving that the relationship seemed in question because of a doublet or hose. It is with the example of Friedrich Behaim that we shall begin.

Negotiating Dress

Friedrich Behaim was born into an economically successful and politically influential Nuremberg merchant family in 1563. When he was five years old, he lost his father, Paul Behaim. Friedrich's mother had been Paul's second wife, and would remain widowed up to her death, nearly twenty years later. Her chief task during these decades was to prudently maintain the wealth left behind by her husband for his seven children and to prevent any material decline or moral dishonour. The girls needed good dowries to marry well; the boys needed land, money, goods, and a distinguished education. Patricians now were meant to go to university if they ever wished to become high office holders in their city, even though, strikingly, they were also expected not to take their academic interests too far. Anyone with a doctoral degree was excluded from membership of the Nuremberg council.[4] Moreover, they were also expected to see some of the world beyond their hometown. As we have seen, this typically was no longer done by way of a pilgrimage via Venice to the Holy Land, but through visiting foreign universities and new forms of tourism to important places and illustrious men.

So, aged fourteen, Friedrich first went to study at the small local academy of Altdorf, which wealthy Nuremberg burghers had founded in 1575 as a mixture of a fee-paying high school and university. Here, Lutheran youths were to improve their Latin, music, and general grasp of the humanities removed from the distractions of urban life. Friedrich went to the Altdorf academy for three years, and during this time he did something exceedingly rare: he kept his mother's letters. Sons and men usually were much more likely to throw away women's family letters, while women more often perfumed them, tied ribbons around them, and stored them away. Thus Luther's letters to Katharine of Bora, on the rare occasions when he travelled, still can be treasured today; but none of her's or the children's survive.

In many ways, however, it is not entirely surprising that many letters were seen as irrelevant for posterity. Historians now often attempt to detect the growth of 'modern' intimacy in terms of love and care in such correspondence, and sure enough feelings of this kind were expressed. Early modern people were no cold automata, because they were so aware that the plague or other diseases might take their earthly lives away all too soon. Friedrich, for example, assured his mother of his filial loyalty, and he cared for her physical wellbeing. He sent special greetings to the maid who had wept when he had left for Altdorf, and wished for news from his siblings. But mostly his letters focused on his own needs and development—as one would expect from a youth who had just moved out of the family home and rooted himself in a new environment. It is therefore important not to try to fit these letters into an account of the successive development of a modern romanticized familial intimacy. The letters from and to the mother essentially constituted a relationship in terms of demand, negotiation, and provision. They emphasized the experience of a child dependent on a parent to obtain rent, food, candles, paper, books, washed clothes, new clothes, and shoes. Hence they reveal why the material and immaterial, interest and emotion must not be thought of in opposition to each other. As the sociologist Eva Illouz argues, economic processes such as the acquisition of, bargaining for, and possession of, goods generate intensely emotional cultures and impact on family relations.[5] Exchanges and emotions, we might formulate, conditioned each other in historically specific ways. The greater relevance of commodified items provided new dimensions to the emotional life of children, couples, and kin—from manipulation to moral anxiety or mutual pleasure in possessions.

Hence the relationship of mother and son in these family letters emerges as one in which a parent oversaw responsibilities of material and physical as interlinked with moral care. Friedrich's mother, for instance, worried about his eyes and bloodletting, and she was adamant that he should keep his distance from noble pretensions. She looked after his learning in terms of a process of intellectual development through sourcing books he asked for, but otherwise mainly sought assurance of his conformity to requirements and diligent achievement. Neither was there a sense that there should be any spiritual development, rather more a spiritual routine. It was taken for granted that her son would uphold a pious status quo by attending church on Sundays. This type of bourgeois education was to realize for Friedrich exactly the kind of position he obtained when he returned via some northern Italian cities to his Nuremberg home territory in his early twenties: he became a respected town manager in Gräfenberg and Hilpoldstein, which belonged to Nuremberg's vast civic territory. He also married into a powerful Nuremberg patrician family and had ten children.

The bulk of these relatively short letters, which his mother, née Magdalena Römer, only signed once, as 'Mrs Paul Behaim', was about material transactions from Nuremberg to Altdorf. What do they tell us about the circulation of goods, clothing practices, and their role in a family's emotional life? One of the first items Magdalena sent was a satin cap, alongside a small fork as new tool of culinary civility which had spread from Italy. She therefore, to some extent, supported her son's embodiment of social distinction through luxury accessory. She also immediately sent three new shirts, which had been made at home by various people, including a man who worked at the household for particular crafts jobs from time to time. Friedrich expressed his esteem for these home produced shirts: 'Nothing more for now except my greetings to all the household and to Martin, and to all who have worked on my shirts. God Bless.'[6] Bed-clothes were also made at home, taking 'a while to make'.[7] After little more than three months at Altdorf, Friedrich complained in October that 'my everyday hose are full of holes and hardly worth patching; I can barely cover my rear, although the stockings are still good. Winter is almost here, so I still need a lined coat. All I have is a woven *Arlas*, which is also full of holes. So would you have my buckram smock lined as you think best? I have not worn it more than twice.'[8] His mother again employed Martin to make these clothes. She distinguished between leather hose, which would be worn on holidays, and woollen everyday ones. She decided to have another coat made for him, but meanwhile instructed him to keep the smock unlined for another summer and to receive his old coat until the new one was made. He was told to keep one coat brushed and clean, and to use cleaning flakes on his leather hose once he had worn them three times. The old hose she wished to have returned.[9] In early November, however, Friedrich remarked that the new hose were 'completely too small', and that he would have to use a tailor to let them out.[10] Before January, his mother sent Friedrich new shirts, caps, and handkerchiefs, and asked him to return his old coat so that she could give it to a schoolboy as a New Year's gift.[11] The beginning of each year was a time of ritual gift exchanges and charity, and it turned out that Friedrich himself had already given the coat to a poor Altdorf student. Such charitable giving, then, was another of the myriad ways through which clothing circulated. Hence, it was not necessarily the kind of cut or cloth that distinguished different status groups, but whether or not an item was new or worn, torn, patched, or pristine, and how well it was dyed.

Meanwhile Friedrich requested more money for beer, because his mouth got so dry 'from reading'. In early April he was sent a new pair of hose. His mother was worried that the price of fabric might double within weeks. She asked him to send his leather and woollen hose home to see whether they might be let out: 'I cannot always be buying new hose.'[12] To govern a household well was a matter of constant oversight in these ways—to keep track of what items of clothing each child had, to get a sense of how prices would fluctuate and what could be renewed rather than replaced, but also to make decisions about what items were essential to keep up decent appearances. Dependants were requested to be cooperative and sensible in the adjustment to constraints on expenditure—and to share an ethics of wise spending and maintaining which made one honourable, not someone who squandered. This was one of the ways in which 'filial love' became concrete. But then again, none of this was necessarily straightforward if a child or husband was not there to have clothes or shoes properly fitted. It is astonishing that no measurements were sent in advance, for on 18 April 1579 Friedrich complained again that he was returning the new hose, because they were much too short and tight. 'The stockings are so tight', he added, 'that I cannot get them on at all. And the hose are also too tight. The doublet is a complete misfit. Would you have it let out and lengthened for me? I prefer it too loose than too tight. The leather hose I am sending to you are much too short and the seat too tight ever to be much improved...I must have a fustian doublet, for now I have no such doublet at all. The ones I have are too small for me.'[13]

In other words: it was a fiasco, far more expensive than Mrs Behaim had thought, and the labour that had gone into the new items seemed lost. In May, one month in advance, Friedrich next let his mother know that he was no longer able to refuse to take part in a play. His part was to be the queen. Anticipating her concern, he wrote: 'you need not worry about clothes; I only need necklaces, a wig, and a skullcap'.[14] She promptly replied that she had no intention of helping him to decorate the stage and would not send anything fine that might be stolen. But a later letter implies that she had indeed sent a wig and skullcap and some costumes, which Friedrich stated had not been harmed in the play, had been stored by him 'neatly and safely' afterwards and he was taking good care of them, ready to be sent back in boxes at a later date. So, the value of theatre clothes and the need to look after them was respected—clothing was inter-linked with a whole set of care practices that would allow the clothes to last. This was in the form of appropriate storage, cleaning, skilled mending, and patching, for which Friedrich's tailor charged the same price he paid for five books. Stored clothes and linen were kept clean and perfumed through rosewater or rose leaves, which his mother sent in abundance and he promised to dry and put in his linen chest.

Such cleanliness at the same time was a symbolic practice: it could take on metaphor-ical meanings to denote morality. If everything was clean, then everything was in order. Spotless behaviour resided in the act of maintaining such appearances even against con-straints and through a joint household effort. 'As for your behaviour' Mrs Behaim thus wrote in 1579, 'just do not venture behind any castle'—where prostitutes were found—'regardless of what your roommates do. And always keep a clean shirt on your back.'[15] And because his mother had developed an anxiety that her maturing son might go to prostitutes, a clean shirt took on these moral meanings and perhaps not just represented cleanliness but was thought in part to uphold the moral substance of its wearer. This is how we can think of objects as active in relationships and exchanges, creating an identity rather than representing it. Hence Mrs Behaim seemed to suddenly send quite a lot of white shirts. 'Dear Mother', Friedrich penned in January 1580, 'I have now received a shirt, then another, and thereafter two shirts. But I am puzzled why you do not send me shoes? Would you let me know about them?'[16] It turned out that she had overlooked this request, but she kept track from Nuremberg of whether her son would have a washed shirt to wear: 'I think you still have a white shirt to wear this Sunday. I will send two new shirts next week. Send your dirty laundry home to be washed. No more for now.' (Unsigned.)[17] So in principle, then, Friedrich was expected to dress to a plan and with regularity, and so as to make absolutely sure that he would ensure to wear fresh white shirts for the day of the Lord. Clothing practices of this kind thus reinforced a shared evaluation of religion and honourable society.

And while her son never failed to use loving words and formula to write to her, Mrs Behaim only rarely wrote 'Dear Son', or a nickname, 'Fritz'. Usually the letters began

'Friedrich'. Letter 69, for instance, reads: 'Friedrich. I am herewith sending you the hose and the money. Have the hose cleaned. There is no need to alter them until the stockings become torn. However, you may not mischievously tear them, for they cost a lot. Keep them clean and they will last you a long time. No more for now.' (Unsigned.)[18] So while shirts were evidently in plentiful supply and in a very controlled way constituted an agreed conformity, hose clearly were a source of anxiety for the mother. She still needed to remind him of their value, and to imply that he might even mischievously destroy them. After all the cooperation he had shown, this seemed to call into question her trust in his maturity. The tone was commanding. But the problem evidently was that shirts had a wide fit, whereas hose were fitted more precisely to the body. As the body changed, they became useless, a source of instability, and hence of further communication. Already some weeks later in May, Friedrich wrote demandingly that he needed shoes

> Also, it was almost Easter when anyone last did anything to improve my clothing
> a little. My stretched-out hose become smaller each day. When I walk or bend
> over, they split on every side. If you do not let them out, I maintain they will
> become completely useless. If you will allow me the cheapest fustian hose or
> galliot without any trim that would be good enough for me on workdays during
> the summer. And you could repair the other hose so that I might have them on
> holidays and spare my new ones.[19]

Whereas shirts stood for predictable controlled civility, if they were washed and their folds kept reasonably sharp, hose could be used to evoke images of an involuntary grotesque display of the lower body, bulging, protruding, or even worse, naked. The reply was instant, practical, and surprisingly understanding: 'Friedrich. I am herewith sending you five eln of fustian for hose and four eln for a doublet…Do have it made large enough, for you are now having your greatest growth.'[20] These exchanges reaffirmed trust. Needs and realistic, cost-effective procedures to ensure decency had to be established jointly by mother and son. They both followed the same goal, ordering the year into seasons, workdays, holidays, and feast-days, avoiding extravagance.

This was until Friedrich took his leave from Altdorf and travelled in a large party to a place called Neuenmarkt, where he watched a noble wedding and took part in a student wedding, and generally spent a larger amount of money. On top of this there were his accumulated bills from Altdorf. Everything came to eighteen florins. It 'is a lot of money' he justified himself, 'but one cannot always be spinning silk'. This was not an obvious proverb to use at this point, unless he meant that instead of always spinning silk one should sometime wear something made of silk. Indeed, Friedrich next daringly proposed: 'One must at some time in his life live it up, although I have done so more out of necessity. I ask you not to be annoyed with me and to send me (the money) at the earliest.'[21] So even now it was crucial that he tried to justify himself at least in part through the necessity of social pressure rather than a mere argument for pleasure and a material dimension to an occasional exuberant expression of a love of life—'one must at some point in his life live it up'. No reply is preserved.

Seven months later, Friedrich was in Venice when he heard that his mother had perished. Now orphaned, he wrote to his uncle, and appointed guardian, Sigmund Heldt for the first time. He let him know that he knew that his mother had been taken to God, wishing her and all 'of us a joyful resurrection'. Immediately after, he described what he wore: 'I am dressed in simple mourning clothes because I brought no clothes whatsoever here with me. In the winter, when I could have arranged [to have clothes made] I needed only one clean suit of clothes, so I chose to have two simple articles of clothing made, the only ones since I have been in Italy.'[22] And a doublet, in fact, the letter later revealed. Friedrich, in other words, did not elaborate on how he felt, as people nowadays would be likely to. He described how he dressed and thereby displayed that his values were continuous to those at home. This description of embodied plainness and civility in an expensive city of sumptuous possibility and hundreds of prostitutes moreover mediated new claims for financial support. To Heldt, he was not going to assert that life sometimes needed living up or that it was a while since anyone had cared about his clothing. The rhetoric to be deployed was one of humble responsibility and restraint, in which he showed that all the constraints on expenditure were external. His own limited choices revealed to the guardian how trustworthy, frugal, and well behaved he was as a son who had lost his mother.

Paul Behaim II

Friedrich had a brother, six years older than himself, named Paul, after their father. He was the oldest of the four sons whom Magdalena Römer had to provide for alongside four daughters after her husband's death. Paul II, too, first studied in Leipzig for three years, and then lived in northern Italian cities for another full three years, from 1575 to 1578. Even though he did not keep his mother's letters to him, it is obvious that issues of clothing and fears about expenditure loomed even larger in them.[23] Paul was a confident spender. Whereas his younger brother would, on the whole, try to be careful and seek agreements with his mother, Paul told her what he had spent, provided eloquent reasons for purchases, and worked through ensuing arguments with her. He regularly provided lists of his expenditure, and at Leipzig showed remorse and improvement during a time of sharp price rises, which he knew affected his family.

Paul was well-read and schooled, and highly talented rhetorically. This made him brilliantly effective in deploying the imagery of the torn in order to get his mother to agree to expenses. In June 1573, for instance, aged sixteen, he told her that he really needed some new clothes this year if he wanted to walk around 'a little clean' (*sauber*). Moreover the problem was that Leipzig tailors were unwilling to use 'one stitch' to mend clothes if one never bought anything new. So he had always mended them himself, 'but what kind of mending is this', he lamented, 'if one mends something today it is torn tomorrow and afterwards one walks around with hose which are just lots of patches'. The mending dissolved, it was on the move, about to reveal what clothing was meant to conceal. However, he continued wisely, 'I am not writing you this because I wish to wear stately clothes with velvet and silk. No, not at all. I would like to follow your opinion that I should be able to wear clothes for 3, 4, 5, 6 years, like you. But I know that you would not approve if one walks around like someone who has fallen off the gallows.' He thus asked for her permission to have new clothes made, including a gown for feast days.[24]

In August he requested specific kinds of fabric from her, so that he could order new clothes from tailors at the autumn fair, who worked more cheaply.[25] The bill arrived in October, exceeded eight Thaler, and included spending on bits of velvet, which were used for trims on two hats and one coat, as well as new doublets with twelve buttons.[26] Paul received her response within seven days, and wrote back in dismay. She had accused him of overspending, especially for his 'daily penny', which he said was unfair, because the most he did was to sometimes order some beer if someone from Nuremberg or one of the students he shared a table with dropped by. But, he continued, 'if you are cross and unforgiving about the eight Thaler which I have spent to make the doublet and hose and adjust the coat, and wondered whether I used the money for these or foolishly, I have followed your order and sent them out to you.' So all new clothes were gone again—sent to Nuremberg to be inspected. Paul dutifully acknowledged that it was a mother's duty to punish misbehaving children, and that he had spent too much at the fair and sinned against her. He accepted her punishment and his reduced allowance, merely asking her to let her 'motherly fury' go. He only hoped to be able to be granted a long enough life by God to repay her for some of the pain and work she experienced with him.[27] Paul had already set out in another letter that he knew full well that she invested in him and his future career on behalf of the family, assuring her that he did wish to repay her, to make good, morally as well as materially. He signalled his sense of moral obligation to her through this rhetoric of remorse in the strongest terms—he had sinned against his mother through indulgence.

During the summer of the following year, 1574, Paul used a further strategy to uphold her confidence in him by sending a detailed description of another son of a patrician Nuremberg family, Jeremias Imhoff. Imhoff lived a loose life in Wittenberg, and Paul had visited him because someone had told him Jeremias was close to death. It turned out that Imhoff's brother-in-law had given him a tiny room at the back of his house, so that he would not be able to look out of the window and get friends in to gamble and feast. But this admittedly friendly young man still did nothing other than gamble. Paul stated, rather shocked, that he had twice found him with his similarly disposed wife still in bed at eight o'clock in the morning—two hours before early modern Germans normally had their lunch! This impression of Jeremias's squandering was fittingly rounded off by a description of his clothes: 'He has a very stately manner of clothing. During weekdays his dress is: all velvet baggy hose and a red atlas doublet, on Sunday: a yellow damask outfit.' Imhoff had shown him all the university as well as Luther's and Melanchthon's tombs, but otherwise entertained him and his friends in such a way that Paul had not managed to stay sober one single day.[28] For Paul, 'stateliness', *Stadtlichkeit*, was the category that marked the divide between the honourable decency and decorousness he could aspire to as a student and impressively luxurious dress. Imhoff clearly did not distinguish strongly in terms of the materials he used between weekdays and feast-days. This also documented that he did not seem to work at all. In the act of wearing weekday clothing, then, honourable people showed that they were among those who worked to earn a living, rather than people of leisure and sin. Paul's letter showed his mother that Jeremias Imhoff embodied charming immorality, while he himself was not an inch like this dissolute young man.

By September, however, Magdalena Behaim received a letter from Paul announcing that he now wished to have the coat turned inside out for winter, because it had taken on a blue colour, and also to have new clothes made. Two weeks later he announced that he had had baggy hose made for nine Thaler, and was looking forward to the trip to Italy, if she was still happy to let him go. 'That should be my greatest joy in life', he frankly exclaimed, 'to see something through travelling.'[29] In another letter, he soon elaborated:

> about the clothes I had made you need to know that it was not without reason that I took these kinds of hose, the baggy hose [*Pumphosen*] as one calls them, and also Italian [*welsch*] hose, because they are really worn in Italy, and you may gather from Ketzel's hose what shape they are. And because I wish to look at this country and stay there for a while, I have chosen these kinds of hose. As regards the shoes there is also a reason, which I wish to let you know about another time.[30]

The point of travelling, he argued elsewhere, was to get to know other customs and manners (*gebrauch und artt*). Baggy hose were not at all 'lumpen', as his mother alleged, but 'clean and durable in the Italian way according to their customs'.[31] So off he went.

From Italy, Paul continued to send records of his expenses to his mother. As Matthias Beer has shown, young men of the burgher and upper classes in early modern Germany obviously gained greater independence as they now routinely left their families for such extended periods of time. It is also important to emphasize that this experience marked gender differences in these status groups in a new way. As more and more young men left to go to university and to study and travel abroad, this left bourgeois young women much more clearly tied to their hometown and household—to familiar worlds, in short. For men, by contrast, this allowed for a new social role as well-informed, adventurous 'men of the world', who entertained others with narratives of risks they had mastered and impressed them with the insights they had gathered. It gave men something to talk about to an audience for the rest of their lives, to dialogue with other men who had had similar experiences, and cultivate an interest in travel literature. It affirmed their standing, while women's prestige in this respect became more second-hand; it was related to them being part of a household of well-travelled men and, increasingly, to consuming travel literature. Even so, young men's temporary independence would be closely supervised through regular private correspondence and curbed through their remaining financial dependence. If children wished to remain a valued member of the family network, which of course was never a nuclear one, but had been carefully extended and institutionalized through marriages, god-parentage, and guardianships, they needed to convince in their spending and conform. In other words: these young men had to argue their cases well, choose what to explain now and what to leave for later, when to show remorse and betterment, when to ask for permission and when to take courage and act according to their own desires. If we might describe households in pragmatic terms as 'site[s] of alliances between husband and wife and of implicit contracts between parents and children', then the time when young men left the family household was the time when those implicit contracts were dramatically put to the test.[32]

Paul Behaim travelled to Italy in a trio of Nuremberg sons and was put up with a Nuremberg relative of one of them, Gabriel Gienger, who had known the country and oversaw their introduction to Italian living as well as their expenditure. Like his brother Friedrich a few years later, Paul had left some debts in Leipzig unsettled. He knew that he needed to display frugality in his first letter from Italy anyway, while making two essential points: first, that his companions spent more; and second, that everything here was more expensive. This was artfully achieved in a letter from Padua:

> Dear Mother...I have used the money from the sale (of a horse) to have the simplest coarse green clothing made for myself—a doublet with modest trim, pleatless hose (like those Gienger [the tutor] wears at home), and a hooded coat...Lest you think things are cheap here, all this has cost me approximately seventeen or eighteen crowns, even though it was as plain and simple as it could be. I could not have been more amazed when I saw (that bill) than you will be when I send it to you.[33]

Still more convincing was needed, however, and it promptly followed in a further letter. Paul reminded his mother that the parents of the trio had in fact decided 'unanimously' before they left Nuremberg that the boys should wear 'only clothing made from coarse green and from neither a grander or a lesser fabric, saying that a better fabric was not appropriate for us young men, nor any other as strong and neat in appearance'. So why did she suddenly insist that he should have bought linen? He had been the only one who had kept to the rule in buying coarse material; linen was expensive in Italy, and, as he added only at the end, 'not in style here'. Next followed his larger argument, that one should adopt the customs of the country one lived in. Once more he proceeded by taking account of her emotional reactions, signalling that he understood how she felt. Yet he also needed to tell her just what the world was like here that one needed to adjust to. 'It will astonish you even more to learn that it is the custom here (indeed, it is all one knows) to wear only simple stockings...detached from the hose, which, moreover, cost more than two gulden.'[34]

Sons were usually fitted out before they set out on their studies, and this seems often to have led to disagreement. Count Christoph von Zimmern, for instance, was perfectly happy to have his son fitted out in 'good, silken dress' before he went to study in Freiburg, but he instructed his tailor to cut everything large in respect of his son's expected growth. When his son prevailed upon the tailor to make fashionable short garments, he was scolded as a fool by the count and firmly reminded whom to obey.[35] While

Paul Behaim had himself decided on the fashionable breeches, it is important to note that the parents and guardians—not only the mothers—had made a collective decision about what colour and fabric was to be appropriate for these young Nuremberg men.

Paul soon produced evidence that at least Gienger dressed more costly. In August 1575, many of their belongings in Padua were stolen. Their money was gone, as well as 'a small necklace with a malachite heart worth about forty crowns, and a pair of velvet hose with silver trim'—these belonged to their tutor. Soon it was time to think about winter clothes. The students had borrowed almost everything they needed from local Jews, from books to furniture. Jews were also at the node of trade in hiring clothes. Their second-hand clothes shops were called *strazzaria* and remained located right in the centre of Padua both before and after the Jewish ghetto was founded in 1603.[36] But it is also possible that Jewish salesmen in addition peddled in the streets and specifically targeted German students, who by far outnumbered students from other countries. Pietro Bertelli's costume book *Diversarum nationum habitus*, printed in Padua between 1594–1596, depicted a 'Judeus mercator patavinus' carrying an arm full of clothes and rudely beckoning in German 'What do you want to give' (*Was welt ier geben*).[37] This manner of speech, which in its direct demanding tone reduced an exchange of goods to a monetary transaction, harked back to the much older anti-Semitic stereotypes that depicted Jews as usurers, which we encountered in Luther's early image campaign against them (Fig. 60). Here there was no interaction with nice words describing the qualities of what was on sale and seeking to establish a more personal relation with a client, whom one honoured for his ability to distinguish different qualities and the character of goods. It was represented as a disturbingly de-personalized relationship with merchandise and customers, which focused on getting deals done fast with gain and goods that would quickly circulate from one owner to the next.

In a city like Padua with a mobile student population, renting out clothes as well as furniture was the obvious thing to do: Paul's companions were moving on further south in autumn, and nobody wanted to carry heavy winter robes around with them before or after the cold season. Paul, meanwhile, calculated whether it was cheaper to hire or to invest in buying and reselling: 'looking ahead to winter', he reported rather belatedly in December, 'I have bought a camel's hair coat lined with fox fur for four crowns, which, depending on my circumstances later, I can resell at a good price. Otherwise, I would have to pay the Jew ten Batzen a month just for the loan of such a good.'[38]

THE FRIENDSHIP ALBUM

In 1576, Gienger and one of the Nuremberg trio moved on, while the other one together with eighteen-year-old Paul stayed on in Padua, but lived in different places. Since August, Gienger and others had spent money on very special entries in Paul's friendship album, which is preserved in the British Library, to commemorate their connection. These albums were small books with empty pages, to be filled with mottoes, coats of arms or images by friends and mentors. The custom of having such albums was a relatively recent one. It had first become common in Wittenberg, and remained particularly popular among students and travelling noblemen. Around 1,500 of these alba survive.[39] Paul's album nonetheless was special in that it was one among a smaller group with costume figures.[40] How do we make sense of this new visual practice? It is to be assumed that local illuminists carried out such work and offered particular models appealing to the taste of their customers. They were likely to be interested in creating visual icons that had a particular hold on young, male foreigners and could quickly be churned out time and again.

The friendship album of a Nuremberg man called Sigmund Ortellius or Örtel, whose stay in Italy overlapped with Paul's, showed a scene of what appears to be a humoristic depiction of two quarrelling young men. One looked like a student, but both wore torn clothes. This contrasted to figurines of splendid, politically influential Venetian and Roman men and seductively elegant women with their gloves and fans. Italian women were imaginary complements of confident elegance, ease, and often sexual appeal. Their breasts were usually depicted uncovered, and even more accentuated if dark veils were worn over the face, merely leaving the chest uncovered. These vignettes, in other words, newly attached symbolic meanings and identifications to particular kinds of masculinity and femininity in Italian society just as the printed costume book was emerging. They pioneered these visual moral geographies.

Travelling young men who showed these figures in their alba displayed their knowledge of what counted as honourable and good mannered, or, as in the case of courtesans, was tolerated in a society so different to theirs. The women were abstract figures, not women they had met. This enabled them to fit men and women into a familiar 'moral cosmography', in which they figured as 'walking ideas'.[41] Yet these depictions were not just about rationally conceived 'ideas' and 'concepts'. They ambivalently cast these foreign icons of femininity as objects of desire, while associating them with immorality at the same time. Images managed the partly conscious attractions and fears of groups of young men who lived in much more homo-social environments than they would have done at home for this particular stage of their education, before they returned home to marry. And it was absolutely clear that these Protestant men would now be firmly told not to have any illicit sex.

The album of Jona and Petri Portner of Nuremberg shows entries for the years 1567–1608. One image merrily celebrates joy, love, and laughter in the figure of a man with long baggy hose, a red hat with bushy feathers, and a long glass of wine. 'Laugh: love: laugh' is inscribed above, and the same words again are rendered upside down above it. The page facing this scene shows coat of arms depicting a happy virgin, dressed in red, with long blonde hair (Fig. 129).[42] The next entries, however, depict buttoned-up honourable German women, one dressed in black and gold, with flowers in her hand (Fig. 130), the other one in black and white, with the inscription 'Honour to God alone'.[43] German female dress once more seemed to come with a guarantee of virtue, whereas Italian dress, as represented in Weigel's costume book, indicated greater sensuousness, luxurious sophistication, and dramatic playfulness, but far less transparency and reliability (Figs. 131–132).

130. Album Amicorum of Portner, honourable lady, Eg.1186, 28v. © The British Library, London

High-ranking Italian men served as identificatory figures for younger men attracted by their office, women ambivalently through allure. During their stay, young Nurembergers would have had no personal contact with a Venetian doge, but the best of them aspired to become something akin to these illustrious republican urban governors furthering the common weal. Their future success and honour would later express itself in such representational robes and gowns signalling authority and integrity. It is easy to see how Paul, too, might have identified with such a vision of male responsibility in an urban world, so removed though it was for the moment from his life in hired clothes, items to be sold, and rags, but nonetheless connected with his heritage and ideal future. After all, his own father had been senior burghermaster of Nuremberg, as well as leading a civic delegation to an important meeting of Lutheran territories.

In Paul Behaim's own album, Gienger had an enticing Florentine woman entered, with a low cut décolleté, and a striking red gown with a decorous belt, as well as different necklaces, emphasizing the volume of her breasts.[44] In 1576, Paul acquired three further vignettes paid for by Nuremberg men in Italy: a doge; a dogeressa with a low-cut gown, a multicoloured feather fan, a decorous handkerchief, and belt; and a Venetian *consigliero*—a man of the council of ten, attired in a glorious red robe with gold brocade. Once more though we need to ask: Why Venice and Florence? Paul had arrived in Venice in April 1575, but only stayed there for four days, before his group had wanted to move on to Ferrara. He nonetheless had ended up in Padua, because the flooded Po had cut off their access route. Less than one year later, in March 1576, Paul was desperate to move on—but not back to Venice. He wished to see Bologna, Siena, and Rome, as seeing these cities seemed essential for the 'pursuit of my studies and good manners'.[45]

None of this worked out, for the plague spread from Venice and into Padua. Paul escaped to a village, but was infected by a visiting German nobleman, whom he witnessed dying within days. Paul himself would be seriously ill for months, returning to Padua

131.   Album Amicorum of Johannes Thomas Örtel, Italian lady with ostrich feather fan, Eg.1225, 23r. © The British Library, London

132.   Album Amicorum, The German gentleman chooses the German lady over Italian women, Staatsbibliothek Bamberg, I Qc 41, 129r. © Staatsbibliothek Bamberg, Photo: Gerald Raab

in autumn 1576, and soon renewed his plan to go to Verona. His mother suspiciously asked for an academic progress report, and in the end decided to cut his allowance. So once again, it was time to defiantly deploy the rhetoric of the ragged, which he now linked to a new argument: his process of learning and discovery depended on being close to noble people and others leading honourable lives. All these people were 'tidy and neat, and they expect those they associate with to be so as well'. 'One does not', he lectured his mother and sisters, who read this at home, 'put oneself in such company in tatters and rags', so that, in sum, 'one must at times do a bit more and not count the cost'.[46]

In August 1577, still in Padua and after having fallen out with a cousin and his mother, he refused to stay any longer on her budget.[47] He was aware that he had already drawn more heavily on income from their paternal inheritance than his siblings. His mother received precise advice in Nuremberg on how much the best sons of the city usually spent on a trip to Rome. She was horrified, alongside his guardian. But surprisingly, his sisters now supported him—if he did not go, none of them ever would. In the end, Paul had actually hardly seen Venice, and had been stuck in Padua and even in an Italian village. He had obtained no degree—which was not really problematic—but, worse, no real experience of Italy either. Would he be able to convincingly talk about Italian institutions, sites, and people? No! They did not even know yet that his album amicorum in fact would look quite pitiful—there were hardly any entries apart from the initial trio around Gienger. Most pages remained empty, merely a mute testimony to his lack of funds to engage in sociability and build up solid friendships among educated men. Yet after everything that had been spent on him already, his sisters concluded that his new travel expenditure would not matter so much in proportion, hoping that he would pay everything back to them at some point.[48]

Paul, for his part, began to make up with his mother, arguing that the devil himself had caused their division. Her 'happiness' and welfare as well as 'the honour of us all' were now his principal concerns.[49] Yet again he overspent on his allowance, only to rebut her protest with an affirmation of his filial indebtedness to her, followed by some more rhetoric of the ragged: 'I must tell you that I have never in my life been filthier or more dishevelled...and if your will remains inflexible and I cannot have made a new suit of clothes made here, I will come home to you in rags.'[50] The infested, dirty, ragged state of high-born travellers returning home was topical: 'See our louse-bitten Travellers ragged device/ Of case, shoes, and stockings, and Canniball lice' ran one rhyme elucidating the travellers' depiction on the frontispiece of Thomas Coryat's later travel reports.[51]

Yet something else was at stake in this exchange between mother and son. In presenting an image of his return in rags, Paul evoked a scene everyone in this culture across Europe knew well, though, as in Matthäus Schwarz's case, it had previously applied to adventures in one's home country: the tale of the prodigal son. The prodigal son had travelled, squandered his money on meals, drink, expensive clothes, and frivolous company. Now, he returned clad merely in a torn shirt. The dramatic endpoint of his departure from a moral life was whether he would be welcomed back into his parental household and, as in the biblical tale, generously be given beautiful clothing, or be driven away.[52] This imagery clearly exercised a strong fascination on people at this time. It allowed them to project their anxieties about a lack of control over travelling young men, who, after all, had survived all diseases up to then to grow into strong youths. Would they bring shame or honour onto their family during this time and upon their return? How far could forgiveness stretch? (Fig. 133) Had they taken up this life from the start to deny their parents and live selfishly and sinfully, so that they deserved to be driven away like the richly clad Lazarus by Abraham (Lk 16, 19)? The violent tale of a thirteenth century author called Wernher 'the Gardener' still circulated, which told about a peasant son called Helmbrecht who came home ragged and blind from his life as robber-knight. His father turned him away.[53]

'Imaging work' through story-telling, embroidery, water-colouring, or art purchases seems to have been a way for contemporaries to express, and therefore perhaps to some extent manage, emotions and expectations around such dramatic turning points in family life. Women of the wealthy Nuremberg Tucher family, for instance, neatly embroidered this familiar scene early in the century with a morally determined and wholly unsentimental ending: the son clad in a short shift was driven away by three beautifully clad young women with a stick, presumably his indignant sisters.[54] The Dutch painter Pieter Cornelius Kunst, by contrast, went on the art market with a large oil painting simply representing the lost son in the simplest of rags at the moment of return. This pictorial mode invited a narrative imagination as those looking at the picture could now imagine possible endings to the scene. It invited onlookers into a dialogue about what ought to happen, of how one should deal with sons who had been estranged from family values while they were trying to define their independence.

Students time and again used images to deal with guilt. One Leipzig student was dismissed from his alma mater in 1606 because of a violent fight with a tailor and had a ragged figure, shamefully hiding under bits of cloth, painted into his friendship album under the heading 'Repenting', with golden letters and in beautiful calligraphy. Two quotations from Cicero balanced the notion that 'The wise man never does anything he might repent' with the more practical advice that 'The best thing to do if you do repent something is to change your behaviour.'[55] In such cases, then, an image and inscriptions in the album allowed a student to visually work through some of the conflicting feelings generated by parental expectations for filial obedience, and a wish for independence and specific socially sanctioned expressions of manliness, and to document how he saw this resolved. 'No cash, just torn hose', (*Nunquam pargelt semper zrißen hosßen*), a 1625 album depiction of another ragged German student dryly commented, representing him with his walking stick, a card game, glass, and a gambling board thrown to the ground.[56]

All of this represented not just anxieties over a decline in social status through material failure. These images show how rags once more functioned as a metaphor for a disordered, literally disintegrating life, making young men depend on charity and great

133. Abraham Bach, Parable of the Prodigal Son, Augsburg Broadsheet, Inv. No. HB 26465 ©
Germanisches Nationalmuseum, Nürnberg

parental gestures of generosity and goodwill. They also reveal that visual practices in the
alba were topical, but not rigorously uniform. Rather, they took on a variety of topoi
in relation to different owners, as well as available illuminists, or the owner's drawing
skills.

Paul's mother in the end remained entirely unshaken by the vision that Paul might
really return in rags. She insisted that he would have that outfit made in Nuremberg. He
retorted that the only 'more respectable' fabric was camel hair, which was more expensive in Nuremberg, so could he please bring some back to Nuremberg with him. And in
the closing lines of his letter dated 2 April 1578, Paul still asks her to 'look around for a
good material for a waistcoat, one like that worn by a great many people here. Or if it
pleases you, I could have a finely tailored one made for myself there from a piece of the

leftover camel's hair. . . .'[57] He thought it would take him two to four weeks once he was back in Nuremberg to be outfitted with new clothes. Until then he asked to see nobody and entertain himself with books in the garden.[58]

The idea that he would hide in the family's garden house until new clothes arrived was not as odd or unlikely as it may sound. In 1640, for instance, a Danish ambassador stayed in a small town near Madrid for a full three weeks waiting for appropriate liveries to be made for his servants before he displayed himself at court. Representatives of the Hanseatic towns once even found to their dismay that the king had moved on because he would no longer wait for them to change their travelling clothes for new black clothes according to Spanish custom.[59] Paul, too, had to accept that his culture allowed for the process of travelling as gradual de-vestiture. His re-entry into local society in turn was preceded by an act of investiture for which his mother now once again decided what was considered appropriate and fashionable locally, instructed the tailor what to do, and how much to spend. And Paul did make good after his return. He became a major figure in local politics with its Imperial extension, further expanding the power and honour of the Behaim network through three wives and eighteen children.

CONCLUSION

Nearly fifty years after Friedrich Behaim penned his letters, another young man of this clan wrote from another public school near Nuremberg. The tone was utterly different: 'Would you', Stephan Carl Behaim pressured his mother in a rash rhythm of excited prose, 'God willing, send me my good black coat and my gold silk garters on Saturday for sure, for sure? Also, fix up my gold doublet so that the new taffeta on the sleeves juts forward. And let's risk sending my white doublet. And for sure send me hand-towels, two goblets, a decorative bed-cover, handkerchiefs, and a pewter tankard—all these things for sure, for sure, for sure. And answer my letter today for sure.'[60] This demanding teenager obviously did not keep his mother's letters, and was seen as reckless throughout his life. Nobody was surprised when his brother received notice in 1639 that Stephan Carl had died in Brazil, to where he had fled as a low-ranking officer in a desperate final attempt to escape debts and improve his career opportunities. Barely two years after his arrival, a Nuremberg man met him down and out in the burgeoning colonial settlement of Recife, in a tattered coat, 'filthy and fevered', without stockings and shoes.[61] This despondent image captured all that was expected at the end of a rake's progress, the antithesis against which respectability held up its morale and grammar of vestimentary codes: the clean and mended against the tattered; decent coverage against the uncovered; shoes against bare feet on the ground, in dirt and disorder, spreading disease and death. The possibility of downward mobility through overspending, debt-making, or corruption was something real to every family. And it seemed far more fearsome as the world of goods diversified.

134.   Medal of Lucia Dorer wearing a beret, as an ornament of Germany, 1523, Inv. No. Med 6766. © Germanisches Nationalmuseum, Nürnberg

CHAPTER 7

Bourgeois Taste
and Emotional Styles

DIVINE BEAUTY

In 1522, the goldsmith's wife Lucia Dorer was the first Nuremberg woman below the patriciate to be portrayed on a medal wearing a beret[1] (Fig. 134). Urban women from Venice to Nuremberg, as we shall see, showed their hair and campaigned to wear such berets, which moralists, such as the Strasbourg preacher Geiler von Kaisersberg, dismissed as lascivious.[2] They created a more open look, and made it easier for women to look at others. This new look was guided by Renaissance ideals of female beauty as something to be treasured, which defied misogynist notions that women were an error of nature, while men embodied perfection. Many Renaissance feminists argued that female ornamentation was not necessarily vain and damnable. In 1504, Agrippa von Nettesheim even used neo-Platonist ideas to posit that women were the more perfect sex, and his argument partly relied on the nature of hair. Women's hair was abundant, beautiful, and grew in the right place. Men's grew on the face and was unclean, while all too soon it disappeared from the head. Agrippa's popular treatise, *On the nobility of the female sex*, was translated into several languages, and argued that men were generally inferior and less clean because they had been created from earth. He proposed that beauty was a brilliant light that shone from God's face to touch humans and emanated especially from women. This spiritualization of female beauty allowed Agrippa to lavishly describe it. While he considered a woman's body, hands, voice, gestures, and movements in a summary fashion, he commented on her hair and all the parts of a woman's face in detail, from her forehead to her cheeks, eyebrows, eyes, gaze, lips, and teeth.[3] All this rendered a visualization of chastity through veiling techniques less important: beauty itself could be divine!

Given such debates, women's involvement with fashion was not necessarily idle consumption either, it could help them to visualize new identities in which virtue and beauty went together, to offer esteem and a startling public visibility on urban streets or at dances. Lucia Dorer's medal was even inscribed with the claim that she was a muse and an ornament of Germany. A hole allowed for the medal to be hung on a chain, rather than to be tucked away in a coin cabinet. This was a striking visual act, especially for a woman below the patriciate, which implicitly claimed that women did not need to be high-born to claim such esteem. Beauty ideals could be one way for women to have a Renaissance. Accessories such as berets could lead to experiments with gender roles, which were used by men as much as by women and could be seen as masculine. Lucia Dorer, in any case, did not seem to wish to project a notion of delicate female beauty; her features were large and her look determined. More traditionally, women's ornamentation materialized their honour in service of their family and the increasingly important home.[4]

Magdalena Behaim

How can we find out about urban women's experiences as consumers and in households? The Behaims once more are of help. Magdalena Behaim was Friedrich and Paul Behaim's oldest sibling. In 1583, aged twenty-eight, and thus perfectly in time, she married into a well-off and politically active Nuremberg merchant family, the Paumgartners. Balthasar Paumgartner carried on business in a whole network of northern Italian cities, especially in Florence, Venice, Bologna, Genoa, and Lucca. From here, Balthasar reported on delicious melons, parmesan, artichokes, fennel, pumpkins, and lemon seeds, female theatre performers, famished poor people, spa trips, and work. He would then regularly travel to the two annual Frankfurt fairs, and hope to see Magdalena on the way. While Balthasar was away, Magdalena would not be lonely and housebound. She continued the couple's presence in Nuremberg society and among relatives as well as managing orders and distributing goods Balthasar sent. Their relationship began at the tail end of two horrible decades in which 20,000 Nuremberg people had fallen victim to the plague. Yet as early as 1600, Nuremberg once more proudly counted 40,000 inhabitants, the same number as in 1561.[5]

Magdalena cultivated their clientele and signed as Magdalena Balthasar Paumgartt-nerin, even to her own husband. As wife she represented a composite unit that was rooted in both their families' achievements and honour. Balthasar took it for granted that both their coats of arms should be cut into wood and embellished with gold. So Magdalena Balthasar Paumgarttnerin went to dances, weddings, a big banquet in the castle, funerals, baptisms, and visited lying-in women, she lent equipment for garden parties and went to numerable garden parties that involved musicians or entertainers herself. She lodged a sick acquaintance, hosted meals, and once more managed communication about purchases of goods, sent cloth samples to Balthasar for him to take orders from, and managed a network of creditors and debtors. During the years 1582–98, up to her early forties, he kept her letters, as she kept his, a total of 172.[6] This makes the Behaims the best documented of any sibling group and Magdalena and her husband Balthasar the best documented couple in the early modern world. Magdalena's letters open a unique window onto an urban culture of bourgeois decorum, buying, and sociability, in which women played such major roles. They can be complemented with rich information from inventories, sumptuary laws, court depositions, as well as images of the kinds of clothes and accessories consumed by Nuremberg men and women across society. Magdalena's and Balthasar's letters also reveal how appearances became part of new emotional styles for couples who endorsed ideas of mutual love and material life as pleasure. Finally, the letters provide a rare glimpse of a woman in business, for Magdalena traded in fabrics and particular items of dress.

RAGGED DEALINGS AND CRIMSON CLOTH

Balthasar had a brother called Yerg, whom he experienced as quarrelsome at particular times and, frankly, 'full of shit'. The single term to characterize his practices was 'ragged dealings' (*lumpenhandel*)—the rough, ragged, used, torn, and morally degenerate once more thought of in opposition to an aesthetics and ethics of respectable form and decorous civility, which extended from manners of speech to comportment, dress, and interlinked with honourable moral conduct.[7] Years after Balthasar had talked so damningly about his brother, Magdalena reported the following story. Yerg had begged his father to lend him money. He had seen a nice outfit at the pigs' market, the *Saumarkt*, where much of the second-hand trade took place, which he wanted to buy for winter. By 1572, at least thirty-eight women worked as second-hand clothes dealers in Nuremberg.[8] The father requested that Magdalena should hand the money for the outfit to the woman who kept the second-hand stall, and she decided to inspect whether it was worth it. The woman arrived with the outfit and Magdalena saw that it was completely new, made from a lesser silk cloth and worth the money. She bought it, but determinedly told Yerg that he was going to get an outfit made from stone if he took this one to the next tavern and gambled on it. No, he replied, then 'the devil should take me—I need it and soon want to go away in it'. A mere three days later, Magdalena went to the market and saw the outfit again hanging at the same stall. On that very day, the woman reported, Yerg had asked for the money to be returned to him, because the outfit did not please him. Magdalena suspected that all this had been arranged with the second-hand dealer for some reward, as they usually were not allowed to take back what they had sold. 'It's not going to get better until he goes to prison', Magdalena sighed—though for a Paumgartner this was most unlikely.[9]

Most of the couple's communication about clothing focused on materials and dyes. Magdalena would request cloths in particular qualities from the northern Italian market for herself and a whole network of clients, or send Balthasar other people's requests by letter straightaway; Balthasar would attempt to acquire these and also independently buy good stock. They knew how to buy well, a key skill for a merchant, and one shared by men and women. They had to look out for new materials and goods, get information about the mixture of fabrics from which they were produced and how well they absorbed dye, how durable they were, where to best source them in terms of price and quality, and find out who would process them most reliably. They maintained social bonds with customers and producers to ensure ongoing trust. This knowledge enabled one to present oneself as a discerning customer and a competent enough agent to purchase for others. This in turn influenced prices and commissions. In this period, prices were rarely fixed. They were adjusted to individual customers in terms of status, knowledge, and their relationship with the buyer.

Magdalena and Balthasar first of all used measurements—her brother, for instance, had asked for grey and black stockings from Bologna, and Balthasar had taken the measurements down, but had had to order them from elsewhere as he could not find any suitable material.[10] Timing evidently mattered as well, because more expensive textiles were bought for particular occasions or seasons, and this had to be planned and secured with care and through quick and responsible merchants and middlemen. Magdalena hence was to tell a Frau Lochnerin that Balthasar had sourced expensive red crimson and two-coloured cloths. When the red crimson was ready one month later, in January 1583, he promised to send it carefully and noted that now no more was to be had.[11] In July 1584, he asked Magdalena to communicate that he had instantly sent green velvet to the Scheurls and taffeta for another woman, so that it would reach them as they had requested. Magdalena would start to think in August of what repairs the lining of her fur coat for winter needed, to ensure it would be in a presentable condition in good time.

Balthasar next wrote that the first attempt to use crimson red atlas had failed, he had taken the fabric for himself and Magdalena to be turned into a blanket, but he had asked for another cloth, which would be sent to Jakob Welser at Genoa that week. He had seen the fabric being woven, but nobody in Lucca or Florence was able to then process it in the way he wanted. Many Nurembergers were clearly highly attracted to red: Magdalena's sister wanted red velvet and silk, and one of the Scheurls another two eln of red velvet. At the end of his long letter, the very same in which he reflected on his brother's ragged dealings, Balthasar returned to crimson red cloth, which he had received as he was writing, a whole 25 eln of it, shining in the evening light. 'It is a beautiful, high colour, pleases me well', he wrote with a mixture of awe and deep aesthetic pleasure.[12] In her reply, Magdalena however immediately raised the anxiety this caused her in the tersest of phrasings: 'I am afraid it will cost too much.'[13] But this colour and smoothness was rich and imparted this sensation on one's life, it defied the ragged; Magdalena meanwhile was busy shopping for pure white linen and cotton cloths to swaddle the baby she was expecting and put cushions under its little head. Balthasar assured her that he had chosen this 'desired, red crimson smooth velvet full well and hoped it would once please your sister'. Once again he was about to finish the letter when he received news from Welser in Genoa, who had received the cloth, telling him how and when he was going to process it. Balthasar added:

> I have no doubt that this is going to be like the most beautiful (thing) as we ourselves desire it. But what it costs, we are not allowed to say. He has already sent me a bill, according to which it will cost between R.66 and R.67. Do not

tell anyone. What this clever boy further writes about it I shall let you sometime (if God will) read for yourself in his letter. He just wants the best for you.[14]

Magdalena felt deeply confused and still more anxious upon this cheerfully conveyed news. Whereas Balthasar valued the item primarily in terms of its prestige and aesthetic value, her worries led her to see this cloth mostly in terms of its exchange value, although she still tried to approach the matter with some humour:

> You are writing me that the blanket is not going to cost more than a suma laud. I was shocked in my heart. Another time we will think about this better before hand. Of course we must not talk about this. It seems to me that if such money was bound up in a piece of silver the value would be there again, but here it is not. Now we both have to be silent. I would really like to know what the clever boy writes. If you write to me that he wants all to be well for me I don't understand in what way. I can hardly wait to hear the price.[15]

Reason was needed to tame vainglorious desire, even if Balthasar suggested they could use it as a family gift rather than for themselves. But this largesse, in any case, made Magdalena fraught, took all joy from the purchase, and now above all created a terrible secret between the couple, which needed to be repeatedly affirmed. Alongside love, which they clearly shared and knew how to make alive, the experience of coupledom was now also constituted through their shared and secret knowledge and shame about on what and how much they spent. Coupledom measured fantasies about a domestic display they wished to establish beyond concerns about exchange value: fantasies of sheer luxury, in other words, because cloth lost value through use, whereas silver stored it. Cloth, moreover, was a 'consumable' commodity, whereas silver was durable, unbreakable even. To communicate views about such objects and their role in life was thus a process of forming a view on how a couple could ideally reach a consensus on what constituted value and the legitimacy of expenditure, what would count as necessity (*Nothurft*), and what as extravagance. In this sense, material consumption and the definition of consumption strategies constituted a married relationship in part, as a couple needed to set up a household and furnish it and themselves according to the social role they assumed at different stages in their lives.

To be married obviously was nothing immaterial in any case—after all marriage in itself was a contract and material transaction. This became particularly obvious when in the northern German city of Stralsund the esteemed mayor, Bartholomäus Sastrow, married his own maidservant in 1598, after his wife had died. Sastrow was adamant that the maidservant deserved to be well dressed according to her new rank and to 'honour himself'. He even specified what kind of jewellery he wanted to have made for her. Sastrow was not going to have her look poorer than his children, or other mayors' wives. His children and the Stralsund council agreed grudgingly.[16] Clothes and jewellery were key establishers of a material and social identity that could evidently be adjusted through marriage (Fig. 135).

Marriage, then, was also the beginning of a household's lifecycle of consumption. In urban bourgeois circles this began to matter much more as entertainment throughout much of the year became the cement of sociability. This was so especially through the sixteenth-century advent of urban gardens, which allowed for several tables of guests to be placed in the open air amidst the sweet smells of flowers, while music, singing, drinking, dancing, laughter, and conversation did not disturb any neighbours. Woodcuts of such scenes would be coloured, cut, and pasted onto storage boxes in bourgeois households, so much did they encapsulate a new emotional style and ideal of ease, love, and leisure.[17] By 1680, there were more than 350 gardens outside the Nuremberg city walls, typically divided into pleasure, fruit, and vegetable gardens.[18] Garden parties provided new and enlarged venues for consumption, where taste could be formed and new ideas exchanged. Bourgeois sociability of this kind was key to an ongoing sense that new consumption ideas were to be discovered, and formed what economists call 'consumption clusters' in like-minded groups.[19]

Much entertaining meanwhile was also done at home, and Magdalena clearly had a keen eye for beautiful cutlery she had seen in large numbers at one house, and tried to get Balthasar to source a decent quantity himself; until he gave up and told her it was better to have them made by a local craftsman. Magdalena's father himself had taken great care in the mid sixteenth century to furnish his household with English tin as well as copper plates, nice drinking mugs, some porcelain bowls from Flanders, tablecloths, and napkins. He had bought rugs to cover tables and beds; good, colourfully painted furniture; lights; and in 1548 spent seven florins on nine painted canvases, while just over one florin went to the carpenter for framing them.[20] Alongside tableware, delicatessen such as the best Bolognese olives, parmesan, and Parma ham, good wine, and the quality of interior decoration clearly had come to matter. Dining itself became more ambitious as women as well as men collected recipes or even, like Susanna Harsdörferin of Nuremberg in 1580, put together cookbooks.[21] Much of the domestic decorations on display alongside paintings were indeed textile hangings or rugs, which explains why Balthasar was so keen to invest in them. The story of the crimson velvet shows how a colour and object occasioned particular desire and esteem among their social circle, and could unbalance principles of bourgeois restraint. Just as Friedrich decided to 'live it up' at one point, the question here too was how and whether to justify deep aesthetic joy and showy luxuriousness. But Magdalena, like her own mother, anxiously had only wanted the bill.

Meanwhile Balthasar nonetheless on many occasions demonstrated a clever merchant's care about spending and a clear sense that objects mattered less in themselves, than in terms of the context in which they were put to use. He sent four eln of the worst damask, so that Magdalena could cover her expanding upper body during pregnancy. He surprisingly asked her to send him only 'five old shirts, two pairs of socks, a night cap, a pair of green padded house-shoes and a pair of thick shoes, to walk in the dirt and rainy weather of Frankfurt' during the fair.[22] Early on in their marriage he had reminded her of what he had already told her in person, namely not to spend much effort on making his wedding shirt. Such gold embroidered wedding shirts in Nuremberg were amorous garments that all brides gave to their husbands—the embroidery a woman's labour of love. They were

135. Wedding-bowl of the Augsburg Pahler–Imhof families, 1572, Augsburg, Städtische Kunstsammlungen. © Städtische Kunstsammlungen

inventorized across society, and thus clearly kept to memorize the wedding. Yet Balthasar thought that this only cost Magdalena useless time and sleep. He simply needed a shirt made from clean, pure linen, with a smooth collar, but otherwise just ordinary (*schlecht und gerecht*).[23] He explicitly justified that he needed his brother's help to source Polish wolf fur for a coat out of necessity. On another occasion, however, Balthasar bought a large amount of expensive and thin striped silk cloth in Mantua, suited for a unified domestic display of curtains, blankets for the day-bed, table-rugs, and cushions. He advised that one needed to be very careful in the cutting of it, so as not to show that the stripes were sewn together, and finally told Magdalena that she could use it if she liked or otherwise use a female dealer (*Käuflin*) to sell it well.[24] This affirms again that these women were not only second-hand dealers, but traded with new items. Just as the proliferating Parisian *revende-uses*, they benefited from a society in which tastes had diversified and mattered.

Dyes changed. Balthasar had spotted a new and, in Nuremberg, unusual colour in which he wanted to dress the male servants—a good yellowish saffron colour.[25] Then Magdalena complained about stockings he sent to her, because they had an unusual colour, a sort of blue, and also because they were bad quality. It looked as if it was linen, but actually it was cotton. She told the man who transported their wares from Lucca to take them straight back, so that Balthasar could perhaps sell them on without any loss there. 'If only you had written to me about the colour, I would have told you that it wasn't the right thing', she added, wishing they were green.[26] Magdalena liked green. So much so that her idea for the important domestic decoration of beds with blankets and curtains was that it would be 'green in green'. Beds, in this period, were representational objects too, rather than 'private', and she emphasized that she would not even use the high quality green taffeta she was asking for to decorate the special lying-in bed, in which new mothers received constant visitors, but for the permanent guest-bed. In addition there was a 'lazy' day-bed, the *Faulbett*, on which people rested or snoozed during the day, and this was put up in one of the reception rooms. *Arlas*, a silk cloth, was no good, because insects would eat it. And it was also important that Balthasar should buy the taffeta at Frankfurt, because this was the cleanest place and again the cockroaches would not eat it.[27] Her next letter urged once more that curtains were customarily green in Nuremberg and that the fringes should also be nicely green. But the green velvet he had sourced seemed too costly to her—she was going to use some old *Pubensamet*, faux velvet.[28]

RENEWING THE WORLD

Any innovation, that is in terms of colour, was clearly not welcomed by Magdalena in these years—she did not want a new and innovative look, but what fitted in with her taste community, would last well, and was not too expensive. Consumption is frequently thought of primarily as emulation of those who are more wealthy, but Magdalena certainly confirms Keith Thomas's sense that the

> consumption of goods was as much conformist in spirit as competitive. Most people bought commodities out of a desire to keep in line with the accepted standards of their own peer group rather than to emulate those of the one above: similarity in living styles was an important source of social cohesion; and anxiety to do the right thing was more common than the urge to stand out.[29]

Georg Simmel observed that people who look similar usually behave in the same way—so that appearances function in part to signal that a person wishes to belong to a particular set of values and hence to generate trust in her or his behaviour among peers.

Yet, again and again there was evidence also for that passionate investment in possessing beautiful and special objects, which strained boundaries of restraint to find some flexibility in treats and occasional largesse. The Behaims' little boy, Balthasarle, was soon fixated, and in 1589 Magdalena wrote that his father needed to bring him a small velvet bag as a gift when he returned—their son talked about it every night.[30] Predictably, his desire for the velvet bag became an ideal tool to manipulate him to behave like a 'pious' boy: 'just tell Balthasarle', his father wrote, 'that he should be pious for a while, for if he is bad than I shall give the nice velvet bag, two pairs of shoes and the red knitted stockings to another pious boy.'[31] The desire for these objects in anticipation would thus mix with fear that they might be withdrawn, given to a better boy. But because they were taken to measure and manipulate behaviour, the stakes accordingly became much higher and the father felt that he could no longer just promise the velvet bag, but also not even one, but two pairs of shoes and special red stockings on top to elicit the desired behaviour. He thought of the objects Balthasarle might like, imagining new needs and wishes. These emotional dynamics within parent–child relations fuelled consumption choices. In 1592, Balthasar likewise wrote to Magdalena that he had had a white doublet made for Balthasarle from cheaper cuts he had obtained, and a pair of pinkish damask breeches with a small flower pattern, which he would bring if 'he is pious for a while and learns fast'.[32] These mechanisms ironically turned luxurious, fashionable goods, rather than toys, for instance, into a materialized reward system for 'pious' and industrious behaviour and thus were emotionally and morally charged in a peculiar way. This socialized a child early on into thinking of clothing and other items of appearance as displaying piety and civility. Other Lutherans were dismayed by such an education: Joachim Westphal in his lengthy 1565 book against the devil of vanity clearly pointed out that there was nothing worse than small children who were hardly able to talk but received

> a new pair of little shoes with gold, a new coat etc. and look at themselves in
> it, and display it and wish that everyone sees and praises it, yes the children are
> contemptuous amongst each other and say, yes, I have a father who is richer than
> yours, he has bought this for me etc. I have a nicer coat than you.[33]

For Westphal, fine clothes only stimulated pride and God's anger. But the daily practices of Lutheran families in Nuremberg could turn fine clothes into a reward, even though little about this would have surprised Westphal, who thought that Nuremberg bred vanity.[34] Balthasarle's taste, in any case, was already shaped by young men of his status he identified with: Magdalena was in the middle of writing a letter to his father when Balthasarle entered and said he wanted two pairs of stockings, especially one like the Altdorf students had. He meant, the mother explained, flesh- or saffron-coloured. Delicate colours were the new trend. To keep these unstained, a boy would need to discipline his movements; these objects necessitated the learning of civilized corporeal behaviour to retain their beauty.[35] At the same time, as we have earlier seen, parents in these milieus also held on to a sense that there had to be clear limits to spending once young men became independent, and that they needed to be firmly educated into judicious forms of spending and consuming. After Balthasarle had tragically died of an illness, his father was asked to look after a son of the Imhoff family, and explicitly 'not to dress him in any costly way nor in silken clothes'.[36]

Magdalena, meanwhile, now wanted 'shiny stuff' for an apron—which probably means that she was referring to a new type of fabric, without knowing its name. Usually, however, Magdalena was extremely well-informed and specific. In 1584, for example, she asked 'friendly, dear Paumgartner', as she called her husband, to get a clean table-rug from the Netherlands, as they were available in Italy, and in Germany only at Frankfurt. She wanted them black and green and in a delicate weave, which she had seen in another household. The striped one they currently had was too big for a table, and the ones one could buy in Nuremberg were coarse. A blanket for the day-bed of the same kind would also be appreciated.[37] In 1591, again, she asked for a blanket and sent measurements for it. She wanted one side to be brown or green, and the other side of two-coloured daffet, such as golden and green or flesh-coloured and white, or anything he liked.[38] She also asked for costly *Arlas* to replace a 'bad', worn upper garment, and reiterated that there was none to be had in Nuremberg.[39] She reminded him for the need of this with reference to the meals she was invited to, and what she had was so used she could 'not wear it during the day'.[40]

As Magdalena aged, she clearly became comfortable in asking for luxurious items, though never of velvet, and usually with reference to need or similar models among Nuremberg society. In 1591, she requested Balthasar not to forget 'my Italian gown, like the one Wilhelm Imhoff has brought his wife from Venice, which one wears instead of fur [apparently as a warm under-gown U.R.]. And please do not mind that I am asking you for something in every letter.'[41] In the same year, she attended a patrician wedding of the Pfinzing family, and reported on the clothes worn by some of the men they knew well: 'Paulus Scheurl, Bendict and Hans Imhoff wore three beautiful completely new saffron-coloured atlas breeches and doublets with golden trims; at the after-wedding event Anthony Tucher wore the same kind of breeches and doublet.' Then followed an astonishing sentence: 'And so the old world has renewed.'[42] Seven years had passed since she had been so shocked about the expense for the red velvet blanket, one precious perfect object. Now it was her turn to affirm the aesthetics of fashion in remarkable terms: it could make the world new by extending what one thought possible and lending it beauty. And to make such an impression, the clothes indeed had to be 'completely' new, never used, premiered for the wedding, and, above all, in the new delicate colours. They were an event, in other words, to regenerate spiritedness, *Muth*, which early modern people could see as interrelated with material innovation and its transformation of what it was like to be in this world. In this way, fashion could not just be seen in negative moral terms as an example of fanciful change, but also as positive, skilled, decorous inventiveness which did show that the world could renew itself purposefully in aesthetic terms, and not just be foolish, sinful, and vain. This was the moment of triumph of bourgeois tasteful fashion in light colours and just a trim of gold against small-spiritedness in petit-bourgeois clothing, *Kleinmuth*, which Cochläus had criticized in Wittenberg, or any brash aristocratic expenditure. These new bourgeois classes found their way of looking 'ahead' rather than 'above' through the formation of taste, and could do so as early as the sixteenth century.[43]

Balthasar, apart from red, particularly appreciated fine, lightly-coloured, and thus visible, clean fabrics with small flower patterns. These 'small motifs' were produced in Italy, but aesthetically influenced by Ottoman, Persian, and Indian patterns. They were cheaper and quicker to weave than previous luxury fabrics, and hence encouraged aristocratic as well as bourgeois customers to buy them and more of them.[44] Flower patterns in addition matched these people's aesthetic preferences because flowers had come to play such an important role in their lives: they were a sign of Eastern delicacy as much as of the sophistication of natural, divinely crafted beauty and graciousness and hence were regarded as a source of acceptable sensuous delight. Plant books had proliferated alongside gardening, and everyone in these circles would have sought to know much about how to cultivate flowers. Vases became more common. Delicacy and delicatessen, decorousness, high quality workshop production, cleanliness, tasteful quality innovation or novelties from elsewhere were what a bourgeois world appreciated about a commercial culture that they regarded as developing a refined civilization.

Hyper-masculinity by the end of the century was no longer on show through indelicate codpieces. Stripes in loud colours set against each other were finally unfashionable. These aesthetics clearly embraced part of the urban upper and middle classes of Lutheran Nuremberg not just in their values, but in their practices of everyday life for maturing householders: shopping with a discerning eye for quality and appropriate expenditure given what was on offer and needed, or lucrative to sell on; talking to a wide range of craftsmen and their wives in workshops as well as female embroiderers or second-hand dealers; changing domestic decoration; writing at length about these goods in letters.[45] Men were involved in this as much as women, but if we look at daily practices there is no sense that any of these activities or skills were thought of as gender specific, apart from the fact that it was clear that men went abroad and almost exclusively to fairs. Every Lutheran bourgeois nonetheless would need to signal that his or her heart was not tied to novel objects, for that would have been truly vainglorious: 'Bring me something strange if you see it. If you don't find it, you will be enough for me!', Magdalena once exuberantly penned to her travelling husband.[46]

Nuremberg Trades

The French humanist Henri Estienne, too, praised innovation in such terms in a treatise he wrote on the Frankfurt fair:

> …if anyone should wish to fit out a whole city with every sort of merchandise
> suited to times of peace, he will see displayed there not only everything he will
> be looking for, but many things of which he never thought, and of which he and
> many others never heard, and all this in such an abundance, that he will think
> that they have been controlled and gathered not simply from many cities, but
> from every part of the whole world.[47]

What makes Estienne's account particularly interesting is that we note once more how a new sense of the global had shifted a European understanding of their work and world. The discoveries had enlarged what they had thought as existent, as well as the materials they could work with. Estienne saw this constant novelty and innovation as linked to craft competition, which displayed itself as much in Nuremberg shops as at the Frankfurt Fair:

> And it is not strange, indeed, that so many wonderful and such excellently wrought wares are for sale there, and that from each market there comes forth some new product, as once from Africa there was continually appearing some new sort of wild beast, since many cities, as if great prizes were offered, struggle in this contention (the desire for glory alone applying the keen incentives,) that the hands of their citizens may win this palm of victory. Among these by no means the last is Nuremberg, whose very shops, crowded with the various wares, anyone who had ever been there would readily believe had been transported bodily to the Frankfort Fair. Indeed, anyone who has passed through Frankfort at the time of the Fair, may say that in the same act he had been to Nuremberg.[48]

Nuremberg with its shops still stood at the apex of this world in the late sixteenth century, while a city like London had just established its distinctive luxury shopping area around the Royal Exchange. Balthasar knew the two faces of this burgeoning market economy and once showed himself truly depressed by a Frankfurt fair that had only bred animosity and jealousy in a climate of great insecurity about the value of coinage. But this was also why conversely in good times commerce could be celebrated as an agent of global exchange and social stability. Thomas Coryat was to judge the bi-annual Frankfurt fairs 'the richest meeting place of any place of Christendom' against its European competitors.[49] Jost Amman's and Hans Sachs's famous 1568 *Book of Trades* celebrated page after page the refinement achieved by glorious Nuremberg craftsmen in luminous workshops with enormous windows, although at the end they included four fools (Fig. 136).

Who were these fools? First came the money-fool, who just wanted to amass riches for his own sake through Jewish practices of usury, but without spending a penny, not even on the deserving poor. Next came the gluttonous fool, who would just rashly gulp down endless amounts of fine food and wine if invited to a rich man's table. Then came the dead stupid fool, depicted as a rural pedlar of small fashion accessories, such as mirrors, gloves, and necklaces, presumably of questionable quality and price. Finally there was the clever fool who earned his money through comedy, but also because he mastered the art of pretence. The first three figures, in other words, illustrated traditional ideas about wrong ways of consuming or distributing goods: to consume out of meanness, or indiscriminately and intemperately, or to buy and sell without any specific knowledge and esteem of the quality of what one was selling. Only the intimate knowledge of making and merchandising related consumption to civility.

This knowledge was cultivated above all, so the book seemed to claim through detailed woodcuts of workshop interiors, among highly skilled, specialized, and diversified urban artisans and knowledgeable shopkeepers (Figs. 137–139). The woodcuts show

136–139. (*opposite*) Jost Amman, *Ständebuch* (*Book of Trades*), fool (*top left*); furrier (*top right*); mirror-maker (*bottom left*); silk-embroiderer (*bottom right*). © Germanisches Nationalmuseum, Nürnberg

Der Schalcksnarr.

Jch brauch mancherley Narren weiß/
Darmit ich verdien Tranck vnd Speiß/
Doch weiß ich durch ein zaun mein Maß/
Mit meim fatzwerck zu greiffen an.
Da ich mit mein närrischen Sachn/
Die Herrschafft kan fein frölich machn/
Mit heuchlerey die Leut ich blendt/
Drum man mich ein Schalcksnarren neñt.
  g   Der

Der Kürschner.

Wol her/ich fütter Röck vnd Schaubn/
Mach schürtzbeltz/brusttüch/Behehaubn/
Von Zöbel/Marder/Vehe vnd Lüchsen/
Von Hermlein/Jlter/Wölff vnd Füchsn/
Von Welschen Kröpffen vnd Geißfeln/
Von Waißen/Rücken/Klaw vnd Keln/
Wer mir thut seines Geltes gönnen/
Der thut mich allzeit willig finden.
  N ij   Der

Der Spiegler.

Jch mach das helle Spiegelglaß/
Mit Bley ichs vnderziehen laß/
Vnd drehe darnach die Hültzen Scheibn/
Darinn die Spiegelgläser bleibn/
Die Mal ich denn mit Farben frey/
Feuwer Spiegel mach ich darbey/
Darinn das Angsicht groß erschein/
Daß mans sicht eigentlich vnd fein.
  y iij   Der

Der Seydensticker.

Jch aber kan wol Seyden stickn/
Mit Gold die brüst vnd Ermel rückn/
Versetzet mit Edlem gestein/
Auch mach ich güldin Hauben rein/
Krentz vnd harband von perlein weiß/
Künstlich Mödel mit hohem fleiß/
Auch Kirchen gweht Meßgwant vnd Albn
Kan ich wol schmückn allenthalben.
  H   Der

several of the small industries that were needed to make up appearances: iron for metal threads and pins, textile fastenings (*Nestler*) to fashion the points and laces that tied the upper to the lower garment; girdle-makers. The book created its own visual myth in depicting an almost exclusively masculinized world, despite the fact that women had several formalized niches in this production, for instance as beret- and bodice-makers for Nuremberg women, and were competent in selling goods.[50] Amman depicted most of the craftsmen in baggy hose and slashed doublets, i.e. in high-quality clothes. So were their customers depicted, not least neatly dressed women, except for one type of illustration depicting stereotypically rustic peasant women with an eye on a beautifully crafted purse, or shoes (Fig. 140). This displayed Nuremberg male craftsmen and their bourgeois clients as arbiters of taste for all society, rather than peasants challenging their aesthetic norms through a counter-culture of their own. It was a controlled world of civilized commerce, rather than open market trading, little stalls, local fairs, second-

140.   Jost Amman, *Ständebuch* (*Book of Trades*), bag-makers. © Germanisches Nationalmuseum, Nürnberg

hand trading and peddling, which, as we have seen, was also integral to early modern consumption.

Christopher Friedrich has argued that, had printing techniques already been available, 'much of the *Ständebuch* [*Book of Trades*] could have been published 200 years earlier'. He therefore uses its images as evidence that 'the basic contours of German structure remained intact between 1300 and 1600'. Friedrich acknowledges that the spread of capitalism, the growing influence of the legal profession, and of course the Protestant Reformation significantly transformed some aspects of German social structure in the fifteenth and sixteenth centuries. But even so, the overall framework remained stable. Most Germans in 1600 would have understood the structure of their society in much the same way as their ancestors had three centuries before.[51]

But was there a unified sense of how that society saw itself and its history? What about women, who had been present in many trades in the Middle Ages but in Amman's publication at best appeared as working alongside a male master or bringing spun wool in a basket, and not even as selling to customers? How could women possibly have seen their working lives in terms of stability, or even that these images reflected what they actually did? Amman's book mainly served to advertise the high quality and diversification of Nuremberg's male artisanal production and pleasures of shopping in an urban centre of this kind. Here were bodices and skirts hanging high up on threads in workshops while men made trims for them, or lined them with fur. There were the beautiful bags in great variety, here specialized instrument-makers, clock-makers, and next a well-clad barber with a luxurious chair on which his older male client sat down for his hair cut. Here was the mirror-maker and a man selling arms to the Landsquenets in his impressive baggy breeches. In sum, then, this was the largest ever visual presentation in print of some of the hundreds of specialized traders and shopworkers, sustained by civic consumer demand, which flourished by this time in Nuremberg and made for its specific milieu and prosperity of a middle class. It was meant to advertise and visualize its progressive civilization and technological advance not least through high standards of clothing. This was the world of ingenious craftsmanship for which the pedagogical reformer Petrus Ramus had come especially to visit from Paris in 1568 for four days, exclaiming he would have liked to stay for four years.[52] The *Book of Trades* associated order with prized male craftwork, control, and independence as the basis of urban prosperity, rather than with the derelict looking cast of Catholic clergymen that had been put at the front of the book. It was not, we can take it, about a society that had changed little for two hundred years.

NUREMBERG DRESS

How much then do we know about clothes that Nuremberg people actually owned? Fortunately, thanks to one pioneering monograph on 'textile belongings' in sixteenth- and seventeenth-century Nuremberg we do know a lot. It is the only such study for any German city, and clearly demonstrates that if one wishes to understand anything

about clothing practices at this time it is imperative to look at sumptuary legislation in conjunction with civic council minutes, inventories, court records, and visual
documentation. We also need to work from a detailed understanding of the production, merchandising, and layered look of fabrics, cuts, and accessories.[53] Nuremberg
sumptuary laws since 1490 were absolutely clear that they wished women to completely cover their upper-body. This equation of covered arms, shoulders, and chests with
decency, as we have already seen, remained characteristic of German dress, in contrast
to what Italian, French, but also Protestant English women could wear. In addition
sumptuary laws were highly restrictive about the use of velvet and other high quality
silk fabrics for their gowns, that is, their everyday garment for which most material was
needed. Even the upper ranks of society were only allowed to use woollen and linen
fabrics, which of course included high quality woollen material such as *Schamlott* and
Arlas, until 1618.[54]

Decorousness in dress was then achieved mostly through trims as well as partlets.
Partlets were pieces of fabric covering the shoulders and upper chest, like a wide collar,
or stretched like a small jacket up to the breasts. 'Chest-cloths' similarly were smaller
pieces of fabric worn over the shirt and under the gown. Then there were coloured
linings for dark coats, as well as a range of accessories, such as belts and girdles, but especially the emerging culture of fashionable headwear. For trims, sumptuary legislation
distinguished until the seventeenth century between the upper classes, who were allowed
to use silk fabrics of all kinds and in any colour, but only of a prescribed width, while
all other women were only allowed black or dark-brown trims. Middle- and lower-class
women appeared in court to justify their more precious and coloured trims as well as
whole gowns in livelier colours from the second half of the sixteenth century onwards.
Inventories show that a knife-maker's wife, for instance, could own a dark-brown gown
with woollen lining and a velvet trim down to her feet in 1538.[55]

During the sixteenth century, black or red belts, often made from velvet, or metal
belts, helped to hold the gown in place and hold purses, sets of keys, or needle cushions
on long strings[56] (Fig. 141). Women wore a skirt under these gowns, which was tied to
a bodice, and an ensemble equalling what is called a kirtle or petticoat in English. It was
often combined with an apron. This skirt was meant to be partly or fully visible, and
here, again, trims came into their own: they were much broader, came in many colours
and were sewn in diverse and innovative ways. It was with reference to these excessive
decorations that the city council in 1557 called 'for a return to bourgeois standards', a
'*bürgerliches mass*'.[57]

The bodices that fastened on to the petticoat were made by women, and these too
came in a range of lively colours. They would often be matched by the trim on the
lower part of the skirt, and thus contrast with the black or brown gown worn above
these garments and the white shirt worn underneath.[58] The more precious woollen and
linen fabrics were used with greater frequency even by women from the lower orders,
and upper-class women were allowed to wear all silk fabrics except for pure velvet. By

141. (*opposite*) Leather-bag with seams using gold-thread, south-German, mid-sixteenth
century. © Bayerisches Nationalmuseum, München

1618, a clothing ordinance permitted all except the women of the lowest rank to wear silk fabrics.[59] These bodices, then, made by female artisans, allowed for a relatively un-licensed engagement with fashion. It was here that small flower patterns made their entry, silk trims shone, and different colours were skilfully combined. In regard to part-lets, clothing ordinances similarly proposed a surprisingly permissive view. From 1506 onwards all women right up to the lower bourgeoisie were allowed silk fabrics such as damask. In 1529 we thus find the wife of a grinder or polisher legally owning yellow- and salmon-coloured partlets with fastenings.[60] Black velvet was to be restricted to the upper ranks, and, of course, beautifully set off jewellery. In 1577, nonetheless, even a beret-maker's wife was caught with one of these.[61]

Finally, as has already been mentioned, the appearance of the head was transformed during the early decades of the century. A new fashion for berets and golden haircaps now fascinated many women. They either replaced or were used alternatively to veils, hoods, and coifs. Berets and caps opened up a woman's profile and face, which could then be publicly displayed with far greater effect on streets, individual portrait medals, statues, and paintings. Northern Italian women and their artists had explored these possibilities since the mid-fifteenth century in their return to classical visualizations of female beauty. Venetian women however were reminded by their government in 1533 to wear simple veils; 'they were not "to innovate or change the said method of covering the head, nor wear berets or hats"'.[62] In 1497, one Fugger daughter in Augsburg was sharply commented on by a chronicler when she went to her wedding 'with a bare head with attached braids, in an aristocratic manner', instead of the customary brown veil and just showing her head with her natural hair.[63] Yet by the time Maximilian I attended a dance of the best Augsburg families in its town hall in 1518, he himself requested all women to lay down their vast hoods and veils.[64] Berets gave women a truly striking look, because they were objects used mostly by men, and thus allowed for gender fluidity. In 1522, Nuremberg women successfully lobbied Archduke Ferdinand I to support them against their council's view that they should wear elaborate old-fashioned hoods around their bound hair for the sake of tradition.[65]

1522 meanwhile saw the publication of Johannes de Indagine's treatise on the art of physiognomy in Strasbourg, which was to become one of the most important in all of Europe, was translated into German within one year, and had been preceded by two of his treatises on skin complexion.[66] If physiognomic knowledge about foreheads, lines, and chins in this period was one of the 'pre-verbal "prisms" through which people came to interpret each other', then women's unveiling was likely to promise complete 'audio-visual' information about the size and nature of their face, head, and hair. Artificial hair and dyes of course raised new concerns about women's deluding masquerade.[67] It was during the 1520s then, that the look of German women in urban centres dramatically opened up on many, if not all, occasions, and they began to use a wide variety of berets made from different fabrics and other types of small or large bonnets and hairbands across all ranks of society.[68] Hoods were mostly white and sometimes red, whereas bon-nets and the like exhibited a far greater chromatic spectrum. In addition, there was a range of jewellery or cheaper decorative items, such as feathers, which could be attached to headwear.

Berets were often made and sold locally by women, but also ordered in large quantities from Italy alongside bonnets. Barrels with fifty-one red bonnets arrived for one Nuremberg merchant in 1533. The account book of an Augsburg merchant for 1533–1551 reveals a lively trade with a whole variety of berets and bonnets for a wide market segment in a whole range of colours from red, blue, green, black, to 'liver-coloured, grey and white from Verona' to be sold in Augsburg and other upper-Swabian towns.[69] Italian mercers across the cities translated the tastes of aristocrats to builders' wives

142.   Hans Weigel, *Trachtenbuch*, Nuremberg daughter of a craftsman going to a dance, L.11.33. © The Master and Fellows of Trinity College, Cambridge

143.   Lorenz Strauch, *Portrait of Clara Praun* (1565–1638) with red braided hairpiece and beret without brim, 1589, Inv. No. Gm 1540. © Germanisches Nationalmuseum, Nürnberg

144. (*opposite*)   *Hausbuch der Landauer Zwölfbrüderstiftung*, the braid maker Wolff Rummel (d. 1663), Amb. 279.2°, 130r. © Stadtbibliothek Nürnberg

into constant fashion novelties. In Italy, this, too, was often unguilded work, allowing women to participate in their making with their own ideas. Entrepreneurial merchants would then bring the products of this interchange of creativity to Germany.[70]

The final effect of this gradual rejection of coifs and hoods, as the introduction to this chapter discussed, was that hair became much more visible. In addition to men's interest in dyeing their hair and beards (as Hieronymus Köler's example showed), this makes one instantly understand why so many recipes for haircare and dyes circulated, as did a profusion of braided hairpieces. Hairbands accordingly rose as fashionable items, and could be beautifully embroidered (Fig. 142). Particular hair fashions now allowed women to create visible communities and become fashion inventors.[71] Even Nuremberg shopkeepers (although not maidservants until the seventeenth century) were allowed to have pearls on their hairbands and could usually afford cheaper varieties of pearls to be found abundantly in the Nuremberg shops.[72]

The new prominence of face, hair, and head at least for women up to their old age was also accomplished through artificial braids, made by specialized craftsmen from precious silken, linen, or woollen fabrics, and then stuffed with leftover pieces of wool. They came in a striking variety of colours: mostly red, green, as well as blonde or purple. Red braids feature on several portraits, but were not at all costly (Figs. 143–144). One woman thus entered marriage with a smith wearing a 'green silken pair of braids with gold', and a tailor's wife had red braids with golden jewellery on them.[73] An inventory left by the wholesale merchant Elisabeth Krauß when she died in 1639 shows that she kept 609 pairs of linen braids in all sorts of colours as well as twenty-one silken braids and 280 pairs made from cotton and a precious woollen fabric.[74]

All this documents that women of every rank in Nuremberg could find areas of fashionable expression that were affordable and allowed, but nonetheless were contained within a set of regulations stressing the importance of decency rather than luxurious expenditure—manifested through regulations on the gown, made from black or brown woollen and linen fabrics for everyone. It was this combination of, say, a purple braid and dark layering that encapsulated the ideal of a 'bourgeois mean' in its decorous civility.

MEN'S WEAR

Turning to men, the same principle applies. It is misleading to merely look at the usually dark coloured gowns to conclude that an age of 'chromatic austerity' with a true 'horror' of bright colours now dominated European Protestants dressed in black, brown, or grey.[75] Breeches across all ranks frequently came in lively colours, especially in red, yellow, and blue, as well as in white, off-white, green, and multi-coloured makes.[76] Codpieces, as we have seen, were worn until the late sixteenth century. They, as well as doublet and hose, could be fastened with colourful ribbons, and knees, of course, began to be decorated with garters. As we have seen from the Behaim correspondence, delicate colours, such as light yellow or pink, were also held in high esteem.[77] The knee continued to be a key category for people's thinking about male clothes. Long baggy breeches that nearly went down to the feet were most disturbing to moralists because they went over the knee and used too much material. Baggy breeches above the knee perfectly fitted the three categories of what could be 'honourable, decorous and beautiful' dress, which a 1560 Nuremberg ordinance explicitly considered.[78] This in turn explains why stockings in various colours figured so prominently, and male elites were especially keen on Italian silk stockings. The council in 1593 even ordered that Italians living in Nuremberg were to be reprimanded for their use of golden buttons, silken stockings and gowns, as well as velvet breeches, which had clearly caught on among male elites.[79] There was the same general emphasis against the use of velvet or other costly silks for gowns and breeches, while these materials were far more tolerated for trims, borders, headwear, and even doublets. Even artisans such as knife-makers or butchers were let off by the council when they appeared before them for having worn a velvet doublet.[80] When the council discussed its 1568 sumptuary ordinance it added in its minutes that journeymen were allowed to wear 'used' velvet berets without punishment.[81] The council seems to have been typically permissive in regard to male headwear. Thus, in 1537, a man who had been employed carrying sacks left behind a cap with a 'golden star' on it, while in 1545 a man who worked for a bath similarly owned a 'brown silken cap with a golden star'. These clearly resembled the trademark golden caps with star patterns rich merchant men and women, such as members of the Fugger family, wore.[82]

Every married Nuremberg artisan, moreover, received from his wife a wedding shirt with a gold-embroidered collar.[83] Especially in winter, red woollen shirts were often worn over a white linen shirt, or a warming piece of fabric over the chest, the *Brust-tuch*, for which red, too, was a popular colour.[84] Towards the end of the century, white ruffs and lace collars became fashionable. Men could wear caps and berets with inlays, to make their head appear higher, and again towards the end of the century men more often began to wear higher hats to elongate their figure. Taken together, then, such sources bear out that these decades witnessed the commercial evolution of a wide range of goods on offer to almost anyone, as well as the continuous transfer of Italian luxuries across the Alps.

CONCLUSION

Magdalena Behaim had outlived Balthasar and all her siblings when she died in 1642, almost towards the end of the Thirty Years' War. A little more than ten years earlier, one enterprising woman called Anna Köferlin had created an innovation that would be adopted around the world until today: the educative doll's house.[85] She herself was childless, and presumably the wife of a Nuremberg woodcutter, who printed a broadsheet for her in 1631 (Fig. 145). It was printed from two blocks and showed the nine-foot model she had built over several years, fully furnished with a library, musical instruments, paintings, and armoire. This doll's house was displayed in Nuremberg for neat boys and

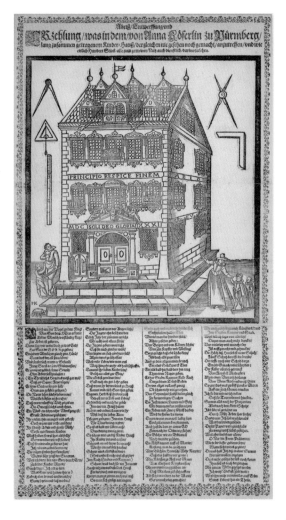

145. *Abriß, Entwerffung vnd Erzehlung, was in dem, von Anna Köferlin zu Nürnberg, lang zusammen getragenem Kinder-Hauß … anzutreffen*, 1631, Broadside made from two blocks, 54.0 × 29.3 cm, AN 145119001. © The Trustees of the British Museum

146. (*opposite*) Doll's house, Nuremberg 1611, original parrot in cage now removed, HG 1592. © Germanisches Nationalmuseum, Nürnberg

girls to be instructed in good housekeeping. The oldest Nuremberg doll's house dates from 1611 (Fig. 146); the only previously known and no longer extant doll's house had been made for Albrecht V of Bavaria in 1558.

The hold of these new, carefully crafted display objects as educative tools emerged out of the culture of bourgeois Nuremberg domesticity this chapter has described. The doll's house, too, was a visual myth, summing up the very ideal of the bourgeois household: everything was in its place, provided for, comfortable, refined, and clean. In an exceptionally preserved Nuremberg doll's house dating from 1639 is a chalk board with drawings of different linen items to be marked if they needed replacing. Hence the fact that linen items were non-durable as well as items likely to be eaten by insects rather than items that lasted and stored value was presented simply as a management task: you needed to monitor constantly what needed to be renewed. There is a heavy suitcase with fine white linen shirts and laced cuffs that the husband would have sent to the places where he would be on business for a long time. Carpenters had supplied beautifully decorated wardrobes for more linen, perfumed and tied with silk ribbons. All these goods were evidently satisfying their owners and were just in the right place.

This home was colourful, with wall decorations everywhere, and an exotic parrot in his cage. It was a house, too, in which sociability, amusement, the enjoyment of food, drink, and the world of coupled love had their place. Down in the 'drinking chamber', the *Trinkstube*, iron tankards are placed on a table of simple and solid oak. Those

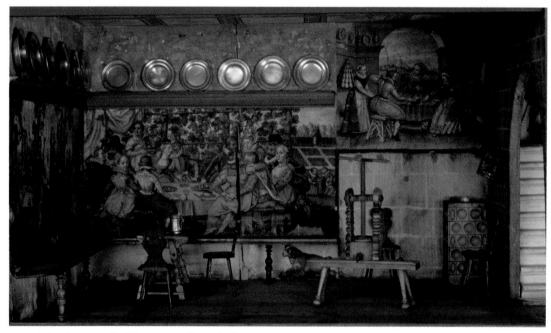

147. (*above*)   Detail of first Nuremberg doll's house, 1611, HG 1952. © Germanisches Nationalmuseum, Nürnberg

participating in such merriment could picture themselves in a garden as if looking out of a window onto a favourite scene, for the wall painting behind the table shows jolly men and women in happy love and companionship[86] (Fig. 147). This, then, was the bourgeois myth of domesticity that was so powerfully visually produced and had emerged out of one strand within the Nuremberg milieu of a Lutheran merchant and craft city. Just across the staircase leading to the drinking chamber, wall paintings just below the ceiling depicted lascivious monks and nuns.

Taste had become part of a way of seeing the world. This view was obviously presented here without the more anxious concerns that, as we have seen, clearly underpinned it: how to keep up the family's honour and appearances in competition with others, how to control expenditure, damage, deal with ill health, or low fertility. Then there was the fact that Magdalena Behaim could also sometimes be simply bored at an invitation, that she once had to ward off the amorous moves of the host at one of the many garden parties she had to attend by herself, as well as Balthasar's keen sense of other men's watchfulness and back-biting. Yet here, nonetheless, was that imaginary glory of the doll's house world with all its advantages and promises: nothing ripped, nothing torn, the right kind of expenditure on skilfully made goods, everyone merry, married women and men as esteemed companions rather than struggling about authority, parrot chattering away, flowers blossoming outside, and the grass groomed neatly by gardeners in perfectly geometrical squares; a world, doubtless, in which people had attached themselves in new ways to things and consumption played its part in creating identities.[87]

Jorg urlaub ain peck nachmals ain puncher vnd lerzich am auffseher in den
mutten ist vns brueder Hans komen den 10 September â 1567 seins allters
bey 7 Jaren / Diser Brueder ist hernach den 4 Jenner â 1568 zu morgens frue
todt for seinem bedtt gefunden worden ist doch den abent zuvor frisch vnd gesundt
Schlaffen gangen / vnd mitt Jederman friedlich vnd ainnig gewest / ist also mitt
4 monatt weniger 6 tag Jm zwolff Brueder Hans gewest / vnd ist der 386 brued
Gott genad Jm .

148.   *Hausbuch der Mendelschen Zwölfbrüderstiftung*, the baker Jorg Urlaub and a maidservant,
1568, Amb.317b.2º, 23r. © Stadtbibliothek Nürnberg

Epilogue: An Old Regime of Dress?

This book has explored the versatility of visual communication through appearances for many Renaissance people, and how it connected with the new presence of figurative images in their lives. It has suggested that dress displays, as well as their representation on printed paper, canvas, metal, vellum, on walls or wood, were symbolic visual techniques that tell us how different groups in this society enacted and remade identities. Changes in the construction of dress and the greater availability of materials and accessories alongside changes in art contributed to people's self awareness of themselves as subjects who visually explored the world and rendered the seen meaningful, as well as their experience of gaining presence through being looked at. Images and appearances both therefore can be treated as a humanly crafted assemblage of forms, which were more than decorative and transformed the way in which men and women came to conceive of themselves (Fig. 148).

Cloth could even mediate thought. Few nowadays would imagine that the seventeenth-century philosopher Leibniz's conception of the process of understanding the universe as a set of folds was stimulated by the contemporary practice of tying garters into elaborate loops and knots. Leibniz drew garters in the margins of his manuscript, they had two loops pointing upwards and one loop in the middle pointing downwards, a variant of the clover-knot.[1] It makes little sense, then, to think about appearances as representations, or of the world as a separate reality they merely reflected rather than shaped.[2]

To consider both dress displays and simulated images as humanly crafted complexes of forms challenges a more traditional understanding of what constitutes 'art'.[3] Modern art, art history, and anthropology, however, have irrevocably taught us that the notion of art applies to any humanly crafted assemblage of forms. These are always part of a society's symbolic systems, rather than subject to objective aesthetic criteria that might convincingly divide 'primitive' from 'non-primitive' art, or 'applied' from 'non-applied' art. Once we approach both images and dress displays as symbolic practice, we are then able to analyse the production and life of visual fictions held together by mutual expectations in particular societies as constitutive of reality. The production of an idolizing, completely immersed, gaze at overwhelmingly beautiful and costly church vestments and jewellery in carefully staged medieval papal ritual would be one example of how perception was structured so as to involve the senses, heighten emotional responsiveness, and hence ideally evoke acclamatory epiphanies in audiences. At the end of the early modern period, by contrast, the Hamburg merchant son Hieronymus Schramm would happily report from Amsterdam in 1769: 'Truly, I am here as at home. Dressed in black and without any pomp I walk through the streets and every twenty steps find someone with whom I have to speak.'[4]

In Schramm's bourgeois circles at this time the symbolic practice of dressing in black and seeing others dressed in black without any pomp and incalculable sartorial competitiveness clearly served as the very basis of mutual expectations about trust and horizontal social bonding, vital to do business and travel easily. It moreover generated a comforting sense of being at home when you were not. Relatively standardized dress practice could be translated into different environments across boundaries so as to make people recognizable to each other as people of the same kind, who held the same cultural and emotional values, especially for anyone watching out for such similarities rather than differences. Mutually held expectations of what someone looking a particular way was going to be like created a powerful visual fiction of identity. This also explains why, as we have seen, Zurich pastors should have pressurized one of their most esteemed preachers and humanists not to walk round like a mercenary soldier—such diversity simply would interfere with the attempt to establish new mutual expectations among reformed Protestants of what trustworthy pastors were to look like and be like. For historians these visual fictions become most fascinating when expectations changed or broke down and conflicted, because this tells us most about the values different groups within society identified with, and what perplexities remained part of everyday life.

This approach explains why the focus of this book has been on cultural arguments about dress displays and different uses of images in an age of accelerated visuality and the intensified commodification of goods. Renaissance cultural arguments explored and sometimes challenged ways in which appearances articulated boundaries between an inner and outer self, appearance and reality, nature and artifice, the sacred and profane, the rich and the ragged. Tighter-fitting clothes, moreover, made many people constantly aware of their weight and age. Dress displays, as this book has shown, in turn were about much more than elite men wanting recognition. They could be a focus for imagining one's relationship to the body, sexuality, religion, society, as well as the evolving idea of the nation and aesthetic domain. Dress displays and images of clothes were attempts to work out how one was linked to the past, how the nation could be linked to or separated from foreign ones, how to be civilized but not affected and pretentious; how to signal sexual identities; how to find aesthetic styles that were not messy and mixed up; how to show successive ingenuity while honouring one's commitment to communal laws; how to be simple without being rough and inept; or how to take pleasure in clothing without becoming enslaved to it obsessively.

It would therefore be wrong to suggest that a growth in consumption and the circulation of goods globally was embraced straightforwardly.[5] This, we need to remember, was a period in which the humanist Guillaume Postel in 1560 would be the first to declare himself a 'cosmopolite', while across Europe powerful patriotic myths were built up to be rekindled in the age of nation-states.[6] It was also a period vigorously inquiring into different conceptions of the human condition. As the chapter on Matthäus Schwarz suggested, these could selectively run alongside each other to make sense of life, or deal with the sensation that it might neither be controllable nor make sense to humans after all.

This book has therefore focused on the question of how people's interaction with more things and visual media added even further complexities to their lives. Images and dress displays had become a more important conduit to publicly proclaim one's values and links to different groups. Image-making practices could sometimes present highly controlled visual acts and arguments to achieve a specific response in large public audiences, but could also be used to explore more openly what was local, regional, and foreign, to manage conflicting emotions, or to reflect on the course of an individual life in terms of how one had tried to appear to others. The book has thus attempted to contribute to a history of the image in the tradition of Aby Warburg with his interest in the emotional resonance of visual products and practices, which asks what images did for people who produced or owned them. Warburg wrote one of his most stimulating essays on precious, huge tapestries depicting nothing but woodcutters after he discovered that one of these had originally hung in the monumental palace of a powerful Burgundian man, Chancellor Rolin.[7]

Such a history of the image recovers as far as possible how images and artefacts were produced, who used images, how, and why within particular visual traditions as much as the wider context of social relations, political fields, and interests in collecting that rendered visual practices meaningful. It treats visual practices as an active medium of cultural experiences that add an important dimension to our sense of past people's emotional lives. It also looks at objects and privately kept illustrated manuscripts as much as finished oil paintings or broadsheets intended for public display. Such diverse visual practices had come to play a greater role for early modern people and need to become more fully part of our historical analysis of how they engaged with human existence, or intervened in particular debates.

A World of Colour

The book has also tried to set out why it makes little sense to characterize the period before 1700 as an 'old regime of dress'. Daniel Roche characterized this 'sartorial ancien régime' by three crucial aspects: 'inertia and immobility, especially among the lower classes and in the countryside; a coincidence of costume and social position; a desire for control, which imposed sumptuary laws on the authorities and norms of etiquette and conformity to custom on everyone'. Roche regarded these characteristics as diluted 'to some extent' by the 'growth of the urban economy and of fashion and the subsequent confusion of ranks' during the seventeenth century. Yet he agreed with Fernand Braudel that these changes truly accelerated from 1700 onwards.[8]

Braudel insisted in 1979, in his pioneering remarks on clothing as part of a global material world during the early modern period, that fashion is not just a matter of quantity and abundance. To him, fashion was 'a question of seasons, days' and particular hours where you would need to wear a particular item to be considered fashionable. Rural dress, according to Braudel, was virtually immobile for centuries. He commented briefly on Dutch market scenes during the sixteenth and up to the early seventeenth centuries which 'curiously' showed that bourgeois clothing changed a great deal, but principally regarded only court and aristocratic dress as subject to fashion before the eighteenth century. The story of how an over-dressed peasant girl from Bretagne pleaded with Mme de Sévigny in 1680 to be relieved of debts amounting to 8,000 livres seemed to him exceptional, though he acknowledged it as evidence for the governmental failure across Europe to cohesively implement sumptuary law. 'Normally', Braudel nonetheless concluded with reference to plentiful reports on nineteenth-century impoverished French peasants, 'everyone in the countryside went barefoot, and on urban markets you could immediately distinguish the bourgeois from common folk'.[9]

More recently, a leading economic historian has affirmed that we should indeed think of the period prior to 1700 as a 'drab sartorial world' in which white linen colours and expensively dyed woollens in red or bright blue 'formed rare exceptions' to demonstrate their wearers' exceptional status.[10] It has even been suggested that a 'kind of black-and-white world' could establish itself in Western Europe after printing dominated over polychromatic manuscript writing and imagery, which took its hold on people's sensibilities at least in some contexts and regardless of their confession.[11] 'The discourse on fashion', affirms another historian, 'was new for the eighteenth century.'[12] This book has called for a review of arguments that portray this age as rigidly socially controlled, or marked by intensely local societies removed from exchange with or knowledge of the wider world. It has also sought to stimulate a fundamental shift in how we imagine the 'look' of these periods in Germany as well as in Europe as a whole.

Textile historians know that this was a world filled with colour. Wool dyed with woad was relatively cheap to produce, and made blue a popular colour, while madder was cheaply used for red dyes. Mix madder and woad, and you achieve shades of violet.[13] In 1548, one humble Basle bathing maid thus left on her death very used clothes, but she owned red boots, a pair of red woollen sleeves and green woollen sleeves as well as a number of pieces of cloth to cover her chest which would also have been colourful. Colourful pieces, such as partlets and neckerchiefs, were typically combined with more subdued, 'respectable' items of clothing.[14] Yellow had turned into a fashion colour since the beginning of the century. Basle inventories show that it was first adopted by wealthy men and women, but within a few years equally so by prostitutes, journeymen, apprentices and maidservants, as well as minor officials and artisans. In 1512, for instance, the widow of the civic piper would own a yellow bodice and yellow and green hose.[15] By 1520, everyone wore yellow and the colour was used in many innovative ways and new colour combinations to keep its appeal alive—yellow-brown, yellow-red, yellow-green, yellow-black.[16] Another inventory-based study for the area of Brunswick in Germany has found that everyone stored such garments in wooden chests painted red and green.[17] We moreover have to be attentive to unexpected terminologies we encounter in written documents: when sixteenth-century Germans wrote 'brown' they usually referred to a broad range of shades between red and blue, such as violet.[18]

This world, then, in many aspects continued the pronounced Gothic love of colour. Copper-water, gall apples, and a range of herbs such as 'wild saffron' were some of the materials used by inventive dyers profiting from a profusion of experiments to determine a plant's qualities. As a result, anyone looking at German pictorial evidence would have a hard time trying to spot dull, undyed fabrics, except, perhaps, when as a matter of principle people wanted to go sheep instead of chic. But in a society that so intensely interacted with nature, 'natural' colours were not yet identified with off-whites. It appreciated the many vibrant colours nature could provide, and the widely documented custom of men and women wearing flower- and grass-wreaths as well as dyed bird feathers is further testimony to this appreciation. In the many vignettes of people of all sorts of professions that decorate the Augsburg book of oaths in the late sixteenth century, blues and reds certainly abound. The same is true for the people depicted in the Nuremberg house-books of the charitable foundation for artisans (Fig. 149), though they were also often shown in black, which was regarded as particularly honourable for mature men.

To imagine peasants, we might wish to turn to the Swiss chronicle of Diebold Schilling, which, unusually so for its time, includes many coloured images of rural life in the first half of the sixteenth century.[19] Or look at Adrian van de Venne's exceptional early seventeenth-century miniatures of Dutch peat-cutters, peasants, and maids in bright clothes.[20] These images clearly functioned to illustrate a more widely shared sense of visual reality, even if the selection of particular scenes and people still makes such documents visual myths rather than something one should interpret as direct evidence of an objective 'reality' experienced as such by everyone. However, quite simply, if all Augsburg and Nuremberg carpenters, Swiss peasants, or Dutch peat-cutters had worn grey and brown, it would not have made sense to depict them here in greens, bright blues, reds, violets, whites, or brilliant blacks often mixed with more colourful accessories. People in this period wore colours and frequently were ingenious rather than inert in displaying themselves. Hence a drab world this was not, in the Swiss case not least because from these same villages came the mercenary soldiers and their female friends who took away Italian or French clothing from battlefields and brought it back home as booty.

149.   *Hausbuch der Mendelschen Zwölfbrüderstiftung*, the carpenter
Hans Stenger, 1607, Amb.317b.2°, 146r. © Stadtbibliothek Nürnberg

FASHION AND CHANGE

From a historical point we therefore need to restate that already since 1300, social assertion, sexual competition, and emotional and creative expression manifested themselves to a remarkable extent and in many settings through the use of appearances.
There is no doubt that European clothing styles had begun to change more rapidly even

outside courts, and these processes began to be documented in chronicles at that time.[21] By 1500, many contemporaries therefore felt that it was quite unclear what clothing customs were. They also more readily associated themselves with a sense that civilization developed constantly and thus had to endorse measured change. Indeed, the more people looked at their own history and at other cultures, the less they were able to escape the sense that they lived in a 'new world' of their own.

New looks included commodified items, such as cloth or second-hand clothes that were bought, as well as hairstyles and 'beard-styles', which were cheaper to achieve. Braiding techniques are a good example of this kind of adornment, and we have seen that at least urban women would use artificial braids dyed red and green.[22] The spectrum of social groups whose appearances expressed their own or their masters' and mistresses' aspirations and aesthetic ideals ranged from revolting peasants who called themselves 'decorous heroes' (zierhelden), to man-servants involuntarily dressed by Balthasar Behaim in fashionable liveries in delicate colours.

An accountant like Matthäus Schwarz, as we have seen, lived many aspects of his life through an engagement with clothing and the technical brilliance that could now be applied to their making. 'Sporting' a fashionable or beautiful style could be a more sporadic event for some, and for many it was associated with the most public display at church on Sundays. As early as 1570, the French had constructed a verb for ordinary people dressing up in their Sunday best: 's'endimancher'.[23] The daughter of one Nuremberg citizen would even be imprisoned in 1610 because she had borrowed many clothes from artisan women for such different social occasions as a wedding, a sermon, holy communion, a dance, or just to go for a walk in. She had then sold the clothes to nearby Jews.[24] Sources occasionally let us glimpse how common such informal exchanges of clothes and jewellery were among all classes, which inventories obscure. You dressed, in other words, not just through what you possessed, but through networks you were able to access. Your social bonds would be cemented through exchanges of this kind.

THE IMPACT OF LAWS

Hence the next point to tackle in response to Roche is whether sumptuary laws were able to impose 'conformity to custom'. It comes as a surprise to note that these laws have in fact been chronically understudied. For, as the last chapter has shown, this involves more than looking at ordinances.[25] It implies the much more laborious task of reconstructing the implementation of these laws through council minutes and court records in different cities and territories, and also of finding out what garments, fabrics, and accessories exactly were referred to. It has been easy to overlook, for instance, that these laws not just issued restrictions of what was not to be done, but often made quite generous allowances. The 1530 Imperial Police Ordinance thus permitted daughters of peasants and unmarried peasant women to wear hairbands of silk.[26] Towns' women were allowed to wear expensive belts with silver decorations, as well as a golden ring and a collar with silk embroidery. Unmarried women were even permitted special velvet hairbands with silver decorations.[27]

There is no doubt that female prettiness in Germany, as in Italy, was fostered as prerequisite for encouraging marriage and the formation of households through the use of precious things.[28] Cities moreover were clearly torn between their wish to use dress to regulate expressions of gender and rank, as well as to forestall an emotional dynamic of social competition and envy, and, on the other hand, the typical Renaissance endorsement that cities were aesthetic communities, and competed not just for the elegance of their buildings and charitable government, but their inhabitants' looks as well. As we have seen, a powerful debate about patriotism generally endorsed the sense that Germany needed to signal that it was an advancing, ingenious civilization. It was supported by an important strand within Lutheranism, which claimed that suitable decorousness rather than uniform dress equality was an important cultural value.

As in other countries, sumptuary laws would be lifted while significant dignitaries visited. Cities, moreover, increasingly competed to be regarded as a 'workshop of the world', in which merchandising documented prosperity and power. Nuremberg council minutes, as we have seen, intriguingly reveal that magistrates often took mild views on sumptuary legislation. Such legislation, we remember, had begun to appear in Europe during the thirteenth century, and became widespread from the late fifteenth century. Yet sixteenth-century sumptuary laws are difficult to identify for many German cities.[29] Augsburg saw no particular effort to implement sumptuary legislation until 1583. Its first sumptuary ordinance seems to date from 1568. This was despite the fact that Imperial Ordinances had demanded since 1548 that authorities should issue dress laws that were appropriate for their territory, or otherwise pay significant fines.[30] From Cologne, one fragment of an ordinance survives from as late as 1697. This grappled with taking on board the 1548 imperial mandate.[31]

The case of Leipzig demonstrates that even its unusually extensive civic and territorial sumptuary legislation could not lock people into sartorial inertia from above. It fascinatingly takes us from the fifteenth century through to the eighteenth century. Protestant Leipzig, as we have seen, had its important fair, and was highly involved in distributing goods from the Atlantic trade on to Eastern Europe. Civic sumptuary legislation started in the late fifteenth century to order the visualization of rank. Yet by 1550, even common artisans had to be forbidden to wear silks or golden bracelets and necklaces, and maidservants all silk, velvet trims, or 'golden' trimmings. In 1595 an ordinance declared such regulations futile, because fashions changed so fast. We remember the richly embroidered hanging discussed in chapter four. It adorned the chimney of the room in which these very Leipzig councillors met, depicting the nude German with a piece of cloth under his arm on his way to a tailor. 'There is little to order and prescribe', a further ordinance lamented after just one year. It specifically referred to its most noble burgher and merchant wives and daughters to once more declare: 'what people wear changes almost every year among the German Nation and from one to the other.'[32]

In 1612, a first territorial ordinance resulted from years of discussion, and distinguished fourteen status groups. It privileged academics with degrees and office-holders. When the ordinance was reinforced in 1628, it threatened extremely harsh punishments, especially against women and tailors. Women had also been a particular target in previous Leipzig legislation. This underlines that such legislation was not necessarily about rank in terms of profession, but tried to order the expenditure on visualizations of masculinity and femininity and hence male and female influence. Alas, in 1640, the Leipzig council still bemoaned that there was almost 'not a month that went by without a new fashion'.[33] Six civic sumptuary ordinances had been issued up to 1625; a further eleven followed up to 1698. Delegated informers were responsible for naming offenders. But these collected very few fines, and those that were came almost exclusively from artisans' wives. Hence the actual surveillance of these exceptionally frequent ordinances was extremely limited.[34]

Civic legislation came to a halt by the end of the seventeenth century, while territorial sumptuary laws continued. At the same time, state officials systematically supported local luxury production.[35] By 1749, twenty-five Leipzig manufacturing firms produced silk and velvet, gold and silver decorations, brocade, and processed tobacco. In addition, English textiles as well as colonial goods traded by the Dutch and French became much more present at the Leipzig fair. In 1747, Saxon officials reported that common people preferred foreign silk.[36] Dresden in turn had already begun to license a wider range of entrepreneurs of luxury wares. A Leipzig professor of philosophy helped local wholesale merchants to champion a politics of free trade.[37] Against this background a new dress code was issued in 1750, to regulate who was allowed to wear what kinds of locally or foreign manufactured goods. Even day-labourers and farmers, for instance, were permitted to wear Saxon fabrics with some silk content.[38] Shopkeepers and craft masters were allowed hat buttons of pure gold, silk, or silver.[39] The code alarmed numerous agents invested in the functioning of the global market. Wholesale merchants instantly argued that such restrictions would damage the fair and hence the wellbeing of the whole city. Further appeals were received from local merchants in other Saxon cities, from several of the biggest German trading cities, such as Cologne and Hamburg. Even the British state secretary wrote. They all claimed that the dress code would make the fair unattractive and cause far wider damage to others who had sold or bought fine fabrics in Leipzig.[40] In response, the Dresden state officials decided to enforce the code only in 1752, by which time they reckoned that the domestic production of luxury goods would be sufficiently developed.[41]

The dress code now served as a mercantilist measure. Yet the wholesale merchants' lobby, which was also strongly represented on the civic council, vocally defended everyone's right to wear 'clean' and 'respectable' clothing. They also argued that they needed a constant consumer demand for a wide selection of fine wares to remain in business, because fashions changed quickly.[42] Pamphlets satirized the sartorial privations maids and low folk like pedlars would now suffer. Two state commissioners were duly sent to Leipzig to control sumptuary deviance. Over one hundred interrogations were conducted during the next six years.[43] These show that 'even the most humble Leipzig residents had begun to assimilate the material culture fostered by Atlantic World commerce, and the perceived flamboyance of their dress clashed with a traditional view of their social position'.[44] Those interrogated showed no signs of guilt. Here as elsewhere, and in earlier periods, they produced elaborate apologies to prove that they had had these items made before the new dress code, were unaware of a particular law, or that it did not apply to them. Many defended their view that their appearance manifested the rank they had achieved in society and hence due difference to social inferiors. By 1762, a governmental commission finally acknowledged that sumptuary competition was a 'social ill that is not to be directed through police-ordinances'. It necessitated a response by 'softer means'.[45]

What the Leipzig sources therefore confirm is that clothing long before 1700 formed a key part of the way in which women went about imagining society and their place within it for themselves—and how they defended this view. They agreed that clothing should visualize one's position in society, and accepted that they had to do this in dialogue with sumptuary rules. Yet they clearly had some scope to use clothes as a cultural resource to enhance their and their families' esteem with the right balance of beauty, modesty, and refinement, rather than undue excess, on which notions of virtue rested. Virtuous, civil conduct was the only basis for claims of their equal or even superior worth to men. Innovative hairstyles, once more, could testify to something akin to artistry and ingenuity, as well as startle through a rejection of hoods. Women could therefore use appearances to resist being defined in their looks and worth from above.[46] They could make themselves visible in and as ornaments of their city.

Costume books endorsed this perspective through the disproportionate number of plates they devoted to women of all classes across Europe and by delighting in their decorousness, or, in Vecellio, abundant details of their 'lovely' looks. Apart from learning, appearances therefore were one of the more accessible conduits for women to 'have' a Renaissance, or later even an Enlightenment. Let's take the grave-digger's daughter Anna Riek, who in 1798 lived in the small Swabian, Pietist town of Laichingen and married a day-labourer. Anna owned three scarlet bodices, a particularly rich collection of silk, half-silk, and cotton neckerchiefs as well as caps, including a 'Parisian'. One of these laced bodices was striped in the colours of the French tricolour.[47]

Obviously there also existed centres and peripheries of fashionable dress consumption within Europe and across Germany. Paris and northern Italian cities such as Lucca, Florence, and Venice, as we have seen, had developed their expertise in manufacturing and trading fashionable materials since the thirteenth century. Spain was the place to get the finest leather; Eastern Europe specialized in furs, Southern German cities supplied elite men with fine arms, which until the eighteenth century were often part of their dress. For a broader demand, merchants and busy pedlars would distribute accessories, such as fine metal buttons or coloured woollen buttons, as well as foreign cloth across Germany. Even for the small Black Forest town of Wildberg we find a single register of no less than one hundred fines for sumptuary offences collected almost exclusively from women during a single year.[48] A rigid notion that European society divided into a rich, bourgeois elite, and a mass of inert, immobile poor in brown or grey, unable to negotiate hierarchies, simply does not adequately capture its realities. Nor is Mack Walker's influential portrayal of the 'two Germanys' any longer plausible, divided into a few 'mover-and-doer towns' such as Hamburg, Leipzig, Frankfurt, Cologne, or Nuremberg, and an overwhelming majority of small 'hometowns' with their distinctive ideals and frozen social life right into the nineteenth century.[49] In these 'hometowns', Walker posited, 'even rules on what clothing who might wear did not actively assert rank and place so much as accept their existence and inhibit the race after status by the display of wealth'.[50] Yet we have seen that dress had become an object of desire everywhere in dynamic European societies since the Middle Ages promising far more than to objectify rank.

My point therefore has not been to argue that everyone looked fashionable or that there existed no constraints on how men, and women in particular, could dress. Many items were still inherited from one generation to another. Women's wages were lower than men's or they were kept in unpaid forms of work altogether. This means that they had less independent access to financial resources to buy what they wanted, and were more dependent on forming networks to lend and exchange clothes and accessories.[51] Sumptuary laws, as we have seen, could be used by male elites to target women especially to curtail their spending, and German territorial sumptuary laws could explicitly restrict lower class men and women from wearing even red stockings.

Customs and excise duties were further governmental measures used across Europe to restrain spending on foreign products. Yet despite such constraints, items of fashionable clothing or accessories, as well as brightly coloured items, nonetheless circulated more widely than historians have often led us to believe.[52] Rags were deeply associated with poverty and shame, so that appearances were a major resource of self-respect and esteem for all social ranks. The 'beggar's coat' had become a metaphor for an indifferently patched together world from lots of pieces that would quickly fall apart under its own weight.[53] One Nuremberg broadsheet depicted a terrifying bogey-woman with a dripping, snotty nose and a gown entirely made from patches. She announced that she would burn girls' dolls, cut and tear up all Sunday dresses, put her snot on their spinning, give them snot to drink, and send lots of bugs to their beds should the girls not be neat, pious, and hard-working in school and at home (Fig. 150). Rags in these ways, as this book has argued throughout, became a powerful metaphor for disorder and could engender social fear.

Everyone in this society therefore would learn to see whether a garment was new and 'fresh' or old, fitted or hung loosely on the body, was impeccable or not, clean or spotty, whether the dye of a shirt was made from bricks, for instance, and therefore less brilliant and lasting, or whether it was a deeper colour that bespoke the value of many hours of skilled labour that had gone into its making. Accessories and precious details had a key role in disseminating a taste for fashion, in which trimmings of velvet or coloured caps with bits of silk materials, belts, or dyed feathers, for instance, became more common and something people would picture themselves as beautiful with. Cheap imitations of precious materials, such as fake gold and silver hat-bands, were especially aimed at

150. Albrecht Schmidt, *Die Butzenbercht*, broadsheet Inv. No. HB 24505. ©Germanisches Nationalmuseum, Nürnberg

lower-class and younger consumers. Vermeer's Delft model for his painting *Girl with the Pearl-Earring* probably wore no more than a varnished glass teardrop in her ear.[54] 'Labouring people' in England, John Styles concludes, were 'already responsive to accessible innovations' before 1700. In a country that had repealed sumptuary legislation as early as 1604, people often strove particularly hard to save up for affordable finery. German eighteenth-century travellers were routinely astonished at how often it was difficult for them to distinguish between the high and the low.[55] People in most societies engage with the possibilities of human adornment. Early modern popular classes were no exception. Beauty services, such as shaving and hairdressing, became more elaborate. Appearances became something more people were keen to spend on, elaborate, document, and even consume books about.

New and Old Luxuries

Within the long view of an intensifying European engagement with the possibilities of adornment through commercial activities, this book has charted how part of the literary elite began to equate decorous clothing with ideals of progressive civilization, social benefit, and a new kind of emotional competence.[56] They could associate dress displays with an appropriate civic and sometimes patriotic display, appropriate expression of piety and civil commitment, innovation, commerce, production skills, aesthetic beauty, as well as spiritedness. This society, therefore, witnessed the genesis of bourgeois ideals. Fashion, to be sure, was created through some dialogue with high aristocratic ideals (which in themselves were clearly variegated according to budgets and the hold of an orientation first towards Spain and then to France), but also independently from them. The strength of the larger German cities was crucial in this process. Germany was not structured around a single monarchical court and one central city in which the nobility resided. It had a strong tradition of commercial entrepreneurship, international information, and trading networks among commercial classes, as well as highly distributed skilled artisans. As in Italy, it could cultivate the notion of regional diversity and healthy competition among cities and among medium sized, aspiring courts.[57]

German readers, in addition, were highly aware of global encounters and the proliferations of customs around the world. As this book has argued, the German Reformation was in many ways continuous to the 'material Renaissance'. Luther's attacks on monastic habits emphasized that costumes were worldly customs and thus part of the way in which society chose to be, rather than anything to do with how God chose it to be. Above all, Luther rejected the moral response that had been so characteristic of many medieval religious movements: that luxury needed to be rejected through total simplicity and poverty. For Luther, neither simplicity nor material spiritual enchantment was anything that mediated God's grace. A vocal strand within Lutheranism and Calvinism rather held that bourgeois, pious gentility was manifested through dress and cultivated through proper decorousness rather than plain simplicity. We can therefore speak about a material Reformation and Renaissance in Northern Europe and not just an Italian material Renaissance to trace that very process in which more people outside courts attached themselves to things and looked for a moral ethic and emotional style that drew on classical as well as Christian notions of how virtue and decorum might hold up against the human drive for selfish, immodest vanity, and competitiveness. Even English Puritans would come to acknowledge that possessions could be God's temporal blessings as 'ornaments and delights'.[58]

Through these arguments a clearer distinction between what Jan de Vries has called 'Old Luxury' and 'New Luxury' gradually emerged to talk about non-necessities.[59] Old Luxury was all about glittering, conspicuous vice as masquerade and concealment to bolster privilege that was not based on merit. Here objects did not really matter in themselves, they were fetishes. Protestants typically identified such consumption negatively with papal, oriental, and monarchical splendour, which built up a false world of fantastic illusion and overwhelmed the eyes of onlookers. The humanist Philip Melanchthon characteristically interpreted the belly and breasts of the terrifying pope-ass monster, which he and Luther turned into an icon of anti-Catholicism, in these terms. As Melanchthon rudely put it, belly and breasts symbolized 'cardinals, bishops, priests, monks, students and such like whorish people and pigs, because their whole life consists of nothing but gobbling food, of drinking and of sex'.[60]

Old Luxury was not accessible to many. It served a narrow elite trapped in a vicious circle of excessive self-love and greed, who cultivated extravagant and often unnatural, effeminate, and over-sensuous tastes, and needed a large class of adulating subservient people to consume in this vainglorious way. It was regarded as cultural practise of pride, which engendered constant envy even among elites. Its emotional style pertained to uncontrollable passions, rather than manageable emotions. As in ancient Rome, Old Luxury was doomed, set to lead to a whole republic's decline, and for Christian writers easily evinced the misery of human nature after the Fall. This depiction of wrongful luxury consumption also related back to the ancient Greek discussion, in which 'much of the discourse of private consumption' likewise played 'not on class antagonism, but on a more direct conflict between public and private uses of private wealth. An inheritance dissipated in vices is not only lost to the individual and his family…it is also lost to the city.'[61] Greek philosophers considered consumption as mostly self-indulgent, consumed in passion for boys by men who drank too much and spirited away estates.

Attitudes to 'New Luxury' were typically established through such caricatures of Old Luxury. New luxury and the defence of new decencies could be declared virtuous rather than decried as an engine of vice. They could be identified with a republican spirit and public gain, gentility, politeness as well as different regimes of spectatorship. This kind of consumption was ideally said to enshrine clear codes of honourable, often more frugal consumption, based on a regular self-examination of whether one needed something or was over-indulgent in unreasonably conspicuous consumption. It was an idea that could be related back to the Greek insistence on personal responsibility in managing passions.[62] In the seventeenth and eighteenth centuries, consumption for a bourgeois first of all qualified as good if it did not encourage travesty—men as effeminate gallants, for instance, or women in breeches. Adriaen van der Venne thus needed to draw a vomiting cat next to a rare miniature of a popular couple having fun in mutual cross-dressing, to explore sexual identities beyond clear divisions into masculine and feminine that this society had come to sanction so rigorously (Fig. 151). Bourgeois consumption was meant to instate men as heterosexual, respectable, who would marry and take on public roles, and women as distinctly feminine as well as destined for fidelity in marriages. Elements like the new small flower patterns and pastel colours, meanwhile, were not yet understood to be gender specific, thus allowing for some gender fluidity through consumption. This softer, delicate style, which took its cues from Persian designs, was an alternative to the German hyper-masculinity of much of the sixteenth century with its bold stripy patterns, daring slashes, and frequently loud colours. Meanwhile, uniform black in its different shades continued as the international unisex currency of restrained sumptuousness in particular settings for a long time.

New luxury models of consumption, however, typically endorsed measured innovation and the notion of aesthetic pleasure as a part of cultural competence.[63] Sensations such as surprise and delight could be regarded as refined, because they were not linked to simple utility or physical pleasure.[64] Necessity directed towards mere functional utility, whereas civilization could lead to honourable decorum and progressive, though 'polite', creativity. Such evaluations typically were connected to the notion that consumers should obtain a high degree of product information and an understanding of intricate cuts and constructions of clothing from artisans, shops, and tradesmen, or books and magazines, and hence cultivate taste based on knowledge as well as civil sociability rather than pompous tastes to advertise conspicuous wealth. A whole series of Nuremberg broadsheets published in 1609, for instance, displayed a woman as just such a knowing customer in a series of crafts-workshops, who supervised the production of goods she had requested with an eagle eye to avoid imperfections (Fig. 152). Bourgeois classes could positively cherish fashion as a forward-looking social institution. It could now be presented as fuelling the wealth of nations and engendering emotional wellbeing.

151. Adriaen van de Venne, *Carousing Couple with Cat*, early seventeenth-century, watercolour and body-colour over black chalk, AN 374179. © The Trustees of the British Museum

WOMEN'S CLAIMS

Women's right to be fashionable in a domesticated bourgeois manner soon was increasingly acknowledged. Dürer's drawings of the neat *Hausfrau* had pioneered this idea. As we have seen for Nuremberg, female merchants and retailers in turn could be at the forefront of building up a fashionable clientele. In seventeenth-century Antwerp designated 'à-la-mode' shops would spring up from 1660. By 1700 there were sixty-one of them. Nearly forty per cent of them were even listed under a woman's name.[65] During the seventeenth century, moreover, the theatre established itself more firmly across urban society and could provide an ideal public space to reimagine characters and sanction or criticize particular emotional styles. Molière's 1661 comedy *The School for Husbands* (*L'Ecole des maris*) is a perfect example of this. This short, entertaining play was a European success. It was not just performed, but published with plentiful captivating engravings. Its whole plot turning on two brothers who had totally different ideas

152.   Albrecht Schmidt, *Der Rothgerber (tanner)*, broadsheet, 19.0 × 31.5 cm Inv. No. HB 26806. © Germanisches Nationalmuseum, Nürnberg

about dress and each had been promised orphaned girls for marriage if they looked after them. The younger brother, Sganarelle, rigorously wanted his girl to be clad in brown and grey wool and remain indoors, while he himself likewise only dressed functionally and traditionally. His older and more relaxed brother, Aristide, by contrast, thought of well-designed social pleasures, such as the theatre and good company, as important in the school of life. Nice clothes to him were a further source of pleasure as well as being acknowledged as a source of female self-esteem, which would make women feel well treated by men who provided money to buy them. It would make them happy and honourable. Commerce and sociability hence were overtly presented as guaranteeing female civility and emotional contentment.

Molière wrote during the reign of Louis XIV, and thus did not advertise this life in any way as republican. Rather, it was linked to the notion of a good monarchy as opposed to tyranny. Sganarelle exemplified such tyranny in the household regiment, which contemporaries thought of as any state's microcosm. Tyranny was presented as resulting from a deep fear of rebellion—in the household this would happen through adultery. Yet an overly restrictive regime would produce just that effect, and hence Sganarelle lost his girl to a fop. His brother's girl, Leonore, instead was given a voice to defend women's dress in terms of a political right crucial to building a virtuous society through encouraging self-regard, in contrast to the situation of enslaved Ottoman women. This is important, because the play could otherwise be seen to merely rehearse a part familiar to European readers through the *Roman de la Rose* (1225–1240), where the Unhappy Husband, the Mal Marié, was already presented as a miser depraving his wife of beautiful apparel, while defending that dress simply needed to be functional. This man denigrated his wife by giving her his own overused, far too big overshoe as well as a blank, undecorated belt. Meanwhile, this medieval miser hoarded money.[66]

More than four hundred years later, Lenore argued for women's liberty and against their subjection to men's will and suspicions. Trust would enable women's natural virtue to manifest itself:

> Yes, all these stern precautions are inhuman.
> Are we in Turkey, where they lock up women?
> It's said that females are slaves or worse,
> And that's why Turks are under Heaven's curse.
> Our honour, Sir, is truly very frail
> If we, to keep it, must be kept in jail.
> …
> All these constraints are vain and ludicrous:
> The best course, always, is to trust in us.
> It's dangerous, Sir, to underrate our gender.
> Our honour likes to be its own defender.[67]

With these qualifications, dress consumption no longer was an emblem of female vanity and fickleness; it could be valued as a constructive part of the societal weave and affirm a woman's competent selfhood. Fops clearly were fools, because they equated 'exterior appearances with the whole man'.[68] Yet it had become easier since Matthäus Schwarz's times to argue that only such fops and cavaliers were fools, whereas judicious, and once more tasteful, moderate spending among men, as much as women, could be part of a civilized, virtuous existence. 'Opposition to luxury and effeminacy', it has been argued, 'promoted, rather than inhibited fashion change.'[69] Aristide himself remained more ambiguous, but knew that the person who would oppose novelty would be the odd one out. Given his age—which made Sganarelle address him as 'old beau'—he presented himself as no fashion inventor, but as someone who waited for a fashion consensus to emerge that could be equated to the more cautious conformist bourgeois ideals, which now became characteristic of much male dress:

> It's best at all times to observe convention
> And not, by being odd, attract attention.
> For all extremes offend, and wise men teach
> Themselves to deal with fashion as with speech,
> Accepting calmly, with no fuss or haste,
> Whatever changes usage has embraced.
> I'm far from recommending those whose passion
> Is always to improve upon the fashion,
> And who are filled with envy and dismay
> If someone else is more extreme than they:
> But it is bad, on any ground, to shun
> The norm, and not to do the thing that's done;
> Better by far to join the foolish throng
> Than stand alone and call the whole world wrong.[70]

Just one year later, in 1662, a didactic poem entitled 'A Dialogue between Fashion and Nature' appeared in France, and its author quite possibly was a woman. It posited that 'charming tenderness' and urbanity as well as fine feeling were engendered by those who liked fashion and fine things. This superseded natural, rigidly rustic looks, and the praise of male rough toughness and violent heroism. The new man did not look back at history to praise the simplicity of his forbears and valued civility over valour. Like Sganarelle, moreover, any man of such rigid principles would stand out as a capricious eccentric in a world that positively valued fashion, while the powerful fear of envy and jealousy, 'could be neutralised by the perpetually changing array of goods and values that fashion displayed'[71] (Figs. 153–154).

This clearly remains the key 'modern cultural value' fashion as a phenomenon slowly and far from linearly enshrined across many societies: an acceptance among most of some degree of constant change, which no longer made it seem frightening, evil, corrupting, or just puzzling and disturbing.[72] To follow those changes and decide within certain parameters on what to wear could now be seen as integral to human

153.   Doublet, south-German (?), c.1625–1640, silk damask with a delicate pattern of leaves and flowers in yellow on green. © Bavarian National Museum, München

154. *Hausbuch der Mendelschen Zwölfbrüderstiftung*, the braid- and glove-maker and piper Hans Zauscher (d. 1655), Amb. 317b.2°, 125r. © Stadtbibliothek Nürnberg

dignity. Yet again, fashion could only be more widely endorsed because it was not linked to a strong notion of individual competition through constant innovation, to the individualistic '*uomo singolare*', the French sociologist Gilles Lipovetsky sees as crucial for the role of fashion as an engine of modernity. Bourgeois legitimations of fashion far more typically opposed notions of depraved selfishness and rather emphasized that tasteful and subtle choices of fashion elements constituted sociability. It was meant to provide women in particular with a topic to talk about in terms of aesthetic appreciation of the intrinsic qualities of a crafted object, seemly pleasure, and information, rather than something that threw them into envy the minute they took sight of each other. In Japan, pattern books were very much part of this process—the first one, published in 1666, contained two hundred kimono patterns to choose from.[73] For men, it was vital to appear neither as a fashion slave nor as driven by rigid and equally irrational hostility to fashion, but rather to present oneself as capable of fitting in and yet cultivating a degree of personal taste in judicious choices from a variety of apparel appropriate to a man's age, body, station, any particular occasion, and current fashion. This kind of consumption legitimated an enjoyment of possession in contrast to miserly austerity, retentive hoarding, or indiscriminate consumption of every invention, which kept being caricatured. Some thought 'decent gallantry' perfectly possible. The now deeply entrenched aesthetic preference for neat and decorous, colourful and pleasing Persian and Indian flower patterns could be perfectly disseminated across society through cheaper, colourfast, and easily washable floral calico cottons in the eighteenth century. Embroidery books meanwhile had featured Eastern ornamental patterns since the seventeenth century. Fashion continued to evolve through cultural exchanges of the East and the West, which, as we saw in this book's Introduction, is how the fashion phenomenon had emerged in the medieval Western world.

ICONS OF STYLE

An important theme of this book, then, has been to show that aesthetic ideals have a history and that parts of Germany participated in the development towards a greater commodification of appearance during this period, rather than remaining wholly over-regulated and static, a backward periphery of style.[74] My aim has been to place early modern German history in a European and global context, as well as to think about the extent to which its history is marked by the awareness of other cultures or cultural exchange.[75] On 22 August 1716, for instance, Mary Wortley Montagu penned the following lines to the countess of Bristol from Nuremberg:

> I have passed a large part of Germany, have seen all that is remarkable in
> Cologne, Frankfort, Wurtsburg, and this place; and 'tis impossible not to
> observe the difference between the free towns and those under the government
> of absolute princes, as all the little sovereigns of Germany are. In the first,
> there appears an air of commerce and plenty. The streets are well built, full of
> people, neatly and plainly dressed. The shops loaded with merchandise, and the
> commonalty clean and cheerful. In the other, a sort of shabby finery, a number
> of dirty people of quality tawdered out; . . . and above half of the common sort
> asking for alms.[76]

The women in Imperial cities to her seemed like 'a handsome clean Dutch citizen's wife', and she commented positively on the fact that Nuremberg in contrast to English cities had sumptuary laws. By November, Montagu found herself in polite Leipzig, a 'town', she reported, 'very considerable for its trade; and I take this opportunity of buying pages' liveries, gold stuffs for myself, &c., all things of that kind being at least double the price at Vienna.'[77]

This was Montagu's version of the Old versus New Luxury and Decencies divide, typical of liberal English people's views of what happened anywhere beyond Calais or Rotterdam. Courts despotically concentrated riches and magnificence among the few and fostered unproductive labour. Merchant communities, such as Frankfurt, Leipzig, and Nuremberg, bred industriousness and inventive genius, distributed wealth more equally, and produced a neat populace.

For Montagu, Old Luxury was epitomized in the figure of the whore, while the Dutch housewife was the figurehead of New Luxury and Decency. This quite extraordinarily reversed the traditional image of the merchant city as whore, which moralists had always used to describe her commercial temptations and allure to the senses.[78] 'I cannot help fancying one [the women of German commercial cities]', Montagu wrote, 'under the figure of a handsome clean Dutch citizen's wife, and the other like a poor town lady of pleasure, painted and ribboned out in her head-dress, with tarnished silver-laced shoes and a ragged under-petticoat, a miserable mixture of vice and poverty.'[79] New ideals of consumption therefore also created icons of approved styles for orientation, rather than a rigorously individualized regime of style. Europeans, after all, wanted consumer happiness, but still to make it into eternity. Hence, while the figure of the whore had changed sides, the Dutch housewife and mother for Montagu and many others had solidly emerged through the genre of travel writing as the European icon of commerce, cleanliness, domesticity, happy as well as eloquent sociable entertainment, health, and thoroughly honourable Protestant femininity. No rags, tears, or stains tarnished her. She would wash them away, buy something new, or at least be quick with her needle to mend things so that no one would notice anything.[80] This Dutch icon had worked through any embarrassment of riches; she was neither too frugal, nor opulent. Her maidservants would be pretty to look at and busy at work. We can perfectly picture her with her nice trims through the many paintings this society so proudly produced.

Yet against the power of such visual fictions we should not forget that this housewife culture necessitated the common prostitute. Even in the sober Dutch Republic, the prostitute worked nearby. She knew all about how appearances were said to make the man. In 1693, an Amsterdam prostitute dealt with one bourgeois customer who did not want to pay by urinating straight onto his wig over her chamber-pot. In the same year, another of these wonderfully lewd women gleefully told her mates in the workhouse how she had got a man very drunk and robbed all his clothes and shoes. Then she had left him at the portal of the Oude Kerk with a woman's cap on.[81] The prostitutes' revenge was sweet, as they expertly unmasked deceptive respectability through the ancient arts of debauchery, sacrilege, travesty, denudation, and defilement.

Clothing the World

Throughout the sixteenth and seventeenth centuries, then, we have seen that defences of gracious consumption and more intensely commodified appearances as an acceptable or even desirable social pursuit, as well as expressions of competent selfhood and emotional wellbeing, slowly gained ground. It was an idea the eighteenth century would vigorously continue to discuss, despite the fact that sumptuary legislation was now abolished where it still existed. Indeed, Europe seems to have diverged from China only at this juncture. In China, consumption 'went out of fashion' in 1644, with the change of the Ming dynasties to the Manchu. Yet it was 'not that it ceased to exist, but it ceased to be a legitimate topic of concern for the elite, an object of discourse able to act as a site of power'.[82] In Japan, by contrast, the eighteenth and first half of the nineteenth centuries were periods of extremely severe campaigns against conspicuous consumption and the implementation of differentiated sumptuary laws to use dress as visualization of rank. As a result, 'restrained tastes and highly hierarchical categories were, at least in part, the result of the social discipline that the Togukawa state implemented'. Despite such restrictions, pleasure districts remained an officially sanctioned alternative world. Pleasure districts were literally called 'floating world', and it was here that actors and prostitutes traditionally experimented with new fashions and involved ordinary people on holiday from their ordinary lives. There also remained a widespread popular interest in fashion, which was additionally produced by contemporary novels, as well as skilled manufacturing and merchandising. This explains why Togukawa Japan 'harboured a growing population of aesthetic individualists who assumed the importance of beauty in their personal attire as a necessity of life'.[83]

Even if state policies both in China and Japan diverged from Europe in the eighteenth century, it would remain a mistake to treat the structuring force of 'materialism' and a greater interest in the use of dress in everyday life as specifically Western phenomena.[84] The Chinese consumed as many textiles as Europeans during the eighteenth century, perhaps even more than Germans.[85] Vividly printed Indian cotton fabrics with their lasting dyes were exported to different parts of the early modern world, including Africa. Here, the Yoruba, for instance, particularly valued dress, 'and the one who donned inappropriate dress was said to *aro'gi l'aso* (wear cloth like wood)'.[86] The English friar Thomas Gage noted in 1625 that Mexican elites used Far Eastern goods such as cloth of gold and Chinese silks to decorate their coaches.[87] In the Spanish Americas, clothing was in great demand because it marked racial status by 'reputation' in flexible ways. The more European you looked through clothes or hairstyles, the less indigenous you were.[88] The Portuguese for their part used European suits, or red jackets and breeches, shoes with buckles, and hats at the turn of the eighteenth century to reward Amazonian Indian collaborators in Brazil.[89] Latin Americans hence themselves increasingly used clothing as a communicative tool to blur clear racial and social categorizations as well as a tool of self-expression.[90] Thomas Gage certainly thought that men and women of early seventeenth century Mexico City looked far too splendid:

> A hat-band and rose made of diamonds in a gentleman's hat is common, and a hat-band of pearls is ordinary in a tradesman. Nay, a blackamoor or tawny young maid and slave will make hard shift, but she will be in fashion with her neck-chain and bracelets of pearls, and her ear-bobs of some considerable jewels. The attire of this baser sort of people of blackamoors and mulattoes…is so light, and their carriage so enticing, that many Spaniards even of the better sort…disdain their wives for them.[91]

Here were the riches of a world that seemed no different to Gage and other early modern travellers to the splendour of European towns, and in these urban outposts of civilization existed no longer naked savages, but Latin American consumers using pearls, pins, and cloth with equal versatility.[92] Despite an intensification of sumptuary legislation in seventeenth and eighteenth century Latin America, two Spanish travellers in the 1740s even commented that 'the finest stuffs made in countries, where industry is always inventing something new, are more generally seen in Lima than in any other place' and observed mechanics or mulattos in fine clothes.[93] In 1772, a German named Ernst Ludwig Carl published his *Treatise on the Wealth of Princes and Their States* in Paris to marvel at the fact that French second-hand garments were eagerly absorbed by neighbouring nations once they had become unfashionable in France, while 'Peru and Mexico also absorb a great quantity' and the poor of France as well. This cycle perfected the arts and enriched the state, because goods were first sold expensively as luxuries, but then transformed into conveniences and eventually even necessities in a broad and internationally successful market economy that generated enough capital to enable future inventions.[94] From the late seventeenth century onwards writers could excitedly endorse that commerce with European manufactured goods spread civilization and Christianity around the globe.[95] This argument confidently integrated consumerism into a self-conscious definition of what the West could bring to the World[96] (Fig. 155).

It would nonetheless be wrong to assume that there was a 'simple progression from disapprobation to endorsement of luxury' or that everyone's clothes steadily became brighter and lighter. Debate still centred 'on questions of individual and national virtue, economic expansion and canons of taste, definitions of the self, and the social redistribution of wealth'.[97] There continued to exist among many a keen sense that access to clothing was not equally distributed, created its own social divisions, and could be ruinous instead of efficiently storing wealth. The great diversification of the press alongside reading publics further fuelled discussions about how the link between consumption, virtuousness, and the good self could be imagined. Hence, when in 1786, Friedrich Justin Bertuch began to publish his hugely successful German fashion magazine for bourgeois and aristocratic circles, the *Journal des Luxus und der Moden*, he energetically set out just how confrontational positions remained:

> According to the followers of the physiocratic system, Luxury is the Scourge
> of the State! It squanders the rich revenues on fruitless expenditures, prevents
> reproduction, enervates the physiocratic forces of the Nation, dissolves all senses
> of Morality and Honour, ruins the well-being of families and supplies the State
> with hordes of beggars! Luxury, says the financier and the technologist, is the
> richest source for the State; the almighty motive force of Industry; and the
> strongest mechanism of Circulation. It erases all traces of Barbarism in Manners,
> creates Arts, Sciences, Commerce and Trades, increases the Population and
> Forces of the State, and leads to Delight and Joy of Living!—Who of the two is
> wrong?—Both, we believe, when they make absolute claims about this important
> matter. The entire dispute rests upon an incorrect, or at least insufficiently pure
> definition of Luxury.[98]

Bertuch was an entrepreneurial writer and publisher as well as treasurer to Duke Carl August of Saxony-Weimar. His wife founded a silk-flower factory. In the initial year of the *Journal*, Bertuch declared that he was happy to invite a debate about whether there should be cheap, non-fantastical, German patriotic national dress. Yet he quickly dropped the idea after an allegedly female reader had written in to protest that such debates only took men to be citizens and wished to deprive women of their joys of conversations about fashions. It would also ruin 'a large proportion of German manufacturers' with their production of velvet, taffeta, and cotton, rather than wool.[99] The 'New Luxury/Decencies' look that the magazine chiefly propagated was restrained, practical, and mostly English. At the end of its

155.   Back of a doublet, Netherlands (?), c.1630–1640. © Bavarian National Museum, München

first year, the *Journal* named 233 English products from just one mail-order catalogue. It helped to shape the identity and bodily habits of liberal men and women from Hamburg to Weimar and Nuremberg.[100] Yet since its audience was both bourgeois and aristocratic, the *Journal*'s messages could also be ambiguous. Women, for instance, were told not to reveal arms and shoulders, as only modest clothes made for healthy mothers and vigorous children. They could then be told also that clothes were a tool of self-transformation that would heighten women's charm and cover Nature's imperfections. 'Like a world-traveller', a woman was to choose from all national costumes.[101]

The minor Margrave Sibylla Augusta had already cheerily experimented with the latter option in the first decades of the eighteenth century. In her summer residence Favorite near Baden-Baden we still see a spectacular display of forty-six surviving large gouache paintings of her and her husband, Ludwig Wilhelm, as well as their children dressed as Turks, Persians, Moors, Slaves, Chinese, Indians, or Romans. Originally, Sibylla commissioned over seventy. Early modern courts typically had been stimulated to invest in festive global dress-ups by costume books and travel reports to claim universal aspirations to rule. Yet Sibylla Augusta blended her pride in her husband's fight against the Ottomans, from whom he had conquered a 'Persian gown of green velvet', with a playful sense that global national dress was now known so comprehensively that it might be put on and taken off to explore how materials could continually re-make identities in different ways. Here was a self that sought recognition through its ability for endless visual transformation (Fig. 156).

In this study we have come a long way from a discussion of how people began to attach themselves in new ways to dress in the Middle Ages to an initial exploration of the way in which appearances could figure in cultural arguments and practices at the end of the early modern period. The most unsettling anxiety philosophers produced from now on was that clothing might not even be a masquerade, as in Sibylla Augusta's case, but a shell of something hollow. Dress was used metaphorically to evoke the notion that there existed a form for matter that had simply disappeared. Hegel attacked the whole institution of the Holy Roman Empire in this way. Here, he argued in a spirited essay in 1802, was that mighty ensemble of the emperor's regalia, clothes, and even shoes, all of which allegedly were still Charlemagne's and had to be worn at coronation rituals. This ridiculously upheld constitutional continuity as visual fiction through ceremonial dress display. The emperor's clothes embodied a contradiction which only political change could resolve.[102] In 1873, Nietzsche would damningly thunder in his *Uses and Abuses of History* that Germans did not care enough about creating adequate forms. They took on something replicating foreign modes, which did not cost too much or take too much time to put on, and it was then declared to be German customary clothing. Germans prided themselves as a nation of interiority and disdained too much care about form. Yet, Nietzsche cunningly continued, 'there famously exists a danger of this commitment to inner values: the inner content itself, from which it is assumed that it is not visible from outside, might sometimes wish to disappear, but from outside you will hardly notice anything, nor that it ever existed'. For Nietzsche there was no doubt that Germany had all the potential to be sensitive, as well as serious, powerful, good, and richer in its inner life than other cultures. 'But', he startlingly concluded, 'as a whole it remains weak, because all the beautiful fibres are not folded into a strong lace bow.'[103]

As with Leibniz, something about men's psychic attachment to beautifully tied bows and knots could clearly become surprisingly important for their accounts of societies or the universe. More seriously, Nietzsche shows us how relevant thinking about clothes remained when reflecting on precarious national and personal identities, on transitions of self-display into self-delusion, or political displays into outdated farce. Visual fictions and emotional styles gained consent for a time, but could be challenged and changed. The wider framework of this book has taken us to the Middle Ages, Renaissance, and into global worlds. It will leave my ideal reader with an understanding of why we can say that clothes made history, and history can be about clothes.

156. *Markgrave Sibylla Augusta as Slave*, tempera on parchment, mounted on wood, German, c.1700–1710, Inv. No. G8451. © Staatliche Schlösser und Gärten Baden-Württemberg, Favorite

Notes

Acknowledgements

1 Robert Ross, *Clothing: A Global History*, Cambridge: Polity 2008, 144.

Prologue

1 Stephen Varick Dock, *Costume and Fashion in the Plays of Jean-Baptiste Poquelin Molière: A Seventeenth-Century Perspective*, Genève: Editions Slatkine 1992, 72.

2 Michael Scholz-Hänsel, *El Greco. Der Großinquisitor. Neues Licht auf eine schwarze Legende*, Frankurt-am-Main: Fischer 1991, 47–60.

Introduction

1 The most recent contribution to this debate has come from an art historian interested in the visual argument of clothing, see Philipp Zitzlsperger, *Dürers Pelz und das Recht im Bild: Kleiderkunde als Methode der Kunstgeschichte*, Berlin: Akademie Verlag 2008, but is over-argued, as Dürer did not wear a Schaube and the painting clearly can be dated to 1500. For the identification of a councillor's gown see Johannes Pietsch, *Zwei Schauben aus dem Bayerischen Nationalmuseum München: Ein Beitrag zur Kostümforschung*, Munich: Siegl 2004.

2 For different positions see Dieter Wuttke, 'Dürer und Celtis. Von der Bedeutung des Jahres 1500 für den deutschen Humanismus: Jahrhundertfeier als symbolische Form', *The Journal of Medieval and Renaissance Studies*, 10 (1980), 73–129; Joseph Leo Koerner, *The Moment of Self-Portraiture in German Renaissance Art*, Chicago: Chicago University Press 1996; Hans Belting, *Das echte Bild: Bildfragen als Glaubensfragen*, Munich: Beck 2005. Over one century later, Rembrandt would choose Northern fashions of the 1520s and 1530s as a retro-look in his self-portraits to place himself in the tradition of his revered models Dürer and Lucas van Leyden; Marieke de Winkel, *Dress and Meaning in Rembrandt's Paintings*, Amsterdam: Amsterdam University Press 2006, ch. 4.

3 Jeffrey Chipps Smith, *The Northern Renaissance*, London: Phaidon 2004, 278.

4 Zitzlsperger, *Dürers Pelz*, 75.

5 See the excellent passages on his hair in Koerner, *Moment of Self-Portraiture*, 169–170.

6 See Chapter 2 in this book on his shoes and the commemorative painting by Hans Lautensack, *Landscape with a Portrait of Albrecht Dürer*, 1553, Niedersächsisches Landesmuseum Hannvover.

7 See the landmark discussion in Erwin Panofsky, *The Life and Art of Albrecht Dürer*, with a new introduction by J. Chipps Smith, Princeton: Princeton University Press 2005, 281.

8 Chandra Mukerji, *From Graven Images: Patterns of Modern Materialism*, New York: Columbia University Press 1983, 3.

9 Richard A. Goldthwaite, *Wealth and the Demand for Art in Italy 1300–1600*, Baltimore and London: Johns Hopkins University Press 1993, 255. For a general account of European trade in this period see Peter Spufford, *Power and Profit: The Merchant in Medieval Europe*, London: Thames & Hudson 2002; for the Renaissance as an age of new consumerism Lisa Jardine, *Worldly Goods: A New History of the Renaissance*, London: Macmillan 1996; and for the global dimensions of trade Fernand Braudel, *Civilization and Capitalism 15th–18th Century, vol. II, The Wheels of Commerce*, trans. Siân Reynolds, London: HarperCollins 1985.

10 Kenneth Pomeranz's landmark study *The Great Divergence: China, Europe, and the Making of the Modern World Economy*, Princeton: Princeton University Press 2009, first reminds us what to look for: 'an increase in the variety of goods

charged with social significance and the velocity with which they changed; an increase in how many people were allowed to possess them, and in the extent to which they could be acquired from strangers; a sharp increase in imitative consumption, and proliferation of discussion about the "proper," "tasteful" way to use various commodities' and finds these processes best documented for urbanized regions of western Europe, China, Japan, and, to some extent, India, see 129–131.

11 See, in particular, Craig Clunas, *Superfluous Things: Material Culture and Social Status in Early Modern China*, Honolulu: University of Hawaii Press 2004; Timothy Brook, *The Confusions of Pleasure: Commerce and Culture in Ming China*, Berkeley: University of California Press 1998, 218–237; Eiko Ikegami, *Bonds of Civility: Aesthetic Networks and the Political Origins of Japanese Culture*, Cambridge: Cambridge University Press 2005; for a pioneering comparative account see Peter Burke, 'Res et Verba: Conspicuous Consumption in the Early Modern World', in John Brewer and Roy Porter (eds.), *Consumption and the World of Goods*, London: Routledge 1993, 148–161.

12 Cat., *Turning Point: Oribe and the Arts of Sixteenth-Century Japan*, ed. Miyeko Murase, Metropolitan Museum of Art, New York, New Haven: Yale University Press 2003, 12.

13 Ikegami, *Bonds of Civility*, 285.

14 For pioneering approaches see Braudel, *Wheels of Commerce*; C. A. Bayly, *The Birth of the Modern World 1780–1914*, Oxford: Blackwell 2004. Recent discussions of clothing include Richard Robb, *Clothing and Global History*, Cambridge: Polity Press 2008; Mario Belfanti, 'Was Fashion a European Invention?', *Journal of Global History*, 3 (2008), 419–443.

15 Heinz Schilling, *Die Stadt in der Frühen Neuzeit*, Munich: Oldenbourg 1993, 6–9, drawing on Jan de Vries's research.

16 Martha Howell, 'Fixing Movables: Gifts by Testament in Late Medieval Douai', *Past and Present*, 150 (1996), 41–42.

17 StAN, Amts- und Standbücher, 15.6.1609, Catherina Försterin.

18 Drebbel was born in North Holland in 1572, cit. in Svetlana Alpers, *The Art of Describing: Dutch Art in the Seventeenth Century*, Chicago: Chicago University Press 1983, 13.

19 See, for instance, Valentin Groebner, *Ökonomie ohne Haus: Zum Wirtschaften armer Leute in Nürnberg am Ende des 15. Jahrhunderts*, Göttingen: Vandenhoeck 1993; Patricia Allerston, 'Clothing and Early Modern Venetian Society', *Continuity and Change*, 15 (1993), 367–390; on lotteries see Evelyn Welch, 'Lotteries in Early Modern Italy', *Past and Present*, 199 (May 2008), 71–111.

20 Howell, 'Fixing Movables', 44.

21 For a forceful rejection of the emulation theory for eighteenth-century England see John Styles, *The Dress of the People: Everyday Fashion in Eighteenth-Century England*, New Haven: Yale University Press 2007.

22 Susan Mosher Stuart, *Gilding the Market: Luxury and Fashion in Fourteenth-Century Italy*, Philadelphia: University of Pennsylvania Press 2006, 222.

23 Carol Collier Frick, *Dressing Renaissance Florence: Families, Fortunes and Fine Clothing*, Baltimore: Johns Hopkins Press 2002.

24 Elizabeth Currie, 'Diversity and Design in the Florentine Tailoring Trade, 1550–1620', in Michelle O'Malley and Evelyn Welch (eds.), *The Material Renaissance*, Manchester: Manchester University Press 2006, 167–169.

25 Evelyn Welch, 'Art on the Edge: Hair and Hands in Renaissance Italy', *Renaissance Studies*, 23 (2008), 268. In thirteenth-century France, likewise, a market for relatively affordable luxury items had emerged.

26 For excellent studies of the role of clothing in twelfth- and thirteenth-century courts see Andreas Kraß, *Geschriebene Kleider: Höfische Identität als literarisches Spiel*, Tübingen: A. Francke Verlag 2006, as well as Gabriele Raudszus, *Die Zeichensprache der Kleidung. Untersuchungen zur Symbolik des Gewandes in der deutschen Epik des Mittelalters*, Hildesheim: Olms 1985. Of particular interest as well is Peter von Moos, 'Das Mittelalterliche Kleid als Identitätssymbol und Identifikationsmittel', in idem (ed.), *Unverwechselbarkeit: Persönliche Identität und Identifikation in der vormodernen Gesellschaft*, Cologne: Böhlau 2004, 123–139.

27 Islamic fabrics and style elements were used by twelfth-century crusaders when they returned, see Janet Snyder, 'Cloth from the Promised Land: Appropriated Islamic Tiraz in Twelfth-Century French Sculpture', in E. Jane Burns (ed.), *Medieval Fabrications: Dress, Textiles, Clothwork, and Other Cultural Imaginings*, New York: Palgrave 2004, 147–164.

28 An excellent study for the twelfth and in particular thirteenth centuries is Sarah-Grace Heller, *Fashion in Medieval France*, Cambridge: D. S. Brewer 2007.

29 Susan Crane, *The Performance of Self: Ritual, Clothing, and Identity During the Hundred Years War*, Philadelphia: University of Pennsylvania Press 2002, 178. As Susan Crane phrases it, royal and aristocratic dress, 'showiness and gesture' 'are not void of commitment but instead mark the moments where commitment is deepest', 4.

30 Joachim Bumke, *Courtly Culture: Literature and Society in the High Middle Ages*, trans. Thomas Dunlap, Berkeley: University of California Press 1991, 133.

31 Anna Muthesius, 'Silk in the Medieval World', in David Jenkins (ed.), *The Cambridge History of Western Textiles*, vol. 1, Cambridge: Cambridge University Press 2003, 325–355; E. Jane Burns, *Courtly Love Undressed: Reading through Clothes in Medieval French Culture*, Philadelphia: University of Pennsylvania Press 2002, Part IV.

32 Burns, *Courtly Love*, 191; David Abulafia, 'The Role of Trade in Muslim–Christian Contact during the Middle Ages', in Dionisius A. Agius and Richard Hitchcock (eds.), *The Arab Influence in Medieval Europe*, Reading: Ithaca Press 1994, 1–24.

33 John H. Munro, 'Medieval Woollens: Textiles, Textile Technology and Industrial Organisation, c.800–1500', in Jenkins (ed.), *The Cambridge History of Western Textiles*, vol. 1, 194–197.

34 For an outstanding study see Simona Slaničká, *Krieg der Zeichen: Die visuelle Politik Johanns ohne Furcht und der armagnakisch-burgundische Bürgerkrieg*, Göttingen: Vandenhoeck 2002.

35 Odile Blanc, 'From Battlefield to Court: The Invention of Fashion in the Fourteenth Century', in Désirée G. Koslin and Janet E. Snyder (eds.), *Encountering Medieval Textiles and Dress: Objects, Texts, Images*, Houndsmill: Palgrave 2002, 161.

36 Peter Burke, *The Fortunes of the Courtier: The European Reception of Castiglione's Cortegiano*, Cambridge: Polity Press 1995.

37 Babur Nama, *Journal of Emperor Babur*, trans. A. S. Beveridge, ed. D. Hiro, London: Penguin Books 2006, 275.

38 C. A. Bayly, 'The Origins of Swadeshi (Home Industry): Cloth and Indian Society, 1700–1930', in Arjun Appadurai (ed.), *The Social Life of Things: Commodities in Cultural Perspective*, Cambridge: Cambridge University Press 1986, 300.

39 Nuno Vassallo e Silva, 'Precious Stones, Jewels and Cameos: Jacques de Coutre's Journey to Goa and Agra', in Jorge Flores and Nuno Vassallo e Silva (eds.), *Goa and the Great Mughal*, London: Scala 2004, 118.

40 Barbara Stollberg-Rilinger, *Des Kaisers alte Kleider: Verfassungsgeschichte und Symbolsprache des Alten Reiches*, Munich: Beck 2008, 58.

41 Maria Hayward, *Dress at the Court of King Henri VIII*, Leeds: Maney Publishing 2007, 233.

42 'On y veut des objets à réjouir les yeux', Stephen Varick Dock, *Costume and Fashion in the Plays of Jean-Baptiste Poquelin Molière: A Seventeenth-Century Perspective*, Geneva: Editions Slatkine 1992, 96.

43 Helmuth Kiesel, *"Bei Hof, bei Höll": Untersuchungen zur literarischen Hofkritik von Sebastian Brant bis Friedrich Schiller*, Tübingen: M. Niemeyer Verlag 1979, on Schiller see 247.

44 Michel de Montaigne, 'On Sumptuary Laws', in *The Complete Essays*, trans. M. A. Screech, London: Penguin 1987, 301; see also 'On Habit', 133.

45 John Bulwer, *Anthropometamorphosis: A View of the People of the Whole World: Or A Short Survey of their Policies, Dispositions, Naturall Deportments, Complexions, Ancient and Moderne Customes, Manners, Habits & Fashions*, London: William Hunt 1654.

46 See Ninya Mikhaila and Jane Malcolm Davies, *The Tudor Tailor: Reconstructing Sixteenth-Century Dress*, London: Batsford 2006, 18, discussing a German example. For German material, in particular, see Gundula Wolter, *Die Verpackung des Geschlechts: Eine illustrierte Kulturgeschichte*, Marburg: Jonas Verlag 1991.

47 Montaigne, *Complete Essays*, 971.

48 (Kawara bakama guni), Ikegami, *Bonds of Civility*, 262.

49 A good exploration of this in relation to dress is Amanda Bailey, *Flaunting: Style and the Subversive Male Body in Renaissance England*, Toronto: University of Toronto Press 2007.

50 Katharina Simon-Muscheid, *Die Dinge im Schnittpunkt sozialer Beziehungsnetze: Reden und Objekte im Alltag (Oberrhein, 14. bis 16. Jahrhundert)*, Göttingen: Vandenhoeck 2004, 176.

51 Simmel's brief essay is an attempt to reflect on fashion as a social phenomenon in antagonistic terms: it enables people to integrate as well as to mark their individual distinctiveness, see

Georg Simmel, *Philosophie der Mode* (1905), in Otthein Rammstedt (ed.), *Georg Simmel: Gesamtausgabe*, vol. 10, Frankfurt-on-Main: Suhrkamp 1995, 9–37.

52 The landmark study for this account is Carol Gilligan, *In a Different Voice: Psychological Theory and Women's Development*, Cambridge, MA: Harvard University Press 1993. For an excellent example of how such perspectives have changed writing on the Italian Renaissance see Guido Ruggiero, *Machiavelli in Love*, Baltimore: John Hopkins University Press 2007.

53 Ruggiero, *Machiavelli in Love*, 21.

54 Gilles Lipovetsky, *The Empire of Fashion: Dressing Modern Democracy*, trans. Catherine Porter, Princeton: Princeton University Press 2004, 224–225.

55 Gerhard Jaritz, 'Kleidung und Prestige-Konkurrenz: Unterschiedliche Identitäten in der städtischen Gesellschaft unter Normierungszwängen', in Neithart Bulst and Robert Jütte (eds.), Zwischen Sein und Schein. Kleidung und Identität in der ständischen Gesellschaft, *Saeculum*, 44 (1993), 23.

56 Thomas Coryat, *Coryats Crudities 1611*, intro. by William M. Schutte, London: Scolar Press 1978, 465.

57 Museu de Arte Antiga, Lisbon.

58 Montaigne, 'On Sumptuary Laws', in *Complete Essays*, 302.

59 For a brilliant study of the meanings given to food, many of which have a bearing on how dress was thought of, see Emily Gowers, *The Loaded Table: Representations of Food in Roman Literature*, Oxford: Clarendon Press 1993.

60 Philipp von Rummel, *Habitus barbarus: Kleidung und Repräsentation spätantiker Eliten im 4. und 5. Jahrhundert*, Berlin: de Gruyter 2005, ch. 4. Ovid advised that 'a casual look suits men' looking for love, as long as they wore a clean toga, got a good haircut, and cleaned their fingernails. Xenophon could praise Cyrus, king of Persia, for requesting decorousness in the form of high shoes and make-up from his noblemen at court, Burke, *The Fortunes*, 10–12.

61 *Juvenal and Persius*, trans. by Susanna Morton Braund, Harvard: Harvard University Press 2004, 472–473, on boys see 412–413.

62 Rummel, *Habitus barbarus*, 95–96, presents the classical tradition of this argument, which was revived many times throughout the early modern period.

63 *Cesare Vecellio's Habiti Antichi et Moderni: The Clothing of the Renaissance World*, ed. and trans.

Margaret F. Rosenthal and Ann Rosalind Jones, London: Thames & Hudson 2008.

64 Cat., *Encounters: The Meeting of Asia and Europe, 1500–1800*, ed. Anna Jackson and Amin Jaffer, London: V&A Publications 2004, 100–102.

65 Ikegami, *Bonds*, Pl. 2 and 365.

66 Cat., *Encounters*, 326–328.

67 Ikegami, *Bonds*, 353–355.

68 Luís Fróis, *Européen & Japonais: Traité sur les contradictions & différences de mœurs*, Préface de Claude Lévi-Strauss, Paris: Chandeigne 1998.

69 *Le Voyage en Chine d'Adriano de las Cortes s.j. (1625)*, ed. Pascale Girard, Paris: Chandeigne 2001; Cat., *Encounters*, Pl. 16.13.

70 Leslie Meral Schick, 'The Place of Dress in Premodern Costume Albums', in Suraiya Faroqhi and Christoph K. Neumann (eds.), *Ottoman Costumes: From Textile to Identity*, Istanbul: Eren 2004, 99.

71 Schick, *The Place*, 100.

72 Schick, *The Place*, 101.

73 This has now been explored by Giorgio Riello and Prasannan Parthasarathi (eds.), *The Spinning World: A Global History of Cotton Textiles, 1200–1850*, Oxford: Oxford University Press 2009.

74 Ikegami, *Bonds*, 252 and 284.

75 For the Ottoman Empire see Suraiya Faroqhi, 'Introduction, or Why and How one might want to Study Ottoman Clothes', in ead. and Neumann (eds.), *Ottoman Costumes*, 31.

76 Styles, *The Dress of the People*, ch. 7.

77 Hans Medick, *Weben und Überleben in Laichingen 1650–1900*, Göttingen: Vandenhoeck 1996, on mortality data see ch. 4.5; for the increase in textiles see 405.

78 Medick, *Weben*, 427–428.

79 For *cointerie* see Heller, *Fashion*, ch. 4.

80 Andrew Boorde, *The Boke of the Introduction of Knowledge . . .*, London: W. Copland, 1550?. The date is also sometimes given as 1542, and sometimes as 1568.

81 Brook, *Confusions of Pleasure*, 220 'shiyang'.

82 Ikegami, *Bonds*, 247.

83 Paul Behaim, *Briefe eines Leipziger Studenten aus den Jahren 1572 bis 1574*, ed. Wilhelm Loose, Meißen: 1880, 6.

84 Bailey, *Flaunting*, 116.

85 Halil Inalcik, 'Bursa and the Silk Trade', in idem and Donald Quataert (eds.), *An Economic and Social History of the Ottoman Empire*, vol. 1, Cambridge: Cambridge University Press 1994, 218.

86 This has been explored by Amy Butler Green-field, *A Perfect Red: Empires, Espionage, and the Quest for the Color of Desire*, New York: Harper-Collins 2005.

87 The latter process is well set out in Tom Scott, *Society and Economy in Germany, 1300–1600*, Houndsmill: Palgrave 2002, 99.

88 Ulinka Rublack, *The Crimes of Women in Early Modern Germany*, Oxford: Oxford University Press 1999.

89 This point is discussed in the Epilogue.

90 The nobilities of Poland and Hungary had adopted national dress, and Greek national dress was introduced as late as 1821.

91 For a pioneering account over such a long time period see Chris Bayly, 'The Origins', in Appadurai (ed.), *The Social Life*; Philip Mansel, *Dressed to Rule: Royal and Court Costume from Louis XIV to Elizabeth II*, New Haven: Yale University Press 2005, which includes many non-European examples; an excellent collection with a wide geographical and chronological range is Wendy Parkins (ed.), *Fashioning the Body Politic: Dress, Gender, Citizenship*, Oxford: Berg 2002; on Russia see also Oksana Sekatcheva, 'The Formation of Russian Women's Costume at the Time before the Reforms of Peter the Great', in Catherine Richardson (ed.), *Clothing Culture, 1350–1650*, Aldershot: Ashgate 2004, 77–94; on the French Revolution see Cissie Fairchilds, 'Fashion and Freedom in the French Revolution', *Continuity & Change*, 15 (2000), 419–433; Michael Sonenscher, *Sans-Culottes: An Eighteenth-Century Emblem in the French Revolution*, Princeton: Princeton University Press 2008, esp. ch. 2; on America; cf. Michael Zakim, *Ready-Made Democracy: A History of Men's Dress in the American Republic*, Chicago: Chicago University Press 2003.

92 For an overview see Bumke, *Courtly Culture*, 128–155.

93 Stella Mary Newton, *Fashion in the Age of the Black Prince: A Study of the Years 1340–1365*, Woodbridge: The Boydell Press 1980, 10; see also Slanićka, *Zeichen*, 92–95.

94 'Seyt willenchomen, her Hindenploz!', the poet was Peter Suchenwirt, Ulrike Lehmann-Langholz, *Kleiderkritik in mittelalterlicher Dichtung. Der Arme Hartmann, Heinrich 'von Melk', Neidhart, Wernher der Gaertenaere und ein Ausblick auf die Stellungnahmen spätmittelalterlicher Dichter*, Frankfurt-on-Main: Peter Lang 1985, 80.

95 Odile Blanc, 'From Battlefield to Court: The Invention of Fashion in the Fourteenth Century', in Désirée G. Koslin and Janet E. Snyder (eds.), *Encountering Medieval Textiles and Dress: Objects, Texts, Images*, Houndsmill: Palgrave 2002, 165.

96 Desiderius Erasmus, *The Collected Works of Erasmus*, 'On Good Manners in Boys', vol. 25, 278.

97 Bumke, *Courtly Culture*, 140.

98 Odile Blanc, *Parades et Parures: L'invention du corps de mode à la fin du Moyen Age*, Paris: Éditions Gallimard 1997.

99 Cit. in Medick, *Weben*, 379.

100 On the relation of dress and gender see Blanc, *From Battlefield to Court*, 170.

101 Hayward, *Dress*, 10–13.

102 Bumke, *Courtly Society*, 146.

103 Hayward, *Dress*, 16–17; Cat., *Turks: A Journey of a Thousand Years, 600–1600*, ed. David J. Roxburgh, London: Royal Academy of Art 2005, Pl. 293.

104 K. N. Chaudhuri, *Asia Before Europe: Economy and Civilisation of the Indian Ocean from the Rise of Islam to 1750*, Cambridge: Cambridge University Press 1990, 182–189.

105 Ibn Khaldûn, *The Muqaddimah: An Introduction to History*, trans. Franz Rosenthal, ed. N. J. Dawood, Princeton: Princeton University Press 1967, 322.

106 Belfanti, *Was Fashion a European Invention?*, 423.

107 The man was Jean Palerne Forézien, see Matthew Elliot, 'Dress Codes in the Ottoman Empire: The Case of the Franks', in Faroqhi and Neumann (eds.), *Ottoman Costumes*, 117.

108 Ruggiero, *Machiavelli in Love*, 146.

109 A consistent exploration of this theme can be found in Stuard, *Gilding the Market*, esp. chs. 4 and 8. See also the Conclusion to this book.

110 An important exploration of this can be found in contributions to Flores and Vassallo e Silva (eds.), *Goa and the Great Mughal*.

111 Lehmann-Langholz, *Kleiderkritik in mittelalterlicher Dichtung*, 80.

112 Catherine Kovesi Killerby, ' "Heralds of a Well-instructed Mind": Nicolosa Sanuti's Defence of Women and their Clothes', *Renaissance Studies*, 13 (1999), 255–282, here 268. Perhaps this comment purposefully rejected a particular pagan Roman moralization of gemstones, which through the early Christian

writer Tertullian's work on female adornment, too, had narrowly rejected them as signs of worldly sumptuousness. On Tertullian's discussion of gemstones see Lehmann-Langholz, *Kleiderkritik in mittelalterlicher Dichtung*, 83–86.

113 Kovesi Killerby, 'Heralds', 263.

114 Georg Steinhausen (ed.), *Privatbriefe aus dem deutschen Mittelalter*, vol. 1, n.p. 1899, 141.

115 Gülru Neçipoglu, 'Süleyman the Magnificent and the Representation of Power in the Context of Ottoman-Habsburg–Papal Rivalry', *The Art Bulletin*, 71 (1989), 407–427.

116 Hannah S. M. Amburger, *Die Familiengeschichte der Koeler: Ein Beitrag zur Autobiographie des 16. Jahrhunderts*, Nuremberg: J. L. Stich 1930, 230.

117 Evelyn Welch, *Shopping in the Renaissance: Consumer Cultures in Italy, 1400–1600*, New Haven: Yale University Press 2005, 12.

118 Douglas Biow, *The Culture of Cleanliness in Renaissance Italy*, Ithaca: Cornell University Press 2006, 183–185. In 1512, the German Franciscan Thomas Murner hilariously turned himself into an advocate of lice, who, he wrote, used to have imperial rights to ascend from the heat of the body into the airy freedom of the neck. Now every woman who thought she was infested used glittering jewellery, pearls, and golden necklaces on which no louse could climb. Gold was too cold for lice and all this shininess made these poor white animals just as invisible as black cloths. This forced them to stay down under in the clothes. This is ch. 34 of his *Narrenbeschwörung*, discussed in Lehmann-Langholz, *Kleiderkritik*, 286–291.

119 Cit. in Alpers, *The Art of Describing*, 13.

120 Craig Clunas, *Empire of Great Brightness: Visual and Material Cultures of Ming China, 1368–1644*, London: Reaktion 2007, 12.

121 Ernst Hartwig Kantorowicz, *The King's Two Bodies: A Study in Medieval Political Theology*, Princeton: Princeton University Press 1957, 415–418. For a recent study see Kristin Marek, *Die Körper des Königs: Effigies, Bildpolitik und Heiligkeit*, Munich: Fink 2009.

122 Most members of the Augsburg weavers' guild, for example, were far from well off, but the guild nonetheless commissioned significant local artists to paint an elaborate programme of historical and biblical scenes, Jewish prophets,

and pagan philosophers onto the conifer wood covering the walls and vaulted ceiling of their meeting room. This Augsburg weavers' room is on display in the Bavarian Nationalmuseum, Munich, and one of the painters was Jörg Breu; see *Bayrisches Nationalmuseum: Handbook of the Art and Cultural History Collection*, ed. Renate Eikelmann, Munich: Hirmer Verlag, no date, 74.

123 Horst Bredekamp, 'Bild – Akt – Geschichte', in Clemens Wischermann et al. (eds.), *Geschichtsbilder, 46. Deutscher Historikertag in Konstanz 2006, Berichtsband*, Constance: Universitätsverlag 2007, 309.

124 Goldthwaite, *Wealth*, 255.

125 Bredekamp, 'Bild – Akt – Geschichte', '…Bilder…mitbewirken, was erst gespiegelt und reflektiert werden kann', 291.

126 Anne Hollander, *Seeing through Clothes*, Los Angeles: University of California Press 1993, 452. Hollander therefore concluded that changes in fashion were interrelated with 'vital activity in representational art—in the nineteenth and twentieth centuries no less than in the fifteenth and sixteenth'.

127 Hollander, *Seeing*, xv.

128 Hollander, *Seeing*, xvi, 454.

129 He sold devotional images of Mary for five florins, too, while a *Judgement of Paris* earned Cranach twenty florins; see the pioneering work of Gunnar Heydenreich, *Lucas Cranach the Elder: Painting Materials, Techniques and Workshop Practise*, Amsterdam: Amsterdam University Press 2007, contract 316 in Appendix II, 451.

130 Matthias Weber (ed.), *Die Reichspolizeiordnungen von 1530, 1548 und 1577: Historische Einführung und Edition*, Frankfurt-on-Main: V. Klostermann 2002, 142–143.

131 Lisa Monnas, *Merchants, Princes and Painters: Silk Fabrics in Italian and Northern Paintings 1300–1550*, New Haven: Yale University Press 2009, 267.

132 Valerius Anshelm, *Die Berner Chronik*, ed. Historischen Verein des Kantons Bern, vols. 1–6, Bern 1884–1901, vol. 2, 390.

133 Ibn Khaldûn, *History*, 116.

134 See his path-breaking book: Keith Moxey, *Peasants, Warriors and Wives: Popular Imagery in the Reformation*, Chicago: University of Chicago Press 1989, 5. For an excellent introduction to different approaches within

the new field of visual culture studies see Joanne Morra and Marquard Smith (eds.), *Visual Culture: Critical Concepts in Media and Cultural Studies*, vol. 1, London: Routledge 2008.

135 See, for instance, the discussion in relation to fashion in Margaret Dikovitskaya, 'An Interview with W. J. T. Mitchell', in ead., *The Study of the Visual after the Cultural Turn*, Cambridge, MA: MIT Press 2005, 245.

136 See the pioneering work of Michael Baxandall, *The Limewood Sculptors of Renaissance Germany*, New Haven: Yale University Press 1980; Clunas, *Superfluous Things*, 165.

137 Valentin Lötscher (ed.), *Felix Platter, Tagebuch (Lebensbeschreibung) 1536–1567*, Basle: Schwabe & Co. 1976, 350: 'Do war ein schiiterbigen, doruf satzt der nachrichter den todtenbaum, zerreis in, dass der cörpel allerdingen sichtbar war, dorüber ein schamlater rock, hatt ein sammete spitzhauben auf, mit rotem scharlch ausgefieteret. Er richtet in auf; war noch ziemlich gantz und kantlich, hatt die augen ingefallen und beschlossen. man legt die biecher neben in und richtet sein contrafetung uf, an der stange uf der biige, zundt das feur an und verbrant alles zu äschen.' On the painting and Joris's prophetic gesture see briefly Paul Burckhardt, *David Joris und seine Gemeinde in Basel*, Basel: [n.p.] 1949, 37.

138 This position is further explored by Stuart Clark, *Vanities of the Eye: Vision in Early Modern European Culture*, Oxford: Oxford University Press 2007.

139 Peter Burke, 'Imagining Identity in the Early Modern City', in Christian Emden et al. (eds.), *Imagining the City, vol. 1., The Art of Urban Living*, Frankfurt-on-Main: Peter Lang 2006, 23–37.

140 'Declaring that his clothes should enjoy the meal, since they, not he, had been invited', see Pamela H. Smith, 'Science and Taste: Painting, Passions, and the New Philosophy in Seventeenth-Century Leiden', *Isis*, 90 (1999), 432–435. For an excellent discussion of medieval literature which reveals similar tropes see Jan-Dirk Müller, 'Writing – Speech – Image: The Competition of Signs', in Kathryn Starkey and Horst Wenzel (eds.), *Visual Culture and the German Middle Ages*, New York: Palgrave 2005, 35–52 as well as Peter von Moos, 'Das mittelalterliche Kleid als Identitätssymbol und Identifikationsmittel', 123–124, where he discusses the Arab origins of the trope and some of its medieval usages.

141 Caroline Evans, *Fashion at the Edge: Spectacle, Modernity and Deathliness*, New Haven: Yale University Press 2007. For an outstanding account of cloth in art see Monika Wagner, *Das Material der Kunst. Eine andere Geschichte der Moderne*, Munich: C. H. Beck 2001, esp. ch. III.

142 J. R. Hale, *Artists and Warfare in the Renaissance*, New Haven: Yale University Press 1990.

143 Hale, *Artists and Warfare*, 134.

144 Chipps Smith, *Northern Renaissance*, 12.

145 Panofsky, *The Life and Art*, 280.

146 Chipps Smith, *Northern Renaissance*, 245–246.

147 Larry Silver, *Marketing Maximilian: The Visual Ideology of a Holy Roman Emperor*, Princeton: Princeton University Press 2008.

148 Giulia Bartrum (ed.), *German Renaissance Prints 1490–1550*, London: British Museum Press 1995, 161.

149 Quentin Skinner sees the depiction as a pairing of vice (tristitia) and virtue (belief in the republic), see idem., *Visions of Politics, vol. 2, Renaissance Virtues*, Cambridge: Cambridge University Press 2002, 106–117.

150 Cat., *Welt im Umbruch: Augsburg zwischen Renaissance und Barock*, vol. 1, Augsburg: Augsburger Druck- und Verlagshaus 1980, 274–275.

151 See the sixteenth-century coloured woodcut 'Vom Wucher, Furkauff und Tryegerey', printed in Cat., *Kurzweil viel ohn 'Maß und Ziel': Alltag und Festtag auf den Augsburger Monatsbildern der Renaissance*, Berlin: Hirmer 1994, 62 as well as Luther's comparison of government to a 'bad beggar's fur', ch. 3.

Chapter Two

1 Joseph Leo Koerner, *The Moment of Self-Portraiture in German Renaissance Art*, Chicago: Chicago University Press 1993, 40.

2 For this figure see Tom Scott, *Society and Economy in Germany, 1300–1600*, Houndsmill: Palgrave 2002, 64.

3 For Italy see Guido Rugiero, *Machiavelli in Love: Sex, Self, and Society in the Italian Renaissance*, Baltimore: Johns Hopkins University Press 2007, 27–28.

4 On beards as material markers of boyishness or manhood in English literature see Will Fisher, *Materializing Gender in Early Modern English Literature and Culture*, Cambridge: Cambridge University Press 2006.

5 A pioneering volume which looks at the meanings of visual practices for male self-enactments is Mechtild Fend and Marianne Koos (eds.), *Männlichkeit im Blick: Visuelle Inszenierungen in der Kunst seit der Frühen Neuzeit*, Cologne: Böhlau 2004.

6 Hans Belting, *Florenz und Bagdad: Eine westöstliche Geschichte des Blicks*, Munich: Beck 2008.

7 This is brought out, in particular, by Ludmilla Jordanova's forthcoming monograph on History and Images for Cambridge University Press.

8 Chris Pinney and Nicolas Peterson (eds.), *Photography's Other History*, Durham: Duke University Press 2003, 13.

9 Michail Bakhtin, *Rabelais and his World*, trans. Helene Iswolsky, Bloomington: Indiana University Press 1984.

10 Valentin Groebner, 'Inside Out: Clothes, Dissimulation, and the Arts of Accounting in the Autobiography of Matthäus Schwarz, 1496–1574', *Representations*, 66 (Spring 1999), 100–121, here 105.

11 Groebner, 'Inside Out', 101.

12 Groebner, 'Inside Out', 115.

13 Gabriele Mentges, 'Fashion, Time and the Consumption of a Renaissance Man in Germany: The Costume Book of Matthäus Schwarz of Augsburg, 1496–1564', *Gender and History*, 14 (2002), 382–402, here 397.

14 Mentges, 'Fashion', 397 and 399.

15 'Quid tum', Belting, *Florenz und Bagdad*, 229–232; Horst Bredekamp, *Bilder bewegen: Von der Kunstkammer zum Endspiel. Aufsätze und Reden*, ed. Jörg Probst, Berlin: Wagenbach 2007, 9–22.

16 'Da sprich ich, das ich all mein tag gern was bey den alten, und ire antwurt meyner frag was mir ein grose freud zö hern. Und under anderm ward wyr etwa auch zö röd der trachtung und monier der klaydungen, wie sy sich also teglich verkerete. Und etwa zaigten sy mir ir trachtencontrofat, so sy vor 30, 40 in 50 jarn getragen hetten, das mich ser wundert... Das ursacht mich, die meyne auch zu contrafaten, zu sehen uber ein zeit als 5, in 10 oder mer jarn, was noch daraus werden wölle.' See August Fink (ed.), *Die Schwarzschen Trachtenbücher*, Berlin: Deutscher Verein für Kunstwissenschaft 1963, 98.

17 Fink, *Trachtenbücher*, 98.

18 Wilhelm Rem, 'Chronica newer Geschichten', in *Die Chroniken der schwäbischen Städte: Augsburg*, vol. 5, Leipzig: Hirzel 1896, 119.

19 Claus-Peter Clasen, *Textilherstellung in Augsburg in der frühen Neuzeit*, Augsburg: B. Wissner 1995.

20 Other than this there are three background scenes featuring archery men and a parade for Ferdinand of Austria; tiny background scenes of a boat, sledge, or walks in the snow; a dog raising his leg against a house; his son and his three children once each; and finally once, as a matter of cause, his coachman.

21 For an excellent recent synthesis see Mark Häberlein, *Die Fugger: Geschichte einer Augsburger Familie (1367–1650)*, Stuttgart: Kohlhammer 2006.

22 Norbert Lieb, *Die Fugger und die Kunst, vol. 2: Im Zeitalter der hohen Renaissance*, Munich: Schnell & Steiner 1958, 155.

23 Lieb, *Fugger und die Kunst*, 181.

24 Lieb, *Fugger und die Kunst*, 180.

25 Lieb, *Fugger und die Kunst*, 122.

26 Häberlein, *Fugger*, 61.

27 Lieb, *Fugger und die Kunst*, 87.

28 Cat., *Kurzweil viel ohn 'Maß und Ziel': Alltag und Festtag auf den Augsburger Monatsbildern der Renaissance*, Munich: Hirmer 1994; Cat., *Welt im Umbruch: Augsburg zwischen Renaissance und Barock*, Augsburg: Augsburger Druck- und Verlagshaus 1980, vol. 1, 119.

29 For excellent accounts of art in Augsburg see Andrew Morrall, *Jörg Breu the Elder: Art, Culture and Belief in Reformation Augsburg*, Aldershot: Ashgate 2002; Pia Cuneo, *Art and Politics in Early Modern Germany: Jörg Breu the Elder and the Fashioning of Political Identity, c.1475–1536*, Leiden: Brill 1998.

30 *Welt im Umbruch*, vol. 1, 217 f.

31 Groebner, 'Inside Out', 100.

32 Fink, *Trachtenbücher*, 76–79.

33 Fink, *Trachtenbücher*, 164, I 116.

34 Fink, *Trachtenbücher*, 167, I 121.

35 *Die Korrespondenz Hans Fuggers von 1566 bis 1594*, vol. 2, Part 2, *1582–1594*, ed. Christl Karnehm, Munich: Kommission für Bayerische Landesgeschichte 2003, 1542.

36 Karnehm, *Korrespondenz*, 1365, 1397.

37 Carlo Mario Belfanti and Fabio Gisuberti, 'Clothing and Social Inequality in Early Modern Europe: Introductory Remarks', in *Continuity and Change*, 15/3 (2000), 361.

38 Karnehm, *Korrespondenz*, 1416.

39 Karnehm, *Korrespondenz*, 1424.

40 Karnehm, *Korresponenz*, 1424.

41 A brilliant engagement with the contemporary meaning of fur is Philipp Zitzlsperger, *Dürer's Pelz und das Recht im Bild. Kleiderkunde als Methode der Kunstgeschichte*, Berlin: Akademie Verlag 2008.

42 Jutta Zander-Seidel, *Textiler Hausrat: Kleidung und Haustextilien in Nürnberg von 1500 bis 1650*, Munich: Deutscher Kunstverlag 1990, 218.

43 Zander-Seidel, *Textiler Hausrat*, 217–218.

44 Fink, *Trachtenbücher*, 156, I 104.

45 Fink, *Trachtenbücher*, 138–139, I 66.

46 Fink, *Trachtenbücher*, 139, I 67.

47 Fink, *Trachtenbücher*, 148, I 86.

48 Fink, *Trachtenbücher*, 143, I 74.

49 Fink, *Trachtenbücher*, 149, I 87.

50 Fink, *Trachtenbücher*, 258–259.

51 Fink, *Trachtenbücher*, 150, I 90.

52 Fink, *Trachtenbücher*, 142, I 74.

53 'sonder sich mit der kleydung/ wie dieselbe jnen von jrer Herrschafft gegeben wirdt/ benuegen lassen', *Eines Ersamen Raths der Statt Augspurg der Gezierd und Kleydung halben auffgerichte Policeyordnung*, Augsburg 1582. The first ordinance that has been traced dates from 1568, whereas before this these matters were treated in a summary way by police ordinances, see Stéphanie Chapuis, 'Juges et Jupons: Les lois vestimentaires et les femmes à Augsbourg au XVIe siècle', in Marie Viallon (ed.), *Paraître et se vêtir au XVIe siècle: Actes du XIIIe Colloque du Puy-en-Velay*, Saint Étienne: Publications de L'Université de Saint-Étienne 2006, 199.

54 Chapuis, 'Juges et Jupons', 209–211; and, in greater detail, Thomas Lüttenberg, 'Législation symbolique ou contrainte efficace?: Les lois vestimentaires dans les villes allemandes au XVIe siècle', in Christine Aribaud and Sylvie Mouysset (eds.), *Vêture & Pouvoir XIIIe–XX siècle*, Toulouse: Framespa 2003, esp. 147. Such attempts to implement sumptuary laws were typically sporadic, and therefore demonstrate their failure to act as an institution which would homogenize societal groups. In the middle sized Imperial city of Schwäbisch-Hall, for instance, women were fined during 1687 and 1688, when the council tried to round up especially those wearing velvet headbands with small pearls or golden lace trimmings. The women pestered the council for mitigations with all imaginable qualifications of why they had worn these. An inn-keeper's wife even told the constable that she was absolutely right to wear expensive clothes on Sunday and 'now she wanted to wear them even more and see who would keep her from doing so, because her husband was not only an innkeeper, but a doctor', Ulinka Rublack, *The Crimes of Women in Early Modern Germany*, Oxford: Oxford University Press 1999, 40. These depositions have also been analysed by Renate Dürr, 'Die Ehre der Mägde zwischen Selbstdefinition und Fremdbestimmung', in B. Ann Tlusty (ed.), *Ehrkonzepte der Frühen Neuzeit. Identitäten und Abgrenzungen*, Berlin: Akademie Verlag 1998, 170–184.

55 An exploration on the possible bearing of imperial ordinances on Augsburg paintings can be found in Neithart Bulst, Thomas Lüttenberg, and Andreas Priever, 'Abbild oder Wunschbild?: Bildnisse des Christoph Ambergers im Spannungsfeld von Rechtsnorm und gesellschaftlichem Anspruch', *Saeculum*, 53 (2002), 21–73. See also the discussion in the Epilogue.

56 Barbara Stollberg-Rilinger, *Des Kaisers alte Kleider: Verfassungsgeschichte und Symbolsprache des Alten Reiches*, Munich: Beck 2008, 126.

57 Wolfgang Behringer, 'Arena and Pall Mall: Sport in the Early Modern Period', *German History*, 27 (2009), 331–357.

58 Fink, *Trachtenbücher*, 258, II 41.

59 Lyndal Roper, *The Holy Household: Women and Morals in Reformation Augsburg*, Oxford: Oxford University Press 1989.

60 Fink, *Trachtenbücher*, 58–59.

61 See the important discussion in Karin Orchard, *Annäherung der Geschlechter: Androgynie in der Kunst des Cinquecento*, Münster: Lit Verlag 1992, here 48.

62 Roper, *Holy Household*, 151

63 Zitzlsperger, *Dürer's Pelz*, 35–37, 42–45.

64 Anette Kranz, *Christoph Amberger: Bildnismaler zu Augsburg. Städtische Eliten im Spiegel ihrer Porträts*, Regensburg: Schnell & Steiner 2004, 113–115.

65 Kranz, *Amberger*, 322–324.

66 Clemens Sender, *Die Chronik von C. Sender von den ältesten Zeiten der Stadt Augsburg bis 1536*, ed. F. Roth, Munich: Königliche Akademie der Wissenschaften 1894, 177.

67 Sender, *Chronik*, 186.

68 Sender, *Chronik*, 340.

69 Sender, *Chronik*, 355.

70 Sender, *Chronik*, 388.

71 Sender, *Chronik*, 337.

72 Sender, *Chronik*, 389.

73 Stollberg-Rilinger, *Des Kaisers*, 300.

74 Sender, *Chronik*, 266.

75 See, in particular, Jörg Rogge, *Für den gemeinen Nutzen: Politisches Handeln und Politikverständnis von Rat und Bürgerschaft in Augsburg im Spätmittlelalter*, Tübingen: M. Niemayer Verlag 1996, ch. 2.

76 'Er hatte ainen schamaloten rockh, mit marder gefuettert, deren dieser zeyt nicht vil in Augsburg gewesen, den geschlechtern zu layd an, ain ruckmarderine hauben mit zwayen grossen berline knopffen hatt er auff, und ain samatin wamas truge er dismals an seinem layb', see Rogge, *Gemeinen Nutzen*, fn. 324.

77 Fink, *Trachtenbücher*, 12.

78 Paul Hector Mair, *Zwei Chroniken des Augsburger Ratsdieners Paul Hector Mair von 1548 bis 1564*, Die Chroniken der deutschen Städte, Munich: Königliche Akademie der Wissenschaften 1917.

79 Mair, *Zwei Chroniken*, 126.

80 See the magnificent edition by Gregor Rohmann, *Das Ehrenbuch der Fugger: Darstellung – Transkription – Kommentar*, 2 vols., Augsburg: Wißner 2004.

81 See Hartmut Bock, *Die Chronik Eisenberger, Edition und Kommentar: bebilderte Geschichte einer Beamtenfamilie der deutschen Renaissance – Aufstieg in den Wetterauer Niederadel und das Frankfurter Patriziat*, Frankfurt-on-Main: Historisches Museum 2001, 404–417.

82 M. Channing Linthicum, *Costume in the Drama of Shakespeare and his Contemporaries*, Oxford: Clarendon Press 1936, 16–23; Desiderius Erasmus, 'On Good Manners in Boys', in *Collected Works of Erasmus, Literary and Educational Writings 3*, ed. J. K. Sowards, Toronto: University of Toronto Press, 279.

83 Sender, *Chronik*, 208.

84 Götz Freiherr von Pöllnitz, *Anton Fugger*, 3 vols., Tübingen: Mohr 1958–1986, vol. 3, 427.

85 Pöllnitz, *Anton Fugger*, vol. 3, 429.

86 Lyndal Roper, *Oedipus and the Devil: Witchcraft, Sexuality and Religion in Early Modern Europe*, London: Routledge 1994, 128.

87 Lieb, *Fugger und die Kunst*, 78, 'zu prächtig, zu reich in seinen Dingen'.

88 Häberlein, *Fugger*, 92, 'sich der hanndl selb abschneidt unnd ausgeet.'

89 Paul Hector Mair, *Geschlechter Buch: darinn der loblichen Kaiserliche Reichs Statt Augspurg so vor fünffhundert vnd mehr Jahren hero, dasselbst gewonet, vnd biss auff acht abgestorben, auch deren so an der Abgestorbnen stat eingenommen vnd erhöhet worden seyn*, Frankfurt-on-Main: S. Feyerabend 1580.

90 Alexandra Shepard, *Meanings of Manhood in Early Modern England*, Oxford: Oxford University Press 2003.

91 Evelyn Welch, *Shopping in the Renaissance: Consumer Cultures in Italy 1400–1600*, New Haven: Yale University Press 2005, 220.

92 Anna Rapp Buir and Monica Stucky-Schürer, *Die Sieben Planeten: Eine 1547–1549 datierte Tapisseriefolge in der Fondation Martin Bodmer*, Basle: Schwaber Verlag 2008, 27–28; A. Weitnauer, *Venezianischer Handel der Fugger: Nach der Musterbuchhaltung des Matthäus Schwarz*, Munich: Duncker & Humblot 1931.

93 For a similar criticism see the stimulating article by John Martin, 'Inventing Sincerity, Refashioning Prudence: The Discovery of the Individual in Renaissance Europe', *American Historical Review*, 102 (1997), 1309–1342.

94 H. C. Erik Midelfort, *A History of Madness in Sixteenth-Century Germany*, Stanford: Stanford University Press 1999, 238.

95 Cf. Roper, *Oedipus and the Devil*, Introduction.

96 'Better still, since most luxury goods are used (…), it might make more sense to regard luxury as a special "register" of consumption (…). The signs of this register…are some or all of the following attributes: (1) restriction, either by price or by law, to elites; (2) complexity of acquisition, which may or may not be a function of real scarcity; (3) semiotic virtuosity, that is, the capacity to signal fairly complex social messages (as do pepper in cuisine, silk in dress, jewels in adornment, and relics in worship); (4) specialised knowledge as a prerequisite for their "appropriate" consumption, that is, regulation by fashion; and (5) a high degree of linkage of their consumption to body, person, and personality', see Arjun Appadurai, 'Introduction: Commodities and the Politics of Value' in idem (ed.), *The Social Life of Things: Commodities in Cultural Perspective*, Cambridge: Cambridge University Press 1986, 3–64, here 38.

97 Albrecht Dürer, *Schriftlicher Nachlass*, ed. Hans Rupprich, vol. 1, Berlin: Deutscher Verein für Kunstwissenschaft 1956, 57, 23 Sep-

tember 1506, 'Mein frantzossischer mantell, dy…husseck vnd der prawn rock lassen vch fast grüssen', Original BM Sloane, Harl. 4935, fol. 41.

98 Fink, *Trachtenbücher*, 18.

Chapter Three

1 Cat., *Martin Luther und die Reformation in Deutschland*, Germanisches Nationalmuseum, Frankfurt-on-Main: Insel Verlag 1983, 67.

2 For a brief overview see, for instance, Françoise Piponnier and Perrine Mane, *Dress in the Middle Ages*, New Haven: Yale University Press 1995, ch. 8.

3 For plurality in an age which used to be thought of in terms of 'Lutheran orthodoxy' see Thomas Kaufmann, *Konfession und Kultur: Lutherischer Protestantismus in der zweiten Hälfte des Reformationsjahrhunderts*, Tübingen: Mohr Siebeck 2006.

4 St Thomas Aquinas, *Summa theologiae: A Concise Translation*, ed. Timothy McDermott, London: Eyre and Spottiswoode 1989, 232.

5 Barbara Stollberg-Rilinger, *Des Kaisers alte Kleider: Verfassungsgeschichte und Symbolsprache des Alten Reiches*, Munich: Beck 2008, ch. VI.

6 Simona Slanicka, *Krieg der Zeichen: Die visuelle Politik Johanns ohne Furcht und der armagnakisch-burgundische Bürgerkrieg*, Göttingen: Vandenhoeck & Ruprecht 2002, 97 f., with reference to a quote by Philippe de Mézières.

7 Andreas Kraß, *Geschriebene Kleider: Höfische Identität als literarisches Spiel*, Tübingen: A. Franke 2006, Part II.

8 Luca Molà, *The Silk Industry of Renaissance Venice*, Baltimore: Johns Hopkins University Press 2000, 89.

9 There were three basic types of dress: Priests wore a chasuble, a circular cloak with only an opening for the head; deacons a dalmatic, a richly decorated tunic with sleeves; while copes opened in the front and developed into equally sumptuous ceremonial mantles. Churches and convents were often given precious textiles by the wealthy, which were reused.

10 See the pioneering work of Juliane von Fircks, *Liturgische Gewänder des Mittelalters aus St. Nicolai in Stralsund*, Riggisberg: Abegg Stiftung 2008, 73, Cat. No. 1.

11 This is an analogy to Michel Baxandall's observations on polychrome altarpieces in *The Limewood Sculptors of Renaissance Germany*, New Haven: Yale University Press 1980, 42.

12 von Fircks, *Gewänder*, 106, Cat. No. 4, – AMOR MERCE DAMA.

13 von Fircks, *Gewänder*, Cat. No. 17.

14 Karen Stolleis, *Messgewänder aus deutschen Kirchenschätzen des Mittelalters bis zur Gegenwart: Geschichte – Form – Material*, Regensburg: Schnell & Steiner 2001, Cat. Nos. 12, 14. These ironically only survive because in some parts of Lutheran Germany they were carefully tidied away into chests.

15 Andrea von Hülsen-Esch, *Gelehrte im Bild: Repräsentation, Darstellung und Wahrnehmung einer sozialen Gruppe im Mittelalter*, Göttingen: Vandenhoeck 2006, 135.

16 'Se l'evesque, faisant l'office solennel et divin, estoit parez comme un pauvre chappelain, le peuple en perdroit la moitie ou plus de sa devocion', cit. in Slanicka, *Krieg*, 98, fn. 124.

17 Charles VI of France was likened to a precious jewel, Slanicka, *Krieg*, 95.

18 *Enea Silvio Piccolomini Papst Pius II: Ausgewählte Texte*, ed. Berthe Widmer, Basle: Schwaber 1960, 182. On acclamations see Ernst H. Kantorowicz, *Laudes Regiae: A Study in Liturgical Acclamations and Medieval Ruler Worship*, Berkeley: University of California Press 1946.

19 Enea Silvio Piccolomini, *Deutschland: Der Brieftraktat an Martin Mayer*, ed. Adolf Schmidt, Cologne: Böhlau 1962, 179–186.

20 Cited in William A. Dyrness, *Reformed Theology and Visual Culture: The Protestant Imagination from Calvin to Edwards*, Cambridge: Cambridge University Press 2004, 31.

21 Michel Pastoureau, *Black: The History of a Color*, Princeton: Princeton University Press 2009, 64–66.

22 'omnis habitus est licitus', cit. by Jörg Jochen Berns, 'Luthers Papstkritik als Zeremoniellkritik. Zur Bedeutung des päpstlichen Zeremoniells für das fürstliche Hofzeremoniell der Frühen Neuzeit', in Jörg Jochen Berns and Thomas Rahn (eds.), *Zeremoniell als höfische Ästhetik in Spätmittelalter und Früher Neuzeit*, Tübingen: Niemeyer 1995, 166, fn. 24.

23 'bonus pro laicis liber', cited in Heiko Oberman, 'Teufelsdreck: Eschatology and Scatology in the "Old" Luther', *Sixteenth Century Journal*, xix (Fall 1988), 443.

24 Cranach the Elder's *Passional Christi und Antichristi*, 'Von Gold der Papst drey Kronen tregt' is the title, and the verse ran: 'Der Kaiser Constantinus hat uns die kaiserlic Krone, Gezierde, allen anderen Geschmuck, inmassen wie ihn der

Kaiser trägt, Purpurkleid, alle andere Kleider und Scepter zu tragen und zu brauchen geben', see, for instance, Joseph Leo Koerner, *The Reformation of the Image*, Chicago: University of Chicago Press 2004, 121.

25 'Zum andern, da auch nun der gemeyn man so weyt bericht und in verstandt kummen ist, wie der geystlich nichts sey, wie der wol und all zu vil beweysen so mancherley lieder, spruech, spoeterey, da man an alle wende, auff allerley zettel, zu letzt auch auff den karten spilen pfaffen und muenich malet, und gleych eyn eckel worden ist, wo man eyn geystlich person sicht und hört, was ists dann, das man wider den strom fechten will und halten', *D. Martin Luthers Werke: Kritische Gesamtausgabe, 1883–1978, Weimarer Ausgabe (WA)*, 1883, vol. 18, 409.

26 A particularly useful discussion of prices throughout the sixteenth century, which remained relatively stable, is *Wunderzeichen und Winkeldrucker 1543–1586: Einblattdrucke aus der Sammlung Wikiana in der Zentralbibliothek Zürich*, ed. Bruno Weber, Zurich: Urs Graf-Verlag 1972, 29–31, fn. 71.

27 Miriam Chrisman contends that 'an illustrated book was a book designed for lay use, whether laymen would read or not', *Lay Culture, Learned Culture: Books and Social Change in Strasbourg, c.1480–1599*, New Haven: Yale University Press 1982, 69, 106.

28 Linda B. Parshall and Peter W. Parshall, *Art and the Reformation: An Annotated Bibliography*, Boston, MA: G. K. Hall 1986, xxxii–xxxvii. Andrew Pettegree's more recent criticisms of Bob Scribner's work are unfortunately based on the first, 1981, edition of his book, and only a few pages of it, and does not take into account his far more nuanced reflections in ch. 8 and esp. ch. 9 of R. W. Scribner, *For the Sake of the Simple Folk: Popular Propaganda for the German Reformation*, Oxford: Clarendon Press 1994. These show that they are in far greater agreement than Pettegree assumes, while the woodcuts Pettegree selects to depict the great complexity of all Lutheran propaganda are not the most popular ones which were produced, see Andrew Pettegree, *Reformation and the Culture of Persuasion*, Cambridge: Cambridge University Press 2005.

29 Many of the most original explorations of this theme can be seen in the final essays by Bob Scribner, see R. W. Scribner, *Religion and Culture in Germany (1400–1800)*, ed. Lyndal Roper, Leiden: Brill 2001.

30 Luther, *WA*, vol. 19, 1–43.

31 Bibliotheque Nationale, Paris, MS Allemand 95, Boniface Dieffenbach's chronicle, 74r.

32 Scribner, *For the Sake*, 143–147.

33 Luther, *WA*, vol. 19, 7.

34 Cit. in Susan Mosher Stuard, *Gilding the Market: Luxury and Fashion in Fourteenth-Century Italy*, Philadelphia: University of Pennsylvania Press 2006, 66.

35 Agrippa von Nettesheim, *Über die Fragwürdigkeit, ja Nichtigkeit des Wissenschaften, Künste und Gewerbe*, transl. G. Güper and ed. Siegfried Wollgast, Berlin: Akademie Verlag 1993, 62, see also 134–135.

36 Luther, *WA*, vol. 19, 9, 'Diese seckt ganz rot gekleydet war, An der haut was nicht gut ein har.'

37 Luther, *WA*, vol. 19, 'gut gestalt und fromen scheyn'.

38 Luther, *WA*, vol. 19, 11, 'Nur keyn fromer nicht steckt ym kleyd.'

39 Luther, *WA*, vol. 19, 20.

40 Luther, *WA*, vol. 19, 41.

41 Luther, *WA*, vol. 19, 43. He ended wishing that God might let the 'bats' see and know themselves.

42 The humorous sensation if you feel this is not proper English, than please adjust Q: SEE Q IN TEXT of unmasking evil was further enhanced in a broadsheet from *c.*1550 attacking the Interim through a critique of the long white linen surplice, which different kinds of Roman clergy wore over a gown. A flap over the surplice revealed a devil underneath, see, for instance, Koerner, *The Reformation*, Ill. 161.

43 Cit. in Michael G. Baylor (ed. and transl.), *The Radical Reformation*, Cambridge: Cambridge University Press 1991, 108.

44 *Tagebuch des Hans Lutz, aus Augsburg: Ein Beitrag zur Geschichte des Bauern-Kriegs im Jahre 1525*, ed. Benedikt Greiff, Augsburg: Lauter 1849, 15.

45 Cit. in Marion Kobelt-Groch, *Aufsässige Töchter Gottes: Frauen im Bauernkrieg und in den Täuferbewegungen*, Frankfurt-on-Main: Campus 1993, 34.

46 Hans-Christoph Rublack,...*hat die Nonne den Pfarrer geküsst? Aus dem Alltag der Reformationszeit*, Gütersloh: GTB Siebenstern 1991, 129.

47 Martin Luther, *Von Herrn Lenhard Keiser in Baiern*, WA, vol. 23, 466. On the medieval tradition of degradations see Dyan Elliott, 'Dressing and Undressing the Clergy: Rites of Ordination

and Degradation', in E. Jane Burns (ed.), *Medieval Fabrications: Dress, Textiles, Clothwork, and Other Cultural Imaginings*, New York: Palgrave 2004, 55–70.

48 Bob Scribner and Tom Scott (eds. and transl.), *The German Peasants' War: A History in Documents*, London: Humanities Press 1991, 200.

49 Petra Roettig, *Reformation als Apokalypse: Die Holzschnitte von Matthias Gerung im Codex germanicus 6592 der Bayrischen Staatsbibliothek in München*, Bern: Peter Lang 1991, 201, Ill. 96.

50 Anna Rapp Buri and Monica Stucky-Schürer, *Die Sieben Planeten und ihre Kinder: Eine 1547–1549 datierte Tapisseriefolge in der Fondation Martin Bodmer*, Basle: Schwabe Verlag 2008, Ill. 16.

51 Robert W. Scribner, 'Anticlericalism and the Cities', in Scribner, *Religion and Culture*, 171.

52 For the following see Helga Scheible, 'Willibald Pirckheimers Persönlichkeit im Spiegel seines Briefwechsels am Beispiel seines Verhältnisses zum Klosterwesen', in Franz Fuchs (ed.), *Die Pirckheimer: Humanismus in einer Nürnberger Patrizierfamilie*, Wiesbaden: Harrassowitz 2006, 73–88.

53 Scheible, 'Pirckheimers', 76.

54 Scheible, 'Pirckheimers', 78.

55 Scheible, 'Pirckheimers', 80.

56 Scheible, 'Pirckheimers', 80–1, 'Wie wol ich nye in mein kutten hab gehoft, dar innen selig zu werden, glaub ich doch, das ich meinem gesponßen paß darinnen gefal dann inn einem perlein rock.'

57 Franz Freiherr von Soden, *Beiträge zur Geschichte der Reformation und der Sitten jener Zeit mit besonderem Hinblick auf Christoph Scheurl II*, Nuremberg: Bauer & Raspe 1855, 48.

58 This argument is set out by Barbara Stollberg-Rilinger, 'Knien vor Gott—Knien vor dem Kaiser: Zum Ritualwandel im Konfessionskonflikt', in Andrea von Hülsen-Esch (ed.), *Inszenierung und Ritual im Mittelalter und Renaissance*, Düsseldorf: Droste Verlag 2005, 263–292.

59 Gottfried Seebaß, *Das reformatorische Werk des Andreas Osiander*, Nürnberg: Verein für Kirchengeschichte 1967, 210.

60 Seebaß, *Osiander*, 216.

61 Seebaß, *Osiander*, 211 and 281.

62 BNP, Ms Allemand 95, Boniface Dieffenbach, 74r.

63 Maidservants and lying-in maids, for instance, cost an additional six florins per year, because one customarily gave them beer, Andreas Osiander the Elder, *Gesamtausgabe*, ed. Gerhard Mül-

ler and Gottfried Seebaß, vol. 5, Gütersloh: Mohn 1982, 521.

64 Müller and Seebaß, *Osiander*, 523–524.

65 Seebaß, *Osiander*, 214–216.

66 Cat., *Martin Luther und die Reformation*, 133.

67 Pamela Johnston and Bob Scribner (eds.), *The Reformation in Germany and Switzerland*, Cambridge: Cambridge University Press 1993, 30.

68 Cat., *Martin Luther und die Reformation*, cover, 1522/4.

69 See, for instance, his dress when he left the Wartburg briefly in 1521, Martin Brecht, *Martin Luther*, vol. 2, *Ordnung und Abgrenzung der Reformation 1521–1532*, Stuttgart: Calwer Verlag 1986, 50.

70 Brecht, *Luther*, 204.

71 Gunnar Heydenreich, *Lucas Cranach the Elder: Painting Materials, Techniques and Workshop Practise*, Amsterdam: Amsterdam University Press 2007.

72 Brecht, *Luther*, 200.

73 Ulrike Lehmann-Langholz, *Kleiderkritik in mittelalterlicher Dichtung: Der Arme Hartmann, Heinrich 'von Melk', Neidhart, Wernher der Gaertenaere und ein Ausblick auf die Stellungnahmen spätmittelalterlicher Dichter*, Frankfurt-on-Main: Peter Lang 1985, 92.

74 Hülsen-Esch, *Gelehrte im Bild*, 191–193.

75 P. Zinsli (ed.), *Der Berner Totentanz des Niklaus Manuel in den Nachbildungen von Albrecht Kauw (1649)*, Bern: Paul Haupt 1953, final fold-out.

76 Thomas Eser and Anja Grebe, *Heilige und Hasen: Bücherschätze der Dürerzeit*, Nürnberg: Germanisches Nationalmuseum 2008, 43.

77 'geistlicher leerer Martin Luther unserem Bruder in Christo', *Luthers Werke*, WA, vol. 15, 343, account of Heinrich Vogtherr.

78 *Luthers Werke*, WA, vol. 15, 345: 'Ferner ir habt mir einen feindeßbrief geschryben, ir gebt mir meinen title nicht, den mir doch etliche fürsten und herrn, so meine feinde seindt, geben und nicht abbrechen.'

79 'rotzypffelich'—It was overtly used in this colour as a mark of social rank 'Standeszeichen'. Doctors had begun to receive red berets since the mid-fourteenth century.

80 Phillip Melanchthon, 'Oratio contra affectationem novitatis in vestitu (1527)', in *Corpus Reformatorum*, vol. 11, Halle: Schwetschke 1843, 139–149.

81 Hannah S. Amberger, *Die Familiengeschichte der Koeler: Ein Beitrag zur Autobiographie des*

16. Jahrhunderts, Nuremberg: J. L. Stich 1930, 220.

82 Amberger, *Koeler*, 221.

83 On academic dress see especially Andrea von Hülsen-Esch, 'Kleider machen Leute. Zur Gruppenrepräsentation von Gelehrten im Spätmittelalter', in Otto Gerhard Oexle and Andrea von Hülsen-Esch (eds.), *Die Repräsentation der Gruppen: Texte – Bilder – Objekte*, Göttingen: Vandenhoeck 1999, 225–258.

84 Walter Friedensburg, *Geschichte der Universität Wittenberg*, Halle a. S.: Niemeyer 1917, 245.

85 See Stollberg-Rilinger, *Des Kaisers*, 9.

86 Klaus Deppermann, *Melchior Hoffman: Soziale Unruhen und apokalyptische Visionen im Zeitalter der Reformation*, Göttingen: Vandenhoeck 1979, 45.

87 Deppermann, *Hoffman*, 75.

88 Lee Palmer Wandel, *Always Among Us: Images of the Poor in Zwingli's Zurich*, Cambridge: Cambridge University Press 1990.

89 Johnston and Scribner, *The Reformation*, 56.

90 Thus Eberlin von Günzburg in his 1521 'Wolfaria' demanded that 'all men for fear of punishment should wear long beards, nobody shall have a smooth face like a woman. It shall be a shame not to wear a beard. Everyone shall have short, cut hair', in Adolf Laube and Sigrid Looß (eds.), *Flugschriften der frühen Reformationsbewegung (1518–1524)*, vol. 2, Berlin: Akademie Verlag 1983, 725.

91 Agrippa von Nettesheim, *Von dem Vorzug und der Fürtrefflichkeit des weiblichen Geschlechts vor dem männlichen (1509)*, Tübingen: Edition Diskord 1987, 20.

92 Thomas Kaufmann, *Das Ende der Reformation. Magdeburgs 'Herrgotts Kanzlei' (1548–1551/2)*, Tübingen: Mohr Siebeck 2003, 267, fn. 290.

93 Will Fisher, *Materializing Gender in Early Modern English Literature and Culture*, Cambridge: Cambridge University Press 2006, esp. 122.

94 Deppermann, *Hoffman*, 87.

95 Scribner, *Popular Movements*, 53.

96 Roettig, *Reformation als Apokalypse*, 31.

97 Verena Schmid Blumer, *Ikonographie und Sprachbild: Zur reformatorischen Flugschrift 'Der gestryfft Schwitzer Baur'*, Tübingen: Niemeyer 2004, esp. ch. 10.

98 Blumer, *Ikonographie*, 239.

99 Michel Pastoureau, *The Devil's Cloth: A History of Stripes and Striped Fabric*, transl. Jody Gladding, New York: Columbia University Press 2001.

100 'mit aller varb wild/ über wild', quoted in Blumer, *Ikonographie*, 233.

101 Blumer, *Ikonographie*, 242–243

102 Blumer, *Ikonographie*, 249.

103 Thus, Lorenz Fries's handbook of medicine, first published in 1518, addressed the 'gestreifleten leyen', Blumer, *Ikonographie*, 250, 253.

104 For the following see Blumer, *Ikonographie*, 255–276. Murner's pamphlet *Great Lutheran Fool* dates from 1520 and includes a chapter on the 'striped laymen'. The printer of the Basel pamphlet was Pamphilius Gengenbach.

105 The woodcut, especially in its symbolization of the fertile/infertile tree, is analysed in Blumer, *Ikonographie*, ch. 6.

106 Blumer, *Ikonographie*, 255.

107 Blumer, *Ikonographie*, 256.

108 Blumer, *Ikonographie*, 257.

109 Blumer, *Ikonographie*, 263; 'Sieben fromme, aber trostlose Pfaffen klagen ihre Not'.

110 Blumer, *Ikonographie*, 265.

111 *Luthers Werke, WA*, vol. 28, 517.

112 Jakob und Wilhelm Grimm (eds.), *Deutsches Wörterbuch*, vol. 15, Leipzig: Hirzel 1956, 1193.

113 This was not an abstract aim: the chronicle of a sixteenth-century Lutheran ennobled family of office-holders thus records the story of the shameful conversion of one of its members to Judaism and includes a picture of him as 'noble rabbi', see *Die Chronik Eisenberger: Bebilderte Geschichte einer Beamtenfamilie der deutschen Renaissance – Aufstieg in den Wetterauer Niederadel und das Frankfurter Patriziat*, ed. Hartmut Bock, Frankfurt-on-Main: Historisches Museum 1992, 112.

114 These can be located via the Wolfenbüttel Lutherdatenbank under the keyword-search 'Wucher' for the images on Luther's prints.

115 Laube and Looß, *Flugschriften*, vol. 2, 681.

116 Martin Luther, *Von Kauffshandlung und Wucher*, Wittenberg: Lufft 1524, 2.

117 Laube and Looß, *Flugschriften*, vol. 2, 1121–1155.

118 Laube and Looß, *Flugschriften*, vol. 2, 1125.

119 Laube and Looß, *Flugschriften*, vol. 2, 1131.

120 S. Sumberg, *The Nuremberg Schembart Carnival*, New York: Columbia University Press 1941.

121 *Die Wickiana: Johann Jakob Wicks Nachrichtensammlung aus dem 16. Jahrhundert,*

ed. Matthias Senn, Zurich: Leeman 1975, 165–167. The story became a stock example in sermons, see E. H. Rehermann, *Das Predigtexempel bei protestantischen Theologen des 16. und 17. Jahrhunderts*, Göttingen: Otto Schwartz & Co. 1977, 564–565.

122 We find the discussion of 'ubirmûte' in connection with sumptuous clothing since the first ambitious 'moral–theological' work in German, *Der Arme Hartmann*, from the middle of the twelfth century, Lehmann-Langholz, *Kleiderkritik*, 78.

123 Joachim Bumke, *Courtly Culture: Literature and Society in the High Middle Ages*, transl. Thomas Dunlap, Berkeley: University of California Press 1991, 138.

124 Scheible, 'Pirckheimer', 88.

125 So that social discipline might sometimes best be analysed in Foucauldian terms as productive obsession rather than silencing repression, Lyndal Roper, *Oedipus and the Devil: Witchcraft, Sexuality and Religion in Early Modern Europe*, London: Routledge 1994, 117–119, on clothing and the devil-books.

126 In this context see in particular Melchior Lorch's drawing of 1555 where the pope hands money to a Turkish warrior, discussed in Roettig, *Reformation als Apokalypse*, and Ill. 45.

127 Philip M. Soergel, 'Baggy Pants and Demons: Andreas Musculus's Condemnation of the Evils of Sixteenth-Century Dress', in Andrea Bendlage et al. (eds.), *Recht und Verhalten in vormodernen Gesellschaften*, Bielefeld: Verlag für Regionalgeschichte 2008, 139–154.

128 Ria Stambaugh (ed.), *Teufelbücher in Auswahl*, vol. 4, Berlin: de Gruyter 1978, 274; the incident is referred to by Musculus himself.

129 Stambaugh, *Teufelbücher* vol. 4, 277.

130 Stambaugh, *Teufelbücher*, vol. 4, not paginated.

131 Stambaugh, *Teufelbücher*, vol. 4, 25.

132 Stambaugh, *Teufelbücher*, vol. 4, 31.

133 Stambaugh, *Teufelbücher*, vol. 4, 28.

134 Stambaugh, *Teufelbücher*, vol. 4, 27–28.

135 Stambaugh, *Teufelbücher*, vol. 4, 25.

136 Stambaugh, *Teufelbücher*, vol. 4, 25–26.

137 Stambaugh, *Teufelbücher*, vol. 4, 6.

138 Erika Thiel, *Geschichte des Kostüms: Europäische Mode von der Antike bis zur Gegenwart*, Berlin: Henschelverlag 1960, Ill. 201.

139 Christian Wilhelm Spieker, *Lebensgeschichte des Andreas Musculus: Ein Beitrag zur Reformations- und Sittengeschichte des sechzehnten Jahrhunderts*, Frankfurt-on-the-Oder: Verlag der Hofbuchdruckerei von Trowitzsch und Sohn 1858, esp. 197.

140 Johannes Strauss, 'Kleiderteufel', in Ria Stambaugh (ed.), *Teufelbücher Q: SPELLING*, without s vol. 2, Berlin: de Gruyter 1972, 16, 'Feine Bürgerßröcke zu Winter und Sommer / Sonderlich die feinen langen und erbarn Kappen oder Mäntel / ohne und mit Ermeln / die kleyden und zieren wol alte und junge Leute.'

141 Theodor Hampe (ed.), *Gedichte vom Hausrat aus dem XV. und XVI. Jahrhundert in Facsimiledruck herausgegeben*, Strassburg: J. H. E. Heitz 1899.

142 This series was only fully reconstituted and contextualized in 1991, Roettig, *Reformation als Apokalypse*.

143 Roettig, *Reformation*, Ill. 7b and 90.

144 The Wittenberg New Testament by Cranach had first illustrated the prophets as old, bearded men in richer robes and only in 1534, for the complete translation of the bible, made them look younger, simplifying their gowns so as to make them look like contemporary evangelical preachers, and emphasizing their upright, confident comportment. Cranach adjusted the setting to Wittenberg itself. Both are illustrated together in Koerner, *Reformation of the Image*, 174.

145 Roettig, *Reformation*, 171, 'Angethan mit secken. Das ist mit ein schlechten und lieblosen Cleide versehn.'

146 For a particularly interesting recent contribution see Thomas Packeiser, 'Pathoseformel einer "christlichen Stadt"? Ausgleich und Heilsanspruch im Sakramentsretabel der Wittenberger Stadtpfarrkirche', in Andreas Tacke (ed.), *Lucas Cranach d. Ä. Zum 450. Todesjahr*, Leipzig: Evangelische Verlagsanstalt 2007, 233–277.

147 Ulinka Rublack, *Reformation Europe*, Cambridge: Cambridge University Press 2005, ch. 1.

148 A sermon that expresses such a view is Lucas Osiander, *Ein predig/ Von hoffertiger/ ungestalter Kleidung/ der Weibs und Manns Personen*, Tübingen: Georg Gruppenbach 1586, 16.

149 Wolfgang Sommer, *Gottesfurcht und Fürsten-herrschaft: Studien zum Obrigkeitsverständnis Johann Arndts und lutherischer Hofprediger zur Zeit der altprotestantischen Orthodoxie*, Göttingen: Vandenhoeck 1988, 67–68.

150 Johannes Cochläus, 'Eine heilige Vermahnung der heiligen Stadt Rom an Deutschland', in Adolf Laube (ed.), *Flugschriften gegen die Reformation (1518–1524)*, Berlin: Akademie Verlag 1997, 627.

151 Cochläus, 'Vermahnung', 614–646.

152 Cochläus, 'Vermahnung', 629, 'Nun volget dieser statt nach in boßheiten, ja gat ir auch in etlichen stücken vor, das elend, arm, katticht stätlyn Wittenberg, gegen Prag kaum ein statt dryer heller wertt, ja nit wert, das sie söl in teütschen landt ein statt genant werden, welche vorzwaintzig jaren gelerten und ungelerten unbekant was, ein ungesunt, unlieblich erd, on wyngarten, on baumgarten, on fruchtbar baum, ein bierische kamer, rauch (rau), frosthalb, on freid, gantz kotticht, waz ist doch Wittenberg, wenn das schloß, stifft und schul nit weren. Sehest on zwyfel nichts anders do denn lutherische, daz ist kottichte heüser, unrein gassen, alle weg, steg und strassen vol kotß, ein barbarisch volck, die kein ander bierische hendel dryen und dryerhellerische kauffmannschafft, ir marckt ist on volck, stadt on burger, kleinbürgerliche kleidung do grosser mangel und armut aller ynwoner.'

153 Brecht, *Luther*, vol. 2, 201.

154 Brecht, *Luther*, vol. 3, *Die Erhaltung der Kirche 1532–46*, Stuttgart: Calwer Verlag 1988, 240–242.

155 Richard A. Goldthwaite, *Wealth and the Demand for Art in Italy 1300–1600*, Baltimore and London: Johns Hopkins University Press 1993, 255.

156 Uwe Rieseken-Braun, *Duellum mirabile: Studien zum Kampfmotiv in Martin Luthers Theologie*, Göttingen: Vandenhoeck 1999, 255.

157 'Reformator Ecclesiae Oder Deren in dieser Welt…Erretter', in *Deutsche Flugblätter des 16. und 17. Jahrhunderts*, ed. Wolfgang Harms, vol. 2, Tübingen: Niemeyer 1986, 203, 360–361.

158 This paraphrases Lorraine Daston and Peter Galison's immensely useful approach to scientific objectivity, and thus the interaction with the natural, in *Objectivity*, New York: Zone Books 2007, 52.

159 William G. Naphy (transl. and ed.), *Documents on the Continental Reformation*, Houndsmill: Macmillan Press 1996, 72.

160 Graeme Murdock, 'Did Calvinists have a Guilt Complex?: Reformed Religion, Conscience and Regulation in Early Modern Europe', in Kate Cooper and Jeremy Gregory (eds.), *Retribution, Repentance, and Reconciliation*, Woodbridge: The Boydell Press 2004, 138–158; idem, 'Dressed to Repress? Protestant Clergy Dress and the Regulation of Morality in Early Modern Europe', *Fashion Theory*, 2 (2000) 179–199.

161 Valerius Anshelm, *Die Berner Chronik*, ed. Historischen Verein des Kantons Bern, vols. 1–6, Bern: Haller 1884–1901, vol. II, IV, 462.

162 Friedrich Nicolai, *Über den Gebrauch der falschen Haare und Perrucken in alten und neuen Zeiten: Eine Historische Untersuchung*, Berlin: n.p. 1801, 101.

163 Mary Hollingsworth, *The Cardinal's Hat: Money, Ambition and Housekeeping in a Renaissance Court*, London: Profile Books 2004, 179.

164 For a brilliant study see Markus Völkel, *Römische Kardinalshaushalte des 17. Jahrhundert: Borghese, Barberini, Chigi*, Tübingen: Niemeyer 1993.

165 Elfriede Moser-Rath, *Dem Kirchenvolk die Leviten gelesen: Alltag im Spiegel süddeutscher Barockpredigten*, Stuttgart: Metzler 1992, 262–278.

166 Fernand Braudel, *Civilisation matérielle, économie et capitalisme, XVe-VIIIe siècle*, vol. 1, Paris: Flammarion 1979, 362.

Chapter 4

1 Elizabeth Currie, 'Prescribing Fashion: Dress, Politics and Gender in Sixteenth-Century Conduct Literature', *Fashion Theory*, 4 (2000), 159.

2 Julian Raby, *Venice, Dürer and the Oriental Mode*, London: Islamic Art Publications 1982.

3 Cf. Dieter Wuttke, *Dazwischen: Kulturwissenschaft auf Warburgs Spuren*, vol. 1, Baden-Baden: V. Koerner 1996, 367; Jane Campbell Hutchinson, *Albrecht Dürer: A Biography*, Princeton: Princeton University Press 1990, 68.

4 Erwin Panofsky, *The Life and Art of Albrecht Dürer*, first published in 1943, with a new introduction by Jeffrey Chipps Smith, Princeton: Princeton University Press 2005, 36.

5 Panofsky, *Life and Art*, 36, xxxiii.

6 Panofsky, *Life and Art*, xxxii.

7 Cf. Cesare Vecellio, *Vecellio's Renaissance Costume Book: All 500 Woodcut Illustrations from the Famous Sixteenth-Century Compendium of World Costume*, New York: Dover 1977, 28–33.

8 Benjamin Isaac, *The Invention of Racism in Classical Antiquity*, Princeton: Princeton University Press 2004, esp. 436 and 439: 'In the eyes of Tacitus and other Romans, the failure to subdue all of the Germans was the single worst failure of the empire. It was a matter of safety as well as honour. The logic of ancient imperialism describes here a vicious circle: subject people eventually lose their independence of mind and become natural born subjects; conversely those who are not subjected remain dangerous.'

9 Herbert W. Benario (ed. and trans.), *Tacitus: Germany, Germania*, Warminster: Q Aris & Phillips 1999, 30–32, 50.

10 Cit. in Kurt Stadtwald, *Roman Popes and German Patriots: Antipapalism in the Politics of the German Humanist Movement from Gregor Heimburg to Martin Luther*, Geneva: Droz 1996, 61.

11 Isaac, *Invention of Racism*, 438, 'The Germans constitute more of an object of stereotypical thinking than almost any other people.'

12 Cit. in Caspar Hirschi, *Wettkampf der Nationen: Konstruktionen einer deutschen Ehrgemeinschaft an der Wende vom Mittelalter zur Neuzeit*, Göttingen: Wallstein 2005, 306–307, fn. 14.

13 Campbell Hutchinson, *Albrecht Dürer*, 72–74.

14 Isaac, *Invention of Racism*, 431.

15 Enea Silvio Piccolomini, *Papst Pius II: Ausgewählte Texte aus seinen Schriften*, ed. Berthe Widmer, Basel: Schwaber 1963, 412–414.

16 For the debate surrounding the 'Germania' see Gerald Strauss (ed. and trans.), *Manifestations of Discontents on the Eve of the Reformation*, Bloomington: Indiana University Press 1971, 35–47.

17 Hirschi, *Wettkampf*, 151.

18 Gernot Michael Müller, *Die 'Germania generalis' des Conrad Celtis: Studien mit Edition, Übersetzung und Kommentar*, Tübingen: Niemayer 2001, 94–96.

19 Müller, *Celtis*, 94.

20 Müller, *Celtis*, 416.

21 Müller, *Celtis*, 421.

22 Müller, *Celtis*, 429.

23 Müller, *Celtis*, 108.

24 Johann Eberlin von Günzburg, *Ein zamengelesen buochlin von der Teutschen Nation gelegenheit, Sitten vnd gebrauche, durch Cornelium Tacitum vnd etliche andere verzeichnet (1526)*, ed. Achim Masse it's Masser, Innsbruck: University of Innsbruck 1986, 57.

25 Philipp von Rummel, *Habitus barbarus: Kleidung und Repräsentation spätantiker Eliten im 4. und 5. Jahrhundert*, Berlin: de Gruyter 2005, 145, 222.

26 Selections from *Conrad Celtis 1459–1508*, ed. and trans. Leonard Forster, Cambridge: Cambridge University Press 1948, 46–50.

27 Forster, *Celtis*, 53–54.

28 Jörg Robert, *Konrad Celtis und das Projekt der deutschen Dichtung: Studien zur humanistischen Konstitution von Poetik, Philosophie, Nation und Ich*, Tübingen: Niemayer 2003, 430.

29 *Juvenal and Persius*, ed. and trans. Susanna Morton Braund, Cambridge, MA: Harvard University Press 2004, 472.

30 Robert, *Konrad Celtis*, fn. 343.

31 Isaac, *Racism*, 432.

32 In the same period, the Protestant and politically influential Augsburg couple Anton and Magdalena Rudolf chose an almost identical representation when they had themselves portrayed by the local master painter Christopher Amberger. They were depicted wearing black gowns, heavy fur over their shoulders, exactly the same finely pleated shirts, and each wore one ring. Strikingly, the husband displayed the decorous element of a small, beautifully crafted silver shaft which held white and red carnations, while Magdalena's portrait hinted at a gold chain worn over her shirt—this usually was the key male attribute of wealth and political influence; Annette Kranz, *Christoph Amberger: Bildnismaler zu Augsburg*, Regensburg: Schnell & Steiner 2004, Pls. 58/59, Cat. 16/17.

33 Robert, *Celtis*, fn. 381.

34 Benario, *Tacitus*,

35 Robert, *Celtis*, 437.

36 Ulrike Lehmann-Langholz, *Kleiderkritik in mittelalterlicher Dichtung: Der Arme Hartmann, Heinrich 'von Melk', Neidhart, Wernher der Gaertenaere und ein Ausblick auf die Stellungnahmen spätmittelalterlicher Dichter*, Frankfurt-on-Main: Peter Lang 1985, 271.

37 Müller, *Germania generalis*, 435.

38 Hirschi, *Wettkampf*, 118.

39 Hirschi, *Wettkampf*, 306, fn. 15.

40 Georg Forster, *Ein außbund schooner Teutscher Liedlein*, Nürnberg: Johann vom Berg, Nuremberg: Berg 1550, Discantus, 'S'ist ein frag/ und grosse klag/ wies gelt kombt auß dem lands/ auß dem lands/ Soliches frag loß/ darff nit vil

gloß/ man gibt's umb seyden gwande/ Der welte bracht/ ist vbermacht/ die hoffart bricht herfüre/ ein yeder will/ on maß und zil/ on maß vnd zil/ sich kleiden vber bure vber bure' n.p.

41 Einhard, *Vita Karoli Magni, The Life of Charlemagne*, ed. and trans. Evelyn Scherabon Firchow and Edwin H. Zeydel, Coral Gables: University of Miami Press 1974, ch. 23.

42 Hirschi, *Wettkampf*, 318.

43 Hirschi, *Wettkampf*, 339–340.

44 On the imperial level, luxury in clothing was first prohibited in 1497 and 1498. Maximilian I adopted the argument that Germany was drained of all 'blood' and life through expenses for gold and silk, and wished to strengthen the flow of German capital to German textile production, Hirschi, *Wettkampf*, 321–323.

45 Helmut Puff, *Sodomy in Reformation Germany and Switzerland 1400–1600*, Chicago: University of Chicago Press 2003.

46 Cit. in Bronwen Wilson, *The World in Venice: Print, the City, and Early Modern Identity*, Toronto: University of Toronto Press 2005, 71.

47 A particularly good example is Christoph Amberger's full-length painting of an Augsburg patrician with a *Schaube* and mi-parti striped hose in 1525, Vienna, Kunsthistorisches Museum. On the subject see Johannes Pietsch, *Zwei Schauben aus dem Bayerischen Nationalmuseum München: Ein Beitrag zur Kostümforschung*, München: Siegl 2004.

48 There is a large literature on this subject. Some of the most interesting discussions are provided by Keith Moxey, *Peasants, Warriors and Wives: Popular Imagery in the Reformation*, Chicago: Chicago University Press 1989, ch. 4; Larry Silver, 'Shining Armor: Emperor Maximilian, Chivalry, and War', in Pia Cuneo (ed.), *Artful Armies, Beautiful Battles: Art and Warfare in Early Modern Europe*, Leiden: Brill 2002, 61–86; J. R. Hale, *Artists and Warfare in the Renaissance*, New Haven: Yale University Press; Jan Willem Huntebrinker, *'fromme Knechte' und 'gartteufel': Sölnder als soziale Gruppe im 16. und 17. Jahrhundert*, D.Phil. dissertation, Dresden 2008.

49 Flacius Venegati, *Vier Bücher der Ritterschaft*, Augsburg: Stainer 1529.

50 Convivium Musicum, Ensemble Villanella, Stefan Berger, *Tugend und Untugend. German Secular Songs and Instrumental Music from the Time of Luther*, Naxos 8.553352, Songs 36, 37.

51 John A. Lyn II, *Women, Armies, and Warfare in Early Modern Europe,* Cambridge: Cambridge University Press 2008.

52 Walter L. Strauss (ed.), *The German Single-Leaf Woodcut 1550–1600*, vol. 1, New York: Hacker Art Books 1975, 353.

53 In contrast to Matthias Rogg's sense that there was a large degree of overlap between military and civilian fashions, based on broadsheet depictions of Landsquenets, see his ' "Zerhauen und zerschnitten, nach adelichen Sitten": Herkunft, Entwicklung und Funktion soldatischer Tracht des 16. Jahrhunderts im Spiegel zeitgenössischer Kunst', in Bernhard R. Kroener and Ralf Pove (eds.), *Krieg und Frieden: Militär und Gesellschaft in der Frühen Neuzeit*, Paderborn: Ferdinand Schöningh 1996, 109–135.

54 Strauss, *Woodcut*, vol. 3, 1070.

55 'So bin ich der hohe Deutsche genan aller nation Kleidung gfelt mir wol weis doch nicht wie ichs machen sol mir doch eine bas dan die ander gefelt da mit ich ein ansehen hab als ein helt do will ich hin zum werckman gan und im die sache selber zeigen an.'

56 'So Schav Nvn dise Biltnvs an wie seltsam es in der Welt tvt stan mit der kleidung dvrch alle Lant helt sich avch niemant nach seinem Stant dann es vor Alters so nicht gewesen ist wie man in allen Historien list.'

57 Ch. 1, p.6.

58 Isabelle Paresys, 'Paraître et se vêtir au XVIe siècle: morales vestimentaires', in Marie Viallon (ed.), *Paraître et se vêtir au XVIe siècle. Actes du XIIIe Colloque du Puy-en-Velay*, Saint Étienne: Publications de L'Université de Saint-Étienne 2006, 15.

59 Gábor Klaniczay, 'Everyday Life and Elites in the later Middle Ages: The Civilised and the Barbarian', in Peter Linehan and Janet L. Nelson (eds.), *The Medieval World*, London: Routledge 2001, 671–690. Much of this fascinating article actually refers to early modern material; Janusz Tazbir, 'Culture of the Baroque in Poland', in Antoni Maczak, Henryk Samsonowicz, and Peter Burke (eds.), *East-Central Europe in Transition: From the Fourteenth to the Seventeenth Century*, Cambridge: Cambridge University Press 1985, 167–181, esp. 178 on French observers.

60 Hans Weigel, *Habitvs Praeciptvorum Popvlorvm… Trachtenbuch*, Nuremberg: Hans Weigel 1577.

61 Odile Blanc, 'Ethnologie et merveille dans quelque livres de costumes Français', in Viallon (ed.), *Paraître*, 82, 86.

62 François Desprez, *Receuil de la diversité des habits, qui sont de present en usage, tant es pays d'Europe, Asie, Affrique, & Isles sauvages, le tout fait après le naturel*, Paris: Richard Breton 1562.

63 Ulrike Ilg, 'The Cultural Significance of Costume Books in Sixteenth-Century Europe', in Catherine Richardson (ed.), *Clothing Culture 1350–1650*, Aldershot: Ashgate 2004, 29–48.

64 Ilg, 'Costume Books', 37.

65 For a brief overview cf. K. Pilz, 'Jost Amman', in Andreas Klimt and Michael Steppe (ed.), *Allgemeines Künstlerlexikon*, vol. 3, Munich-Leipzig: K. G. Saur 1992, 246–249.

66 This argument is well developed in Thomas Lüttenberg, 'Der Nackte Mann mit Schere und Tuchballen: Ein Sinnbild der Verhaltensnormierung und seine Entwicklung im 16. Jahrhundert', in Andrea Bentlage, Andreas Priever, and Peter Schuster (eds.), *Recht und Verhalten in vormodernen Gesellschaften: Festschrift für Neithart Bulst*, Bielefeld: Verlag für Regionalgeschichte 2008, esp. 134–137.

67 Weigel, *Trachtenbuch*, 2.

68 Weigel, *Trachtenbuch*, 2.

69 Weigel, *Trachtenbuch*, 3, 'was bey vnseren zeiten in unserem allgemeinen Vatterland/ für seltzame wunderbarliche verenderungen zugleich mit dem frembden vnnd außlendischen kleidungen/ erfolget seien/ ...'.

70 Weigel, *Trachtenbuch*, 3.

71 Weigel, *Trachtenbuch*, 6.

72 For the classical position see Rummel, *Habitus barbarus*, 95–96.

73 Alexander Schmidt, *Vaterlandsliebe und Religionskonflikt: Politische Diskurse im Alten Reich (1555–1648)*, Leiden: Brill 2007.

74 Weigel, *Trachtenbuch*, 3.

75 Weigel, *Trachtenbuch*, CLXXIII.

76 Weigel, *Trachtenbuch*, CLV.

77 Weigel, *Trachtenbuch*, LXXVI.

78 Weigel, *Trachtenbuch*, XCVII, 'Ehrbarkeit/ Tugent vnd Frombkeit/ Ist eins Weibs gröste zier allzeit./ Das sieht man zu Genff an den Frawen./ Die lassen sich so fein züchtig schauen.'

79 See Ch. 5.

80 Weigel, *Trachtenbuch*, XCIX, 'In Metz wol in der vesten Stadt/ Die Kayser Carl belagert hat/ Will sie vor hat gehört zum Reich/ Gehen die Frawen also gleich.'

81 Weigel, *Trachtenbuch*, CLXXXIII, 'In Indi der Frawen Tracht/ Vnd Klaidung ist alle gemacht/ Von schönen Federn ander art/ Drinn düncken sie sich schön vnd zart./ Das ding so sie trägt in

der Hendt/ Ist hol wird Tammaracta genendt./ Drein thun sie steinlein rasseln darmit/ Sind ir Götter ander wissens nit.'

82 Weigel, *Trachtenbuch*, CV.

83 Weigel, *Trachtenbuch*, CLXXIX.

84 Weigel, *Trachtenbuch*, CXCVII.

85 Weigel, *Trachtenbuch*, LXXXVVII.

86 Weigel, *Trachtenbuch*, CLVI.

87 Weigel, *Trachtenbuch*, LXVI.

88 Wilson, *The World in Venice*, 265.

89 See also Martin Dinges, 'Von der "Lesbarkeit der Welt" zum universalisierten Wandel durch individuelle Strategien: Die soziale Funktion der Kleidung in der höfischen Gesellschaft', in Neithard Bulst and Robert Jütte (eds.), *Zwischen Sein und Schein: Kleidung und Identität in der ständischen Gesellschaft*, Saeculum, 44 (1993), 93–95, with reference to Weigel's book.

90 Johannes C. Stracke, *Tracht und Schmuck Altfrieslands nach den Darstellungen im Hausbuch des Häuptlings Unico Manninga*, Aurich: Verlag ostfriesische Landschaft 1967.

91 Stracke, *Tracht*, 72.

92 Dirk Niefanger, *Geschichtsdrama in der Frühen Neuzeit 1495–1773*, Tübingen: Niemeyer 2005, 81–86.

93 '*Julius Redivivus*: Julius Caesars Rückkehr ins Erdenleben', in Nicodemus Frischlin, *Sämtliche Werke*, ed. and trans. Christoph Jungck and Lothar Mundt, vol. 3, Part I, Stuttgart–Bad Cannstatt: frommann-holzbog 2003, 564, 'Ehem, quam pannis obsitus Est!'.

94 Frischlin, *Julius Redivivus*, 586.

95 Frischlin, *Julius Redivivus*, 586.

96 Hirschi, *Wettkampf*, 298.

97 Schmidt, *Vaterlandsliebe*, 403.

98 These are discussed by various authors, but not systematically connected to the earlier patriotic discourse; see, for instance, Thomas Lüttenberg and Andreas Priever, ' "...Hergegen macht das kleyd oft einen Mann und Helden": Deutsche Alamode-Flugblätter des 17. Jahrhunderts im europäischen Kontext', in Adelheid Rasche and Gundula Wolter (eds.), *Ridikül! Mode in der Karikatur 1600 bis 1900*, Cologne: DuMont 1993, 153–168.

99 See, for instance, Will Fisher's *Materializing Gender in Early Modern English Literature and Culture*, Cambridge: Cambridge University Press 2006, ch. 4, esp. 143. A good example of rendering the Cavalier hairstyle as visual act is Bernini's bust of Thomas Baker.

100 For an outstanding study see David Kuchta, *The Three-Piece Suit and Modern Masculinity: England, 1550–1850*, Berkeley: California University Press 2002, 1.

101 John Roger Paas (ed.), *The German Political Broadsheet*, Wiesbaden: Harrassowitz 1985, vol. 3, *1620–21*, 308.

102 Wolfgang Harms, Cornelai Kemp eds., Deutsche illustrierte Flugblätter des 16. und 17. Jahrhunderts, vol. 4, Tübingen: Niemeyer 1987, *Druckgraphik*, IV, 32, 54: 'Wie wenig besonders die Graphik zur Kritik beiträgt, macht die Beobachtung deutlich, dass die einzelnen Figuren kaum karikierende Züge aufweisen, umso mehr, als die beiden äußeren Figuren auf die Stichserie *La noblesse de Lorraine*(1624) von Jacques Callot (1592–1635) zurückgehen... Hierin offenbart sich ein hinter der wortreichen Kritik verborgener normativer Impuls, der dem Reiz der neuen Mode bereits erlegen ist; in einer Zeit, da Kleiderordnungen individuelle Luxusbedürfnisse auf ein allgemeines, von der Ständeordnung bestimmtes Maß beschränkten, konnte diese Faszination jedoch nur unter dem Schutz der Moralsatire weitergegeben werden.'

103 Harms, so this needs to be changed to Deutsche illustrierte Flugblatter subsequently *Druckgraphik*, IV, 39, 64–65.

104 Paas, *German Political Broadsheet*, vol. 4, *1622–29*, 313.

105 Paas, *German Political Broadsheet*, vol. 4, 317.

106 See, for instance, Paas, *German Political Broadsheet*, 305.

107 Paas, *German Political Broadsheet*, vol. 5, *1630–31*, 102; Harms, *Druckgraphik*, II, 284, 496.

108 Paas, *German Political Broadsheet*, vol. 6, *1632*, 85.

109 Paas, *German Political Broadsheet*, vol. 6, 89.

110 Harms, *Druckgraphik*, IV, 40, 66–67.

111 Paas, *German Political Broadsheet*, vol. 2, *1616–1619*, 240.

112 It also added the old anecdote of how Paracelsus had been called by the emperor, but not been admitted because he was badly dressed. He returned dressed in silk and sat silently in front of the emperor. When asked by him why he did not speak Paracelsus replied he thought the clothes should do so, as everyone seemed to think that all art lay in them. Paas, *German Political Broadsheet*, vol. 4, 316.

113 Harms, *Druckgraphik*, IV, 36, 60–61.

114 Harms, *Druckgraphik*, IV, 37, 62–63.

115 Karen Stolleis, *Die Gewänder aus der Lauinger Fürstengruft*, Munich: Deutscher Kunstverlag 1977.

116 Ecole française, *Portrait de Madame de Ventadour avec les portraits de louis XIV et de ses descendants, 1715–1720*, London, Wallace Collection.

117 For Moscherosch's prominent anti-court criticism through the à-la-mode idiom to depict selfishness, flattery, and corruption see Johann Michael Moscherosch, *Visiones de Don Quevedo: Wunderliche vnd Wahrhafftige Gesichte Philanders von Sittewald...*, Strassburg: Johann Phillip Mülben 1642.

118 Thomas Coryat, *Coryats Crudities 1611*, intro. William M. Schutte, London: Scolar Press 1978, 444.

119 Seven Deadly Sins of London, see Ann Rosalind Jones and Peter Stallybrass, *Renaissance Clothing and the Material of Memory*, Cambridge: Cambridge University Press 2000, 1. A host of fears about national identity similar to German developments are explored in Roze Hentzschell, *The Culture of Cloth in Early Modern England: Textual Construction of a National Identity*, Aldershot: Ashgate 2008, esp. ch. 4.

120 Seventeenth-century court dress has been comparatively explored by Cat., *Fastes de cour et ceremonies Royales: Le Costume de cour en Europe 1650–1800*, eds. Pierre Arizzoli-Clémentel and Pascale Gorguet Ballesteros, Paris: Réunion des Musées Nationaux 2009.

Chapter 5

1 Jean Michel Massing, 'Hans Burgkmair's Depiction of Native Africans', in idem, *Studies in Imagery*, vol. II, London: Pindar Press 2007, 114–141.

2 Modelled on the Triumph of Caesar by Benedetto Bordon and Jacobus Argentoratensis in Venice in 1504, Massing, 'Burgkmair's Depiction', fn. 27.

3 Massing, 'Burgkmair's Depiction', 43. For Peutinger's enthusiasm see Folker Reichert, *Erfahrung der Welt: Reisen und Kulturbegegnung im späten Mittelalter*, Stuttgart: Kohlhammer 2001, 176.

4 *Balthasar Springer's Indienfahrt 1505/06. Wissenschaftliche Würdigung der Reiseberichte Springers zur Einführung in den Neudruck seiner 'Meerfahrt' vom Jahre 1509*, ed. Franz Schulze, n.p.: J. H. E. Heitz 1899.

5 Schulze, *Meerfahrt*, 8, my emphasis.

6 Larry Silver, *Marketing Maximilian: The Visual Ideology of a Holy Roman Emperor*, Princeton: Princeton University Press 2008, ch. 3.

7 Jean Michel Massing, 'Early European Images of America', in Massing, *Studies in Imagery*, vol. II, London: Pindar Press 2007, 103.

8 For two important recent contributions see Harald Kleinschmidt, *Ruling the Waves: Emperor Maximilian I, the Search for Islands and the Transformation of the European World Picture c.1500*, Utrecht: Hes & de Graaf 2008; and Christine R. Johnson's study *The German Discovery of the World: Renaissance Encounters with the Strange and Marvellous*, Charlottesville: University of Virginia Press 2008.

9 Economic historians have, of course, been active in exploring these trade links, see, in particular, the work of Hermann Kellenbenz; see also Walter Grosshaupt, 'Commercial Relations between Portugal and the Merchants of Augsburg and Nuremberg', in Jean Aubin (ed.), *La Decouverte, le Portugal et L'Europe*, Paris: Fondation Gulbenkian 1990, 359–397.

10 Johnson, *German Discovery of the World*, 112.

11 For a brief summary and commentary see Tom Scott, *Society and Economy in Germany, 1300–1600*, Houndsmill: Palgrave 2002, 208–212.

12 Thomas Eser and Anja Grebe (eds.), *Heilige und Hasen: Bücherschätze der Dürerzeit*, Nürnberg: Germanisches Nationalmuseum 2008, 122.

13 Reichert, *Erfahrung der Welt*, 100–101.

14 Bernhard von Breydenbach, *Die fart oder reysz über mere zu dem heiligen grab…*Augsburg: A. Sorgen 1488.

15 On the following see Klaus A. Vogel, 'Cultural Variety in a Renaissance Perspective: Johannes Boemus on "The manners, laws and customs of all people" (1520)', in G. Brugge and J. P. Rubiès (eds.), *Shifting Culture: Interaction and Discourse in the Expansion of Europe*, Münster: Lit Velag 1995, 17–34; Erich Schmidt, *Deutsche Volkskunde im Zeitalter des Humanismus und der Reformation*, Berlin: E. Ebering 1904.

16 Simon Grynaeus, *Die New Welt der Landschaften unnd Insulen, so bis hie…unbekant…*, Strassburg: G. Ulricher 1534 (translated from the first Latin 1532 edition).

17 Sebastian Münster, *Briefe Sebastian Münsters*, ed. Karl Heinz Burmeister, Frankfurt-on-Main: Insel Verlag 1964.

18 Wolfgang Neuber, *Fremde Welt im europäischen Horizont: Zur Topik der deutschen Amerika-Reiseberichte der Frühen Neuzeit*, Berlin: E. Schmidt 1991; Marília dos Santos Lopes, *Afrika: Eine neue Welt in deutschen Schriften des 16. und 17. Jahrhunderts*, Stuttgart: Steiner 1992; Carl Göllner, *Die europäischen Türkendrucke des 16. Jahrhunderts*, 2 vols, Bukarest–Baden: Academiei Republicii Socialiste România 1961–1968.

19 Johnson, *German Discovery of the World*, ch. 4, specifically with reference to Hieronymus Bock's herbal, first published in 1539, which replicated many of the arguments that were also made against the wearing of foreign clothes; Alix Cooper, *Inventing the Indigenous: Local Knowledge and Natural History in Early Modern Europe*, Cambridge: Cambridge University Press 2007, esp. 1–86.

20 Donald J. Harreld, *High Germans in the Low Countries: German Merchants and Commerce in Golden Age Antwerp*, Leiden: Brill 2004, 4, 7, 133.

21 Harreld, *High Germans*, ch. 7.

22 Jeffrey Chipps Smith, *The Northern Renaissance*, London: Phaidon 2004, 27–29.

23 Horst Pohl (ed.), *Willibald Imhoff, Enkel und Erbe Willibald Pirckheimers*, Nuremberg: Stadtrat Selbstverlag 1992, 83, 311.

24 Hans Rupprich (ed.), *Albrecht Dürer, Schriftlicher Nachlass*, 3 vols., Berlin: Deutscher Verein für Kunstwissenschaft 1956–1970, vol. 1, 164–165.

25 Rupprich, *Dürer*, 167.

26 Massing, 'Early European Images'. An important essay on methodological issues involved in the matching of attributes and the geographical origin of overseas subjects depicted is Peter Mason, *The Lives of Images*, London: Reaktion Books 2001, ch. 3.

27 Rupperich, *Dürer*, 155.

28 Dagmar Eichberger and Charles Zika (eds.), *Dürer and his Culture*, Cambridge: Cambridge University Press 1998, ch. 1.

29 Martin Kemp, ' "Wrought by No Artist's Hand": The Natural, the Artifical, the Exotic, and the Scientific in Some Artifacts from the Renaissance', in Claire Farago (ed.), *Reframing the Renaissance: Visual Culture in Europe and Latin America 1450–1650*, New Haven: Yale University Press 1995, 177–196.

30 Julian Raby, *Venice, Dürer and the Oriental Mode*, London: Islamic Art Publications 1982.

31 'Dürer', Elliott writes, 'gazed in wonder on Montezuma's treasures, but these exotic objects were curiosities to be admired, not models to be

imitated. As the handiwork of "barbarians", the artistic creations of the peoples of America exercised virtually no influence on sixteenth-century European art. They were simply consigned to the cabinets of curiosities—mute witnesses to the alien customs of non-European man', John Elliott, *The Old World and the New 1492–1650*, Cambridge: Cambridge University Press 1970, 32.

32 Rupprich, *Dürer*, 170.

33 Pamela H. Smith, *The Body of the Artisan: Art and Experience in the Scientific Revolution*, Chicago: Chicago University Press 2004, 74.

34 Smith, *The Body*, 74.

35 Massing, 'European Images', 97.

36 But almost for the next forty years, up to his death in 1559, Weiditz continued to face the goldsmith's guilds insistence that they needed to ensure their unrivalled reputation in all of Europe through rigorous rules. Charles's letter did little to help.

37 And presented to the Germanic National Museum in 1868; see *Christoph Weiditz, Authentic Everyday Dress of the Renaissance: All 154 Plates from the 'Trachtenbuch'*, ed. Theodor Hampe, Toronto: Dover 1994.

38 Martin Warnke, *Political Landscape: The Art History of Nature*, London: Reaktion 1994.

39 Hampe, *Weiditz*, CXV.

40 Holger Kürbis, *Hispania descripta: Von der Reise zum Bericht. Deutschsprachige Reiseberichte des 16. und 17. Jahrhundert über Spanien. Ein Beitrag zur Struktur und Funktion der frühneuzeitlichen Reiseliteratur*, Frankfurt-on-Main: Peter Lang 2003, 172: '…und ist fast kein Dorf so klein, darinnen nicht etwas Absonderliches erdacht würde'; he was travelling with Phillip I of Spain.

41 Kate Lowe, 'The Stereotyping of Black Africans in Renaissance Europe', in K. J. P. Lowe and T. F. Earle (eds.), *Black Africans in Europe*, Cambridge: Cambridge University Press 2005, 47.

42 Smith, *The Body*, 99.

43 Hannah S. Amburger, *Die Familiengeschichte der Köler: Ein Beitrag zur Autobiographie des 16. Jahrhunderts*, Nuremberg: J. L. Stich 1930, 214.

44 Amburger, *Köler*, 215.

45 Amburger, *Köler*, 216.

46 Amburger, *Köler*, 219.

47 Beard styles have been productively explored by Will Fisher, *Materializing Gender in Early Modern English Literature and Culture*, Cambridge: Cambridge University Press 2006.

48 Balthasar Schnurr, *Vollständiges und schon aller Orten bekandtes Kunst= Hausz = und Wunder = Buch*, Frankfurt-on-Main: Zubrodt und Haass 1676 provides relevant examples.

49 See Ch. 2 of this book and Amburger, *Köler*, 225.

50 Amburger, *Köler*, 230.

51 Damião de Góis, *Lisbon in the Renaissance: A New Translation of the Urbis Olisiponis Descriptio*, ed. and trans. Jeffrey S. Ruth, New York: Ithaca Press 1996, 29.

52 Góis, *Lisbon*, 30.

53 Góis, *Lisbon*, 30.

54 Góis, *Lisbon*, 230.

55 For the general context see Jörg Denzer, 'Die Welser in Venezuela—Das Scheitern ihrer wirtschaftlichen Ziele', in Mark Häberlein and Johannes Burkhardt (eds.), *Die Welser: Neue Forschungen zur Geschichte und Kultur des oberdeutschen Handelshauses*, Berlin: Akademie Verlag 2002, 285–319.

56 Amburger, *Köler*, 232.

57 Amburger, *Köler*, 233.

58 Amburger, *Köler*, 235.

59 Amburger, *Köler*, 241, 243.

60 Denzer, 'Welser in Venezuela', 287.

61 Jeffrey Chipps Smith (ed.), *New Perspectives on the Art of Renaissance Nuremberg: Five Essays*, Texas: The Archer M. Huntington Art Gallery 1985; John Roger Paas (ed.), *Der Franken Rom: Nürnbergs Blütezeit in der zweiten Hälfte des 17. Jahrhunderts*, Wiesbaden: Harrassowitz 1996; replacing the story of decline in Gerald Strauss's classic study *Nuremberg in the Sixteenth Century*, Bloomington: Indiana University Press 1976.

62 Kemp, *'Wrought by no Artist's Hand'*, 191; Smith, *The Body*, 74–80.

63 Rainer Gömmel, 'Die Vermittlerrolle Nürnbergs zwischen Italien und Deutschlands vom Spätmittelalter bis zum 18. Jahrhundert aus wirtschaftshistorischer Sicht', in Volker Kapp and Frank-Rutger Hausmann (eds.), *Nürnberg und Italien: Begegnungen, Einflüsse und Ideen*, Tübingen: Stauffenburg Verlag 1991, 42.

64 Jeffrey Chipps Smith, 'The Transformation in Patrician Tastes in Renaissance Nuremberg', in idem (ed.), *New Perspectives on the Art of Renaissance Nuremberg*, 92–94.

65 Chipps Smith, 'The Transformation', 95.

66 Giulia Bartrum (ed.), *The New Hollstein German Engravings, Etchings and Woodcuts 1400–1700, Jost Amman*, Part II, Rotterdam: Sound & Vision 2001, Intaglio Prints by Amman, nos. 53, 45.

67 Their works were *De peregrinatione et agro Nea-politano*, published 1574 in Strasbourg and in English in 1575; *Commentariolus de arte apodemica*, Ingolstadt: 1577; *Methodus apodemica*, Basel: 1577; cf. Justin Stagl's excellent essay 'Ars apodemica: Bildungsreise und Reisemethodik von 1560 bis 1600', in Xenja von Ertzdorff and Dieter Neukirch (eds.), *Reisen und Reiseliteratur im Mittelalter und in der Frühen Neuzeit*, Amsterdam: Rodopi 1992, 141–191.

68 Jutta Zander-Seidel, *Textiler Hausrat: Kleidung und Haustextilien in Nürnberg von 1500–1650*, Munich: Deutscher Kunstverlag 1990, 289–291.

69 *Katalog der Lipperheidischen Kostümbibliothek*, ed. Eva Nienholdt and G. Wagner-Neumann, 2nd edn., Berlin: Kunstbibliothek 1965, vol. 1, 1, Lipp Aa2.

70 *Lipperheidische Kostümbibliothek*, Aa2, 3.

71 Hans von Staden, *Wahrhaftige Historia und beschreibung eyner Landtschafft der Wilden, Nackten, Grimmigen Menschenfresser Leuthen, in der Newenwelt America gelegen*, Frankfurt-on-Main: Weygandt Han 1557.

72 Richard L. Kagan, *Urban Images of the Hispanic World 1493–1793*, New Haven: Yale University Press 2000, 9–11.

73 *Lipperheidische Kostümbibliothek*, Aa2, 435r.

74 These are now digitalized and searchable in German and English under http://www.nuernberger-hausbuecher.de.

75 Michel de Montaigne, *The Complete Essays*, trans. and ed. M. A. Screech, London: Penguin Books 1991, 241.

76 Cit. in Odile Blanc, 'Ethnologie et merveille dans quelque livres de costumes Français', in Marie Viallon (ed.), *Paraître et se vêtir au XVIᵉ siècle. Actes du XIIIᵉ Colloque du Puy-en-Velay*, Saint Étienne: Publications de L'Université de Saint-Étienne 2006, 86.

77 Montaigne, *Complete Essays*, 256.

78 Montaigne, *Complete Essays*, 255.

79 *Cesare Vecellio's Habiti Antichi et Moderni: The Clothing of the Renaissance World*, ed. Margaret F. Rosenthal and Ann Rosalind Jones, London: Thames & Hudson 2008, esp. 34–42, 493.

80 Paul Hulton and David B. Quinn, *The American Drawings of John White*, 2 vols., London: British Museum Press 1964.

81 Ernst van den Boogart (ed.), *Civil and Corrupt Asia: Image and Text in the Itinerario and the Icones of Jan Huygens van Linschoten*, Chicago: University of Chicago Press 2003, 33.

Chapter 6

1 For a pioneering essay see Amanda Vickery, 'Women and the World of Goods: A Lancashire Consumer and her Possessions', in John Brewer and Roy Porter (eds.), *Consumption and the World of Goods*, London: Routledge 1993, 247–301.

2 Contemporary Zambian youths, too, 'pick' from overseas second-hand clothes to try out a particular look and 'explore who they are and who they would like to become'. Karen Tranberg Hansen, 'From Thrift to Fashion: Materiality and Aesthetics in Dress Practises in Zambia', in Susanne Küchler and Daniel Miller (eds.), *Clothing as Material Culture*, Oxford: Berg 2005, 114, 117.

3 The author was deeply worried about the economic effects of the Reformation's onslaught on Aristotelian and scholastic learning; Simon and Wolfgang Blick, 'Verderben und Schaden der Lande und Leute an Gut, Leib, Ehre und der Seelen Seligkeit aus Luthers und der seines Anhangs Lehre', in Adolf Laube (ed.), *Flugschriften gegen die Reformation (1518–1524)*, Berlin: Akademie Verlag 1997, 668–669.

4 Julia Lehner, *Die Mode im alten Nürnberg*, Nuremberg: Schriftenreihe des Stadtarchivs 1984, 26.

5 See, for instance, Eva Illouz, *Cold Intimacies: The Making of Emotional Capitalism*, Cambridge: Polity Press 2007.

6 Steven Ozment (ed. and narrator), *Three Behaim Boys: Growing Up in Early Modern Germany: A Chronicle of their Lives*, New Haven: Yale University Press 1990, 101.

7 Ozment, *Behaim Boys*, 102.

8 Ozment, *Behaim Boys*, 106.

9 Ozment, *Behaim Boys*, 107.

10 Ozment, *Behaim Boys*, 113.

11 Ozment, *Behaim Boys*, 115.

12 Ozment, *Behaim Boys*, 121.

13 Ozment, *Behaim Boys*, 122.

14 Ozment, *Behaim Boys*, 123.

15 Ozment, *Behaim Boys*, 131.

16 Ozment, *Behaim Boys*, 134.

17 Ozment, *Behaim Boys*, 137.

18 Ozment, *Behaim Boys*, 139.

19 Ozment, *Behaim Boys*, 140.

20 Ozment, *Behaim Boys*, 140.

21 Ozment, *Behaim Boys*, 154.

22 Ozment, *Behaim Boys*, 158.

23 Cf. Mathias Beer, 'Migration, Kommunikation und Jugend: Studenten und Kaufmannslehrlinge

der Frühen Neuzeit in ihren Briefen', *Archiv für Kulturgeschichte*, 88 (2/2006), 355–387; Steven Ozment, *Flesh and Spirit: Private Life in Early Modern Germany*, New York: Knopf 1999, ch. 3.

24 Paul Behaim, *Briefe eines Leipziger Studenten aus den Jahren 1572 bis 1574*, ed. Wilhelm Loose, Meißen: 1880, 6.

25 Loose, *Briefe*, 7.

26 Loose, *Briefe*, 8–9.

27 Loose, *Briefe*, 9.

28 Loose, *Briefe*, 16–17.

29 Loose, *Briefe*, 18.

30 Loose, *Briefe*, 20.

31 Cit. in Beer, 'Migration', 384: 'Derhalben…hab ich mich nicht in lumpen gekleidet, sondern den welschen brauch nach in sauberen und werendten zeug (…) eben man muß sich nach landtgeprauch halten.'

32 See Jan de Vries, *The Industrious Revolution: Consumer Behaviour and the Household Economy, 1650 to the Present*, Cambridge: Cambridge University Press 2008, 14, following David Sabean's discussion in his *Property, Production, and Family in Neckarhausen, 1700–1870*, Cambridge: Cambridge University Press 1990, 97–98.

33 Ozment, *Flesh and Spirit*, 142.

34 Ozment, *Flesh and Spirit*, 144.

35 Hansmartin Decker-Hauff, *Die Chronik der Grafen von Zimmern*, vol. 3, Sigmaringen: Jan Thorbecke Verlag 1981, 101.

36 Stefano Zaggia, 'Foreign Students in the City, *c.*500–1700', in Donatella Calabri and Stephen Turk Christensen (eds.), *Cultural Exchange in Early Modern Europe, vol. 2: Cities and Cultural Exchange in Europe, 1400–1700*, Cambridge: Cambridge University Press 2007, 191.

37 Reproduced in Evelyn Welch, *Shopping in the Renaissance: Consumer Cultures in Italy, 1400–1600*, New Haven: Yale University Press 2005, 41, Ill. 39.

38 Ozment, *Flesh and Spirit*, 157.

39 Werner Wilhelm Schnabel, *Das Stammbuch: Konstitution und Geschichte einer textsortenbezogenen Sammelform bis ins erste Drittel des 18. Jahrhunderts*, Tübingen: Niemeyer 2003.

40 For an excellent edition of a French album from 1575 with 105 illustrations from Italy, a number of them with ethnographic content under headings such as 'How wine is carried in Padua', or 'Peasants on their way to the market', see Maurizio Rippa Bonati and Valeria Finucci (eds.),

Mores Italiae: Costume and Life in the Renaissance, Cittadella: Biblios 2007.

41 The 'accumulation of painted costume illustrations by travellers may have operated similarly (to emblems), the figures were valued for the ideas they emblematized. The migration of Venetian types into what were essentially moral guidebooks brings to the fore those concepts that were important to foreigners about Venice'; Bronwen Wilson, *The World in Venice: Print, the City, and Early Modern Identity*, Toronto: University of Toronto Press 2005, 118.

42 British Library (BL), Egerton 1, 186, 26v, 27r.

43 BL, Egerton 1, 186, 27v–30v.

44 BL, Egerton 1, 192, 4r.

45 Ozment, *Flesh and Spirit*, 160.

46 Ozment, *Flesh and Spirit*, 174.

47 Ozment, *Flesh and Spirit*, 181.

48 Ozment, *Flesh and Spirit*, 182–183.

49 Ozment, *Flesh and Spirit*, 197.

50 Ozment, *Flesh and Spirit*, 188.

51 Thomas Coryat, *Coryats Crudities 1611*, intro. William M. Schutte, Scolar Press: London 1978, a2.

52 Konrad Renger, *Lockere Gesellschaft. Zur Ikonographie des Verlorenen Sohnes und von Wirtshausszenen in der niederländischen Malerei*, Berlin: Gebrüder Mann Verlag 1970.

53 Ulrike Lehmann-Langholz, *Kleiderkritik in mittelalterlicher Dichtung: Der Arme Hartmann, Heinrich 'von Melk', Neidhart, Wernher der Gaertenaere und ein Ausblick auf die Stellungnahmen spätmittelalterlicher Dichter*, Frankfurt-on-Main: Peter Lang 1985, 194–225.

54 Cat., *Deutsche Kunst und Kultur im Germanischen Nationalmuseum*, Nuremberg: Karl Ulrich & Co 1972, n.p. *c.*1460.

55 *Edler Schatz holden Erinnerns: Bilder in Stammbüchern der Staatsbibliothek Bamberg aus vier Jahrhunderten*, Bamberg: Die Bibliothek 1995.

56 *Zu gutem Gedenken. Kulturhistorische Miniaturen aus Stammbüchern des Germanischen Nationalmuseums 1570–1770*, ed. Lotte Kurras, Munich: Prestl 1995, no. 9.

57 Kurras, *Gedenken*, 189.

58 Kurras, *Gedenken*, 190–192.

59 Holger Kürbis, *Hispania descripta: Von der Reise zum Bericht. Deutschsprachige Reiseberichte des 16. und 17. Jahrhunderts über Spanien. Ein Beitrag zur Struktur und Funktion der frühneuzeitlichen Reiseliteratur*, Frankfurt-on-Main: Peter Lang 2004, 220.

60 Ozment, *Behaim Boys*, 179.

61 Ozment, *Behaim Boys*, 283.

Chapter 7

1 Jutta Zander-Seidel, *Textiler Hausrat: Kleidung und Haustextilien in Nürnberg von 1500–1650*, Munich: Deutscher Kunstverlag 1990, 120, Ill. 106.

2 L. C. Eisenbart, *Kleiderordnungen der deutschen Städte zwischen 1350 und 1700: Ein Beitrag zur Kulturgeschichte des Bürgertums*, Göttingen: Musterschmidt 1962, 97.

3 Agrippa von Nettesheim, *Von dem Vorzug und der Fürtrefflichkeit des weiblichen Geschlechts vor dem männlichen*, Tübingen: edition diskord 1987, 15–17.

4 Cat., *At Home in Renaissance Italy*, ed. Marta Ajmar-Wollheim and Flora Dennis, London: Victoria & Albert Museum 2006.

5 Heinz Schilling, *Die Stadt in der Frühen Neuzeit*, Munich: Oldenburg 1993, 13–14.

6 *Briefwechsel Balthasar Baumgartners des jüngeren mit seiner Gattin Magdalena geb: Behaim (1582–1598)*, ed. Georg Steinhausen, Tübingen: Litterarischer Verein 1895. For a discussion and selection of representative letters with a correction of Balthasar's biographical data see Steven Ozment, *Magdalena and Balthasar: An Intimate Portrait of Life in Sixteenth-Century Europe Revealed in the Letters of a Nuremberg Husband and Wife*, New Haven: Yale University Press 1986.

7 Steinhausen, *Briefwechsel*, 54.

8 Zander-Seidel, *Textiler Hausrat*, 393.

9 Steinhausen, *Briefwechsel*, 136.

10 Steinhausen, *Briefwechsel*, 6.

11 Steinhausen, *Briefwechsel*, 9 10, 21.

12 Steinhausen, *Briefwechsel*, 58.

13 Steinhausen, *Briefwechsel*, 27.

14 Steinhausen, *Briefwechsel*, 61.

15 Steinhausen, *Briefwechsel*, 64.

16 Bartholomäi Sastrow, *Herkommen, Geburt und Lauff seines gantzen Lebens…*, ed. Gottlieb Mohnike, 3 vols., Greifswald: Universitätsbuchhandlung 1823, vol. 3, 220–223.

17 See, for instance, Giulia Bartrum (ed.), *The New Hollstein German Engravings, Etchings and Woodcuts 1400–1700, Jost Amman*, Part II, Rotterdam: Sound & Vision 2001, 50, 51.

18 Michael North, '*Material Delight and the Joy of Living': Cultural Consumption in the Age of Enlightenment in Germany*, transl. Pamela Selwyn, Aldershot: Ashgate 2008, 82.

19 Jan de Vries, *The Industrious Revolution: Consumer Behaviour and the Household Economy, 1650 to the Present*, Cambridge: Cambridge University Press 2008, 25.

20 Johann Kamann (ed.), 'Aus Nürnberger Haushalts-und Rechnungsbüchern des 15. und 16. Jahrhunderts, Part 2', in *Mitteilungen des Vereins für die Geschichte der Stadt Nürnberg*, 8 (1888), 39–168, esp. 41–43

21 Germanisches Nationalmuseum, HS 18909.

22 Steinhausen, *Briefwechsel*, 60.

23 Steinhausen, *Briefwechsel*, 21.

24 Steinhausen, *Briefwechsel*, 45.

25 Steinhausen, *Briefwechsel*, 21.

26 Steinhausen, *Briefwechsel*, 65.

27 Steinhausen, *Briefwechsel*, 67.

28 Steinhausen, *Briefwechsel*, 67.

29 Keith Thomas, *The Ends of Life: Roads to Fulfilment in Early Modern England*, Oxford: Oxford University Press 2009, 126.

30 Steinhausen, *Briefwechsel*, 101.

31 Steinhausen, *Briefwechsel*, 103.

32 Steinhausen, *Briefwechsel*, 160.

33 Ria Stambaugh (ed.), *Teufelsbücher in Auswahl, vol. 3, Joachim Westphals Hoffartsteufel*, Berlin: Walter de Gruyter 1973, 110.

34 Steinhausen, *Briefwechsel*, 99.

35 Steinhausen, *Briefwechsel*, 117.

36 Steinhausen, *Briefwechsel*, 225.

37 Steinhausen, *Briefwechsel*, 39.

38 Steinhausen, *Briefwechsel*, 124.

39 Steinhausen, *Briefwechsel*, 126.

40 Steinhausen, *Briefwechsel*, 139.

41 Steinhausen, *Briefwechsel*, 142.

42 'Ist also die alte welt wider ney worn', Steinhausen, *Briefwechsel*, 150.

43 For the notion of looking ahead rather than above see de Vries, *Industrious Revolution*, 52, who nonetheless sees this process starting during the later seventeenth and eighteenth centuries.

44 M.-A. Privat-Savigny and M.-H. Guelton, 'Fleurons et palmettes: Quelques tissus à petits motifs des années 1560–1630 destinés à l'habillement', in Marie Viallon (ed.), *Paraître et se vêtir au XVIe siècle: Actes du XIIIe Colloque du Puy-en-Velay*, Saint Étienne: Publications de L'Université de Saint-Étienne 2006, 225.

45 For a pioneering account centred on Nuremberg in a later period see Rebekka Habermas, *Frauen und Männer des Bürgertums: Eine Familiengeschichte (1750–1850)*, Göttingen: Vandenhoeck, 2000.

46 Steinhausen, *Briefwechsel*.

47 *The Frankfurt Book Fair of Henri Estienne*, ed. James W. Thompson, New York 1968, 158–159.

48 Thompson, *Estienne*, 162–164.

49 Thomas Coryat, *Coryats Crudities 1611*, intro. William M. Schutte, London: Scolar Press 1978, 564–565.

50 See below, Zander-Seidel, *Textiler Hausrat*, 64.

51 Christopher R. Friedrichs, 'German Social Structure, 1300–1600', in Bob Scribner (ed.), *Germany: A New Social and Economic History, 1450–1630*, London: Arnold 1996, 234.

52 Pamela Smith, *The Body of the Artisan: Art and Experience in the Scientific Revolution*, Chicago: Chicago University Press 2004, 66–67.

53 Zander-Seidel, *Textiler Hausrat*.

54 Zander-Seidel, *Textiler Hausrat*, 49.

55 Zander-Seidel, *Textiler Hausrat*, 60, 57, fn. 45.

56 Zander-Seidel, *Textiler Hausrat*, 144.

57 Zander-Seidel, *Textiler Hausrat*, 63.

58 Zander-Seidel, *Textiler Hausrat*, 64, 74–80.

59 Zander-Seidel, *Textiler Hausrat*, 78.

60 Zander-Seidel, *Textiler Hausrat*, 81.

61 Zander-Seidel, *Textiler Hausrat*, 83.

62 Evelyn Welch, 'Art on the Edge: Hair and Hands in Renaissance Italy', *Renaissance Studies*, 23 (2008), 242.

63 Mark Häberlein, *Die Fugger: Geschichte einer Augsburger Familie (1367–1650)*, Stuttgart: Kohlhammer 2006, 167.

64 Zander-Seidel, *Textiler Hausrat*, 168.

65 These were the 'Stürze', Zander-Seidel, *Textiler Hausrat*, 117.

66 Johannes Indagine, *Die kunst der chiromantzey, usz besehung der hend. Physiognomey, usz anblick des menschen…*, Strassburg: J. Schott 1523; his two earlier treatises were published in 1511 and 1515.

67 For the awareness of physiognomy in this culture see Martin Porter, *Windows of the Soul: The Art of Physiognomy in European Culture 1470–1780*, Oxford: Oxford University Press 2005, 322.

68 Zander-Seidel, *Textiler Hausrat*, 131. This is also revealed by the Augsburg Monatsbilder.

69 Zander-Seidel, *Textiler Hausrat*, 135.

70 On mercers see Welch, 'Art on the Edge', 256–258.

71 Welch, 'Art on the Edge', 245.

72 Zander-Seidel, *Textiler Hausrat*, 140.

73 Zander-Seidel, *Textiler Hausrat*, 142.

74 Zander-Seidel, *Textiler Hausrat*, 143.

75 See the ill-informed discussion of Michel Pastoureau, *Black: The History of a Color*, Princeton: Princeton University Press 2008, 130–135 and Zander-Seidel's rightly very different stance, *Textiler Hausrat*, 298–300.

76 Zander-Seidel, *Textiler Hausrat*, 183.

77 Zander-Seidel, *Textiler Hausrat*, 193.

78 Zander-Seidel, *Textiler Hausrat*, 188 and Chs. 2 and 3 of this book.

79 Zander-Seidel, *Textiler Hausrat*, 194.

80 Zander-Seidel, *Textiler Hausrat*, 197.

81 Zander-Seidel, *Textiler Hausrat*, 220–221, 'abgetragen Sammaten pireten'.

82 Zander-Seidel, *Textiler Hausrat*, 231.

83 Zander-Seidel, *Textiler Hausrat*, 204.

84 Zander-Seidel, *Textiler Hausrat*, 203 and 236.

85 For the following see Leonie von Wilckens, *Tageslauf im Puppenhaus: Bürgerliches Leben vor dreihundert Jahren*, Munich: Prestel 1956.

86 Wilckens, *Puppenhaus*.

87 Some of its sixteenth-century German centres were Nuremberg, Leipzig, Frankfurt, and Cologne, as well as Hamburg, Dresden, and Berlin in the seventeenth century, joined by Weimar and others during the age of Enlightenment. This argument is explored for eighteenth-century Germany by North, 'Material Delight and the Joy of Living'. See also the map for the distribution of the *Journal für Luxus und der Moden* in 1791 in German towns, 16, and North's argument that the journal sought a 'rapprochement of aristocratic and middle class tastes', 170, so that in contrast to Maxine Berg's findings (in *Luxury and Pleasure in Eighteenth-Century Britain*, Oxford: Oxford University Press 2005) for England we generally do not find that only the middle classes pioneered bourgeois consumption. More research is needed on this aspect. The Thirty Years' War (1618–1648) in this respect certainly does not need to be regarded as the mythical destructor of German life that threw a society into stagnation. Historians now rather point to the possibilities it opened up for social mobility in a society that had previously begun to offer limited employment opportunities for a consistently increasing population. One example is a boy called Johann Merkel, born in a village near Nuremberg when the war was well under way, in 1627. His father was a shoemaker, his mother a peasant's daughter. In 1643 we find Johann a man in his early twenties who has lost his father and finds his stepfather difficult. He went to Nuremberg and immediately

found work in the merchant house of a family called Schröck. By 1658, Johann had saved enough money and earned the right to become a citizen of Nuremberg and to independently trade with salt and metal. Eight years later, aged thirty-nine, he married one of the Schröcks' daughters. Her money finalized his social ascent. One of Johann's sons would get married to the daughter of an Altdorf professor of philology and hold key political offices in Nuremberg. Children of the Merkel family would regularly achieve positions of significant commercial and political influence, right up to the nineteenth century; Habermas, *Frauen und Männer des Bürgertums*, 1–7. A similar narrative around the Bassermann family in Hanau and Mannheim unfolds in Lothar Gall, *Bürgertum in Deutschland*, Berlin: Siedler 1989.

Epilogue

1 Horst Bredekamp, *Die Fenster der Monade: Gottfried Wilhelm Leibniz's Theater der Natur und Kunst*, Berlin: Akademie Verlag 2004, 12–14.

2 See Amiria Henare, Martin Holbraad, and Sari Wastell, 'Introduction: Thinking Through Things', in ead. (eds.), *Thinking Through Things: Theorising Artefacts Ethnographically*, London: Routledge 2007, 11.

3 Images, as the anthropologist Alfred Gell argued, as well as dress displays, could affect or even control the lives of their creators in ways that are intriguing to explore, Alfred Gell, *Art and Agency: An Anthropological Theory*, Oxford: Clarendon Press 1998.

4 'Wahrhaftig, ich bin hier wie zu Hause. Im schwarzen Kleide ohn allen Pomp durchwandere ich die Gassen und finde bei jeden 20 Schritten einen, mit dem ich sprechen muß', cit. in Lothar Gall, *Bürgertum in Deutschland*, Berlin: Siedler 1989, 46.

5 Contrary to Timothy Brook, *Vermeer's Hat: The Seventeenth Century Dawn of the Global World*, London: Profile Books 2008, 82.

6 On Postel see Margaret C. Jacob, *Strangers Nowhere in the World: The Rise of Cosmopolitanism in Early Modern Europe*, Philadelphia: University of Philadelphia Press 2006, 5.

7 Aby M. Warburg, *Ausgewählte Schriften und Würdigungen*, ed. Dieter Wuttke, Baden-Baden: V. Koerner 1980.

8 Daniel Roche, *The Culture of Clothing: Dress and Fashion in the Ancien Regime*, trans. Jean Birrell, Cambridge: Cambridge University Press 1994, 56.

9 Fernand Braudel, *Civilisation and Capitalism 15th–18th Centuries, vol. 2: The Wheels of Commerce*, transl. Sian Reynolds, London: HarperCollins 1982, 352. The sociologist Richard Sennett had earlier posited that even in the eighteenth century there persisted a 'desire to observe the codes of dressing to station. In doing so, people hoped to bring order to the mixture of strangers in the street', Sennett, *The Fall of Public Man*, New York: Knopf 1974, 66.

10 Jan de Vries, *The Industrious Revolution: Consumer Behaviour and the Household Economy, 1650 to the Present*, Cambridge: Cambridge University Press 2008, 135. The French sociologist Pierre Bourdieu meanwhile argued that common people continued to actively resist the aesthetisization of clothing and a capitalist grind that constantly produces new needs through fashion. Their clothing style is positively marked by 'realism' and a functional, rather than symbolic, use of dress; see the apt criticism by Hans Medick, *Weben und Überleben in Laichingen 1650–1900: Lokalgeschichte als Allgemeine Geschichte*, Göttingen: Vandenhoeck 1996, 381.

11 Michel Pastoureau, *Black: The History of a Color*, Princeton: Princeton University Press 2009, 113.

12 Michael North, *'Material Delight and the Joy of Living': Cultural Consumption in the Age of Enlightenment in Germany*, transl. Pamela Selwyn, Aldershot: Ashgate 2008, 46.

13 Essex wills between 1577–1584 described 52 per cent of 1,123 petticoats as red, and 40 per cent as russet, a kind of violet. An excellent publication is Ninya Mikhaila and Jane Malcolm Davies, *The Tudor Tailor: Reconstructing Sixteenth-Century Dress*, Batsford: Anova Books 2006, 40–42.

14 Katharina Simon-Muscheid, ' "und ob sie schon einen dienst finden, so sind sit nit bekleidet dernoc": Die Kleidung der städtischen Unterschichten zwischen Projektionen und Realität im Spätmittelalter und in der frühen Neuzeit', in Neithard Bulst and Robert Jütte (eds.), 'Zwischen Sein und Schein: Kleidung und Identität in der ständischen Gesellschaft', *Saeculum*, 44 (1/1993), 63; see also ch. 5.

15 Katharina Simon-Muscheid, *Die Dinge im Schnittpunkt sozialer Beziehungsnetze: Reden und Objekte im Alltag (Oberrhein, 14. bis 16.*

Jahrhundert), Göttingen: Vandenhoeck 2004, 337–340, here 339.

16 Simon-Muscheid, *Dinge*, 340.

17 Ruth Mohrmann, *Alltagswelt im Land Braunschweig: städtische und ländliche Wohnkultur vom 16. bis zum frühen 20. Jahrhundert*, 2 vols., Münster: Coppenrath 1990.

18 August Fink (ed.), *Die Schwarzschen Trachtenbücher*, Berlin: Deutscher Verlag für Kunstwissenschaft 1963, 79.

19 *Faksimile-Ausgabe der Luzerner Chronik des Diebold Schilling 1513 und Kommentarband*, ed. Alfred A. Schmidt, Luzern: 1979–1981.

20 *Adriaen van de Venne's Album in the Department of Prints and Drawings in the British Museum*, ed. Martin Royalton-Kisch, London: British Museum Publications 1988.

21 For a range of citations see Gerhard Jaritz, 'Kleidung und Prestige-Konkurrenz: Unterschiedliche Identitäten in der städtischen Gesellschaft unter Normierungszwängen', in Bulst and Jütte, 'Zwischen Sein und Schein: Kleidung und Identität in der ständischen Gesellschaft', *Saeculum*, 44 (1993), 11–12.

22 On the medieval fashions for wreaths see Sarah-Grace Heller, *Fashion in Medieval France*, Woodbridge: D. S. Brewer 2007, 79.

23 Robert Beck, 'Paraître dominical et jeu des apparences dans les villes françaises de la fin du XVIIIe siècle à celle du Second Empire', in Isabelle Paresys (ed.), *Paraître et apparences en Europe occidentale: Du Moyen Âge à nos jours*, Villeneuv d'Ascq: Presses du Septentrion 2008, 59–72.

24 StAN, Amts-und Standbücher, 29.12.1610, Margaretha Beckenhoferin.

25 For Europe, Alan Hunt, *Governance of the Consuming Passions: A History of Sumptuary Laws*, Houndsmill: Macmillan, 1996 is a brave and interesting attempt to survey the field, yet based on a limited knowledge of literature translated into English.

26 Matthias Weber, *Die Reichspolizeiordnungen von 1530, 1548 und 1577: Historische Einführung und Edition*, Frankfurt-on-Main: Klostermann 2002, 142.

27 Weber, *Reichspolizeiordnungen*, 143: 'Ehefrauen, unverheiratet Frauen und Kinder: Deßgleichen sollen sich ire haußfrawen und kinder inn irer kleydung auch halten / doch mögen ire haußfrawen eyn gulden rinck nit über fünff oder sechs gulden werth / on Edel gesteyn / eynn kragen mit seiden vernedt / eyn schleyer mit eynem gulden leistlin nit über zwen finger breyt (/) eyn damascken oder athlaß koller / eyn gürtel nit über zehen gulden werth den sie mit silber / doch unvergüldt/beschlagen / Deßgleichen die junckfrawen eyn sammet bendlin mit silber unvergültem beschlechts tragen möchten.'

28 For Italy see Diane Owen Hughes, 'Sumptuary Law and Social Relations in Renaissance Italy', in John Bossy (ed.), *Disputes and Settlements: Law and Human Relations in the West*, Cambridge: Cambridge University Press, 93.

29 See the list provided by Liselotte Constanze Eisenbart, *Kleiderordnungen der deutschen Städte zwischen 1350 und 1700: Ein Beitrag zur Kulturgeschichte des Bürgertums*, Göttingen: Musterschmidt 1962, 163–167, which is not meant to be inclusive, but nonetheless seems indicative. Neithart Bulst's figures do not distinguish between cities, and the kind of ordinance which was issued, but Bulst rightly underlines the need for further research, see Bulst, 'Zum Problem städtischer und territorialer Kleider-, Aufwands- und Luxusgesetzgebung in Deutschland (13. bis Mitte des 16. Jahrhundert)', in André Gouron and Albert Rigaudière (eds.), *Renaissance du pouvoir législatif et genèse de l'Etat*, Montpellier 1988, 29–57.

30 Weber, *Reichspolizeiordnungen*, 181, 229.

31 Johannes Pietsch and Karen Stolleis (eds.), *Kölner Patrizier-und Bürgerkleidung des 17. Jahrhunders. Die Kostümsammlung Hüpsch im Hessischen Landesmuseum Darmstadt*, Riggis: Abegg-Stiftung 2008, 21.

32 Thomas Weller, *Theatrum Praecedentiae: Zeremonieller Rang und gesellschaftliche Ordnung in der frühneuzeitlichen Stadt: Leipzig 1500–1800*, Darmstadt: Wissenschaftliche Buchgesellschaft 2006, 97.

33 Weller, *Theatrum*, 109.

34 Thus, in 1665/6 the council collected ten fines, in 1666/7 eleven, in 1667/8 only three and in 1674 only three as well, Weller, *Theatrum*, 361.

35 Robert Beachy, *The Soul of Commerce: Credit, Property, and Politics in Leipzig, 1750–1840*, Leiden: Brill 2005, 26–27.

36 Beachy, *Commerce*, 26.

37 Beachy, *Commerce*, 27, Carl Günther Ludovici.

38 Beachy, *Commerce*, 28, n. 23.

39 Beachy, *Commerce*, 28, n. 23.

40 Beachy, *Commerce*, 29.

41 Beachy, *Commerce*, 29.

42 Beachy, *Commerce*, 30–31.

43 Beachy counts 100 fines and 112 cases, see Beachy, *Commerce* 30 and n. 29.

44 Beachy, *Commerce*, 31.

45 Weller, *Theatrum*, 381.

46 An analogy for the Middle Ages is discussed by E. Jane Burns, *Courtly Love Undressed: Reading through Clothes in Medieval French Culture*, Philadelphia: University of Pennsylvania Press 2002, 80–84. We can see this in pamphlets that belong to the Querelles des Femmes, see Catherine Kovesi Killerby, ' "Heralds of a Well-Instructed Mind": Nicolosa Sanuti's Defence of Women and their Clothes', *Renaissance Studies*, 13 (3/1999), 255–282.

47 For Medick 'a clear sign that this day-labourer's wife was trying to question the boundaries of the local culture of respectable appearance', Medick, *Weben und Überleben*, 428–429.

48 February 1713–February 1714, Sheilagh Ogilvie, *A Bitter Living: Women, Markets, and Social Capital in Early Modern Germany*, Oxford: Oxford University Press 2003, 202–203.

49 Mack Walker, *German Home Towns: Community, State and General Estate, 1648–1871*, Ithaca: Cornell University Press 1971. For a new approach see also Ulrich Rosseaux, *Freiräume: Unterhaltung, Vergnügen und Erholung in Dresden (1694–1830)*, Cologne: Böhlau 2007.

50 Walker, *Home Towns*, 135.

51 These issues are discussed in Ogilvie, *Bitter Living*.

52 See the above; for a highly nuanced discussion see Medick, *Weben*, ch. 5; for England, Beverly Lemire has presented a number of pioneering works on the textile trade in this vein.

53 See, for instance, Paracelsus's use of it, as quoted by Alix Cooper, *Inventing the Indigenous: Local Knowledge and Natural History in Early Modern Europe*, Cambridge: Cambridge University Press 2007, 25.

54 Brook, *Vermeer's Hat*, 22.

55 John Styles, *The Dress of the People: Everyday Fashion in Eighteenth-Century England*, New Haven: Yale University Press 2007, 6 and ch. 1.

56 I am influenced here by the work of the sociologist Eva Illouz, *Cold Intimacies: The Making of Emotional Capitalism*, Cambridge: Polity Press 2008.

57 Evelyn Welch, *Shopping in the Renaissance: Consumer Cultures in Italy 1400–1600*, New Haven: Yale University Press 2005, 9.

58 Keith Thomas, *The Ends of Life: Roads to Fulfilment in Early Modern England*, Oxford: Oxford University Press 2009, 139.

59 de Vries, *Industrious Revolution*, 58–72. This is with particular reference to Johan and Pieter de la Court, who since 1685 published in Amsterdam on the difference between 'Monarchical' and 'Republican' Luxury and influenced the Dutchman Mandeville.

60 Ulinka Rublack, *Reformation Europe*, Cambridge: Cambridge University Press 2005, 1–2.

61 James Davidson, *Courtesans and Fishcakes: The Consuming Passions of Classical Athens*, London: HarperCollins 1997, 245.

62 Davidson, *Courtesans*, 314. Indeed, one might argue that the French philosopher Michel Foucault could have equally written about the care taken to find the right kind of consumption alongside sex as an essential 'technique of the self' that found its origin in Greek writing and further developed in subsequent centuries. It increasingly seemed plausible to think of consumption as something every person was centrally engaged in. This was thought of as a process in which the passions were deeply involved and had to be managed in complex ways that would need to involve a society's institutional resources as well as great individual resolve. Failures to establish whatever was regarded as measured responses would increasingly be pathologized.

63 Particularly relevant for this study is Karin Wurst, *Fabricating Pleasure: Fashion, Entertainment, and Cultural Consumption in Germany, 1780–1830*, Detroit: Wayne State University Press 2005.

64 See the discussion in Michael Sonenscher, *Sans-Culottes: An Eighteenth-Century Emblem in the French Revolution*, Princeton: Princeton University Press 2008, 10.

65 Laura Van Aert and Ilja Van Damme, 'Retail Dynamics of a City in Crisis: The Mercer Guild in Pre-industrial Antwerp (c.1648—c.1748)', in Bruno Blondé et al. (eds.), *Retailers and Consumer Changes in Early Modern Europe: England, France, Italy and the Low Countries*, Tours: Presses Universitaires 2005, 153.

66 'For the unhappy husband', as Sarah-Grace Heller puts it, 'the opposites of fashion are a complex constellation of situations denying self-expression, including poverty, miserliness, poor materials, inferior workmanship, overuse, poor fit, and plainness', Heller, *Fashion*, 118.

67 Jean Baptiste Poquelin de Molière, *The School for Husbands*, transl. Richard Wilbur, New York: Jovanovich 1992, 20.

68 John Brewer, *The Pleasures of the Imagination: English Culture in the Eighteenth Century*, London: HarperCollins 1997, 112. See also Philip Carter, *Men and the Emergence of Polite Society, Britain 1660–1800*, Harlow: Longman 2001, 137–162. This explains the enduring popularity since the twelfth century of a moral example of dowdy philosophers or doctors, who were refused entry into courts unless they dressed up, and then pointed out that it seemed as if their clothes rather than they had been let in.

69 David Kuchta, *The Three-Piece Suit and Modern Masculinity: England, 1550–1850*, Berkeley: University of California Press 2002, 173.

70 Molière, *School*, 13.

71 Sonenscher, *Sans-Culottes*, 79.

72 In this respect in particular, Gilles Lipovetsky, *The Empire of Fashion: Dressing Modern Democracy*, transl. Catherine Porter, Princeton: Princeton University Press 1994, remains important. We might add to this with some caution a greater sense of choice to reject or adapt novelties in self or group displays.

73 Eiko Ikegami, *Bonds of Civility: Aesthetic Networks and the Political Origins of Japanese Culture*, Cambridge: Cambridge University Press 2005, 272.

74 Winfried Schulze has drawn out attention to the tentative beginnings of liberal economic thinking in sixteenth-century Germany which related to such ideas, Winfried Schulze, 'Vom Gemeinnutz zum Eigennutz: Über den Normenwandel in der ständischen Gesellschaft der Frühen Neuzeit', *Historische Zeitschrift*, 243 (1986), 591–626. One of the first expositions of the argument that individual selfishness and gain could not be restrained but nonetheless benefit social harmony was made in 1564 in a publication jointly authored by the Ulm citizen Leonhard Fronsperger and a lawyer and politician called Oswalt Gut, who stood in the service of the Markgrave of Baden. The pamphlet was provocatively entitled '*Praise of one's own good*' (*Eigennutz*)—in obvious distinction to the common good, which had been the key category of all social ethics up to then. Many sixteenth and seventeenth century authors openly acknowledged people's 'love to acquire', the '*cupiditas acquirendi*', while a text published in 1625 in Frankfurt by one Jakob Bornitz frankly argued that material things could be used for one's immediate needs and used as well for 'pleasure and joy', Schulze, 'Eigennutz', 611 ('*Lust, Ergetz- und Herligkeit*').

75 For a pioneering monograph in this emerging field of research in early modern German history see Christian Hochmuth, *Globale Güter – lokale Aneignung: Kaffee, Tee, Schokolade und Tabak im frühneuzeitlichen Dresden*, Constance: UVK 2008.

76 Mary Wortley Montagu, *Letters*, intro. Clare Brant, London: Everyman 1992, 60–61.

77 The fair here is one of the most considerable in Germany, and the resort of all persons of quality, as well as the merchants, Montagu, *Letters*, 82.

78 Welch, *Shopping*, 33.

79 Montagu, *Letters*, 61.

80 Simon Schama, *The Embarrassment of Riches: An Interpretation of Dutch Culture in the Golden Age*, New York: Knopf 1987.

81 These examples date from court cases in 1693, Lotte van de Pol, *Der Bürger und die Hure: Das Sündige Gewerbe in Amsterdam in der Frühen Neuzeit*, transl. Rosemarie Still, Frankfurt-on-Main: Campus 2006, 65.

82 Craig Clunas, *Superfluous Things: Material Culture and Social Status in Early Modern China*, Honolulu: University of Hawaii Press 2004, 173.

83 This to her explains why images of Japan as a country defined by aesthetic excellence could be endorsed in the nineteenth century, Ikegami, *Bonds*, 285.

84 On this question see Carlo Marco Belfanti, 'Was Fashion a European Invention', *Journal of Global History*, 3 (2008), 419–443.

85 Kenneth Pomeranz, *The Great Divergence: China, Europe, and the Making of the Modern World Economy*, Princeton: Princeton University Press 2000, 141–142.

86 Steeve O. Buckridge, *The Language of Dress: Resistance and Accommodation in Jamaica 1760–1890*, Jamaica: University of the West Indies Press 2004, 19.

87 Araceli Tinajero, 'Far Eastern Influences in Latin American Fashions', in Regina A. Root (ed.), *The Latin American Fashion Reader*, Oxford: Berg 2005, 66–75, here 66.

88 Rebecca Earle, 'Nationalism and National Dress in Spanish America', in Mina Roces and Louise

Edwards (eds.), *The Politics of Dress in Asia and the Americas*, Brighton: Sussex Academic Press 2007, 163–181, here 166.

89 Barbara A. Sommer, 'Wigs, Weapons, Tattoos and Shoes: Getting Dressed in Colonial Brazil', in Roces and Edwards, *Politics of Dress*, 208–209.

90 Mariselle Meléndez, 'Visualising Difference: The Rhetoric of Clothing in Colonial Spanish America', in Root, *Latin American Fashion Reader*, 17–30.

91 Extracts from his writings are reproduced in Susan Migden Socolow, *The Women of Colonial Latin America*, Cambridge: Cambridge University Press 2000, 184.

92 Ilona Katzew, *Casta Painting: Images of Race in Eighteenth-Century Mexico*, New Haven: Yale University Press 2004, 67.

93 Rebecca Earle, 'Luxury, Clothing and Race in Colonial Spanish America', in Maxine Berg and Elizabeth Eger (eds.), *Luxury in the Eighteenth Century: Debates, Desires and Delectable Goods*, Houndsmill: Palgrave 2008, 219–227, here 219.

94 Sonenscher, *Sans-Culottes*, 92.

95 Thomas, *Ends of Life*, 146.

96 See also Chandra Mukerji, *From Graven Images: Patterns of Modern Materialism*, New York: Columbia University Press 1983, 261.

97 Maxine Berg and Elizabeth Eger, 'The Rise and Fall of the Luxury Debates', in idem, *Luxury in the Eighteenth Century*, 7–27, here 7.

98 For an excellent discussion of the eighteenth-century debates conducted by English magazines on the question of property and conduct see James Raven, 'Defending Conduct and Property: The London Press and the Luxury Debate', in John Brewer and Susan Staves (eds.), *Early Modern Conceptions of Property*, London: Routledge 1995, 301–322.

99 North, *'Material Delight'*, 55–57; Wurst, *Fabricating Pleasure*, ch. 6.

100 See the excellent book by Daniel L. Purdy, *The Tyranny of Elegance: Consumer Cosmopolitanism in the Era of Goethe*, Baltimore: Johns Hopkins University Press 1998, 20.

101 Wurst, *Fabricating Pleasure*, 152; 176, 'Wie ein großer Reisender hüllt sie sich in alle Nationaltrachten'.

102 G. W. F. Hegel, 'Die Verfassung Deutschlands (1802)', in *Politische Schriften*, ed. Jürgen Habermas, Frankfurt-on-Main: 1966, 86; see Barbara Stollberg-Rilinger, *Des Kaisers alte Kleider: Verfassungsgeschichte als Symbolgeschichte des Alten Reiches*, Munich: Beck 2008, 7–9.

103 Friedrich Nietzsche, *Vom Nutzen und Nachteil der Historie für das Leben*, Basel: Diogenes 1984, 40–41.

Select Bibliography

MANUSCRIPT SOURCES

Lipperheidische Kostümbibliothek, Berlin:

Aa2 Sigmund Heldt, *Abconterfaittung allerlei Ordenspersonen in iren klaidungen vnd dan viler alter klaidungen, so vor zeiten von Fursten, Furstin vnd herrn, auch Burger vnd Burgerin, alhie zu Nurmberg vnd vilen andern orten getragen sinnt worden. Vnd an eins theils orten noch getragen werden. Deßgleichen allerlei Turnier vnd Gestech von hohen vnd Nidern Stenden. Letzlich die Baurschafft waß ire klaidung, grosse arbeit, vnd widerum ergetzlichkeit gewesen ist*, Nuremberg 1560–1580

Aa4 Trachtenbuch, German, *c.*1560–1594

Aa21 Trachtenbuch, German ?, *c.*1580

Aa22 Trachtenbuch, German, *c.*1580–1600

OZ 136, Stammbuch Julius Bayr, Nuremberg 1577–1592

OZ 13, Stammbuch Leonhard Hayder, Nuremberg 1589–1645

Staatsbibliothek, Berlin:

Ms. Germ. Fol 442 Nürnberger Schembart-Turnier und Wappenbuch *c.*1583

Staatsbibliothek, Munich:

Cgm 1951, Cgm 1952, Hofkleiderbuch und Hof-Livreen der Herzoge Wilhelm IV und Albrecht V, 1508–1551

Cod. iconogr. 341, Kostüme u. Sittenbilder der Männer und Frauen im 16. Jahrhundert in Augsburg und Nürnberg, Deutschland, Europa, Afrika und Asien (late sixteenth century)

Cod. iconogr. 342, Trachtenbuch nach Christoph Weiditz, Hans Römer of Erfurt (1523–1529)

Cod. iconogr. 361, Kostüme und Sittenbilder des 16. Jahrhunderts aus West- und Osteuropa, dem Orient, der Neuen Welt und Afrika, Augsburg *c.*1560–1570

Germanisches Nationalmuseum, Nuremberg:

HS 7177 Der Heldten Geschlechter- und Stammbuch

HS 18909 Susanna Harsdörferin, Kochbuch

HS 20805 Rechnungsbuch Harsdörferin

Stadtbibliothek, Nuremberg:

Amb. 317.2°, 317b.2°, 318.2° Hausbücher der Mendelschen Zwölfbrüderstiftung, I–III

Amb. 279.2° Hausbücher der Landauer Stiftung I

Bibliothéque National, Paris:
Ms Allemands, No 211, Copy of Matthäus Schwarz's Klaidungsbüchlein
Ms Allemands, No 95, Boniface Dieffenbach's chronicle

Trinity College Library, Cambridge:
R.14.23 Greek and Turkish Costumes

British Library, London:
Add. Ms., 27,579 Album Amicorum Johann Cellarius
Add. Ms., 15, 217 Cöler Family
Add. Ms., 78167, William Smith, A Breef Description of the Famous and Bewtifull Cittie of
  Noremberg
Add. Ms., 18973 Album Amicorum Tucher
Add. Ms., 19067 Album Amicorum Miller
Eg. 1184, Album Amicorum Cöler
Eg. 1192, Album Amicorum Paul Behaim II
Eg. 1186, Album Amicorum Jona and Petri Portner
Eg. 1209, Album Amicorum Holzschuher
Eg. 1191, Album Amicorum Sigmund Ortellius
Eg. 1225, Album Amicorum Joh. Tho. Ortellius
Eg. 1269, Album Amicorum Oelhafen

Warburg Library, London:
Dheere, Luc, Theatre de tous les peuples et nations de la terre avec leurs habits,..., n.p., n.d.
  c.1560, Ghent Library MS2466, copy.

ARCHIVAL SOURCES

Stadtarchiv Nuremberg:
Amts-und Standbücher 1609–13
B 14/III vol. 6 Liber Testamentarium
Pellerarchiv PA Nr. 20, Verrechnungsbuch Martin Peller 1587–1609; 1609–1629

Familienarchiv Behaim:
E 11/II Nr. 818, Georg Christoph Behaim, Einnahmen und Ausgaben 1653–1671
E 29/III Nr. 258 Das Große Tucherbuch

Stadtarchiv Augsburg:
Schätze 194B, Herwartsches Ehrenbuch 1544–1558
Schätze, Eidbuch 1590
Schätze 82, Fechtbuch Rast.
2/6 Reichsstadt Zünfte 253 Schneiderarbeitsbuch 1552–1556

Stadtarchiv Schwäbisch Hall:
4/553, Einunger-Gerichtsakten

SELECTED PRIMARY PRINTED SOURCES

Albertinus, Aegidius, *Der Welt Thurnierplatz darinn erstlich der geistlichen Manns- und Weibs Personen in ihren Zierden und Eigenschafften, folgends die weltlichen…auffziehn*, Munich: N. Henricum 1614.

Amman, Jost, *Das Ständebuch: 114 Holzschnitte von Jost Amman mit Reimen von Hans Sachs*, Leipzig: Insel n.d.

—— *Gynaecum: Sive Theatrum mulierum…*, Frankfurt-on-Main: S. Feyerabend 1586.

—— *Im Frauwenzimmer Wirt vermeldt von allerley schönen Kleidungen vnnd Trachten der Weiber/ hohes vnd niders Stands/ wie man fast an allen orten geschmückt vnnd gezieret ist/ Als Teutsche/ Welsche/ Franntzösische/ Engelländische/ Niderländische/ Böhemische/ Vngerische/ vnd alle anstossende Länder…*, Frankfurt-on-Main: S. Feyerabend 1586.

Anshelm, Valerius, *Die Berner Chronik*, vols. 1–6, ed. Historischen Verein des Kantons Bern, Bern: Haller 1884–1901.

Aquinas, St Thomas, *Summa Theologiae: A Concise Translation*, ed. Timothy McDermott, London: Eyre and Spottiswoode 1989.

Babur Nama, *Journal of Emperor Babur*, trans. A. S. Beveridge, ed. D. Hiro, London: Penguin Books 2006.

Bartrum, Giulia (ed.), *The New Hollstein German Engravings, Etchings and Woodcuts 1400–1700, Jost Amman, Part II*, Rotterdam: Sound & Vision 2001.

Baylor, Michael G. (ed. and trans.), *The Radical Reformation*, Cambridge: Cambridge University Press 1991.

Behaim, Paul, *Briefe eines Leipziger Studenten aus den Jahren 1572 bis 1574*, ed. Wilhelm Loose, Meißen: 1880.

Bergmann, Joseph, *Das Ambraser Liederbuch vom Jahre 1582*, Stuttgart: Literarischer Verein 1845.

Berliner Liedflugschriften: Katalog der bis zu 1650 erschienen Drucke der Staatsbibliothek zu Berlin – Preußischer Kulturbesitz, ed. Bearbeitet von Eberhard Nehlsen, vol. 2, Baden-Baden: V. Koerner 2008.

Bertelli, Pietro, *Omnivm fere gentivm nostrae aetatis habitvs, nvnqvam ante hac aediti*, Venice: P. Bertelli 1563.

—— *Diversarv Nationvm Habitus…opera Petri Bertelli*, 3 vols., Padua: A. Alcia, P. Bertelli 1594–1596.

Blick, Simon and Wolfgang, 'Verderben und Schaden der Lande und Leute an Gut, Leib, Ehre und der Seelen Seligkeit aus Luthers und der seines Anhangs Lehre', in Adolf Laube (ed.), *Flugschriften gegen die Reformation (1518–1524)*, Berlin: Akademie Verlag 1997.

Bock, Hartmut (ed.), *Die Chronik Eisenberger: Bebilderte Geschichte einer Beamtenfamilie der deutschen Renaissance—Aufstieg in den Wetterauer Niederadel und das Frankfurter Patriziat*, Frankfurt-on-Main: Historisches Museum 1992.

Boemus, Johannes, *The fardle of facions conteining the auncient manner, customes, and lawes, of the people enhabiting the two partes of the earth, called Affrika and Asie*, London: I. Kingstone 1555.

Boissard, Jan Jacques, *Habitvs Variarum orbis gentium: Habitz de Nations esträges. Trachten mancherley Völcker des Erdskreysz*, Mecheln: Caspar Rutz 1581.

Bonati, Maurizio Rippa and Finucci, Valeria (eds.), *Mores Italiae: Costume and Life in the Renaissance*, Cittadella: Biblos 2007.

Boogart, Ernst van den (ed.), *Civil and Corrupt Asia: Image and Text in the Itinerario and the Icones of Jan Huygens van Linschoten*, Chicago: University of Chicago Press 2003.

Boorde, Andrew, *The Boke of the Introduction of Knowledge...*, London: W. Copland 1550?.

Brant, Sebastian, *Das Narrenschiff, alle ständt der Welt betreffend, wie man sich in allen Händeln weiszlich halten soll...*, Frankfurt-on-Main: W. Han 1560.

——*Fabeln*, ed. Bernd Schneider, Stuttgart: Frommann-holzboog 1999.

Braun, Georg and Hogenberg, Franz, *Civitates Orbis Terrarum*, ed. R. A. Skelton, 6 vols., Cleveland: The World Publishing Company 1966.

Braunstein, Philippe (ed.), *Un Banquier Mis a Nu: Autobiographie de Matthäus Schwarz Bourgeois d'Augsburg*, Paris: Gallimard 1992.

Breydenbach, Bernhard von, *Die fart oder reysz über mere zu dem heiligen grab...*, Augsburg: A. Sorgen 1488.

Briefwechsel Balthasar Paumgartners des Jüngeren mit seiner Gattin Magdalena, geb. Behaim, 1582–1598, ed. Georg Steinhausen, Tübingen: Litterarischer Verein 1843.

Bruyn, Abraham de, *Imperii ac Sacerdotis Ornatus...*, Cologne: J. Rutz 1578.

——*Omnivm poene Gentivm Imagines, Ubi oris totiusq corporis & vestium habitus...*, Cologne: J. Rutz 1577.

Bulwer, John, *Anthropometamorphosis: A View of the People of the Whole World: Or A Short Survey of their Policies, Dispositions, Naturall Deportments, Complexions, Ancient and Moderne Customes, Manners, Habits & Fashions*, London: William Hunt 1654.

Castiglione, Baldassarre, *The Book of the Courtier*, trans. George Bull, Harmondsworth: Penguin 1976.

Celtis, Conrad, *Selections from Conrad Celtis 1459–1508*, ed. and trans. Leonhard Forster, Cambridge: Cambridge University Press 1948.

Cochläus, Johannes, 'Eine heilige Vermahnung der heiligen Stadt Rom an Deutschland', in Adolf Laube (ed.), *Flugschriften gegen die Reformation (1518–1524)*, Berlin: Akademie Verlag 1997.

Cortes, Adriano, *Le Voyage en Chine d'Adriano de las Cortes s.j. (1625)*, ed. Pascale Girard, Paris: Chandeigne 2001.

Coryate, Thomas, *Coryats Crudities 1611*, intro. William M. Schutte, London: Scolar Press 1978.

Das Nürnberger Schönbartbuch: Nach der Hamburger Handschrift, ed. Karl Drescher, Weimar: Gesellschaft der Bibliophilen 1908.

Deserpz, François, *Receuil de la diversité des habits qui sont de present en vsaige tant es pays d'Europe, Asie, Affrique et illes sauuages, Le tout fait apres le naturel*, Paris: Richard Breton 1562.

——*A Collection of the various Styles of clothing which are Presently Worn in Countries of Europe, Asia, Africa, and the Savage Islands, All Realistically Depicted*, ed. and trans. Sarah Shannon, Minneapolis: James Ford Bell Library 2001.

Deutsche Flugblätter des 16. und 17. Jahrhunderts, ed. Wolfgang Harms, Tübingen: M. Niemeyer 1985–.

Die Limburger Chronik, ed. Otto H. Brandt, Jena: Diedrichs 1922.

Dürer Drawings in the Albertina, ed. Walter Koschatzky and Alice Strob, London: Secker & Warburg 1973.

Dürer, Albrecht, Schriftlicher Nachlass, ed. Hans Rupprich, 3 vols., Berlin: Deutscher Verein für Kunstwissenschaft 1956–1970.

Edler Schatz holden Erinnerns: Bilder in Stammbüchern der Staatsbibliothek Bamberg aus vier Jahrhunderten, ed. L. Kurras, Bamberg: Die Bibliothek 1995.

Eines Ersamen Raths der Statt Augspurg der Gezierd und Kleydung halben auffgerichte Policeyordnung, Augsburg: n.p. 1582.

Einhard, *Vita Karoli Magni, The Life of Charlemagne*, ed. and trans. Evelyn Scherabon Firchow and Edwin H. Zeydel, Coral Gables: University of Miami Press 1974.

Erasmus, Desiderius, 'On Good Manners for Boys/De civilitate morum puerilium', in *Collected Works, Literary and Educational Writings*, ed. J. K. Sowards, vol. 25, Toronto: University of Toronto Press 1985, 269–289.

Eser, Thomas and Grebe, Anja, *Heilige und Hasen: Bücherschätze der Dürerzeit*, Nürnberg: Germanisches Nationalmuseum 2008.

Estienne, Henri, *The Frankfurt Book Fair of Henri Estienne*, ed. James W. Thompson, New York: n.p. 1968.

Fabri, Alexandro de, *Diversarum Nationum ornatus*, Padua: Fabri (?) 1593.

Fink, August (ed.), *Die Schwarzschen Trachtenbücher*, Berlin: Deutscher Verlag für Kunstwissenschaft 1963, 79.

Forster, Georg, *Ein außbund schöner Teutscher Liedlein...*, Nürnberg: Johann vom Berg, Ulrich Newber 1550.

Franck, Sebastian, *Erst Theil dieses Weltbuchs, von newen erfundnen landtschafften...*, Frankfurt-on-Main: n.p. 1567.

—— *Teutscher Nation Chronic...*, Frankfurt-on-Main: S. Feyerabend 1539.

Friedensburg, Walter, *Geschichte der Universität Wittenberg*, Halle: Max Niemeyer 1917.

Frischlin, Nicodemus, *Sämtliche Werke*, vol. 3, Part 1, ed. and trans. Christoph Jungck and Lothar Mundt, Stuttgart-Bad Cannstatt: Frommann-holzbog 2003.

Fróis, Luís, *Européen & Japonais: Traité sur les contradictions & différences de mœurs,* Preface by Claude Lévi-Strauss, Paris: Chandeigne 1998.

Fugger Family, *Das Ehrenbuch der Fugger: Darstellung – Transkription – Kommentar*, 2 vols., ed. Gregor Rohmann, Augsburg: Wißner 2004.

Fugger, Hans, *Die Korrespondenz Hans Fuggers von 1566 bis 1594*, vol. 2, Part 2, *1582–1594*, ed. Christl Karnehm, Munich: Kommission für Bayerische Landesgeschichte 2003.

Góis, Damião de, *Lisbon in the Renaissance: A New Translation of the Urbis Olisiponis Descriptio*, ed. and trans. Jeffrey S. Ruth New York: Ithaca Press 1996.

Grassi, Bartolomeo, *Die veri ritratti degl' habiti: Di tutte le parti del mondo*, Rome: Bartolomeo Grassi 1585.

Grimm, Jakob and Wilhelm (eds.), *Deutsches Wörterbuch*, vol. 15, Leipzig: Hirzel 1956.

Grynaeus, Simon, *Die new welt, der landtschaften vund Insulen, so bis hie her allen Altweltbeschrybern unbekant/ Jungst aber von den Portugalesern und Hispaniern im Nidergenglichen meer befunden. Sambt den sitten und gebreuchen der Inwonenden völker*, Strasbourg: Georg Ulricher 1534.

Günzburg, Johann Eberlin von, *Ein zamengelesen buochlin von der Teutschen Nation gelegenheit, Sitten vnd gebrauche, durch Cornelium Tacitum vnd etliche andere verzeichnet (1526)*, ed. Achim Masse, Innsbruck: Institut für Germanistik, Universität Innsbruck 1986.

Hampe, Theodor (ed.), *Gedichte vom Hausrat aus dem XV. und XVI. Jahrhundert in Facsimiledruck herausgegeben*, Strasbourg: J. H. E. Heitz 1899.

Hegel, G. W. F., 'Die Verfassung Deutschlands (1802)', in idem, *Politische Schriften*, ed. Jürgen Habermas, Frankfurt-on-Main: Suhrkamp 1966, 23–139.

Hollar, Wenzel, *Theatrum Mulierum*, London: Henry Overton 1643.

Hutten, Ulrich von, *Des teutschen Ritters Ulrich von Hutten Sämmtliche Werke,* 5 parts, ed. E. J. H. Münch, Berlin and Leipzig: Hirzel 1821–1825.

Ibn Khaldûn, *The Muqaddimah: An Introduction to History*, trans. Franz Rosenthal, ed. N. J. Dawood, Princeton: Princeton University Press 1967.

Indagine, Johannes, *Die kunst der chiromantzey, usz besehung der hend. Physiognomey, usz anblick des menschen...*, Strasbourg: J. Schott 1523.

Johnston, Pamela and Scribner, Bob (ed.), *The Reformation in Germany and Switzerland*, Cambridge: Cambridge University Press 1993.

Juvenal and Persius, ed. and trans. Susan Morton Brand, Cambridge, MA: Harvard University Press 2004.

Kaiser Maximilians I Weisskunig, ed. H. Theodor Musper et al., Stuttgart: W. Kohlhammer 1956.

Katalog der Lipperheidischen Kostümbibliothek, ed. Eva Nienholdt and G. Wagner-Neumann, vol. 1, 2nd edn., Berlin: Kunstbibliothek 1965.

Kamann, Johann (ed.), 'Aus Nürnberger Haushalts-und Rechnungsbüchern des 15. und 16. Jahrhunderts', Teil 1, *Mitteilungen des Vereins für die Geschichte der Stadt Nürnberg*, 6 (1887), 57–122; Teil 2, *MVGN*, 8 (1888), 39–168.

Kurras, Lotte (ed.), *Zu gutem Gedenken: Kulturhistorische Miniaturen aus Stammbüchern des Germanischen Nationalmuseums 1570–1770*, Munich: Prestel 1987.

Laube, Adolf and Looß, Sigrid (eds.), *Flugschriften der frühen Reformationsbewegung (1518–1524)*, vol. 2, Berlin: Akademie Verlag 1983.

Lazius, Wolfgang, *De Aliquot gentium migrationibus, sedibus fixis, reliquiis, linguarumque initiis & immutationibus ac dialectis, libri xii*, Basle: Oporiniana 1572.

Loose, Wilhelm (ed.), *Anton Tuchers Haushaltsbuch 1507 bis 1517*, Tübingen: Bibliothek des litterarischen Vereins 1877.

Luther, Martin, *Von Kauffshandlung und Wucher*, Wittenberg: Lufft 1524.

—— *Werke: Weimarer Ausgabe*, n.p.: H. Böhlau 1883–.

Lutz, Hans, *Tagebuch des Hans Lutz, aus Augsburg. Ein Beitrag zur Geschichte des Bauern-Kriegs im Jahre 1525*, ed. Benedikt Greiff, Augsburg: Lauter 1849.

Mair, Paul Hector, *Geschlechter Buch: darinn der loblichen Kaiserliche Reichs Statt Augspurg so vor fünffhundert vnd mehr Jahren hero, dasselbst gewonet, vnd biss auff acht abgestorben, auch deren so an der Abgestorbnen stat eingenommen vnd erhöhet worden seyn*, Frankfurt-on-Main: S. Feyerabend 1580.

—— *Zwei Chroniken des Augsburger Ratsdieners Paul Hector Mair von 1548 bis 1564*, Die Chroniken der deutschen Städte, Munich: Königliche Akademie der Wissenschaften 1917.

Martin, Daniel, *New Parlament/ Oder Hundert Kurzweilige/ doch nutzliche/ Gespräch/ Frantzösisch und Teutsch/ in welchen unter den Tituln von allerley Standspersonen und Handwerkern diejenige Wort/Reden/und Discurs vorgebracht werden, so man im täglichen Handel und Wandel zugebrauchen pfleget...*, Strasbourg: n.p. 1660.

Melanchthon, Philipp, 'Oratio contra affectationem novitatis in vestitu (1527)', in *Corpus Reformatorum*, vol. 11, Halle: C. A. Schwetzschke 1843, 139–149.

Melem, Oger, *Das Hausbuch der Familie Melem: Ein Trachtenbuch des Frankfurter Patriziats aus dem 16. Jahrhunderts*, ed. Rudolf Walther, Frankfurt-on-Main: Verlag für Wissenschaftliche Literatur 1968.

Möller, Antonium, *Der Danziger Frawen- und Jungfrawen gebreuchlich Zierheit und Tracht so itziger Zeit zu sehen/…*, Danzig: Jacobo Rhodo 1501, Facsimile ed. Richard Bertling, Danzig: R. Bertling 1886.

Montagu, Mary Wortley, *Letters*, intro. Clare Brant, London: Everyman 1992.

Montaigne, Michel de, *The Complete Essays*, trans. M. A. Screech, London: Penguin, 1987.

Moscherosch, Johann Michael, *Visiones de Don Quevedo: Wunderliche vnd Wahrhafftige Gesichte Philanders von Sittewald…*, Strasbourg: Johann Philipp Mülben 1642.

Müller, Gerhard and Seebaß, Gottfried (eds.), *Andreas Osiander d. Ä., Gesamtausgabe*, Gütersloh: Mohn 1982.

Müller, Gernot Michael, *Die 'Germania generalis' des Conrad Celtis: Studien mit Edition, Übersetzung und Kommentar*, Tübingen: Niemayer 2001.

Münster, Sebastian, *Briefe Sebastian Münsters*, ed. Karl Heinz Burmeister, Frankfurt-on-Main: Insel Verlag 1964.

Müntzer, Wolffgang, *Reyssbeschreibung dess gestrengen und vesten Herrn Wolffgang Müntzers von Babenberg, Ritters…*, Nuremberg: L. Lochner, 1574.

Murner, Thomas, *Die Schelmenzunft*, ed. M. Spanier, Berlin: de Gruyter 1925.

Musculus, Andreas, *Vom zuluderten zucht und her erwegnen Pluderichten Hosen Teuffel vormanung und warnung*, Frankfurt-on-Main: G. Raben, Weygand Hans Erben 1563.

Naphy, William G. (trans. and ed.), *Documents on the Continental Reformation*, Houndsmill: Macmillan Press 1996.

Nettesheim, Agrippa von, *Über die Fragwürdigkeit, ja Nichtigkeit der Wissenschaften, Künste und Gewerbe*, trans. and ed. G. Güpner and Siegfried Wollgast, Tübingen: Akademie Verlag 1993.

—— *Von dem Vorzug und der Fürtrefflichkeit des weiblichen Geschlechts vor dem männlichen, (1509)*, Tübingen: Edition diskord 1987.

Nicolai, Friedrich, *Über den Gebrauch der falschen Haare und Perrucken in alten und neuen Zeiten: Eine Historische Untersuchung*, Berlin: n.p. 1801.

Nicolay, Nicolas de, *Von der Schiffart unnd Raisz in die Türckey unnd gegen Oriennt…*, Nuremberg: C. Saldörfer 1572.

Nietzsche, Friedrich, *Vom Nutzen und Nachteil der Historie für das Leben*, Basel: Diogenes 1984.

Nürnbergische Kleiderarten, Nuremberg: Johann Kramer 1669.

Nürnbergische Trachten und Schauwürdige Stadtgebäude oder Plätze, Nuremberg: n.p. 1690.

Osiander, Lucas, *Ein predig/ Von hoffertiger/ ungestalter Kleidung/ der Weibs und Manns Personen*, Tübingen: Georg Gruppenbach 1586.

Ozment, Steven (ed. and narrator), *Three Behaim Boys: Growing Up in Early Modern Germany: A Chronicle of their Lives*, New Haven: Yale University Press 1990.

Paas, John Roger (ed.), *The German Political Broadsheet*, 9 vols., Wiesbaden: Harrassowitz 1985–.

Petrarca, Francesco, *Von der Artzney bayder Glück, des güten und widerwertigen: Unnd wess sich ain yeder inn Gelück und unglück halten soll*, Augsburg: H. Steyner 1532.

Pius II, Enea Silvio Piccolomini Pope Pius II., *Ausgewählte Texte*, ed. and trans. Berthe Widmer, Basle: Schwaber 1960.

Platter, Felix, *Tagebuch (Lebensbeschreibung) 1536–1567*, ed. Valentin Lötscher, Basel/Stuttgart: Schwabe & Co. 1976.

Reichard, Elias Caspar, *Matthäus und Veit Konrad Schwarz nach ihren merkwürdigsten Lebensumständen und vielfältigsten Lebensumständen*, Magdeburg Marburg: n.p. 1786.

Rem, Wilhelm, 'Chronica newer Geschichten', in *Die Chroniken der schwäbischen Städte: Augsburg*, vol. 5, Leipzig: Hirzel 1896.

Rippa Bonati, Maurizio and Finucci, Valeria (eds.), *Mores Italiae: Costume and Life in the Renaissance*, Cittadella: Biblios 2007.

Royalton-Kisch, Martin, *Adriaen van de Venne's Album in the Department of Prints and Drawings in the British Museum*, London: British Museum Publications 1988.

Santa Clara, Abraham a, *Centi-Folium Stultorum in Quarto: Oder Hundert ausbündige Narren, in Folio*, Vienna: J. C. Megerle 1709.

Sastrow, Bartholomäi, *Herkommen, Geburt und Lauff seines gantzen Lebens…*, ed. Gottlieb Mohnike, 3 vols., Greifswald: Universitätsbuchhandlung 1823.

Schilling, Diebold, *Faksimile-Ausgabe der Luzerner Chronik des Diebold Schilling 1513 und Kommentarband*, ed. Alfred A. Schmidt, Luzern: Kunstkreis 1977.

Schnurr, Balthasar, *Vollständiges und schon aller Orten bekandtes Kunst = Hausz = und Wunder = Buch*, Frankfurt-on-Main: Zubrodt u. Haass 1676.

Schwarz, Matthäus, *Das Gebetbuch des Matthäus Schwarz*, ed. Georg Habich, Munich: Verlag der Bayerischen Akademie der Wissenschaften 1910.

Scribner, Bob and Scott, Tom (eds. and trans.), *The German Peasants War: A History in Documents*, London: Humanities Press 1991.

Sender, Clemens, *Die Chronik von C. Sender von den ältesten Zeiten der Stadt Augsburg bis 1536*, ed. F. Roth, Munich: Königliche Akademie der Wissenschaften 1894.

Springer, Burckhardt, *Balthasar Springer's Indienfahrt 1505/06: Wissenschaftliche Würdigung der Reiseberichte Springers zur Einführung in den Neudruck seiner 'Meerfahrt' vom Jahre 1509*, ed. Franz Schulze, n.p.: J. H. E. Heitz 1899.

Staden, Hans von, *Wahrhaftige Historia und beschreibung eyner Landtschaffi der Wilden, Nacketen, Grimmigen Menschenfresser Leuthen, in der Newenwelt America gelegen*, Frankfurt-on-Main: Weygandt Han 1557.

Stambaugh, Ria (ed.), *Teufelbücher in Auswahl*, vol. 4, *Andreas Musculus Hosenteufel*, Berlin: Walter de Gruyter 1978.

——(ed.), *Teufelsbücher in Auswahl*, vol. 3, *Joachim Westphals Hoffartsteufel*, Berlin: Walter de Gruyter 1973.

Steinhausen, Georg (ed.), *Deutsche Privatbriefe des Mittelalters*, 2 vols., Berlin: R. Gaertner 1899.

Stracke, Johannes C., *Tracht und Schmuck Altfrieslands nach den Darstellungen im Hausbuch des Häuptlings Unico Manninga*, Aurich: Ostfriesische Landschaft 1967.

Straub, Georg, *Trachten oder Stammbuch*, Sankt Gallen: n.p. 1600.

Strauss, Gerald (ed. and trans.), *Manifestations of Discontents on the Eve of the Reformation*, Bloomington: Indiana University Press 1971.

Strauss, Walter L., *The German Single-Leaf Woodcut 1550–1600*, 3 vols., New York: Hacker Art Books 1975.

Stubbes, Phillip, *The Anatomy of Abuses*, London: R. Jones 1585.

Tacitus, *Germany, Germania*, ed. and trans. Herbert W. Benario, Warminster: Aris and Phillips 1999.

Vecellio, Cesare, *De gli Habiti antichi, et moderni di Diuerse parti del Mondo…*, Venice: Zenaro 1590.

——*Habiti antichi, et moderni di tutto il Mondo . . .*, Venice: Sessa 1598.

——*Habiti Antichi et Moderni: The Clothing of the Renaissance World*, ed. and trans. Margaret F. Rosenthal and Ann Rosalind Jones, London: Thames & Hudson 2008.

Vecellio's Renaissance Costume Book: All 500 Woodcut Illustrations from the Famous Sixteenth-Century Compendium of World Costume by Cesare Vecellio, New York: Dover 1977.

Venegati, Flacius, *Vier Bücher der Ritterschaft*, Augsburg: Steyner 1529.

Vos, Lambert, *Das Kostümbuch des Lambert Vos (1574)*, ed. Hans-Albrecht Koch, 2 vols., Graz: Akademie Druck – und Verlaganstalt 1991.

Weber, Matthias (ed.), *Die Reichspolizeiordnungen von 1530, 1548 und 1577. Historische Einführung und Edition*, Frankfurt-on-Main: V. Klostermann 2002.

Weiditz, Christoph, *Authentic Everyday Dress of the Renaissance: All 154 Plates from the 'Trachtenbuch'*, ed. Theodor Hampe, Toronto: Dover 1994.

——*Das Trachtenbuch des Christoph Weiditz von seinen Reisen nach Spanien (1529) und den Niederlanden (1531/32)*, ed. Theodor Hampe, Berlin: de Gruyter 1927.

Weigel, Hans, *Habitvs praecipvorvm popvlorvm, tam virorvm qvam foeminarum Singulari arte depicti. Trachtenbuch: Darin fast allerley vnd der fürnembsten Nationen/ die heutigs tags bekandt sein/ kleidungen/ beyde wie es bey Manns vnd Weibspersonen gebreuchlich/ mit allem vleiß abgerissen sein/ sehr lustig vnd kurzweilig zusehen*, Nuremberg: Hans Weigel 1577.

Welser, Marcus Werlich, Engelbert, *Chronica der Weitberiempten Keyserlichen Freyen und der H. Reichs Statt Augspurg . . .*, Augsburg: Engelbert Werlich 1595.

White, John, *The American Drawings of John White*, 2 vols., ed. Paul Hulton and David B. Quinn, London: British Museum Press 1964.

Wunderzeichen und Winkeldrucker 1543–1586: Einblattdrucke aus der Sammlung Wikiana in der Zentralbibliothek Zürich, ed. Bruno Weber, Zurich: Urs Graf-Verlag 1972.

Zimmern, Froben Christoph von, *Die Chronik der Grafen von Zimmern*, ed. Martin Decker-Hauff, 2 vols., Sigmaringen: Thorbecke 1964–1981.

Zinsli, P. (ed.), *Der Berner Totentanz des Niklaus Manuel in den Nachbildungen von Albrecht Kauw (1649)*, Bern: Paul Haupt 1953.

Selected Secondary Bibliography

Abulafia, David, *Atlantic Encounters in the Age of Columbus*, New Haven: Yale University Press 2008.

——'The Role of Trade in Muslim–Christian Contact during the Middle Ages', in Dionisius A. Agius and Richard Hitchcock (eds.), *The Arab Influence in Medieval Europe*, Reading: Ithaca Press 1994, 1–24.

Allerston, Patricia, 'Clothing and Early Modern Venetian Society', *Continuity & Change* 15 (2000), 367–390.

Alpers, Svetlana, *The Art of Describing: Dutch Art in the Seventeenth Century*, Chicago: Chicago University Press 1983.

Amburger, Hannah S. M., *Die Familiengeschichte der Koeler: Ein Beitrag zur Autobiographie des 16. Jahrhunderts*, Nürnberg: J. L. Stich, 1930.

Appadurai, Arjun, 'Introduction', in idem (ed.), *The Social Life of Things: Commodities in Cultural Perspective*, Cambridge: Cambridge University Press 1986, 3–63.

Arlinghaus, Franz-Josef, 'Gesten, Kleidung und die Etablierung von Diskursräumen im städtisch-en Gerichtswesen (1350–1650)', in Johannes Burkhardt and Christine Werkstetter (eds.), *Kommunikation und Medien in der Frühen Neuzeit*, Munich: Oldenbourg 2005, 461–498.

Arnold, Janet, *Patterns of Fashion, vol. II: The Cut and Construction of Clothing for Men and Women c.1560–1620*, London: Macmillan 2008.

—— *Queen Elizabeth's Wardrobe Unlock'd*, Leeds: Maney 1988.

——Tiramani, Jenny, and Levey, Santina M., *Patterns of Fashion, vol. IV: The Cut and Con-struction of Linen Shirts, Smocks, Neckwear, Headwear and Accessories for Men and Women c.1540–1660*, London: Macmillan 2008.

Backmann, Sybille, 'Italienische Kaufleute in Augsburg 1550–1650', in Johannes Burkhardt (ed.), *Augsburger Handelshäuser im Wandel des historischen Urteils*, Berlin: Akademie Verlag 1996, 224–240.

Bailey, Amanda, *Flaunting: Style and the Subversive Male Body in Renaissance England*, Toronto: University of Toronto Press 2007.

Bake, Kristina, '"Unser Leben währet siebzig Jahre, und wenn's hochkommt, so sind's achtzig Jahre, und wenn's köstlich gewesen ist, so ist's's Mühe und Arbeit gewese." Die zehn Alter von Mann und Frau des Tobias Stimmer (?) als Spiegel des bürgerlichen Lebens um 1575', in Cat., *'Die Güter dieser Welt': Schätze der Lutherzeit aus den Sammlungen der Moritzburg Halle*, Halle: Landeskunstmuseum 2000, 23–38.

Bakhtin, Michail, *Rabelais and his World*, transl. Helene Iswolsky, Bloomington: Indiana Uni-versity Press 1984.

Baltrusch, Ernst, *Regimen morum: Die Reglementierung des Privatlebens der Senatoren und Ritter in der römischen Republik und frühen Kaiserzeit*, Munich: Beck 1988.

Bastl, Beatrix, 'Die Bekleidung der Lebenden und der Toten: Memoria, soziale Identität und aristokratischer Habitus im frühneuzeitlichen Habsburgerreich', *Wiener Geschichtsblätter*, 55 (2000), 102–123.

Baur, Veronika, Kleiderordnungen in Bayern vom 14. bis zum 19. Jahrhundert, Munich: Stadt-archiv 1975.

Baxandall, Michael, *The Limewood Sculptors of Renaissance Germany*, New Haven: Yale Univer-sity Press 1980.

Bayerisches Nationalmuseum: Handbook of the Art and Cultural History Collection, ed. Renate Eikelmann, Munich: Hirmer Verlag, no date.

Bayly, C. A., *The Birth of the Modern World 1780–1914*, Oxford: Blackwell 2004.

—— 'The Origins of Swadeshi (Home Industry): Cloth and Indian Society, 1700–1930', in Ar-jun Appadurai (ed.), *The Social Life of Things: Commodities in Cultural Perspective*, Cambridge: Cambridge University Press 1986, 285–322.

Beachy, Robert, *The Soul of Commerce: Credit, Property, and Politics in Leipzig, 1750–1840*, Le-iden: Brill 2005.

Beck, Robert, 'Paraître dominical et jeu des apparences dans les villes françaises de la fin du XVIIIe siècle à celle du Second Empire', in Isabelle Paresys (ed.), *Paraître et apparences en Europe occidentale: Du Moyen Âge à nos jours*, Villeneuv d'Ascq: Presses du Septentrion 2008, 59–72.

Beer, Mathias, 'Migration, Kommunikation und Jugend: Studenten und Kaufmannslehrlinge der Frühen Neuzeit in ihren Briefen', *Archiv für Kulturgeschichte*, 88 (2006), 355–387.

Behringer, Wolfgang, 'Arena and Pall Mall: Sport in the Early Modern Period', *German History*, 27 (2009), 331–357.

Belfanti, Carlo Mario, 'Was Fashion a European Invention?', *Journal of Global History*, 3 (2008), 419–443.

——and Fabio Gisuberti, 'Clothing and Social Inequality in Early Modern Europe: Introductory Remarks', *Continuity & Change*, 15 (2000) 357–366.

Belting, Hans, *Florenz und Bagdad: Eine westöstliche Geschichte des Blicks*, Munich: Beck 2008.

——(ed.), *Bilderfragen: Die Bildwissenschaften im Aufbruch*, München: Wilhelm Fink Verlag 2007.

——*Das echte Bild: Bildfragen als Glaubensfragen*, Munich: Beck 2005.

——*Bild und Kult: Eine Geschichte der Bilder vor dem Zeitalter der Kunst*, Munich: Beck 1990.

Berg, Maxine, *Luxury and Pleasure in Eighteenth-Century Britain*, Oxford: Oxford University Press 2005.

——and Eger, Elizabeth, 'The Rise and Fall of the Luxury Debates', in idem (eds.), *Luxury in the Eighteenth Century: Debates, Desires and Delectable Goods*, Houndsmill: Palgrave 2008, 7–27.

Bernis Madrazo, Carmen, *Trajes y modas en la España de los Reyes Católicos*, 2 vols., Madrid: Instituto Velásquez 1979.

Berns, Joerg Jochen, 'Luthers Papstkritik als Zeremoniellkritik. Zur Bedeutung des päpstlichen Zeremoniells für das fürstliche Hofzeremoniell der Frühen Neuzeit', in Jörg Jochen Berns and Thomas Rahn (eds.), *Zeremoniell als höfische Ästhetik im Spätmittelalter und Früher Neuzeit*, Tübingen: M. Niemeyer Verlag 1995, 157–173.

Bethencourt, Francisco, 'European Expansion and the New Order of Knowledge', in J. J. Martin (ed.), *The Renaissance World*, New York: Routledge 2007, 118–139.

Biow, Douglas, *The Culture of Cleanliness in Renaissance Italy*, Ithaca: Cornell University Press 2006.

Blanc, Odile, 'Ethnologie et merveille dans quelque livres de costumes Français', in Marie Viallon (ed.), *Paraître et se vêtir au XVIe siècle: Actes du XIIIe Colloque du Puy-en-Velay*, Saint Étienne: Publications de L'Université de Saint Étienne 2006, 79–94.

——'From Battlefield to Court: The Invention of Fashion in the Fourteenth Century', in Désirée G. Koslin and Janet E. Snyder (eds.), *Encountering Medieval Textiles and Dress: Objects, Texts, Images*, Houndsmill: Palgrave 2002, 157–172.

——*Parades et Parures: L'invention du corps de mode à la fin du Moyen Age*, Paris: Éditions Gallimard 1997.

——'Images du monde et portraits d'habits: le receuils de costume à la Renaissance', *Bulletin du Bibliophile*, 2 (1995), 221–261.

Blondé, Bruno et al. (eds.), *Buyers & Sellers: Retail Circuits and Practices in Medieval and Early Modern Europe*, Turnhout: Brepols 2006.

——*Retailers and Consumer Changes in Early Modern Europe: England, France, Italy and the Low Countries*, Tours: Presses Universitaires, 2005.

Bock, Hartmut, 'Die Familiengeschichtsschreibung der Welser', *Mitteilungen des Vereins für die Geschichte der Stadt Nürnberg*, 95 (2008), 93–162.

——'Kette und Wappenhelme: Zur Unterscheidung zwischen Patriziat und Adel in der Frühen Neuzeit', *Zeitschrift des Historischen Vereins für Schwaben*, 97 (2004), 59–120.

Bonnet, Anne-Marie, *'Akt' bei Dürer*, Cologne: Böhlau 2001.

Borkopp-Restle, Birgit, *Textile Schätze aus Renaissance und Barock*, Munich: Bayerisches Nationalmuseum 2002.

Borowka-Clausberg, *Balthasar Sprenger und der frühneuzeitliche Reisebericht*, Munich: Iudicum 1999.

Braudel, Fernand, *Civilization and Capitalism 15th–18th Century*, vol. II, *The Wheels of Commerce*, transl. Siân Reynolds, London: HarperCollins 1985.

——*Civilisation matérielle, économie et capitalisme, XVe–VIIIe siècle*, vol. 1, Paris: Flammarion 1979.

Braun, Josef S. J., *Die liturgische Gewandung in Occident und Orient nach Ursprung und Entwicklung, Verwendung und Symbolik*, Freiburg: Herder 1907.

Braunstein, Philippe (ed.), *Un Banquier mis a nu: Autobiographie de Matthäus Schwarz, Bourgeois d'Augsburg*, Paris: Gallimard 1992.

Brecht, Martin, *Martin Luther, vol. 3, Die Erhaltung der Kirche 1532–46*, Stuttgart: Calwer Verlag 1988.

——*Martin Luther, vol. 2, Ordnung und Abgrenzung der Reformation 1521–1532*, Stuttgart: Calwer Verlag 1986.

Bredekamp, Horst, 'Bild – Akt – Geschichte', in Clemens Wischermann et al. (eds.), *Geschichtsbilder, 46. Deutscher Historikertag in Konstanz 2006, Berichtsband*, Constance: Universitätsverlag 2007, 289–309.

——*Bilder bewegen: Von der Kunstkammer zum Endspiel: Aufsätze und Reden*, ed. Jörg Probst, Berlin: Wagenbach 2007.

——*Die Fenster der Monade: Gottfried Wilhelm Leibniz's Theater der Natur und Kunst*, Berlin: Akademie Verlag 2004.

——'Drehmomente – Merkmale und Ansprüche des Iconic Turn', in Christa Maar and Hubert Burda (eds.), *Iconic Turn: Die Neue Macht der Bilder*, Cologne: DuMont 2004, 15–26.

——'A Neglected Tradition? Art History as Bildwissenschaft', *Critical Inquiry*, 29 (2003), 418–428.

Brewer, John, *The Pleasures of the Imagination: English Culture in the Eighteenth Century*, London: HarperCollins 1997.

Brockmann, Stephen, *Nuremberg: The Imaginary Capital*, Rochester: Camden House 2006.

Brook, Timothy, *Vermeer's Hat: The Seventeenth Century Dawn of the Global World*, London: Profile Books 2008.

——*The Confusions of Pleasure: Commerce and Culture in Ming China*, Berkeley: University of California Press 1998.

Brückner, Wolfgang, 'Fremdheitsstereotypen: Der ethnographische Blick als neues Wahrnehmungsmuster visueller Art in der Frühen Neuzeit', in Wolfgang Harms and Alred Messerli (eds.), *Wahrnehmungsgeschichte und Wissensdiskus im illustrierten Flugblatt der Frühen Neuzeit (1450–1700)*, Basel: Schwabe & Co. 2004, 145–162.

Buckridge, Steve O., *The Language of Dress: Resistance and Accommodation in Jamaica 1760–1890*, Jamaica: University of the West Indies Press 2004.

Bulst, Neithart, 'Zum Problem städtischer und territorialer Kleider-, Aufwands- und Luxusgesetzgebung in Deutschland (13. bis Mitte des 16. Jahrhundert)', in André Gouron and Albert Rigaudière (eds.), *Renaissance du pouvoir législatif et genèse de l'Etat*, Montpellier: Société d' histoire du droit 1988, 29–57.

——'Kleidung als sozialer Konfliktstoff. Probleme kleidergesetzlicher Normierung im sozialen Gefüge', *Saeculum*, 44 (1993), 32–46.

——Lüttenberg, Thomas, and Priever, Andreas, 'Abbild oder Wunschbild? Bildnisse des Christoph Ambergers im Spannungsfeld von Rechtsnorm und gesellschaftlichem Anspruch', *Saeculum*, 53 (2002), 21–73.

Bumke, Joachim, *Courtly Culture: Literature and Society in the High Middle Ages*, transl. Thomas Dunlap, Berkeley: University of California Press 1991.

Burckhardt, Paul, *David Joris und seine Gemeinde in Basel*, Basel: Baseler Zeitschrift für geschichte und Altertumskunde 1949.

Burghartz, Susanna (ed.), *Staging New Worlds: de Brys' Illustrated Travel Reports, 1590–1630*, Basel: Schwabe & Co. 2004.

Burke, Peter, 'Imagining Identity in the Early Modern City', in Christian Emden et al. (eds.), *Imagining the City, vol. 1, The Art of Urban Living*, Frankfurt-on-Main: Peter Lang 2006, 23–37.

—— *The Fortunes of the Courtier: The European Reception of Castiglione's Cortegiano*, Cambridge: Polity Press 1995.

—— 'Res et Verba: Conspicuous Consumption in the Early Modern World', in John Brewer and Roy Porter (eds.), *Consumption and the World of Goods*, London: Routledge 1993, 148–161.

Burns, E. Jane, *Courtly Love Undressed: Reading through Clothes in Medieval French Culture*, Philadelphia: University of Pennsylvania Press 2002.

Campbell Hutchinson, Jane, *Albrecht Dürer: A Biography*, Princeton: Princeton University Press 1990.

Campbell, Louise, *Renaissance Portraits: European Portrait-Paintings in the 14th, 15th and 16th Centuries*, New Haven: Yale University Press 1990.

Campbell, Mary B., *The Witness and the Other World: Exotic European Travel Writing, 400–1600*, Ithaca: Cornell University Press 1988.

Carter, Philip, *Men and the Emergence of Polite Society in Britain 1660–1800*, Harlow: Longman 2001.

Cat., *A Well-Fashioned Image: Clothing and Costume in European Art, 1500–1800*, ed. Elizabeth Rodini and Elissa B. Weaver, Chicago: The David and Alfred Smart Museum of Art 2002.

Cat., *At Home in Renaissance Italy*, ed. Marta Ajmar-Wollheim and Flora Dennis, London: Victoria & Albert Museum 2006.

Cat., *Federschmuck und Kaiserkrone: Das barocke Amerikabild in den habsburgischen Ländern*, ed. Friedrich Polleroß et al., Vienna: Bunderministerium für Wissenschaft und Forschung 1992.

Cat., *Kurzweil viel ohn 'Maß und Ziel': Alltag und Festtag auf den Augsburger Monatsbildern der Renaissance*, Munich: Hirmer 1994.

Cat., *Turning Point: Oribe and the Arts of Sixteenth-Century Japan*, ed. Miyeko Murase, Metropolitan Museum of Art, New York, New Haven: Yale University Press 2003.

Cat., *Welt im Umbruch: Augsburg zwischen Renaissance und Barock*, 2 vols., Augsburg: Augsburger Druck- und Verlagshaus 1980.

Cat., *Deutsche Kunst und Kultur im Germanischen Nationalmuseum*, Nuremberg: Karl Ulrich & Co. 1972.

Cat., *Fastes de cour et ceremonies Royales: Le Costume de cour en Europe 1650–1800*, ed. Pierre Arizzoli-Clémentel and Pascale Gorguet Ballesteros, Paris: Réunion des Musées Nationaux 2009.

Cat., *Graphische Sammlung Staatsgalerie Stuttgart*, ed. Hans Burgkmair: Das Graphische Werk, Stuttgart: Staatsgalerie 1973.

Cat., *Martin Luther und die Reformation in Deutschland*, Germanisches Nationalmuseum, Frankfurt-on-Main: Insel Verlag 1983.

Cat., *Turks: A Journey of a Thousand Years, 600–1600*, ed. David J. Roxburgh, London: Royal Academy of Art 2005.

Chapuis, Stéphanie, 'Juges et Jupons: Les lois vestimentaires et les femmes à Augsburg au XVIe siècle', in Marie Viallon (ed.), *Paraître et se vêtir au XVIe siècle: Actes du XIIIe Colloque du Puy-en-Velay*, Saint Étienne: Publications de L'Université de Saint Étienne, 2006, 193–212.

Chauduri, Kirti N., *Asia Before Europe: Economy and Civilisation of the Indian Ocean from the Rise of Islam to 1750*, Cambridge: Cambridge University Press 1990.

Chipps Smith, Jeffrey, *The Northern Renaissance*, London: Phaidon 2004.

——(ed.), *New Perspectives on the Art of Renaissance Nuremberg: Five Essays*, Texas: The Archer M. Huntington Art Gallery 1985.

——'The Transformation in Patrician Tastes in Renaissance Nuremberg', in idem (ed.), *New Perspectives on the Art of Renaissance Nuremberg, Five Essays*, Texas: The Archer M. Huntington Art Gallery 1985, 83–100.

Chrisman, Miriam, *Lay Culture, Learned Culture: Books and Social Change in Strasbourg, c.1480–1599*, New Haven: Yale University Press 1982.

Clark, Stuart, *Vanities of the Eye: Vision in Early Modern European Culture*, Oxford: Oxford University Press 2007.

Clark, Timothy et al. (eds.), *The Dawn of the Floating World, 1680–1765*, London: Royal Academy 2001.

Clasen, Claus-Peter, *Textilherstellung in Augsburg in der frühen Neuzeit*, Augsburg: B. Wissner 1995.

Clunas, Craig, *Empire of Great Brightness: Visual and Material Cultures of Ming China, 1368–1644*, London: Reaktion 2007.

——*Superfluous Things: Material Culture and Social Status in Early Modern China*, Honolulu: University of Hawaii Press 2004.

Collier Frick, Carol, *Dressing Renaissance Florence: Families, Fortunes, and Fine Clothing*, Baltimore: Johns Hopkins Press 2002.

Cooper, Alix, *Inventing the Indigenous: Local Knowledge and Natural History in Early Modern Europe*, Cambridge: Cambridge University Press 2007.

Crane, Susan, *The Performance of Self: Ritual, Clothing, and Identity During the Hundred Years' War*, Philadelphia: University of Pennsylvania Press 2002.

Cuneo, Pia, *Art and Politics in Early Modern Germany: Jörg Breu the Elder and the Fashioning of Political Identity c.1475–1536*, Leiden: Brill 1998.

Currie, Elizabeth, 'Diversity and Design in the Florentine Tailoring Trade, 1550–1620', in Michelle O'Malley and Evelyn Welch (eds.), *The Material Renaissance*, Manchester: Manchester University Press 2006, 154–173.

——'Prescribing Fashion: Dress, Politics and Gender in Sixteenth-Century Conduct Literature', *Fashion Theory*, 4 (2000), 157–178.

Daston, Lorraine and Galison, Peter, *Objectivity*, New York: Zone 2007.

——and Park, Katherine, *Wonders and the Order of Nature, 1150–1750*, New York: Zone 1998.

Davidson, James, *Courtesans and Fishcakes: The Consuming Passions of Classical Athens*, London: HarperCollins 1997.

Deceulaer, Harald, 'Between Medieval Communities and Early Modern Change: Proto-Industrialization and Consumption in the Southern Low Countries (1300–1800)', *Textile History*, (2006), 123–148.

Defert, Daniel, 'Un genre ethnographique profane au XVIe siècle: les livres d'habits (Essai d'ethno-iconographie)', in Britta Rupp-Eisenreich (ed.), *Histoires de L'Anthropologie (XVIe–XIXe siècles)*, Paris: Université de Paris VII 1984, 25–41.

Denzer, Jörg, 'Die Welser in Venezuela—Das Scheitern ihrer wirtschaftlichen Ziele', in Mark Häberlein and Johannes Burkhardt (eds.), *Die Welser: Neue Forschungen zur Geschichte und Kultur des oberdeutschen Handelshauses*, Berlin: Akademie Verlag 2002, 285–319.

Deppermann, Klaus, *Melchior Hoffman: soiale Unruhen und apokalytische Visionen im Zeitalter der Reformation*, Göttingen: Vandenhoeck 1979.

Destemberg, Antoine, 'Le Paraître universitaire médiéval, une question d'honneur (XIIIe–XVe siècles)', in Isabelle Paresys (ed.), *Paraître et apparences en Europe occidentale: Du Moyen Âge à nos jours*, Villeneuv d'Ascq: Presses du Septentrion 2008, 133–164.

Diers, Michael, *Schlagbilder: Zur politischen Ikonographie der Gegenwart*, Frankfurt-on-Main: Fischer 1997.

Dihle, Helene, 'Kostümbilder und Rechnungsbücher der Sächsisch-Ernestinischen Hofschneiderei 1469–1588', *Zeitschrift für Kostüm- und Waffenkunde*, N.F. 3 (1929–31), 127–137, 152–156.

Dikovitskaya, Margaret, 'An Interview with W. J. T. Mitchell', in ead., *The Study of the Visual after the Cultural Turn*, Cambridge, MA: MIT Press 2005.

Dinges, Martin, 'Von der "Lesbarkeit der Welt" zum universalisierten Wandel durch individuelle Strategien: Die soziale Funktion der Kleidung in der höfischen Gesellschaft', in Neithard Bulst and Robert Jütte (eds.), 'Zwischen Sein und Schein: Kleidung und Identität in der ständischen Gesellschaft', *Saeculum* 44 (1993), 90–112.

Durian-Rees, Saskia, *Textilien–Sammlung Bernheimer. Paramente 15.–19. Jahrhundert*, Munich: Hirmer 1991.

——*Schuhe: Vom späten Mittelalter bis zur Gegenwart*, Munich: Hirmer 1991.

Dürr, Renate, 'Die Ehre der Mägde zwischen Selbstdefinition und Fremdbestimmung', in B. Ann Tlusty (ed.), *Ehrkonzepte der Frühen Neuzeit: Identitäten und Abgrenzungen*, Berlin: Akademie Verlag 1998, 170–184.

Dyan, Elliott, 'Dressing and Undressing the Clergy: Rites of Ordination and Degradation', in E. Jane Burns (ed.), *Medieval Fabrications: Dress, Textiles, Clothwork, and Other Cultural Imaginings*, New York: Palgrave 2004, 55–70.

Dyrness, William A., *Reformed Theology and Visual Culture: The Protestant Imagination from Calvin to Edwards*, Cambridge: Cambridge University Press 2004.

Earle, Rebecca, 'Nationalism and National Dress in Spanish America', in Mina Roces and Louise Edwards (eds.), *The Politics of Dress in Asia and The Americas*, Brighton: Sussex Academic Press 2007, 163–181.

Eichberger, Dagmar, and Zika, Charles (eds.), *Dürer and his Culture*, Cambridge: Cambridge University Press 1998.

Eisenbart, L. C., *Kleiderordnungen der deutschen Städte zwischen 1350 und 1700: Ein Beitrag zur Kulturgeschichte des deutschen Bürgertums*, Göttingen: Musterschmidt-Verlag 1962.

Elliott, John, *The Old World and the New 1492–1650*, Cambridge: Cambridge University Press 1970.

Emich, Birgit, 'Bildlichkeit und Intermedialität in der Frühen Neuzeit: Eine interdisziplinäre Spurensuche', *Zeitschrift für Historische Forschung*, 25 (2008), 31–56.

Evans, Caroline, *Fashion at the Edge: Spectacle, Modernity and Deathliness*, New Haven: Yale University Press 2007.

Fairchilds, Cissie, 'Fashion and Freedom in the French Revolution', *Continuity & Change*, 15 (2000), 419–433.

Faroqhi, Suraiya and Neumann, Christopher K. (eds.), *Ottoman Costumes: From Textiles to Identity*, Istanbul: Eren 2004.

Fend, Metchild and Koos, Marianne (eds.), *Männlichkeit im Blick: Visuelle Inszenierungen in der Kunst seit der Frühen Neuzeit*, Cologne: Böhlau 2004.

Fircks, Juliane von, *Liturgische Gewänder des Mittelalters aus St. Nicolai in Stralsund*, Riggisberg: Abegg Stiftung 2008.

Fisher, Will, *Materializing Gender in Early Modern English Literature and Culture*, Cambridge: Cambridge University Press 2006.

Christensen, S. Flamand, *Die männliche Kleidung in der süddeutschen Renaissance*, Berlin: Deutscher Kunstverlag 1934.

Flores, Jorge and Vassallo e Silva, Nuno (eds.), *Goa and the Great Mughal*, London: Scala 2004.

Freedman, Paul, *Out of the East: Spices and the Medieval Imagination*, New Haven: Yale University Press 2008.

Friedrichs, Christopher R., 'German Social Structure, 1300–1600', in Bob Scribner (ed.), *Germany: A New Social and Economic History, 1450–1630*, London: Arnold 1996, 233–258.

Gall, Lothar, *Bürgertum in Deutschland*, Berlin: Siedler 1989.

Gattineau-Sterr, Susanne, *Die Trachtenbücher des 16. und 17. Jahrhunderts: Eine Untersuchung zu ihrer Entstehung, Entwicklung und Bedeutung im kunsthistorischen Zusammenhang*, D.phil. Bern 1996.

Gell, Alfred, *Art and Agency: An Anthropological Theory*, Oxford: Clarendon Press 1998.

Goldthwaite, Richard A., *Wealth and the Demand for Art in Italy 1300–1600*, Baltimore: Johns Hopkins University Press 1993.

Göllner, Carl, *Die europäischen Türkendrucke des 16. Jahrhunderts*, 2 vols., Bukarest–Baden 1961–1968.

Gömmel, Rainer, 'Die Vermittlerrolle Nürnbergs zwischen Italien und Deutschlands vom Spätmittelalter bis zum 18. Jahrhundert aus wirtschaftshistorischer Sicht', in Volker Kapp and Frank-Rutger Hausmann (eds.), *Nürnberg und Italien: Begegnungen, Einflüsse und Ideen*, Tübingen: Stauffenburg Verlag 1991, 21–43.

Grafton, Anthony, *Cardano's Cosmos: The Worlds and Works of a Renaissance Astrologer*, Cambridge, MA: Harvard University Press 1999.

——*New Worlds, Ancient Texts: The Power of Tradition and the Shock of Discovery*, Cambridge, MA: Harvard University Press 1992.

Greenblatt, Stephen, *Renaissance Self-Fashioning: From More to Shakespeare*, Chicago: Chicago University Press 1980.

Greenfield, Amy Butler, *A Perfect Red: Empires, Espionage, and the Quest for the Color of Desire*, New York: HarperCollins 2005.

Greenfield, Kent R., *Sumptuary Law in Nürnberg: A Study in Paternal Government*, Baltimore: Johns Hopkins Press 1918.

Groebner, Valentin, *Defaced: The Visual Culture of Violence in the late Middle Ages*, transl. Pamela Selwyn, New York: Zone 2004.

——*Der Schein der Person: Steckbrief, Ausweis und Kontrolle im Europa des Mittelalters*, Munich: Beck 2004.

——'Inside Out: Clothes, Dissimulation, and the Arts of Accounting in the Autobiography of Matthäus Schwarz, 1496–1574', *Representations*, 66 (1999), 100–21.

——*Ökonomie ohne Haus: Zum Wirtschaften armer Leute in Nürnberg am Ende des 15. Jahrhunderts*, Göttingen: Vandenhoeck 1993.

Grosshaupt, Walter, 'Commercial Relations between Portugal and the Merchants of Ausgburg and Nuremberg', in Jean Aubin (ed.), *La Decouverte, le Portugal et L'Europe*, Paris: Fondation Gulbenkian 1990, 359–397.

Grote, Andreas, *Macrocosmos in Microcosmos: Die Welt in der Stube: Zur Geschichte des Sammelns 1450 bis 1800*, Opladen: Leske & Budrich 1994.

Guenther, Irene, *Nazi Chic?: Fashioning Women in the Third Reich*, Oxford: Berg 2004.

Häberlein, Mark, *Die Fugger: Geschichte einer Augsburger Familie (1367–1650)*, Stuttgart: Kohlhammer 2006.

Habermas, Rebekka, *Frauen und Männer des Bürgertums: Eine Familiengeschichte (1750–1850)*, Göttingen: Vandenhoeck 2000.

Hackspiel-Mikosch, Elisabeth and Haas, Stefan (eds.), *Die zivile Uniform als symbolische Kommunikation: Kleidung zwischen Repräsentation, Imagination und Konsumption in Europa vom 18. bis zum 21. Jahrhundert*, Stuttgart: Steiner 2006.

Hagenmann, Karen, *'Männlicher Muth und Teutsche Ehre'. Nation, Militär und Geschlecht zur Zeit der Antinapoleonischen Kriege Preußens*, Paderborn: Schöningh 2002.

Hale, J. R., *Artists and Warfare in the Renaissance*, New Haven: Yale University Press 1990.

Hamling, Tara and Williams, Richard L., *Art Reformed: Reassessing the Impact of the Reformation on the Visual Arts*, Cambridge: Scholars Publishing 2007.

Harms, Wolfgang and Messerli, Alfred (eds.), *Wahrnehmungsgeschichten und Wissensdiskurs im illustrierten Flugblatt der Frühen Neuzeit*, Basel: Schwabe & Co. 2002.

Harreld, Donald J., *High Germans in the Low Countries: German Merchants and Commerce in Golden Age Antwerp*, Leiden: Brill 2004.

Harvey, John, *Men in Black*, London: Reaktion 1995.

Hayward, Maria, *Dress at the Court of Henry VIII*, Leeds: Maney 2002.

Heath, Jennifer, *The Veil: Women Writers on its History, Lore, and Politics*, Berkeley: University of California Press 2008.

Heller, Sarah-Grace, *Fashion in Medieval France*, Cambridge: D. S. Brewer 2007.

Henare, Amiria, Holbraad, Martin, and Wastell, Sari, 'Introduction: Thinking Through Things', in idem, *Thinking Through Things: Theorising Artefacts Ethnographically*, London: Routledge 2007, 1–31.

Hentschell, Roze, *The Culture of Cloth in Early Modern England: Textual Constructions of a National Identity*, Aldershot: Ashgate 2008.

Heydenreich, Gunnar, *Lucas Cranach the Elder: Painting Materials, Techniques and Workshop Practices*, Amsterdam: Amsterdam University Press 2007.

Hirschi, Caspar, *Wettkampf der Nationen: Konstruktionen einer deutschen Ehrgemeinschaft an der Wende vom Mittelalter zur Neuzeit*, Göttingen: Wallstein 2005.

Hochmuth, Christian, *Globale Güter – lokale Aneignung. Kaffee, Tee, Schokolade und Tabak im frühneuzeitlichen Dresden*, Konstanz: UVK Verlag 2008.

Hodgen, Margaret T., *Early Anthropology in the Sixteenth and Seventeenth Centuries*, Philadelphia: Pennsylvania University Press 1964.

Hollander, Anne, *Seeing through Clothes*, Los Angeles: University of California Press 1993.

Howell, Martha, 'Fixing Movables: Gifts by Testament in Late Medieval Douai', in *Past & Present*, 150 (1996), 3–45.

Hughes, Diane Owen, 'Distinguishing Signs: Ear-Rings, Jews and Franciscan Regulation in the Italian Renaissance City', *Past & Present*, 112 (1986), 3–59.

——'Sumptuary Law and Social Relations in Renaissance Italy', in John Bossy (ed.), *Disputes and Settlements: Law and Human Relations in the West*, Cambridge: Cambridge University Press 1983, 69–99.

von Hülsen-Esch, Andrea, 'Kleider machen Leute. Zur Gruppenrepräsentation von Gelehrten im Spätmittelalter', in Otto Gerhard Oexle and Andrea von Hülsen-Esch (eds.), *Die Repräsentation der Gruppen. Texte – Bilder – Objekte*, Göttingen: Vandenhoeck 1999, 225–258.

——*Gelehrte im Bild: Repräsentation, Darstellung und Wahrnehmung einer sozialen Gruppe im Mittelalter*, Göttingen: Vandenhoeck 2006.

Hunt, Alan, *Governance of the Consuming Passions: A History of Sumptuary Laws*, Houndsmill: Macmillan 1996.

Huntebrinker, Jan Willem, *'fromme Knechte' und 'gartteufel'. Söldner als soziale Gruppe im 16. und 17. Jahrhundert*, D.Phil. diss. Dresden 2008.

Ikegami, Eiko, *Bonds of Civility: Aesthetic Networks and the Political Origins of Japanese Culture*, Cambridge: Cambridge University Press 2005.

Ilg, Ulrike, 'The Cultural Significance of Costume Books in Sixteenth-Century Europe', in Catherine Richardson (ed.), *Clothing Culture 1350–1650*, Aldershot: Ashgate 2004.

Illouz, Eva, *Cold Intimacies: The Making of Emotional Capitalism*, Cambridge: Polity Press 2007.

Inalcik, Halil, 'Bursa and the Silk Trade', in id. and Donald Quataert (eds.), *An Economic and Social History of the Ottoman Empire*, vol. 1, Cambridge, Cambridge University Press 1994, 218–255.

Isaac, Benjamin, *The Invention of Racism in Classical Antiquity*, Princeton: Princeton University Press 2004.

Jacob, Margaret C., *Strangers Nowhere in the World: The Rise of Cosmopolitanism in Early Modern Europe*, Philadelphia: University of Philadelphia Press 2006.

Jancke, Gabriele, *Autobiographie als soziale Praxis: Beziehungskonzepte in Selbstzeugnissen des 15. und 16. Jahrhunderts im deutschsprachigen Raum*, Vienna: Böhlau 2002.

——and Ulbrich, Claudia (eds.), *Vom Individuum zur Person: neue Konzepte im Spannungsfeld von Autobiographietheorie und Selbstzeugnisforschung*, Göttingen: Wallstein 2005.

Jardine, Lisa, *Worldly Goods: A New History of the Renaissance*, London: Macmillan 1996.

Jaritz, Gerhard, 'Kleidung und Prestige-Konkurrenz: Unterschiedliche Identitäten in der städtischen Gesellschaft unter Normierungszwängen', in Neithard Bulst and Robert Jütte (eds.), 'Zwischen Sein und Schein: Kleidung und Identität in der ständischen Gesellschaft', *Saeculum*, 44 (1993), 8–31.

Jenkins, David (ed.), *The Cambridge History of Western Textiles*, vol. 1, Cambridge: Cambridge University Press 2003.

Joas, Hans, *Die Kreativität des Handelns*, Frankfurt-on-Main: Suhrkamp 1992.

Johnson, Christine R., *The German Discovery of the World: Renaissance Encounters with the Strange and Marvellous*, Charlottesville: University of Virginia Press 2008.

Johnstone, Pauline, *High Fashion in the Church: The Place of Church Vestments in the History of Art from the Ninth to the Nineteenth Century*, Leeds: Maney 2002.

Jones, Ann Rosalind and Stallybrass, Peter, *Renaissance Clothing and the Material of Memory*, Cambridge: Cambridge University Press 2000.

Jordanova, Ludmilla, 'Image Matters', *Historical Journal*, 51 (2008), 777–792.

Junjea, Monica, 'Braided Histories? Visuelle Praktiken des indischen Moghulreiches zwischen Mimesis und Alterität', *Historische Anthropologie*, 16 (2008), 187–204.

Kagan, Richard L., *Urban Images of the Hispanic World 1493–1793*, New Haven: Yale University Press, 2000.

Kantorowicz, Ernst H., *The King's Two Bodies: A Study in Medieval Political Theology*, Princeton: Princeton University Press 1957.

——*Laudes Regiae: A Study in Liturgical Acclamations and Medieval Ruler Worship*, Berkeley: University of California Press 1946.

Katzew, Ilona, *Casta Painting: Images of Race in Eighteenth-Century Mexico*, New Haven: Yale University Press 2004.

Kaufmann, Thomas, *Konfession und Kultur: Lutherischer Protestantismus in der zweiten Hälfte des Reformationsjahrhunderts*, Tübingen: Mohr Siebeck 2006.

——*Das Ende der Reformation: Magdeburgs 'Herrgotts Kanzlei' (1548–1551/2)*, Tübingen: Mohr Siebeck 2003.

Kellenbenz, Hermann, *Fremde Kaufleute auf der Iberischen Halbinsel*, Cologne: Böhlau 1970.

Keller-Drescher, Lioba, *Die Ordnung der Kleider: ländliche Mode in Württemberg 1750–1850*, Tubingen: Vereinigung f. Volkskunde 2003.

Kemp, Martin, ' "Wrought by no Artist's Hand": The Natural, the Artificial, the Exotic, and the Scientific in Artefacts from the Renaissance', in Claire Farago (ed.), *Reframing the Renaissance: Visual Culture in Europe and Latin America, 1450–1650*, New Haven: Yale University Press 1995, 177–196.

Klaniczay, Gábor, 'Everyday Life and Elites in the Later Middle Ages: The Civilised and the Barbarian', in Peter Linehan and Janet L. Nelson (eds.), *The Medieval World*, London: Routledge 2001, 671–690.

Klein, Lawrence E., 'Politeness for Plebes: Consumption and Social Identity in Early Eighteenth-Century England', in Ann Bermingham and John Brewer (eds.), *The Consumption of Culture 1600–1800: Image, Object, Text*, London: Routledge, 1995, 341–361.

Kleinschmidt, Harald, *Ruling the Waves: Emperor Maximilian I, the Search for Islands and the Transformation of the European World Picture c.1500*, Utrecht: Hes & de Graaf 2008.

Kobelt-Groch, Marion, *Aufsässige Töchter Gottes: Frauen im Bauernkrieg und in den Täuferbewegungen*, Frankfurt–on–Main: Campus 1993.

Koch, Ernst, 'Andreas Musculus und die Konfessionalisierung des Luthertums', in Hans-Christoph Rublack (ed.), *Die lutherische Konfessionalisierung in Deutschland: wissenschaftliches Symposium des Vereins für Reformationsgeschichte 1988*, Gütersloh: Gerd Mohn 1992, 250–273.

Koerner, Joseph Leo, *The Reformation of the Image*, Chicago: University of Chicago Press 2004.

——*The Moment of Self-Portraiture in German Renaissance Art*, Chicago: Chicago University Press 1996.

König, René, *A La Mode: On the Social Psychology of Fashion*, transl. F. Bradley, New York: Seabury Press 1973.

Kovesi Killerby, Catherine, ' "Heralds of a well-instructed mind": Nicolosa Sanuti's Defence of Women and their Clothes', *Renaissance Studies*, 13 (1999), 255–282.

Kranz, Anette, *Christoph Amberger: Bildnismaler zu Augsburg. Städtische Eliten im Spiegel ihrer Porträts*, Regensburg: Schnell & Steiner 2004.

Kraß, Andreas, *Geschriebene Kleider: Höfische Identität als literarisches Spiel*, Tübingen: A. Francke Verlag 2006.

Kroos, Renate, *Niedersächsische Bildstickereien des Mittelalters*, Berlin: Deutscher Verlag für Kunstwissenschaft 1970.

Kuchta, David, *The Three-piece Suit and Modern Masculinity*, Berkeley: University of California Press 2002.

Kürbis, Holger, *Hispania descripta: Von der Reise zum Bericht. Deutschsprachige Reiseberichte des 16. und 17. Jahrhundert über Spanien: Ein Beitrag zur Struktur und Funktion der frühneuzeitlichen Reiseliteratur*, Frankfurt-on-Main: Peter Lang 2003.

Kurzel-Runtschneider, Monica, *Glanzvolles Elend: Die Inventare der Herzogin Jacobe von Jülich–Kleve–Berg (1558–1597)*, Vienna: Böhlau 1993.

Landau, David and Parshall, Peter (eds.), *The Renaissance Print, 1470–1550*, New Haven: Yale University Press 1994.

Lehmann-Langholz, Ulrike, *Kleiderkritik in mittelalterlicher Dichtung: Der Arme Hartmann, Heinrich 'von Melk', Neidhart, Wernher der Gaertenaere und ein Ausblick auf die Stellungnahmen spätmittelalterlicher Dichter*, Frankfurt-on-Main: Peter Lang 1985.

Lehner, Julia, *Die Mode im alten Nürnberg*, Nürnberg: Schriftenreihe des Stadtarchivs Nürnberg 1984.

Leitch, Stephanie, 'Burgkmair's People of Africa and India (1508) and the Origins of Ethnography in Print', *Art Bulletin*, XCI (2009), 134–159.

Lemire, Beverly, 'Consumerism in Pre-Industrial and Early Industrial England: The Trade in Second-hand Clothes', *Journal of British Studies*, 27 (1998), 1–24.

——*Dress, Culture and Commerce: The English Clothing Trade before the Factory, 1660–1800*, London: Macmillan 1997.

——*Fashion's Favourite: The Cotton Trade and the Consumer in Britain, 1660–1800*, Oxford: Oxford University Press 1991.

Lieb, Norbert, *Die Fugger und die Kunst*, vol. 2, *Im Zeitalter der hohen Renaissance*, Munich: Schnell & Steiner 1958.

Linthicum, M. Channing, *Costume in the Drama of Shakespeare and his Contemporaries*, Oxford: Clarendon Press 1936.

Lopes, Marília dos Santos, *Afrika: Eine neue Welt in deutschen Schriften des 16. und 17. Jahrhunderts*, Stuttgart: Steiner 1992.

Lowe, Kate, 'The Stereotyping of Black Africans in Renaissance Europe', in K. J. P. Lowe and T. F. Earle (eds.), *Black Africans in Europe*, Cambridge: Cambridge University Press 2005, 17–47.

Lüttenberg, Thomas, 'Der Nackte Mann mit Schere und Tuchballen: Ein Sinnbild der Verhaltensnormierung und seine Entwicklung im 16. Jahrhundert', in Andrea Bentlage, Andreas Priever, and Peter Schuster (eds.), *Recht und Verhalten in vormodernen Gesellschaften. Festschrift für Neithart Bulst*, Bielefeld: Verlag für Regionalgeschichte 2008, 123–138.

——'The Cod-Piece: A Renaissance Fashion between Sign and Artefact', *The Medieval History Journal*, 8 (2005), 49–81.

——'Législation symbolique ou contrainte efficace?: Les lois vestimentaires dans les villes allemandes au XVIe siècle', in Christine Aribaud and Sylvie Mouysset (eds.), *Vêture & Pouvoir XIIIe–XX siècle*, Toulouse: Framespa 2003, 137–148.

——and Priever, Andreas, ' "...Hergegen macht das kleyd oft einen Mann und Helden". Deutsche Alamode–Flugblätter des 17. Jahrhunderts im europäischen Kontext', in Adelheid Rasche and Gundula Wolter (eds.), *Ridikül! Mode in der Karikatur 1600 bis 1900*, Cologne: DuMont 1993, 153–168.

Lyn, John A. II, *Women, Armies, and Warfare in Early Modern Europe*, Cambridge: Cambridge University Press 2008.

Mansel, Philip, *Dressed to Rule: Royal and Court Costume from Louis XIV to Elizabeth II*, New Haven: Yale University Press 2005.

Marek, Kirstin, *Die Körper des Königs: Effigies, Bildpolitik und Heiligkeit*, Munich: W. Fink 2009.

Martin, John Jeffries, 'Inventing Sincerity, Refashioning Prudence: The Discovery of the Individual in Renaissance Europe', *American Historical Review*, 102 (1997), 1309–1342.

Mason, Peter, *The Lives of Images*, London: Reaktion Books 2001.

Massing, Jean Michel, *Studies in Imagery*, vol. II, London: Pindar Press 2007.

Maue, Hermann, Kupper, Christine, Quasi Centrum Europae, Nuremberg: Germanisches Nationalmuseum 2002.

Medick, Hans, *Weben und Überleben in Laichingen 1650–1900: Lokalgeschichte als allgemeine Geschichte*, Göttingen: Vandenhoeck 1996.

Meléndez, Mariselle, 'Visualising Difference: The Rhetoric of Clothing in Colonial Spanish America', in Regina A. Root (ed.), *The Latin American Fashion Reader*, Oxford: Berg 2005, 17–30.

Mentges, Gabriele, 'Fashion, Time and the Consumption of a Renaissance Man in Germany: The Costume Book of Matthäus Schwarz of Augsburg, 1496–1564', *Gender & History*, 14 (2002), 382–402.

Midelfort, H. C. Erik, *A History of Madness in Sixteenth-Century Germany*, Stanford: Stanford University Press 1999.

Mikhaila Ninya and Malcolm Davies, Jane, *The Tudor Tailor: Reconstructing Sixteenth-Century Dress*, Batsford: Anova Books 2006.

Miller, Daniel, 'Consumption and Commmodities', *Annual Review of Anthropology*, 24 (1995), 141–161.

Mitchell, W. J. T., *What Do Pictures Want? The Lives and Loves of Images*, Chicago: University of Chicago Press 2005.

Mohrmann, Ruth-E., *Alltagswelt im Land Braunschweig. Städtische und ländliche Wohnkultur vom 16. bis zum frühen 20. Jahrhundert*, 2 vols., Münster: Coppenrath 1990.

Molà, Luca, *The Silk Industry of Renaissance Venice*, Baltimore: Johns Hopkins University Press 2000.

Molina, Álvaro and Vega, Jesusa, *Vestir la Identidad, Construir la Apariencia: La cuestión del Traje en la España del Siglo XVIII*, Madrid: Ayuntamiento de Madrid 2004.

Monnas, Lisa, *Merchants, Princes and Painters: Silk Fabrics in Italian and Northern Paintings 1300–1550*, New Haven: Yale University Press 2009.

Moos, Peter von, 'Das Mittelalterliche Kleid als Identitätssymbol und Identifikationsmittel', in idem (ed.), *Unverwechselbarkeit: Persönliche Identität und Identifikation in der vormodernen Gesellschaft*, Cologne: Böhlau 2004, 123–139.

Morra, Joanne, and Smith, Marquard, (eds.), *Visual Culture: Critical Concepts in Media and Cultural Studies*, Abingdon, NY: Routledge 2006.

Morrall, Andrew, 'Ornament as Evidence', in Karen Harvey (ed.), *History and Material Culture: A Student's Guide to Approaching Alternative Sources*, London: Routledge 2009, 47–66.

——*Jörg Breu the Elder: Art, Culture and Belief in Reformation Augsburg*, Aldershot: Ashgate 2002.

Moser-Rath, Elfriede, *Dem Kirchenvolk die Leviten gelesen: Alltag im Spiegel süddeutscher Barockpredigten*, Stuttgart: J. B. Metzler 1992.

Mosher Stuart, Susan, *Gilding the Market: Luxury and Fashion in Fourteenth-Century Italy*, Philadelphia: University of Pennsylvania Press 2006.

Moxey, Keith, 'Visual Studies and the Iconic Turn', *Journal of Visual Culture*, 7 (2008), 131–146.

——*Peasants, Warriors and Wives: Popular Imagery in the Reformation*, Chicago: University of Chicago Press 1989.

Mukerji, Chandra, *From Graven Images: Patterns of Modern Materialism*, New York: Columbia University Press 1983.

Müller, Jan-Dirk, 'Writing – Speech – Image: The Competition of Signs', in Kathryn Starkey and Horst Wenzel (eds.), *Visual Culture and the German Middle Ages*, New York: Palgrave 2005, 35–52.

——*Gedechtnus: Literatur und Hofgesellschaft um Maximilian I*, Munich: Beck 1982.

Munro, John H., 'Medieval Woollens: Textiles, Textile Technology and Industrial Organisation, c.800–1500', in David Jenkins (ed.), *The Cambridge History of Western Textiles*, vol. 1, Cambridge: Cambridge University Press 2003, 181–227.

Murdock, Graeme, 'Did Calvinists have a Guilt Complex?: Reformed Religion, Conscience and Regulation in Early Modern Europe', in Kate Cooper and Jeremy Gregory (eds.), *Retribution, Repentance, and Reconciliation*, Woodbridge: The Boydell Press 2004, 138–158.

——'Dressed to Repress?: Protestant Clerical Dress and the Regulation of Morality in Early Modern Europe', *Fashion Theory*, 4 (2000), 179–200.

Muthesius, Anna, 'Silk in the Medieval World', in David Jenkins (ed.), *The Cambridge History of Western Textiles*, vol. 1, Cambridge: Cambridge University Press 2003, 325–355.

Neçipoglu, Gülru, 'Süleyman the Magnificent and the Representation of Power in the Context of Ottoman–Habsburg–Papal Rivalry', *The Art Bulletin*, 71 (1989), 407–427.

Neuber, Wolfgang, *Fremde Welt im europäischen Horizont: Zur Topik der deutschen Amerika–Reiseberichte der Frühen Neuzeit*, Berlin: E. Schmidt 1991.

Newman, Karen, *Fashioning Femininity and English Renaissance Drama*, Chicago: Chicago University Press 1991.

Newton, Stella Mary, *Fashion in the Age of the Black Prince: A Study of the Years 1340–1365*, Woodbridge: The Boydell Press 1980.

Niefanger, Dirk, *Geschichtsdrama in der Frühen Neuzeit 1495–1773*, Tübingen: M. Niemeyer 2005.

North, Michael, *'Material Delight and the Joy of Living': Cultural Consumption in the Age of Enlightenment in Germany*, transl. Pamela Selwyn, Aldershot: Ashgate 2008.

——*Genuss und Glück des Lebens: Kulturkonsum im Zeitalter der Aufklärung*, Vienna: Böhlau 2003.

O'Malley, Michelle and Welch, Evelyn (eds.), *The Material Renaissance*, Manchester: Manchester University Press 2007.

Oberman, Heiko, 'Teufelsdreck: Eschatology and Scatology in the "Old" Luther', *Sixteenth Century Journal*, 19 (1988), 435–450.

Oelke, Harry, *Die Konfessionsbildung des 16. Jahrhunderts im Spiegel illustrierter Flugblätter*, Berlin: de Gruyter 1992.

Ogilvie, Sheilagh, *A Bitter Living: Women, Markets, and Social Capital in Early Modern Germany*, Oxford: Oxford University Press 2003.

Orchard, Karin, *Annäherung der Geschlechter: Androgynie in der Kunst des Cinquecento*, Münster: Lit Verlag 1992.

Ozment, Steven, *Flesh and Spirit: Private Life in Early Modern Germany*, New York: Knopf 1999.

——*Magdalena and Balthasar: An Intimate Portrait of Life in Sixteenth-Century Europe Revealed in the Letters of a Nuremberg Husband and Wife*, New Haven: Yale University Press 1986.

Paas, John Roger (ed.), *Der Franken Rom: Nürnbergs Blütezeit in der zweiten Hälfte des 17. Jahrhunderts*, Wiesbaden: Harrassowitz 1996.

Packeiser, Thomas, 'Pathoseformel einer "christlichen Stadt"? Ausgleich und Heilsanspruch im Sakramentsretabel der Wittenberger Stadtpfarrkirche', in Andreas Tacke (ed.), *Lucas Cranach d. Ä. Zum 450: Todesjahr*, Evangelische Verlagsanstalt, Leipzig 2007, 233–277.

Panofsky, Erwin, *The Life and Art of Albrecht Dürer*, first published in 1943, with a new introduction by Jeffrey Chipps Smith, Princeton: Princeton University Press 2005.

Paresys, Isabelle, 'Apparences vestimentaires et cartographie de l'espace en Europe occidentale aux XVIe et XVIIe siècle', in Isabelle Paresys (ed.), *Paraître et apparences en Europe occidentale: Du Moyen Âge à nos jours*, Villeneuv d'Ascq: Presses du Septentrion 2008, 253–261.

——'Paraître et se vêtir au XVIe siècle : morales vestimentaires', in Marie Viallon (ed.), *Paraître et se vêtir au XVIe siècle: Actes du XIIIe Colloque du Puy-en-Velay*, Saint Étienne: Publications de L'Université de Saint Étienne 2006, 11–36.

Parkins, Wendy, *Fashioning the Body Politic: Dress, Gender, Citizenship*, Oxford: Berg 2002.

Parshall, Linda B. and Peter W., *Art and the Reformation: An Annotated Bibliography*, Boston: G. K. Hall 1986.

Pastoureau, Michel, *Black: The History of a Color*, Princeton: Princeton University Press 2008.

——*The Devil's Cloth: A History of Stripes and Striped Fabric*, transl. Jody Gladding, New York: Columbia University Press 2001.

Pettegree, Andrew, *Reformation and the Culture of Persuasion*, Cambridge: Cambridge University Press 2005.

Pietsch, Johannes and Stolleis, Karen (eds.), *Kölner Patrizier–und Bürgerkleidung des 17. Jahrhunders: Die Kostümsammlung Hüpsch im Hessischen Landesmuseum Darmstadt*, Riggis: Abbegg–Stiftung 2008.

——*Zwei Schauben aus dem Bayerischen Nationalmuseum München: Ein Beitrag zur Kostümforschung*, Munich: Siegl 2004.

Pilz, K., 'Jost Amman', in Andreas Klimt and Michael Steppes (eds.), *Allgemeines Künstlerlexikon*, vol. 3, Munich–Leipzig: K. G. Saur 1992, 246–249.

Pinney, Chris and Peterson, Nicolas (eds.), *Photography's other History*, Durham: Duke University Press 2003.

Piponnier, Françoise and Mane, Perrine, *Dress in the Middle Ages*, New Haven: Yale University Press 1995.

Pohl, Horst (ed.), Willibald Imhof, *Enkel und Erbe Willibald Pirckheimers*, Nuremberg: Selbstverlag Stadtrat 1992.

Pol, Lotte van de, *Der Bürger und die Hure: Das Sündige Gewerbe in Amsterdam in der Frühen Neuzeit*, transl. Rosemarie Still, Frankfurt-on-Main: Campus 2006.

Pölnitz, Götz Freiherr von and Kellenbenz, Hermann, *Anton Fugger*, 3 vols., Tübingen: Mohr Siebeck 1986.

Pomeranz, Kenneth, *The Great Divergence: China, Europe, and the Making of the Modern World Economy*, Princeton: Princeton University Press 2000.

Porter, Martin, *Windows of the Soul: The Art of Physiognomy in European Culture 1470–1780*, Oxford: Oxford University Press 2005.

Privat-Savigny, M.-A., and Guelton, M.-H., 'Fleurons et palmettes: Quelques tissus à petits motifs des années 1560–1630 destinés à l'habillement', in Marie Viallon (ed.), *Paraître et se vêtir au XVIe siècle: Actes du XIIIe Colloque du Puy-en-Velay*, Saint Étienne: Publications de L'Université de Saint-Étienne 2006, 223–242.

Puff, Helmut, *Sodomy in Reformation Germany and Switzerland 1400–1600*, Chicago: University of Chicago Press 2003.

Purdy, Daniel L., *The Tyranny of Elegance: Consumer Cosmopolitanism in the Era of Goethe*, Baltimore: Johns Hopkins Press 1998.

Raby, Julian, *Venice, Dürer and the Oriental Mode*, London: Islamic Art Publications 1982.

Rangström, Lena, *Modelejon Manligt Mode, 1500–Tal, 1600–Tal, 1700–Tal*, Stockholm: Livrustkammaren 2002.

Rapp Buri, Anna, and Stucky-Schürer, Monica, *Die Sieben Planeten und ihre Kinder: Eine 1547–1549 datierte Tapisseriefolge in der Fondation Martin Bodmer*, Basle: Schwabe Verlag 2008.

Raudszus, Gabriele, *Die Zeichensprache der Kleidung: Untersuchungen zur Symbolik des Gewandes in der deutschen Epik des Mittelalters*, Hildesheim: Olms 1985.

Rehermann, Ernst Heinrich, *Das Predigtexempel bei protestantischen Theologen des 16. und 17. Jahrhunderts*, Göttingen: Otto Schwartz & Co. 1977.

Reich, Ann-Kathrin, *Kleidung als Spiegelbild sozialer Differenzierung: Städtische Kleiderordnungen vom 14. bis zum 17. Jahrhundert im Spiegel der Altstadt Hannover*, Hannover: Hahnsche Buchhandlung 2005.

Reichardt, Rolf, 'Bild– und Mediengeschichte', in Joachim Eibach and Günther Lottes (eds.), *Kompass der Geschichtswissenschaft: Ein Handbuch*, Göttingen: Vandenhoeck 2002, 219–230.

Reichert, Folker, *Erfahrung der Welt: Reisen und Kulturbewegung im späten Mittelalter*, Stuttgart: W. Kohlhammer 2001.

Renger, Konrad, *Lockere Gesellschaft: Zur Ikonographie des Verlorenen Sohnes und von Wirtshausszenen in der niederländischen Malerei*, Berlin: Gebrüder Mann Verlag 1970.

Ribeiro, Aileen, *Fashion and Fiction: Dress in the Art and Literature in Stuart England*, New Haven: Yale University Press 2005.

——'Dress in the Early Modern Period, *c.*1500–1780', in David Jenkins (ed.), *The Cambridge History of Textiles*, vol. 1, Cambridge: Cambridge University Press 2003, 659–690.

——*Dress and Morality*, London: Batsford 1986.

Richardson, Catherine (ed.), *Clothing Culture, 1350–1650*, Aldershot: Ashgate 2004.

Riello, Giorgio and Parthasarathi, Prasannan (eds.), *The Spinning World: A Global History of Cotton Textiles, 1200–1850*, Oxford: Oxford University Press 2009.

Rieske-Braun, Uwe, *Duellum mirabile: Studien zum Kampfmotiv in Martin Luthers Theologie*, Göttingen: Vandenhoeck 1999.

Robert, Jörg, *Konrad Celtis und das Projekt der deutschen Dichtung: Studien zur humanistischen Konstitution von Poetik, Philosophie, Nation und Ich*, Tübingen: M. Niemeyer 2003.

Roche, Daniel, *The Culture of Clothing: Dress and Fashion in the 'Ancien Regime'*, transl. Jane Birrell, Cambridge: Cambridge University Press 1994.

Roeck, Bernd, *Das historische Auge: Kunstwerke als Zeugen ihrer Zeit*, Göttingen: Vandenhoeck 2004.

——'Visual Turn? Kulturgeschichte und die Bilder', *Geschichte und Gesellschaft* 29 (2003), 294–315.

Roettig, Petra, *Reformation als Apokalypse: Die Holzschnitte von Matthias Gerung im Codex germanicus 6592 der Bayrischen Staatsbibliothek in München*, Bern: Peter Lang 1998/90.

Rogg, Matthias, '"Zerhauen und zerschnitten, nach adelichen Sitten": Herkunft, Entwicklung und Funktion soldatischer Tracht des 16. Jahrhunderts im Spiegel zeitgenössischer Kunst', in Bernhard R. Kroener and Ralf Pöve (eds.), *Krieg und Frieden: Militär und Gesellschaft in der Frühen Neuzeit*, Paderborn: Ferdinand Schöningh 1996, 109–135.

Rogge, Jörg, *Für den gemeinen Nutzen: Politisches Handeln und Politikverständnis von Rat und Bürgerschaft in Augsburg im Spätmittlelalter*, Tübingen: M. Niemeyer Verlag 1996.

Roller, Hans-Ulrich, *Der Nürnberger Schembartlauf: Studien zum Fest–und Maskenwesen des späten Mittelalter*, Tübingen: Verein F. Volkskunde 1965.

Roper, Lyndal, *Oedipus & the Devil: Witchcraft, Sexuality and Religion in Early Modern Europe*, London: Routledge 1994.

—— *The Holy Household: Women and Morals in Reformation Augsburg*, Oxford: Oxford University Press 1989.

—— ‘“Going to Church and Street”: Weddings in Reformation Augsburg’, *Past & Present*, 106 (1985), 62–101.

Rosenthal, Magaret F., ‘Fashion, Custom, and Culture in Two Early Modern Illustrated Albums’, in Maurizio Rippa Bonati and Valeria Finucci (eds.), *Mores Italiae: Costume and Life in the Renaissance*, Cittadella: Biblos 2007, 79–108.

Ross, Robert, *Clothing: A Global History, Or, The Imperialists' New Clothes*, Cambridge: Polity 2008.

Rosseaux, Ulrich, *Freiräume: Unterhaltung, Vergnügen und Erholung in Dresden (1694–1830)*, Cologne: Böhlau 2007.

Rublack, Hans-Christoph, *...hat die Nonne den Pfarrer geküsst? Aus dem Alltag der Reformationszeit*, Gütersloh: GTB Siebenstern 1991.

Rublack, Ulinka, *Reformation Europe*, Cambridge: Cambridge University Press 2005.

—— *The Crimes of Women in Early Modern Germany*, Oxford: Oxford University Press 1999.

Rummel, Philipp von, *Habitus barbarus: Kleidung und Repräsentation spätantiker Eliten im 4. und 5. Jahrhundert*, Berlin: de Gruyter 2005.

Sabean, David Warren, *Property, Production, and Family in Neckarhausen, 1700–1870*, Cambridge: Cambridge University Press 1990.

Schad, Martha, *Die Frauen des Hauses Fugger von der Lilie (15.–17. Jahrhundert). Augsburg – Ortenburg – Trient*, Tübingen: Mohr Siebeck 1989.

Schama, Simon, *The Embarrassment of Riches: An Interpretation of Dutch Culture in the Golden Age*, New York: Knopf 1987.

Scheible, Helga, ‘Willibald Pirckheimers Persönlickeit im Spiegel seines Briefwechsels am Beispiel seines Verhältnisses zum Klosterwesen’, in Franz Fuchs (ed.), *Die Pirckheimer: Humanismus in einer Nürnberger Patrizierfamilie*, Munich: Fink 2006, 73–88.

Schick, Leslie Meral, ‘The Place of Dress in Pre-modern Costume Albums’, in Suraiya Faroqhi and Christoph K. Neumann (eds.), *Ottoman Costumes: From Textile to Identity*, Istanbul: Eren 2004, 97–116.

Schilling, Heinz, *Die Stadt in der Frühen Neuzeit*, Munich: Oldenbourg 1993.

Schilling, Michael, *Bildpublizistik der frühen Neuzeit: Aufgabe und Leistungen des illustrierten Flugblatts in Deutschland bis um 1700*, Tübingen: M. Niemeyer 1990.

Schmid Blumer, Verena, *Ikonographie und Sprachbild: Zur reformatorischen Flugschrift 'der gestryfft Schwitzer Baur'*, Tübingen: M. Niemeyer 2004.

Schmidt, Alexander, *Vaterlandsliebe und Religionskonflikt: Politische Diskurse im Alten Reich (1555–1648)*, Leiden: Brill 2007.

Schmidt, Erich, *Deutsche Volkskunde im Zeitalter des Huamnismus und der Reformation*, Berlin: E. Ebering 1904.

Schnabel, Werner Wilhelm, *Das Stammbuch: Konstitution und Geschichte einer textsortenbezogenen Sammelform bis ins erste Drittel des 18. Jahrhunderts*, Tübingen: M. Niemeyer 2003.

Schneider, Jane, 'Peacocks and Penguins: The Political Economy of European Cloth and Colors', *American Ethnologist*, 5 (1978), 413–447.

Schnitzer, Claudia, *Höfische Maskeraden: Funktion und Ausstattung von Verkleidungsdivertissements an deutschen Höfen der Frühen Neuzeit*, Tübingen: M. Niemeyer Verlag 1999.

Scholz-Hänsel, Michael, *El Greco: Der Großinquisitor: Neues Licht auf eine schwarze Legende*, Frankurt-on-Main: Fischer 1991.

Schorn-Schuette, Luise, *Evangelische Geistlichkeit in der Frühen Neuzeit: Deren Anteil an der Erfahrung frühmoderner Staatlichkeit und Gesellschaft*, Gütersloh: Gütersloher Verlagshaus 1996.

Schreiner, Klaus and Signori, Gabriela (eds.), *Bilder, Texte, Rituale: Wirklichkeitsbezug und Wirklichkeitskonstruktion politisch–rechtlicher Kommunikationsmedien in Stadt– und Adelsgesellschaften des spätern Mittelalters*, Berlin: Duncker & Humblot 2000.

Schulze, Winfried, 'Vom Gemeinnutz zum Eigennutz: Über den Normenwandel in der ständischen Gesellschaft der Frühen Neuzeit', *Historische Zeitschrift*, 243 (1986), 591–626.

Scott, Tom, *Society and Economy in Germany, 1300–1600*, Houndsmill: Palgrave 2002.

Scribner, R. W., *Religion and Culture in Germany (1400–1800)*, (ed.) Lyndal Roper, Leiden: Brill 2001.

——*For the Sake of the Simple Folk: Popular Propaganda for the German Reformation*, Oxford: Clarendon Press 1994.

——*Popular Culture and Popular Movements in Reformation Germany*, London: Hambledon 1987.

Seebaß, Gottfried, *Das reformatorische Werk des Andreas Osiander*, Nürnberg: Verein F. Kirchengeschichte 1967.

Sekatcheva, Oksana, 'The Formation of Russian Women's Costume at the Time before the Reforms of Peter the Great', in Catherine Richardson (ed.), *Clothing Culture, 1350–1650*, Aldershot: Ashgate 2004, 77–94.

Senn, Matthias (ed.), *Die Wickiana: Johann Jakob Wicks Nachrichtensammlung aus dem 16. Jahrhundert*, Zurich: Raggi Verlag 1975.

Sennett, Richard, *The Fall of Public Man*, New York: Knopf 1974.

Shannon, Brent, *The Cut of His Coat: Men, Dress, and Consumer Culture in Britain, 1860–1914*, Athens: Ohio University Press, 2006.

Shepard, Alexandra, *Meanings of Manhood in Early Modern England*, Oxford: Oxford University Press 2003.

Signori, Gabriela, 'Veil, Hat or Hair?: Reflections on an Asymmetrical Relationship', *The Medieval History Journal*, 8 (2005), 25–48.

Silver, Larry, *Marketing Maximilian: The Visual Ideology of a Holy Roman Emperor*, Princeton: Princeton University Press 2008.

——'Shining Armor: Emperor Maximilian, Chivalry, and War', in Pia Cuneo (ed.), *Artful Armies, Beautiful Battles: Art and Warfare in Early Modern Europe*, Leiden: Brill 2002, 61–86.

Simmel, Georg, 'Philosophie der Mode (1905)', in Otthein Rammstedt (ed.), *Georg Simmel: Gesamtausgabe*, vol. 10, Frankfurt-on-Main: Suhrkamp 1995, 9–37.

Simon-Muscheid, Katharina, *Die Dinge im Schnittpunkt sozialer Beziehungsnetze: Reden und Objekte im Alltag (Oberrhein, 14. bis 16. Jahrhundert)*, Göttingen: Vandenhoeck 2004.

——'"und ob sie schon einen dienst finden, so sind sit nit bekleidet dernoch": Die Kleidung der städtischen Unterschichten zwischen Projektionen und Realität im Spätmittelalter und in der frühen Neuzeit', in Neithard Bulst and Robert Jütte (eds.), 'Zwischen Sein und Schein. Kleidung und Identität in der ständischen Gesellschaft', *Saeculum*, 44 (1993), 47–64.

Skinner, Quentin, *Visions of Politics, vol. 2, Renaissance Virtues*, Cambridge: Cambridge University Press 2002.

Slanicka, Simona, *Krieg der Zeichen: Die visuelle Politik Johanns ohne Furcht und der armagnakisch–burgundische Bürgerkrieg*, Göttingen: Vandenhoeck 2002.

Smith, Pamela H., *The Body of the Artisan: Art and Experience in the Scientific Revolution*, Chicago: Chicago University Press 2004.

——'Art, Science, and Visual Culture in Early Modern Europe', *Isis*, 97 (2006), 83–100.

——'Science and Taste: Painting, Passions, and the New Philosophy in Seventeenth-Century Leiden', *Isis*, 90 (1999), 432–435.

——and Findlen, Paula (eds.), *Merchants & Marvels: Commerce, Science and Art in Early Modern Europe*, New York: Routledge 2002.

Smith, Woodruff D., *Consumption and the Making of Respectability 1600–1800*, New York: Routledge 2002.

Snyder, Janet, 'Cloth from the Promised Land: Appropriated Islamic Tiraz in Twelfth-Century French Sculpture', in E. Jane Burns (ed.), *Medieval Fabrications: Dress, Textiles, Clothwork, and Other Cultural Imaginings*, New York: Palgrave 2004, 147–164.

Socolow, Susan Migden, *The Women of Colonial Latin America*, Cambridge: Cambridge University Press 2000.

Soden, Franz Freiherr von, *Beiträge zur Geschichte der Reformation und der Sitten jener Zeit mit besonderem Hinblick auf Christoph Scheurl II*, Nuremberg: Bauer & Raspe 1855.

Soergel, Philip M., 'Baggy Pants and Demons: Andreas Musculus's Condemnation of the Evils of Sixteenth-Century Dress', in Andrea Bendlage et al. (eds.), *Recht und Verhalten in vormodernen Gesellschaften*, Bielefeld: Verlag für Regionalgeschichte, Bielefeld 2008, 139–154.

Sommer, Barbara A., 'Wigs, Weapons, Tattoos and Shoes: Getting Dressed in Colonial Brazil', in Mina Roces and Louise Edwards (eds.), *The Politics of Dress in Asia and The Americas*, Brighton: Sussex Academic Press 2007, 200–214.

Sommer, Wolfgang, *Gottesfurcht und Fürstenherrschaft: Studien zum Obrigkeitsverständnis Johann Arndts und lutherischer Hofprediger zur Zeit der altprotestantischen Orthodoxie*, Göttingen: Vandenhoeck 1988.

Spieker, Christian Wilhelm, *Lebensgeschichte des Andreas Musculus: Ein Beitrag zur Reformations– und Sittengeschichte des sechzehnten Jahrhunderts*, Frankfurt-on-the-Oder: Verlag der Hofdruckerei von Trowitzsch & Sohn 1858.

Spufford, Margaret, *The Great Reclothing of England: Petty Chapmen and their Wares in the Seventeenth Century*, London: Hambledon, 1984.

Spufford, Peter, *Power and Profit: The Merchant in Medieval Europe*, London: Thames & Hudson 2002.

Stadtwald, Kurt, *Roman Popes and German Patriots: Antipapalism in the Politics of the German Humanist Movement from Gregor Heimburg to Martin Luther*, Geneva: Droz 1996.

Stagl, Justin, 'Ars apodemica: Bildungsreise und Reisemethodik von 1560 bis 1600', in Xenja von Ertzdorff and Dieter Neukirch (eds.), *Reisen und Reiseliteratur im Mittelalter und in der Frühen Neuzeit*, Amsterdam: Rodopi 1992, 141–191.

Staniland, Kay, 'Samuel Pepys and his Wardrobe', *Costume*, 39 (2005), 53–63.

Steele, Valerie, *Paris Fashion: A Cultural History*, 2nd rev. edition, Oxford: Berg 1998.

——and Major, John S. (eds.), *China Chic: East Meets West*, New Haven: Yale University Press 1999.

Stollberg-Rilinger, Barbara, *Des Kaisers alte Kleider: Verfassungsgeschichte als Symbolgeschichte des Alten Reiches*, Munich: Beck 2008.

——'Knien vor Gott – Knien vor dem Kaiser: Zum Ritualwandel im Konfessionskonflikt', in Andrea von Hülsen-Esch (ed.), *Inszenierung und Ritual im Mittelalter und Renaissance*, Düsseldorf: Droste Verlag 2005, 263–292.

Stolleis, Karen, 'Kölner Patrizier– und Bürgerkleidung in der frühen Neuzeit', in Johannes Pietsch and Karen Stolleis (eds.), *Kölner Patrizier– und Bürgerkleidung des 17. Jahrhunderts: Die Kostümsammlung Hüpsch im Hessischen Landesmuseum Darmstadt*, Riggisberg: Abegg Stiftung 2008, 19–37.

——*Messgewänder aus deutschen Kirchenschätzen des Mittelalters bis zur Gegenwart: Geschichte – Form – Material*, Regensburg: Schnell & Steiner 2001.

——*Die Gewänder aus der Lauinger Fürstengruft*, Munich: Deutscher Kunstverlag 1977.

Stone, Lawrence, *The Crisis of the Aristocracy 1558–1641*, Oxford: Clarendon Press 1965.

Strauss, Gerald, *Nuremberg in the Sixteenth Century*, Bloomington: Indiana University Press 1976.

Styles, John, *The Dress of the People: Everyday Fashion in Eighteenth-Century England*, New Haven: Yale University Press 2007.

——and Vickery, Amanda (eds.), *Gender, Taste and Material Culture in Britain and North America, 1700–1830*, New Haven: Yale University Press 2006.

Sumberg, S., *The Nuremberg Schembart Carnival*, New York: Columbia University Press 1941.

Talkenberger, Heike, 'Von der Illustration zur Interpretation: Das Bild als historische Bildkunde', *Zeitschrift für Historische Forschung*, 21 (1994), 289–313.

Tazbir, Janusz, 'Culture of the Baroque in Poland', in Antoni Maczak, Henryk Samsonowicz, and Peter Burke (eds.), *East–Central Europe in Transition: From the Fourteenth to the Seventeenth Century*, Cambridge: Cambridge University Press 1985, 167–181.

Thiel, Erika, *Geschichte des Kostüms: Europäische Mode von der Antike bis zur Gegenwart*, Berlin: Henschelverlag 1960.

Thomas, Keith, *The Ends of Life: Roads to Fulfilment in Early Modern England*, Oxford: Oxford University Press 2009.

Tinajero, Araceli, 'Far Eastern Influences in Latin American Fashions', in Regina A. Root (ed.), *The Latin American Fashion Reader*, Oxford: Berg 2005, 66–75.

Tranberg Hansen, Karen, 'From Thrift to Fashion: Materiality and Aesthetics in Dress Practises in Zambia', in Susanne Küchler and Daniel Miller (eds.), *Clothing as Material Culture*, Oxford: Berg 2005, 107–120.

Trichet, Louis, *La Tonsure: vie et mort d'une pratique ecclésiastique*, Paris: Cerf 1990.

Tschopp, Silvia S., 'Das Unsichtbare begreifen: Die Rekonstruktion historischer Wahrnehmungsmodi als methodische Herausforderung der Kulturgeschichte', *Historische Zeitschrift*, 280 (2005), 39–81.

Tuffal, Jaqueline, *Les receuils de mode graves au XVIe siècle*, 2 vols., D.Phil. Diss. Paris 1951.

Van Aert, Laura and Van Damme, Ilja, 'Retail Dynamics of a City in Crisis: The Mercer Guild in Pre-industrial Antwerp (c.1648–c.1748)', in Bruno Blondé et al. (eds.), *Retailers and Consumer Changes in Early Modern Europe: England, France, Italy and the Low Countries*, Tours: Presses Universitaires, 2005, 139–169.

Varick Dock, Stephen, *Costume & Fashion in the Plays of Jean-Baptiste Poquelin Molière: A Seventeenth-Century Perspective*, Genève: Editions Slatkine 1992.

Vassallo e Silva, Nuno, 'Precious Stones, Jewels and Cameos: Jacques de Coutre's Journey to Goa and Agra', in Jorge Flores and Nuno Vassallo e Silva (eds.), *Goa and the Great Mughal*, London: Scala 2004, 116–133.

Vickery, Amanda, 'Women and the World of Goods: A Lancashire Consumer and her Possessions', in John Brewer and Roy Porter (eds.), *Consumption and the World of Goods*, London: Routledge 1993, 247–301.

Vincent, John Martin, *Costume and Conduct in the Laws of Basel, Bern, and Zurich 1370–1800*, Baltimore: Johns Hopkins Press 1935.

Vincent, Susan, *Dressing the Elite: Clothes in Early Modern England*, Oxford: Berg 2003.

Vogel, Klaus A., 'Cultural Variety in a Renaissance Perspective: Johannes Boermus on "The manners, laws and customs of all people" (1520)', in G. Brugge and J. P. Rubiès (eds.), *Shifting Culture: Interaction and Discourse in the Expansion of Europe*, Münster: Lit Velag 1995, 17–34.

Völkel, Markus, *Römische Kardinalshaushalte des 17. Jahrhundert: Borghese, Barberini, Chigi*, Tübingen: Niemeyer: 1993.

Vries, Jan de, *The Industrious Revolution: Consumer Behaviour and the Household Economy, 1650 to the Present*, Cambridge: Cambridge University Press 2008.

Wagner, Monika, *Das Material der Kunst. Eine andere Geschichte der Moderne*, Munich: Beck 2001.

Walker, Mack, *German Home Towns: Community, State and General Estate, 1648–1871*, Ithaca: Cornell University Press 1971.

Wandel, Lee Palmer, *Always Among Us: Images of the Poor in Zwingli's Zurich*, Cambridge: Cambridge University Press 1990.

Warburg, Aby M., *Ausgewählte Schriften und Würdigungen*, ed. Dieter Wuttke, Baden-Baden: V. Koerner 1980.

Warnke, Martin, *Political Landscape: The Art History of Nature*, London: Reaktion 1994.

Watanabe-O'Kelly, Helen, *Court Culture in Dresden: From Renaissance to Baroque*, London: Macmillan 2002.

Wee, Herman van de, 'The Western European Woollen Industries, 1500–1750', in David Jenkins (ed.), *The Cambridge History of Western Textiles*, vol. 1, Cambridge: Cambridge University Press 2003, 397–472.

Wehrli, Christoph, *Die Reformationskammer: Das Züricher Sittengericht des 17. und 18. Jahrhunderts*, Winterthur: Keller 1963.

Weiss, Hildegard, *Lebenshaltung und Vermögensbildung des mittleren Bürgertums, Nürnberg 1400–1600*, Munich: Beck 1980.

Weitnauer, A., *Venezianischer Handel der Fugger: Nach der Musterbuchhaltung des Matthäus Schwarz*, Munich 1931.

Welch, Evelyn, 'Art on the Egde: Hair and Hands in Renaissance Italy', *Renaissance Studies*, 23 (2008), 241–268.

—— 'Lotteries in Early Modern Italy', *Past & Present*, 199 (2008), 71–111.

—— *Shopping in the Renaissance: Consumer Cultures in Italy 1400–1600*, New Haven: Yale University Press 2005.

Weller, Thomas, *Theatrum Praecedentiae: Zeremonieller Rang und gesellschaftliche Ordnung in der frühneuzeitlichen Stadt: Leipzig 1500–1800*, Darmstadt: Wissenschaftliche Buchgesellschaft 2006.

Wenzel, Horst, *Hören und Sehen, Schrift und Bild: Kultur und Gedächtnis im Mittelalter*, Munich: Beck 1995.

Wiesner, Merry E., 'Spinsters and Seamstresses: Women in Cloth and Clothing Production', in Margaret W. Ferguson, Maureen Quilligan, and Nancy J. Vickers (eds.), *Rewriting the Renaissance: The Discourses of Sexual Difference in Early Modern Europe*, Chicago: Chicago University Press 1986, 191–205.

Wilckens, Leonie von, *Geschichte der deutschen Textilkunst: Vom späten Mittelalter bis in die Gegenwart*, Munich: Beck 1997.

——— *Tageslauf im Puppenhaus: Bürgerliches Leben vor dreihundert Jahren*, Munich: Prestel 1956.

Wilson, Bronwen, *The World in Venice: Print, the City, and Early Modern Identity*, Toronto: University of Toronto Press 2005.

Winkel, Maricke de, *Fashion and Fancy: Dress and Meaning in Rembrandt's Paintings*, Amsterdam: Amsterdam University Press 2006.

Wolter, Gundula, *Teufelshörner und Lustäpfel: Modekritik in Wort und Bild 1150–1620*, Marburg: Jonas Verlag 2002.

——— *Die Verpackung des männlichen Geschlechts: Eine illustrierte Kulturgeschichte der Hose*, Marburg: Jonas Verlag 1991.

Wunder, Heide, 'What made a man a man? Sixteenth- and seventeenth-century findings', in Ulinka Rublack ed., *Gender in Early Modern German History*, Cambridge: Cambridge University Press 2002, 21–48.

Wurst, Karin, *Fabricating Pleasure: Fashion, Entertainment, and Cultural Consumption in Germany, 1780–1830*, Detroit: Wayne State University Press, 2005.

Wuttke, Dieter, *Dazwischen: Kulturwissenschaft auf Warburgs Spuren*, vol. 1, Baden–Baden 1996.

——— 'Dürer und Celtis: Von der Bedeutung des Jahres 1500 für den deutschen Humanismus: Jahrhundertfeier als symbolische Form', *The Journal of Medieval and Renaissance Studies*, 10 (1980), 73–129.

Zaggia, Stefano, 'Foreign Students in the City, *c.*1500–1700', in Donatella Calabri and Stephen Turk Christensen (eds.), *Cultural Exchange in Early Modern Europe, vol. 2: Cities and Cultural Exchange in Europe, 1400–1700*, Cambridge: Cambridge University Press 2007, 175–196.

Zakim, Michael, *Ready-Made Democracy: A History of Men's Dress in the American Republic*, Chicago: Chicago University Press 2003.

Zander-Seidel, Jutta, *Textiler Hausrat: Kleidung und Haustextilien in Nürnberg von 1500–1650*, Munich: Deutscher Kunstverlag 1990.

Zitzlsperger, Philipp, *Dürer Pelz und das Recht im Bild. Kleiderkunde als Methode der Kunstgeschichte*, Berlin: Akademie Verlag 2008.

Index

Aachen 154
academic dress 98, 101
acclamation 82–3
Adolfus, Gustavus of Sweden (king) 166, 168
Adrian VI (pope) 152
Africa 67, 146, 149, 178, 180, 198, 281
Agricola, Laurentius 102
Akbar (Emperor) 7
alba amicorum 221–7
Alberti, Leon Battista 39
Albrecht V of Bavaria (duke) 254
alchemy 70
Aleander, Jerome 128
Alexander the Great 150
Almeida, Francisco de 177
Alpers, Svetlana 27
Altdorf 212–16, 239
Amman, Jost 198, 243, 244–5
ambassadors 229
Amberger, Christoph 64
Americas 148, 149, 159, 180–1, 184, 188–90, 198, 281–2
Amsterdam 26, 260, 280
Antwerp 46, 180, 182–4, 273
Appadurai, Arjun 77
Aquinas, St. Thomas of 82, 135
Arabs 199
architecture 198
Arena chapel 128
Armour 9, 69, 94, 101, 164, 196
    helmets 20

weapons 40, 52–3, 78, 117, 141, 144–5
ars apodemica 199
art 27, 36–7, 259–66, *see also* visuality
art markets 183
ascetism 96
Asia 67, 83, 146, 149, 162, 164, 198, 209
assimilation 13, 133, 138, 185, 220
astrology 64,70,75
Atlantic World 268
auctions 52
Augsburg 12, 24, 33–78, 182, 187, 263
August, Carl of Saxony-Weimar (duke) 282
August, Count Palatinate 171
Austria 127
Aventinus 138
Ayrer family 198

Babur (Emperor) 7
Baden-Baden 284
bags 55, 245
Barbari, Jacopo 128
barbarians 120, 128, 134, 137,146, 165
barbershops 165
Basle 25
Basque people 188, 190–1
beards
    care of 1–2,

clerical 96, 102
    marking maturity 58, 63
    shapes and dyes of 101, 117, 141, 169, 194–5
    ugly and unclean 231
beauty 187
Beer, Matthias 219
beggars 63, 168
Behaim Römer, Magdalena 213–29
Behaim, Friedrich 212–17
Behaim, Paul 14
Behaim, Stephan Carl 229
Bellini, Giovanni 125, 146, 185
belts and girdles 8, 13, 24, 246, 266
Bergamo 164
Berry, Jean de 7, 21, 188
Bertelli, Fernando 146
Bertelli, Pietro 221
Bertuch, Friedrich Justin 282
black and white 66, 69–71, *see also* colour
"blacks" 144–5, 178, 185, 192–3, 195
bodice-makers 244
body politic 174
body weight 60, 141, *see also* posture
Boemus, Johannes von 181
Bohemia 127, 160
Bologna 223
Boorde, Andrew 14, 145
Bora, Katharina von 120, 212

borrowing and lending 265
Bosse, Abraham 166
bourgeois ideals 270–1
braids 252
Brandenburg, Anna von
    (duchess) 20
Brandenburg, Joachim von
    (duke) 110–11
Brant, Sebastian 28, 87, 103,
    135
Braudel, Fernand 262
Braun, Georg 147
Brazil and Brazilians 181–2, 185,
    187, 199, 207, 229
breeches, see hose and breeches
Bredekamp, Horst 22
Breton, Richard 146
Breu, Jörg 140
Breydenbach, Bernhard von 180
British Library 146, 221
broadsheets
    a-la-mode 166–72
    as advertisement 153–4
    astrological 75
    of bogey-woman 269
    ethnographical 135–7, 177,
        199
    of Jakob Fugger 49,
        Reformation satires 86–7
    military 140
brocade 83
Brouwer, Adriaen 26
Bruck, Arnold von 141
Bruges 83
Brunswick 83
Bruyn, Abraham de 147, 199
Bulwer, John 8
Burckhardt, Jacob 2, 9
Burgkmair, Hans 177, 185
Burgundy 127, 160
buttons 16, 268

caftan 18
Cairo 19
Calicut 178, 185
Calvin, Jean 121

Calvinism 121–2, 155
camelhair 47
Carl, Ernst Ludwig 281
carnival and mummery 37, 40,
    108–9, 123, 200, 202
Casa, Giovanni, della 21
Castiglione, Baldessare 7, 125
Castile 188, 201
Catholic Renewal 70, 122–3
Celtis, Conrad 125–38, 182,
    186
Ceylon 182
charity 214
Charlemagne 130, 138, 165,
    284
Charles II of England (king) 166
Charles V (emperor) 46, 56,
    63, 67, 68, 94, 127, 156,
    180, 184, 187, 194, 195
children 184, 238–9
children's clothes 40–7, 238–40
China 3, 13, 21, 23, 280
Chipps Smith, Jeffrey 27
Cicero 227
civility
    and classical discourses 10–11
    and comportment 60
    and courteous behaviour 6
    and dress 18, 35, 40
    and national ideology 130
    in Mughal Empire 7, 40,
        117,
    see also incivility and clothes as
        civilisation
civitas 202
Clairvaux, Bernard of 85
classical discourse 10–11, 131,
    132, 151–2, 271–2
classification 194, 209
cleanliness 5, 215, 269, 279
Cleves, Anne of (queen) 18
cloaks 29
cloth, English 182
clothes as civilisation 133, 154,
    see also civility
clothes, as loveless 114

Cluny 85
Cochin 20, 177–8, 201
Cochläus, Johannes 119–20,
    240
codpieces 9, 10, 18, 19, 25, 110,
    135, 241
Cologne 147, 267, 269, 279
colour
    as false 104
    as honourable 137, 152, 215
    in clothing 70, 97–8, 117,
        175, 220
    and dyes 15, 184, 262–3
    symbolism of 55
comedy 19, 164
Commynes, Philippe de 8
comparative history 3, 12–15,
    16, 18, 27
concubines 140–43
Constantinople (Istanbul) 13,
    20
Consumption
    agents of 3–4, 6, 8
    as civil 120
    as corrupting 12, 108,150
    and household decision-
        making 164–5, 211–84
Cortes, Adriano de las 13
Cortès, Hernan 184, 187
Coryat, Thomas 10, 174, 226,
    243
cosmopolitanism 12, 148, 261
costume books 12, 146–63
cotton 13
courts 7–8, 9–10, 164, 166
    as spaces of display 15, 18,
        229
    staging magnificence 85, 175
    staging restraint 171–2, 175
cowls 81
Cranach the Elder 24, 97–8,
    116–19, 184
crusades 6
curiosities 185
Cusa, Nicholas of 89
Cyprian, St. 97

d´Almada, Rui Fernandes 185
d´Este, Ippolito 122–3
damask 54, 218, 236
decorousness 35, 60, 112, 154,
    219, 241, 246
Dekker, Thomas 174
devices 7, 194, 196
devil books 109–12
devil 111
disillusion 26, 285
dissimulation 8, 18, 25, 26, 90,
    168
diversity 185
doll-houses 254–7
domestic ideal 257
Donauwörth 171
Dorer, Lucia 231
Dorpat 102
doublets 2, 9, 10, 51, 54, 68,
    116, 215, 218, 240
Drebbel, Conrad 4, 21
Dresden 175
dress
    as foreign 112,131, 135, 137,
        187–91, see also fashion as
        cultural exchange
    in Nuremberg 245–53
    shape of 15,138–9, 141,168,
        214–16
dressing and undressing 9, 16,
    92
"dressing up" arguments as
    rhetorical figure 120, 165
Dürer, Agnes126
Dürer, Albrecht 2–3, 5, 27,
    33–5, 36, 53–4, 125–7,
    146, 149, 180, 182–8,
    208
Dutch 13, 14, 267, 279–80

Ebner family of Nuremberg 95
Eck, Johann 181
economic man 38, 75, 92
Edo 3
effigies 21
Ehem, Jermias 58

Ehrenbuch, Fugger family 68
Einhard 138
Elliott, John 185
embroidery 20, 55, 144–5, 147,
    236, 278
emotions
    as ambivalent 75–7
    and exchange 184, 213, 235,
        239
    as expressed in dress 55, 109,
        114, 196
    and national character 129,
        150
    psychic landscapes 10
empire 179, 180, 196
England and English 13, 182,
    267, 270, 282
English Civil War 166
Enlightenment 268
Erasmus of Rotterdam 16, 70
Estienne, Henri 241–2
Ethiopia 199
ethnicity 160, 165, 168, 174–5,
    179–80, 188
ethnography 188, 200–9
European, as naked, figure of
    149, 170
Evelyn, John 166
executioner 68,103
Eyck, Jan van 22

fans 157, 223
fashion
    and change 10, 16, 76,
        145
    as cross-cultural exchange 7,
        8, 144–5, 165
    functions of 56–7, 78, 82,
        98, 114, 132, 184, 276
    and dress semantics 6,
        13–14
    sociology 9
    symbols 12, 51, 157, 252,
        253
feathers 8, 54, 60, 113, 140,
    149, 189

Febvre, Lucien 16
femininity 18, 19, 126, 133,
    152, 162, 178, 222
Ferdinand of Austria (Emperor)
    56, 67, 68, 141
Fernandez, Valentim 180
Ferrara 223
Feyerabend, Sigismund 146, 149
Fez 159
Finland and Finnish 168
Flanders 15, 22, 70
Florence 5, 6, 14, 19, 223
flower patterns 239, 240–1, 272,
    278
flowers 20
food 183
fools and foolishness 37, 58,
    62,70,76, 109, 242,
    276
France and French 14, 15, 16,
    144–6, 156–7, 164–71,
    267, 281–2
Francis I (king) 18
Franck, Sebastian 181
Frankfurt am Main 146, 182,
    236, 269
Frankfurt fair 242
Frankfurt-Oder 111
Frauenfeld 92
Frederick the Wise, of Saxony
    (duke) 28, 88
Frederick V, of the Palatinate
    (duke) 166
Fresne-Canaye, Philippe 13
Friedrich II of the Palatinate
    (Count) 191
Friedrich Wilhelm II (of Prussia)
    175
Friedrich, Christopher 245
Frischlin, Nicodemus 164
Frisia, East 162–3
Fróis, Luis 12
Fugger family 33, 35, 46–9, 68
Fugger, Hans 52
fur 2, 31, 52–3, 60, 62, 63, 68,
    116, 184, 239

Gage, Thomas 281
garden parties 232, 236
Gardener, Werner the 227
garters 57, 167, 259, 285
Garzoni, Tommaso 183
gaze and spectatorship 260, 272
gender and nationhood 130,
    133, 140
gendering of dress 156, 162, 268
    and femininity 126,133–
        5,152, 168, 222, 231–2,
        248, 272–6
    by Henri VIII 18
    in jewellery 20
    and masculinity 60, 139–45,
        168
    and youth 35
genealogies 68
Geneva 154
German history 245
"German Michel" 170
German, naked, figure of 144–5,
    168
Germany 27
Gerung, Matthias 113–15
Gienger, Gabriel 220–1, 223
global exploration 180–2, 185
Glockendon, Georg 180
gloves 1, 8, 25, 83, 157, 184,
    222
Goa 7, 187
Góis, Damião de 195
gold, cloth of 5
goldthread 10, 16, 83
Goldwaithe, Richard 2
Gomera, Lopez de 207
gowns and robes
    clerical 81, 97, 101, 117,
        139–40
    as aspired to by peasants 105
    and political symbolism 2,
        35, 139–40
    value of 184
    variety of 56, 60–3, 72,
Gräfenberg 213
Granada 188, 190

Granvelle, Cardinal de 52
Greeks 185
Grimm, Sigismund 181
Groebner, Valentin 37
group displays 9
Grynaeus, Simon 181
Guevara, Fray Antonio de 8
guildsmen morality 57, 136, 140
Guinea 178, 180
Günzburg, Johann Eberlein von
    108, 131
Gypsies 144–5, 160, 168, 198

Hale, John 27
Hair
    colouring of 194–6, 231
    covering and uncovering of
        126–7, 231, 149–52
    curling of 2–3
    cut for pilgrimage 81
    grown long by men 166–8
hairbands 265
Hallerstein, Bartholomäus Haller
    von 68
Hamburg 122, 267, 269, 284
handkerchiefs 21, 24, 229
Harms, Wolfgang 167
Harsdörffer, Susanna 236
headwear
    berets 248
    caps 2, 8, 25, 213
    hats 123
    ingenuity of 34, 54–5, 68
    turban 22
Hegel, Georg Friedrich Wilhem
    284
Heimburg, Gregor von 129
Heldt, Sigmund 199–209, 217
Henriques, Francisco 60
Henry VIII (king) 8, 18
Herberstein, Sigismund von 181
Herrenstube (Augsburg) 58
Herwart family of Augsburg 134
Herwart, Joachim 58
Hilpoldstein 213
Hindu tradition 19

Hinudstan 7
Hoffman, Melchior 102
Hogarth, William 13
Hogenberg, Franz 147
Hohenlohe 108
Holbein, Hans 94
Hollander, Anne 23
Holy Roman Empire 127–65,
    182, 284
Holzschuher, Lazarus 68
home-towns 269
hose and breeches
    baggy 110–11, 170, 218
    cut of 10, 16, 19, 140–5,
        252–3
    as rite of maturity 40
    slashed 9, 16, 122
    sown on to footwear 54
humanism 152, 164, 177
Hungary 52, 54, 125, 144–6
Hut, Hans 66

ideas, history of 148–9
identity and identification
    as linked to ageing 40, 63
    as linked to the body 60, 63
    as linked to notions
        of materiality and
        immateriality 26, 284
    as linked to spaces 44
    and nationhood 144–5, 165
    as relational 10–11, 211
    as uncertain 20, 38, 74–6
Ilg, Ulrike 148
Illouz, Eva 213
Imhoff, Benedict 240
Imhoff, Hans 240
Imhoff, Jeremias 218–19
Imhoff, Wilhelm 240
Imhoff, Willibald 184, 198
imitations 5, 252, 269–70
Imperial Cities 137, 141
Imperial Diets 56, 68
incivility 37, 119–20, 133, 137,
    149, 159, 164–5
Indagine, Johannes de 248

India 177
indigenous 108, 127, 131, 164,
    184–5
ingenuity 2, 191, 240
inventories 211, 265
Iran 15, 16
Irish 168, 174
Istanbul, *see* Constantinople
Italian fashion 157, 219
Italy 20, 157–8, 169

Jamnitzer, Wenzel 149, 197–8
Japan 3, 9, 12, 13, 14, 278, 281
jerkins 10
Jesuits 70, 169
Jewellery and gemstones
    in bourgeois clothing 53–4,
        67, 78
    in common people's regional
        clothing 162
    as attribute of rule 6, 9, 67,
        85
    global trade in 182, 195
    as object of contemplation
        198
    spread of 20–1
    sumptuary allowance of 24
Jews 221, 265
Johann Friedrich, Count
    Palatinate 171
Jonson, Ben 14
Joris, David 25
Juvenal 11, 132

Kantorowicz, Ernst 21
Karlstadt, Andreas 97–8
Karsthans 113
Kaysersberg, Gailer von 103, 231
Khaldûn, Ibn 18, 24
kimono 13, 18
Klaniczay, Gábor 146
knights and ladies 6, 16, 18, 140
Koberger, Anton 28
Köler, Hieronymus 21, 194–7
Kranz, Anette 66
Krauß, Elisabeth 252

Kunst, Pieter Cornelius 227
Kyoto 9

Laichingen 268
Lamm, Marcus zum 162, 200
Landauer Stiftung 205
Lang, Matthäus 96
Lapps 133–7, 168–70, 174
Lauingen 171
Lazarillo de Tormes 26
Le Roy, Louis 148
leather 9, 214
legs and knees 18, 60, 252–3
Leibniz 259
Leiden, Jan van 120
Leipzig 144–5, 182, 217, 220,
    266, 279
Lévi-Strauss, Claude 16
Lima 281
Limburg brothers 188
lineage 57, 62, 68
linen 166, 220, 238
Lipovetsky, Gilles 10, 278
Lisbon 21, 46, 180, 195–6
London 3, 4, 242
looms 7
Lorenzetti, Ambrogio 29, 119,
    120
Lorraine 156
Louis XIV of France (king) 275
love 55
Ludwig of Bavaria (duke) 150
Ludwig Wilhelm of Baden-
    Baden (margrave) 284
luminosity 82–5
lutes 34–6, 54
Luther, Martin 39, 81–2,
    85–108, 116–21, 182,
    185, 194, 238
luxury *see also* Oriental luxury
    and simplicity v. luxury
    old and new 271–2, 279, 282
    as slavery 131
Lyon 123

Machiavelli, Niccolo 19

Mack, Georg 198
Madeira 182
Madrid 229
maidservants 153, 252, 266
mail-order catalogues 282
Mainz, Albrecht von
    (archbishop) 86
Mair, Hektor 68
Maler, Hans 34
Mangolt, Barbara 62
Manninga, Unico 162
manuscript culture 74
Marbod of Rennes 20
Margiela, Martin 26
marriage 57–8, 60–2, 64, 133,
    152, *see also* weddings
masculinity
    in bourgeois youths 35,
        37–8, 53, 54, 58, 222
    at courts 6, 9, 18–19,
    as delicate 60
    and empire 178
    as mature 66, 74–5
    and nationhood 138, 140–4,
        152, 159–60, 162, 169,
        174–5
    in Reformation satire 102
masquerade 284
materiality 26–7
Maximilian I (Emperor) 8, 28,
    46, 60, 76, 127, 140,
    178–80, 187, 248
measurements 234
Melanchthon, Philipp 120, 174,
    271
Mendelsche Zwölfbrüderstiftung
    205
mending 217–18
Menot, Michel 145
Mentges, Gisela 38
merchants
    as corrupting 139, 165
    female 252
    as entrepreneurs 6, 279
    and global trade 180
    and mercantilism 267–8,

outlook of in crisis 70
Metz 156
Mexico 281
Milan 164
mirrors 20, 37, 46, 208
Molière, Jean Baptiste 8, 19, 273, 275
money 106–8, 137
monks 89–92, 102
monsters 110–11, 146
Montague, Mary Wortley 279–80
Montaigne, Michel de 8, 9, 10, 47, 144, 207–9
Moriscos 188–90, 201
Moritz of Saxony (duke) 68, 71
Moscow 199
Münster, Sebastian 174, 181
Müntzer, Thomas 102
Münzer, Hieronymus 180
Murner, Thomas 103–4
Musculus, Andreas 110–12
music 141–2, 164
Muslims 18, 19, 24
Muth 108, 109, 110, 150, 240

national dress 282
nationhood 53, 78, 120, 122–75, see also patriotism
necklaces, golden 96, 105
Netherlands 160
Nettesheim, Agrippa von 89, 102, 231
Neuenmarkt 216
Nicolai, Friedrich 122
Nicolay, Nicolas de 146, 148, 198, 201
Nietzsche, Friedrich 284–5
Niklashausen, drummer of 102, 103
noblemen 223
Novgorod 83
nudity 37, 66, 141, 144–5, 149, 168
nuns 67, 92, 94–5

Nuremberg 52, 68, 84, 92, 94, 96, 125, 135–7, 140, 146, 152, 161, 182, 186–7, 197–207, 284
Nürnberger, Lazarus 195

object cultures 2–3, 24–5, 36, 77
Oriental luxury 6–7, 20, 22, 83, 146, 164
Orlamünde 98
Örtel, Sigmund 222
Osaka 13
Osiander, Andreas 88–9, 94–6, 108
Ottomans 13, 14, 18, 144–5, 185, 275

Padua 128, 221, 223–6
Palladius, Peder (bishop) 110
Panofsky, Erwin 126–8
paper 166
Paris 281
parrots 153, 181, 257
partlets 55, 246
Passional Christi 86, 94
Pastoureau, Michel 103
patriotism and civic virtue 152
patriotism and Protestant ideas 152
Paul, St. 91, 102, 121
Paumgartner, Balthasar 232–41, 253
Paumgartner, Magdalena 232–41, 253, 257
Peace of Augsburg (1555) 66
pearls 252
Peasant's War 55, 70, 88–9, 92–8, 112
peasants 104–5, 158–9, 188, 262
peas-body 18, 170
pedlars 164, 267, 268
Pencz, Georg 94
Persia and Persians 146, 150–2, 199, 240, 284
Peru 195, 281

Peter the Great (Tsar) 15
Petrarch Master 28, 92–4
Petrarch, Francesco 28
Peutinger, Konrad 177, 180
Pfinzing family 240
physiognomy 167, 231, 248
Piccolomini, Enea Silvio 85, 129–30
Picts 208
Pirckheimer, Caritas 94–6
Pirckheimer, Katharina 95
Pirckheimer, Willibald 94–6, 109, 184
Pisanello, Antonio 146
Pithou, Nicolas 121
Pizzaro, Francisco 195
plague 58, 89, 232
Plato 10, 22
Platter, Felix 25
Pluderhose 114–15
points 9, 244
Poland 146
popes 92–3, 85
Pörtner, Jona 222
Pörtner, Petri 222
portraiture 24, 33–9, 44, 64, 183–5
Portuguese 7, 10, 20, 182
Postel, Guillaume 207, 261
posture and comportment
  and anger 129
  and bulkiness 18, 63
  and cavaliers 166, 168
  and corsetting 17
  in Dürer's Nürnberg woman and Venetian woman 126
  and sports or military service 60, 141
Prague 120
Praun, Paulus 198
printing 28, 74, 86–7, 166
prodigal son 226–8
prostitution 57, 67, 160, 215, 280
proverbs 216
Puritans 271
Pyrckmair, Hilarius 199

Rabelais, François 37
ragged 121, 166, 217, 226–30, 253, 269
Recife 229
Reformation
    in Augsburg 66–8, 70
    and dress 81–123
    and holy household 58
    as "material Reformation" 271
Religion
    definition of 121
religious and clerical attitudes to dress 6, 8, 13, 15, 20, 16–17, 81–123
Renaissance 2, 38, 77, 120
Renner, Narziss 33, 57, 58, 60, 187
Rhegius, Urbanus 66
Rieck, Anna 268
robes *see* gowns
Roche, Daniel 261–2, 265
Roger II of Sicily (king) 6
Roman de la Rose 275
Roman law 152
Rome 86, 119, 123, 129, 150, 152, 194, 223
Römer, Phillip 52
Rouen 207
Royal Exchange 242
ruffs 122, 170, 253
Ruggiero, Guido 9
Russia 15, 146, 185

Sachs, Hans 90, 94, 112, 119, 198, 242
sailors 159
Sancta Clara, Abraham a 123
Sansovino, Franceso 140
Sanuit, Nicolosa 20
São Tomé 182, 195
Sastrow, Bartholomäus 235
satin 5, 8, 213
scents 120
Schedel, Hartmann 28, 137
Schempart books 108, 205

Scheurl, Paulus 95, 240
Schiller, Friedrich 8
Schilling, Diebold 263
Schmid, Salome 86
Schramm, Hieronymus 266
Schwarz, Matthäus 33–78, 159, 184, 211, 226, 269
Schwarz, Ulrich, the Elder 68
Schwarz, Veit Konrad 57, 74, 78
Schwaz 34
Scots 169
second-hand clothes dealers 233, 237
Seld, Jörg 43
self-fashioning approach 10, 38, 74–5, 77
self-portraiture 1–2, 22, 33–5
Sender, Clemens 67
Sévigny, Mme de 262
Seville 194–5
sexuality 57, 58, 139, 141–2, 152
shirts 1, 54, 97, 214–15
shoes and boots
    as matching outfit 9
    as tight 20
    types of 53–4, 69, 105, 127, 167
shopping 168, 184, 221, 242–5, 272–4
Sicily 164
Siena 29–30, 223
silk
    braids made of 252
    contempt of 111, 121, 138
    praise of 83
    production and exchange of 6, 15, 16, 47, 184
    as visually depicted 24
    types of 52, 72
    in sumptuary legislation 265, 267
Simmel, Georg 9, 238
simplicity v. luxury 10–11, 108, 164–5

slashes 1, 6, 8, 51, 70, 111, 113, 122, 174
sledges 58
sleeves 16
soldiers
    as corrupting 108, 110
    as fashion icons 60
    Northern people as 168–9, 174
    as represented visually 27, 140–4
Soto, Pedro de 47
Spain 52, 160, 166, 169, 194
Spalatin, Georg 28
Spengler, Lazarus 120, 186
spices 164
spinning 15
sports dress 57
Springer, Balthasar 177–8
St Andrew´s cross 140
stockings 20, 123, 170, 216, 229, 239
storage 215
Staden, Hans von 201
Strauss, Johann 112
stripes 103–5, 121
students 212, 227, 239
Styles, John 270
Suebi 127
Süleyman the Magnificent (Ottoman ruler) 18, 20
sumptuary legislation xx, 265–70
    in Augsburg 56
    in Berne and Geneva, 122
    in Florence, 6
    globally, 280–2
    in Leipzig, 266–9
    Montaigne *On Sumptuary Law,* 10–11
    in Nuremberg, 199, 246, 253
Sunday best 265
Sweden 52
Swiss 127, 144–5, 159, 165
Sibylla Augusta of Baden-Baden (margrave) 284

table rugs 240
Tacitus 127, 164
taffeta 60, 234, 238
tailors and tailoring 7, 14, 19,
    52, 140, 144–5, 217–18
Tartars 199
taste 5, 82
temporality 60, 63, 66
teutsch and French 171–2
teutsch and *welsch* (Italian) 139,
    141, 182
Thirty Years' War 166
Thomas, Keith 238
tiara, papal 20, 85, 92–3, 113
transculturation 200
Traut, Wolfgang 177
travelling 13, 74, 146, 172,
    177–8, 219–20
trims 52, 56, 246
Tübingen 108
Tucher family 227
Tucher, Anthony 240
Turler, Hieronymus 199
Turks 144–5, 207

Ulm 171
underclothes 67
urbanisation 3, 5, 6, 11, 120
urbs 202

Valignano, Alessandro 12
Valle, Pietro della 13
Vecellio, Cesare 12, 127, 146–7,
    152, 159, 199, 208, 268
velvet
    in dress ensembles 54, 68,
        218

in exchanges 47
as imagined 6,
types of 52, 234, 238, 253
in sumptuary law 248
in vestments 83
Venerable, Peter the 85
Venezuela 195–6
Venice 31, 44, 126, 140, 161–2,
    217, 223, 248
Venne, Adriaen van de 263, 272
Vermeer, Jan 270
Verona 226
Versailles 8
vestments 67, 83, 102
Vico, Enea 146
Virginia 208
visual acts
    and the dollhouse 254
    and effigies 21–2
    in portraiture 35
    in Reformation satire 93,
        105–6
    as theorised 21–5, 31, 148–9
    in the *Wittenberg Altarpiece*
        118
visuality
    changes in 36, 185, 188
    concepts of 21–7, 148–9,
        161–2, 259–61
    implications of 38–9, 48–50,
        227, 231–2, 245
    mediality of 94
Vogelweide, Walther von der 109
Vries, Jan de 271

waistcoat 228
Waldenburg carnival 108

Walker, Mack 269
Warburg, Aby 22, 261
Wartburg 88
weavers 31, 44
weddings 60–2, 78, 152, 164,
    216, 240
Weiditz, Christoph 187–93,
    201
Weiditz, Hans 192
Weigel, Hans 146–61, 175, 199,
    208, 222
Weimar 284
Welser family 177, 180,
    195–6
Wimpfeling, Jakob 128, 137
White, John 208–9
wigs 122
Wildberg 268
Wilhelm IV of Bavaria (duke)
    145
Wilson, Bronwen 151
Wittenberg 98, 116, 119–20,
    200, 218–19, 222,
    240
woodcut collecting 198
woollens 14, 52, 214
wreaths 70, 263
Württemberg 164, 279

Yoruba 281
youth cultures 9, 10, 35

Zeeland 166
Zimmern, Christoph von
    (count) 220–1
Zwinger, Theodor 199
Zwingli, Huldrych 96